Visual Art Design Using Generative AI

Published by Happy Space Art

https://happyspace.art

This work was created with the assistance of artificial intelligence.

Dedication

I dedicate this book to my parents. My mom filled my life with a sense of wonder and gave me the freedom to chase love and adventure with an open heart. My father taught me that while perfection is unattainable, the pursuit of excellence is always worthwhile.

Acknowledgments

I am very grateful to my editor, Melody Noll, whose discerning eye and unwavering dedication have been instrumental in crafting this narrative. Melody's expertise and patience have had an immeasurable impact on my book.

I would also like to extend my heartfelt thanks to my wife and daughter, whose love and support continue to be my constant source of strength and joy.

Preface

Welcome to *Visual Art Design Using Generative AI*, a journey into the fascinating intersection of artificial intelligence and artistic creation. This book is born from a simple yet profound realization: the emergence of generative AI is not just a technological milestone; it's a canvas for boundless creativity.

Art has always reflected human ingenuity and expression, evolving with every major technological leap. From the first cave paintings to the Renaissance masterpieces, and from the camera's invention to the digital revolution, each advancement has expanded the horizons of what art can be. Now, we stand at the threshold of a new era, where AI is a powerful tool in the creative process.

This book is designed for artists, designers, writers, and anyone intrigued by the potential of AI in art. Whether you are a seasoned artist looking to explore new mediums or a curious enthusiast with no background in AI, you will find something of value in these pages.

Through *Visual Art Design Using Generative AI,* you will be introduced to the fundamentals of generative AI and how it is being used to create art that was once unimaginable. You will learn about the various AI platforms available, their unique features, and how to access and use them. At the heart of this book are the prompts – the key to unlocking the vast potential of AI art generators. Crafting an effective prompt is an art, one that requires a blend of clarity, creativity, and understanding of the AI's language. We will delve into techniques for writing prompts that lead to stunning, thought-provoking, and even awe-inspiring art.

Together, we will also explore the ethical, legal, and societal implications of AI-generated art. This new frontier raises important questions about originality, copyright, and the role of the artist, which we will examine in depth.

As you turn these pages, you will find practical tutorials, inspiring case studies, and insights from leading artists in the field. This book is not just a guide but a source of inspiration, encouraging you to experiment and create art that resonates with your unique voice and vision.

In the era of AI, the crucial role of human creativity is underscored as each carefully crafted command entered via a keyboard becomes the essential catalyst, guiding generative AI prompts to realize the artist's envisioned masterpiece. *Visual Art Design Using Generative AI* is your guidebook to this brave new world of artistic expression.

Let's embark on this exciting journey. Let your imagination soar!

Table of Contents

Chapter 1: Introduction to AI in Art

What is Generative AI?

Generative AI, or Generative Artificial Intelligence (GenAI), refers to a type of artificial intelligence that is designed to create content. This could include anything from text, images, and music to synthetic data and more. Unlike traditional AI models that are typically used for analysis or prediction, GenAI models are used to generate new content. Such AI can mimic human creativity and reflect human style.

GenAI models, including those used for tasks like video generation, image generation, text creation, and music composition, learn from extensive datasets during their development and harness the vast expanse of human knowledge and creativity captured in digital form. This training process and the necessity for substantial datasets can be understood through the lens of how these models learn and their ultimate objectives.

The Dawn of AI in the Artistic Realm

The use of GenAI to create visual art marks a revolutionary chapter in the creative domain. This fusion of technology and art has expanded the horizons of artistic expression and challenged our understanding of creativity itself. Initially, AI's role in art was limited to computational assistance and analysis. AI's role has rapidly evolved into a more interactive and generative role, where AI algorithms are not just tools but also collaborators in the creative process.

Understand Your Creative Process

To better understand your creative process when using GenAI for creating fine digital artworks, consider reflective practices such as journaling your experiences with different prompts and outcomes, noting what excites you or challenges you. Analyze the patterns in your preferences for themes, styles, or subjects, and experiment with varying levels of detail and abstraction to see how they influence the generated art. Pay attention to how you iterate on a concept, including how the AI's interpretations of your prompts align with your vision, and make adjustments accordingly. Documenting these insights can reveal your unique creative tendencies and guide you towards mastery in directing the AI to produce work that truly resonates with your artistic intent.

Importance of Understanding Your Creative Process

From an omniscient vantage point, the importance of understanding one's creative process reveals itself as a multifaceted journey pivotal to the evolution of an artist. This process is not merely a sequence of steps leading to the creation of art but a complex interplay of experiences, emotions, and thoughts that define the essence of creativity itself.

In the realm of the creative mind, every idea, emotion, and memory weaves into the fabric of artistic expression, imbuing each creation with depth and meaning. Understanding this process is akin to holding a map of a vast and intricate landscape. It allows the creator to navigate through the terrains of inspiration and the valleys of doubt with a sense of direction and purpose. This comprehensive insight ensures that every step taken is not just a move towards completing a project but a leap towards realizing the fullest potential of their creative vision.

Moreover, the creative process is marked by its ebb and flow, a cycle of productivity and stagnation. Understanding this rhythm is crucial for the creator to maintain balance. Recognizing when to push forward with fervor and when to retreat and seek renewal is essential for sustaining creativity over time. This awareness acts as a safeguard against burnout, ensuring that the well of inspiration remains replenished.

Additionally, this deep understanding of one's creative process opens the door to growth and innovation. As the creator becomes more attuned to their method of expression, they also become more receptive to exploring new techniques, ideas, and perspectives. This openness to experimentation is the lifeblood of artistic evolution, propelling the creator beyond their comfort zones and into realms of uncharted potential.

The relationship between the creator and their audience is also profoundly affected by this understanding. When creators grasp the nuances of their own process, they can more effectively communicate the intent, emotion, and story behind their work. This connection transcends the physicality of the art, fostering a deeper engagement with the audience. It transforms the act of viewing into an experience, inviting others to not just see but to feel and interpret the world through the creator's eyes.

Finally, from an omniscient standpoint, it's clear that understanding one's creative process is a cornerstone of identity and purpose for the artist. It is not just about producing art but about embarking on a continual journey of self-discovery and expression. Each creation is a reflection of the creator's path at that moment, a snapshot of their evolving narrative. This process, with its trials and triumphs, becomes a testament to the creator's resilience, passion, and dedication to their craft.

In essence, understanding the creative process from an omniscient point of view illuminates its role as a critical conduit for growth, expression, and connection. It is the backbone of the creative endeavor, essential for navigating the complex journey of bringing imagination to life.

The transition from a personal exploration of one's creative process to the broader implications of extrapolating creativity through Generative AI marks a pivotal shift in the narrative of artistic evolution. As individuals delve into the depths of their own artistic methodologies, recognizing patterns, inspirations, and obstacles, the introduction of Generative AI stands as a revolutionary tool that extends the boundaries of what's creatively possible. This fusion of human ingenuity and artificial intelligence opens new horizons for creativity, offering a unique lens through which we can further understand and expand our creative processes. It's not just about harnessing technology to generate art; it's about using this collaboration to deepen our insight into the essence of creativity itself. By integrating Generative AI into our creative endeavors, we embark on a journey that not only amplifies our artistic capabilities but also challenges us to rethink the origins of creativity, pushing the envelope of what it means to be creative in the digital age.

How GenAI Models Are Trained

1. **Learning from Examples:** GenAI models learn by example. They analyze the patterns, structures, and nuances within the data they are fed. By training on a large and diverse dataset, these models can capture a wide range of styles, concepts, and information. This training involves adjusting the internal parameters of the model (often millions or even billions) to minimize the difference between its outputs and the real-world examples it tries to emulate.

2. **Pattern Recognition and Prediction:** The core mechanism of these models involves recognizing patterns in the input data and learning to predict the next element in a sequence, whether that sequence is a line of text, a series of musical notes, or pixels in an image. The larger the dataset, the more patterns and variations the model is exposed to, enhancing its ability to generate coherent, diverse, and innovative outputs.

3. **Optimization:** Training involves numerous iterations over the dataset, where the model gradually refines its predictions to become more accurate. This process requires substantial computational resources and time, especially as the size of the model and dataset increases.

Why Large Datasets Are Essential

Diversity and Richness

A large dataset ensures that the model is exposed to a wide array of examples, encompassing different styles, genres, and modalities. This diversity is crucial for the model to learn the breadth of human creativity and expression, allowing it to generate outputs that are novel yet familiar, innovative yet coherent.

Reducing Bias

While no dataset is entirely free from bias, larger datasets can help mitigate the impact of any one source or type of data. By training on a more comprehensive collection of data, models are less likely to produce outputs that reflect narrow or discriminatory perspectives. However, it's essential to curate datasets carefully to address inherent biases actively.

Improving Reliability and Versatility

Models trained on extensive datasets are generally more reliable and versatile, capable of generating high-quality outputs across a broader range of prompts. They are better equipped to handle unexpected inputs and generate outputs that are creative, accurate, and contextually relevant.

Supporting Complex Tasks

Many creative tasks require a deep understanding of context, subtlety, and nuance. Large datasets provide the depth and breadth of examples needed for models to grasp these complexities, enabling them to perform tasks that require a sophisticated understanding of language, visual concepts, or musical theory.

In summary, the training of GenAI models on large datasets is a critical process that equips these models with the ability to generate outputs that are diverse, innovative, and reflective of the complexity of human creativity. It's a process that marries the vast potential of artificial intelligence with the richness of human expression, opening new possibilities for creative exploration and application. GenAI models learn patterns, styles, and structures from this data, which they use to generate new, original content. As you ponder the vast array of possibilities, know that there are numerous art types you can create using AI.

GenAI can be used to create great works of a varied type, including:

- **3D Art and Modeling**
  AI tools can assist you in creating 3D models for games, animation, and virtual reality, potentially streamlining processes like texturing, sculpting, and rigging.

- **AI-assisted Art Restoration and Analysis**
  AI can help you restore old paintings and artifacts as well as analyze original materials and techniques used to suggest accurate restoration methods.

- **Architectural and Interior Design**
  By analyzing vast amounts of data, AI can assist you to create innovative architectural designs or optimize space utilization in interior design.

- **Culinary Arts**
  Although not traditional "art," you can utilize AI to create new recipes and food combinations, pushing the boundaries of culinary creativity.

- **Data and Programming**
  Code is art. Data sets can be transformed and used for foundational training purposes. Our embrace of AI will lead to the creation of original art. Because synthetic datasets can be used to train other AI models, there is no practical limit to iterations and refinements guided by humans with artistic proclivities.

- **Digital Painting and Illustration**
  You can utilize AI algorithms to generate images and illustrations in various styles, from photorealistic to abstract, based on textual descriptions or by learning from existing art styles.

- **Education**
  AI in education personalizes learning experiences through adaptive learning systems and intelligent tutoring, enhancing student engagement and optimizing teaching methodologies.

- **Fashion Design**
  You can utilize AI tools to predict fashion trends, generate novel clothing designs, and customize apparel based on individualized preferences.

- **Game Design and Development**
  You can utilize AI to create new game levels, plotlines, rewards, and dynamic music that adapts to gameplay.

- **Interactive Art**
  You can leverage AI in your creation of interactive installations where your artwork changes in response to audience movements, sounds, or social media inputs.

- **Music Composition**
  Utilize AI systems to help you compose music in various genres, either generating completely original compositions or adapting existing music to create new pieces. Synthetic voices can also be generated.

- **Performance Art**
  Hmmm, yes! Utilized with live performances, AI can enable profoundly interesting responses and interactions with performers in real-time through motion capture and/or sound analysis.

- **Photography Enhancement and Manipulation**
  You can utilize AI to enhance photographs by improving resolution, adjusting lighting and colors, and generating realistic human images from sketches.

- **Poetry and Creative Writing**
  You can employ AI to help you with ideation and creation of poetry, stories, or even entire novels. Your writing will reflect learning from vast databases of text. Transform that into joyful reading material.

- **Robotics**
  You can utilize AI to design and develop specialized robots. AI can help you choreograph robots to perform a wide array of dance styles, including ballet, belly dance, moonwalk, disco, merengue, cha cha, tango, salsa, hip-hop, vogue, improvised, and other all-time favorites.

- **Typography and Graphic Design**
  AI can generate unique fonts and layouts, or assist in creating visual content for websites, applications, and digital advertisements.

- **Video and Film Production**
  AI can assist you with video editing, from color correction to generating visual effects, and can even be utilized to create short films or animations based on specific guidelines.

- **Virtual and Augmented Reality**
  AI can enhance Virtual Reality (VR) and (Augmented Reality (AR) experiences, creating immersive environments or interactive elements that respond to user actions.

Each of these categories encompasses a wide range of techniques, tools, and outcomes, reflecting the versatility of AI as a medium and tool in the creation of art. This is by no means a comprehensive list. AI technology continues to evolve, and artists will invariably find new and innovative ways to incorporate AI into their creative processes. In its own unique way, generative art is a broad category that entails AI algorithms generating complex responses based on human-devised directives, and this process can result in unique and unpredictable artworks.

Historical Context and Evolution

The journey of AI in art began with simple algorithmic designs and pattern generation:

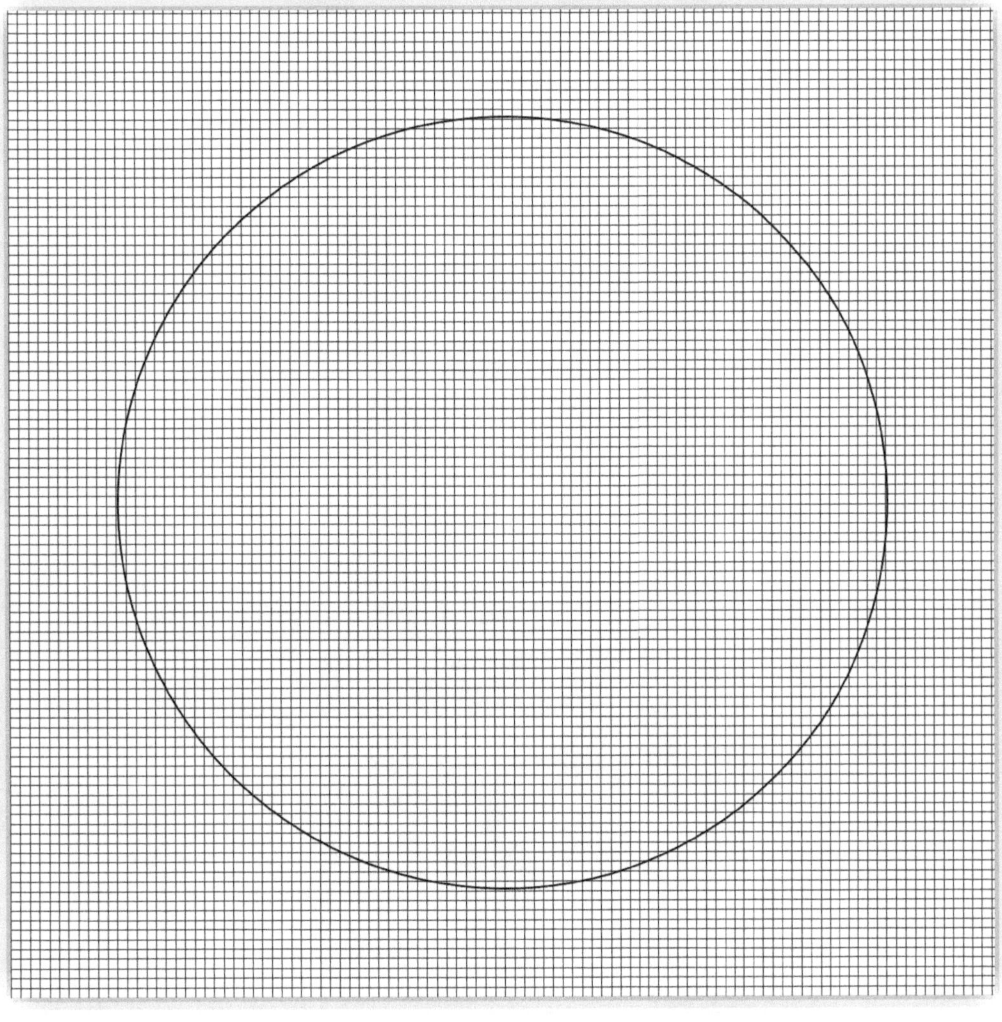

Early experiments in the mid-20th century, such as A. Michael Noll's computer-generated patterns mimicking Piet Mondrian's compositions, paved the way for more complex interactions between AI and art. These artworks below emphasize simplicity, balance, and an abstract, modern aesthetic, reflecting the essence of computer-generated art:

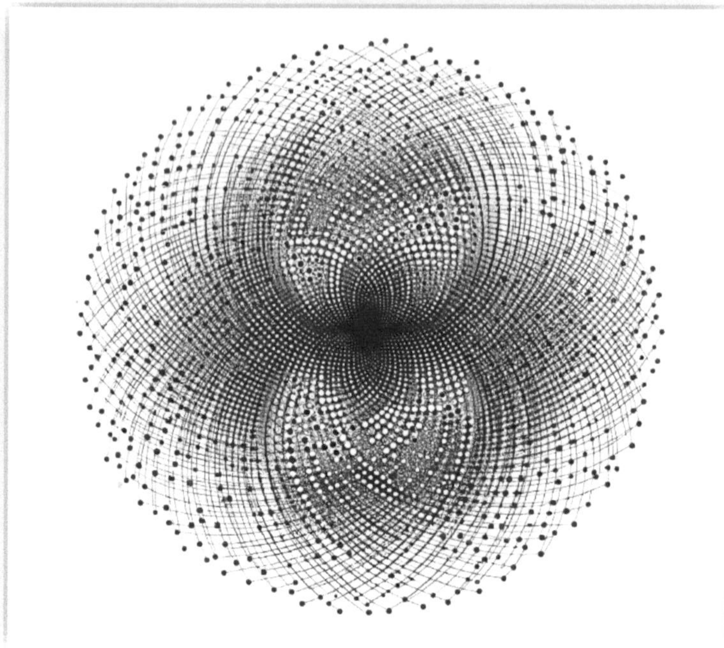

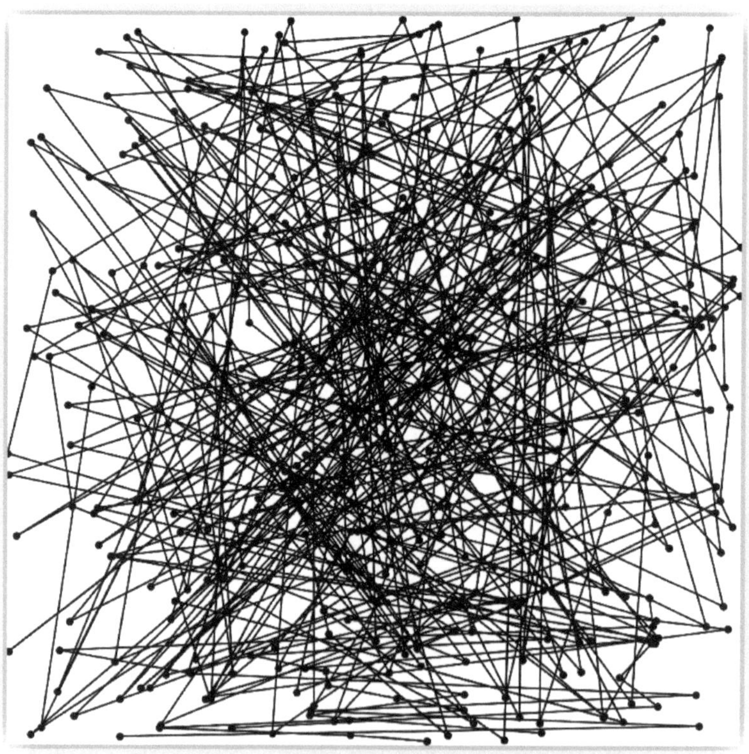

This image is also inspired by the concept of algorithmic patterns. It features a geometric arrangement of rectangles and squares with a limited color palette:

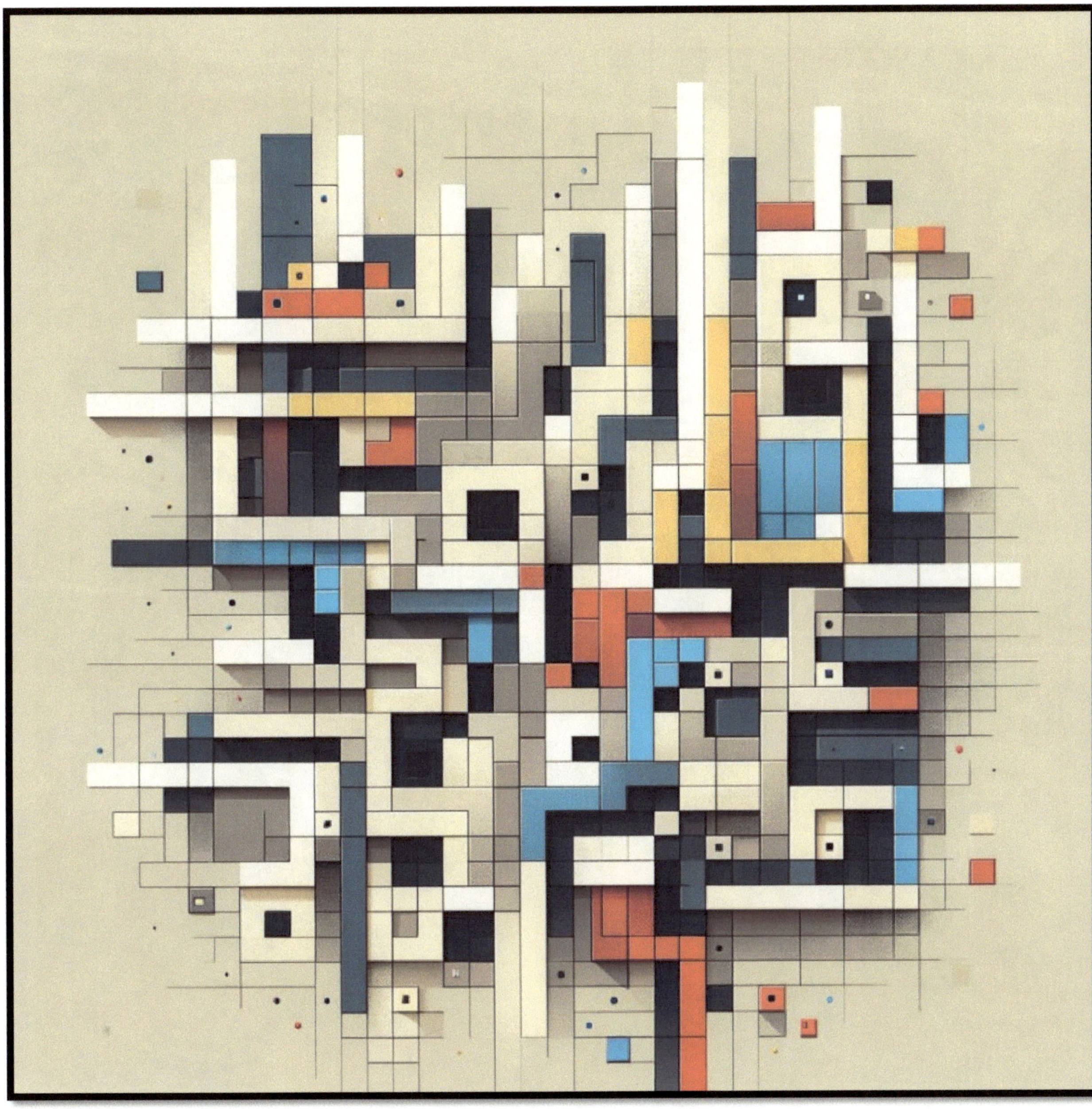

As technology advanced, so did the capabilities of AI in this field. In the late 20th and early 21st centuries, AI began to exhibit capabilities for more nuanced and sophisticated artistic creation, exemplified by projects like AARON, a program developed by Harold Cohen that could produce original paintings.

This AI-generated image resembles the style of art that Harold Cohen's AARON program can create. It features abstract forms and patterns, focusing on organic shapes and a harmonious color palette, reflecting the unique algorithmic approach of the AARON program.

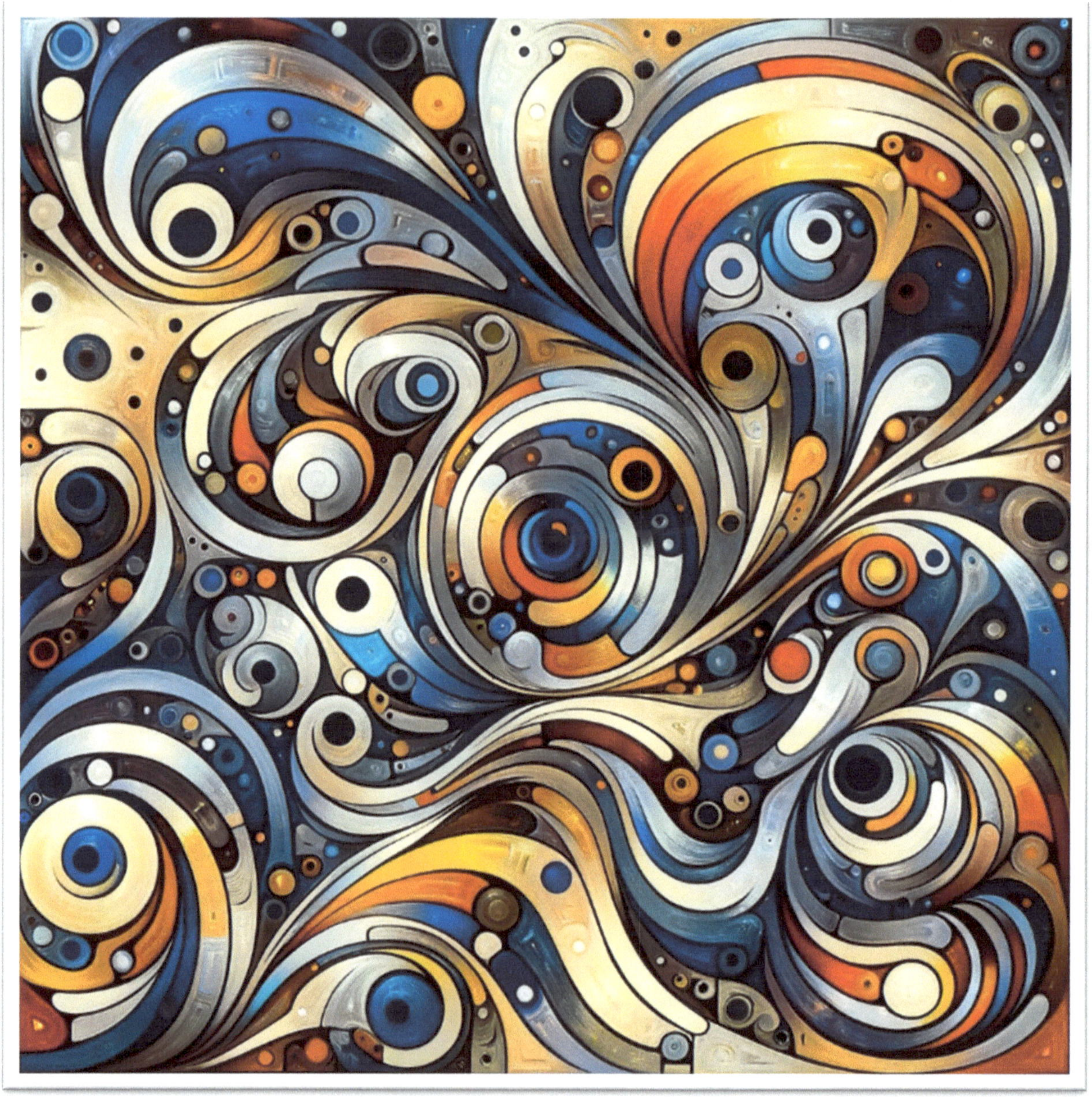

The true paradigm shift occurred with the advent of machine learning and neural networks, which allowed AI to analyze vast datasets of artwork and learn from them, leading to the generation of art that reflected a more profound understanding of styles, techniques, and visual aesthetics.

Basic Principles of AI's Interpretation and Response to Prompts

At the core of AI-generated art is the principle of machine learning. AI systems, through neural networks—layers of algorithms designed to recognize patterns—learn from existing art. They analyze styles, compositions, color schemes, and various artistic elements. When provided with prompts, these AI systems use their 'learned' knowledge to generate new creations.

Prompts act as guiding instructions to the AI. The more specific a prompt, the more targeted the AI's output. For instance, a prompt describing a scene, mood, color scheme, and style will lead the AI to produce art that aligns closely with these specifications. However, the interpretation by AI is not just a straightforward execution of these prompts; it involves a complex process of decision-making, where the AI must balance its learned knowledge with the novelty and creativity inherent in artistic creation.

The AI's response to a prompt is thus a blend of learned patterns and generative creativity, where the output is neither wholly predetermined nor entirely random. This unique interaction between programmed algorithms and artistic spontaneity is what makes AI-generated art both fascinating and, at times, unpredictable.

As we delve deeper into the realm of AI in art, it becomes evident that this technological advance is not just a tool for creation but a paradigm that is redefining the boundaries and possibilities of artistic expression.

Algorithms and Layers

The term "algorithms" in the context of Artificial Intelligence (AI) refers to a set of rules or instructions designed to perform tasks, solve problems, or make decisions based on input data. These algorithms are the building blocks of AI systems, enabling them to process information, learn from data, and undertake complex operations that mimic human intelligence to a certain degree. The sophistication and capabilities of AI systems are often a result of not just individual algorithms but also the integration and layering of multiple algorithms, each contributing to different aspects of the system's overall functionality.

Definition of Algorithms for AI

In AI, algorithms can range from simple decision trees, which follow a straightforward path of yes/no questions to arrive at a decision, to complex deep learning models, which process data through layers of interconnected nodes (neurons) inspired by the human brain. These algorithms are designed to handle specific tasks, such as pattern recognition, natural language processing, prediction, optimization, and more. The choice of algorithm depends on the nature of the task, the type and amount of available data, and the desired outcome.

Layers of Algorithms

The concept of "layers" of algorithms primarily comes from the field of deep learning, a subset of machine learning, where a model is composed of multiple layers of processing units. Each layer transforms its input data in a specific way and passes it on to the next layer, with the output of one layer becoming the input for another. This hierarchical structure allows deep learning models to learn complex patterns and representations from data:

1. **Input Layer:** The input layer receives raw data. In the context of image processing, for instance, this layer would receive the raw pixel data.

2. **Hidden Layers:** These are the layers between the input and output layers. They are called "hidden" because they do not directly interact with the external environment (*i.e.*, they are not exposed to the input or output). Each hidden layer applies transformations to the data, extracting and amplifying features relevant to the task at hand. The complexity and capability of a model increase with the number of hidden layers, hence the term "deep" in deep learning.

3. **Output Layer:** The output layer produces the model's prediction or decision based on the transformed data it receives from the last hidden layer. The output layer is tailored to the specific task, such as classification labels for a classification task or a continuous value for a regression task.

Importance of Layered Algorithms in AI

The layered approach in AI algorithms, especially in deep learning, allows for the handling of highly complex and high-dimensional data. Each layer can learn to recognize different features or aspects of the data, from simple patterns in the initial layers to highly complex concepts in the deeper layers. This enables AI systems to perform tasks with a level of sophistication and nuance that mimics human cognition more closely than simpler algorithms.
Moreover, the arrangement of algorithms into layers facilitates the learning of hierarchical representations of data. This is particularly useful in tasks like image and speech recognition, where early layers might detect simple edges or sounds, while deeper layers interpret complex scenes or semantic content.

In summary, algorithms for AI are the core mechanisms that enable machines to perform intelligent tasks, and the organization of these algorithms into layers, particularly in deep learning models, enhances their ability to process and interpret complex data in a more human-like manner.

Chapter 2: Understanding AI Art Algorithms

The Technology Behind AI Art Generation

At the heart of AI art generation lies a complex interplay of algorithms and computational processes. This technology predominantly revolves around Artificial Neural Networks (ANNs) and Machine Learning (ML), both subsets of Artificial Intelligence. ANNs are designed to mimic the human brain's functioning, enabling the AI to learn from data and make decisions. In the context of art, this means an AI can analyze existing artworks and learn styles, techniques, and patterns to help you create new, original pieces.

Neural Networks and Machine Learning in Art Creation

Neural Networks

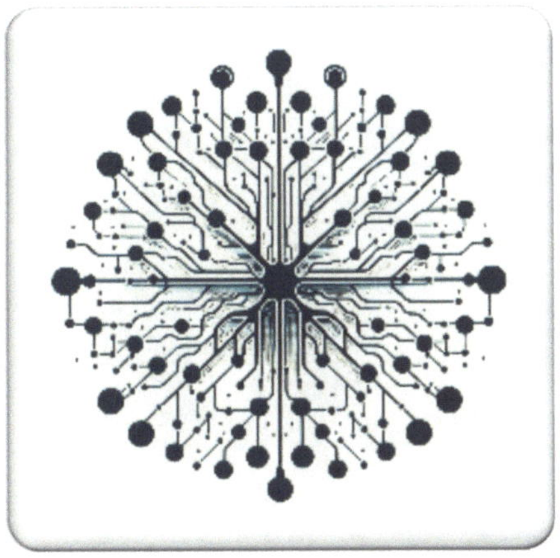

Neural networks in AI art consist of interconnected nodes (like neurons in the human brain) that process and pass on information.

These networks undergo a training phase where they are fed large datasets of art. Through this training, the AI learns to recognize and replicate various artistic styles and elements.

Machine Learning

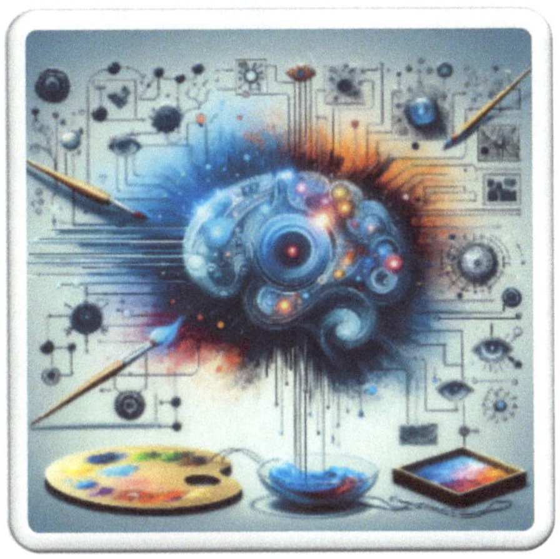

Machine Learning (ML) enables AI to improve its art creation over time autonomously. As it is exposed to more art, it gets better at understanding different artistic nuances.

ML algorithms can identify patterns and styles in art that are too complex for the human eye, allowing for the generation of highly sophisticated and nuanced artworks.

Case Studies of Famous AI Art Pieces

Art is not just about technology but also about how it extends the boundaries of human creativity. Each of the following case studies illustrates the diverse applications of AI in art and the potential of this technology to create works that resonate with human emotions and artistic sensibilities.

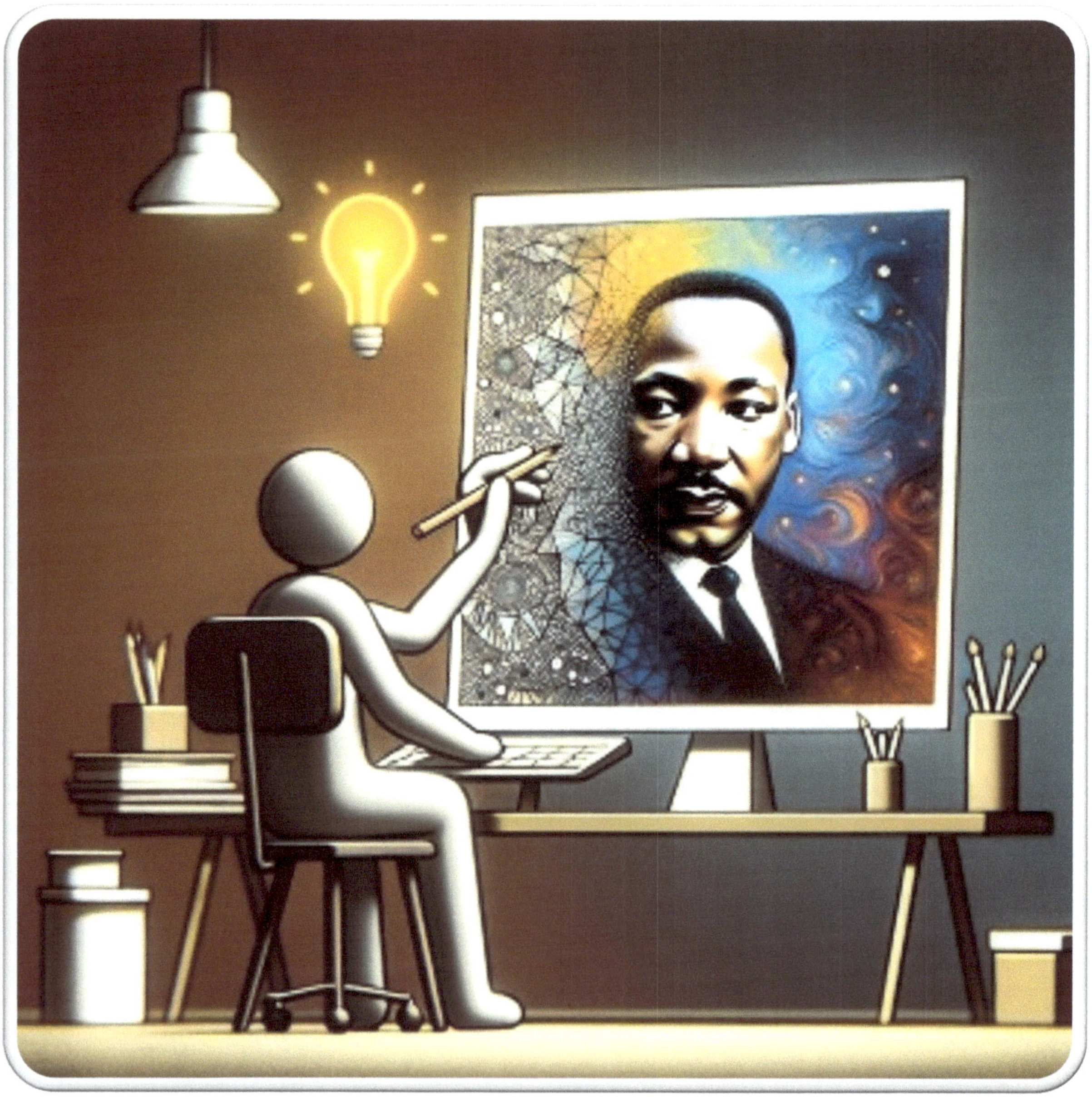

Case Study 1: "The Next Rembrandt"

This project involved training a neural network with Rembrandt's entire body of work to create a new, original painting in the artist's style. This original digital artwork is a stunningly lifelike portrait inspired by Rembrandt's style. This artwork captures the classic and dramatic qualities of Rembrandt's portraits, with attention to detail, lighting, and texture, using his unique color palettes and brushstrokes.

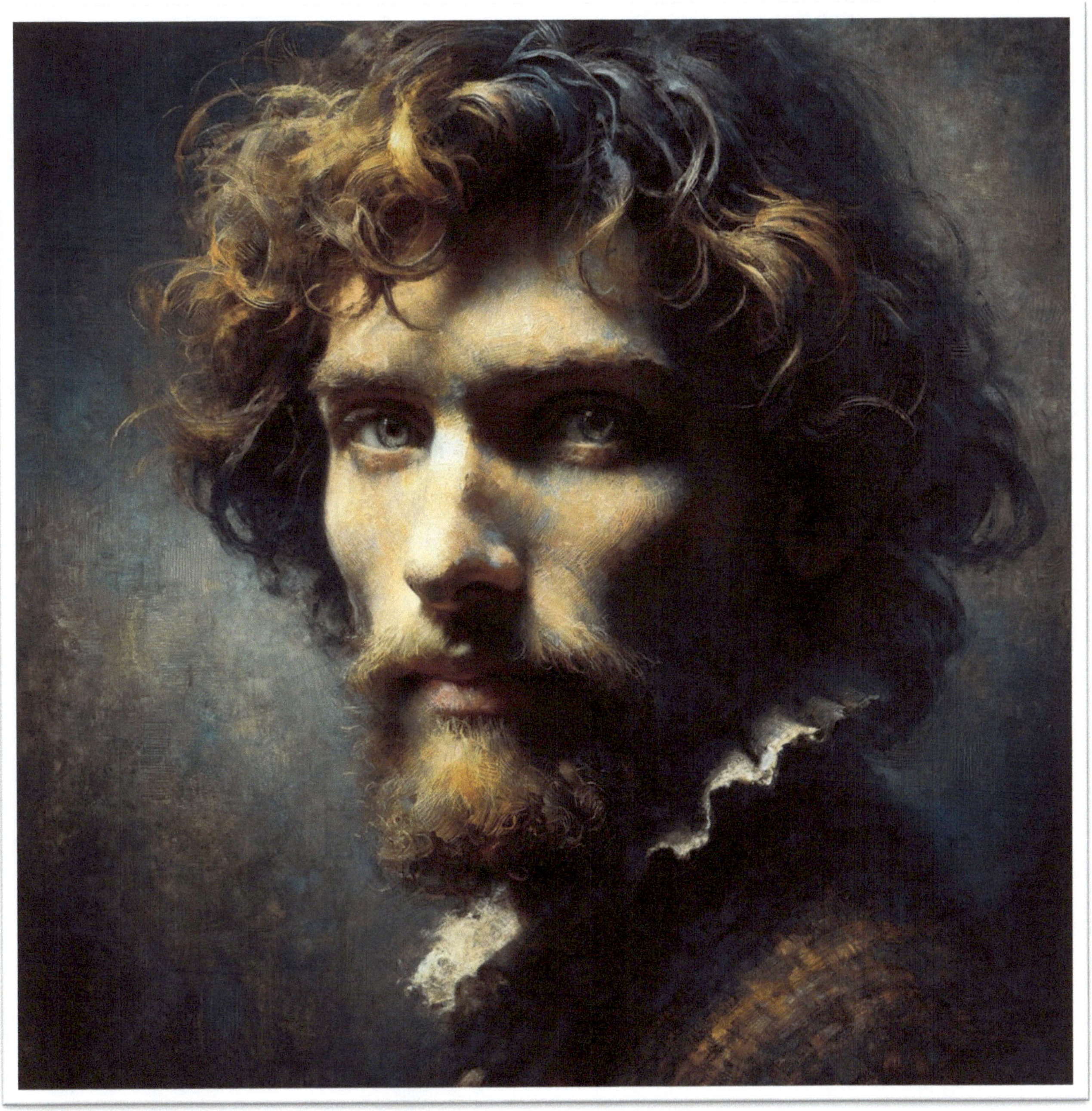

Case Study 2: "DeepArt"

The original digital artwork below illustrates the concept of "DeepArt", reimagining a vintage steamboat scene in a style like early 20th-century cartoons. The composition blends traditional animation with modern digital art techniques, paying homage to the influence of early animation pioneers. This original digital artwork demonstrates how AI can be used to blend contemporary images with historical artistic styles.

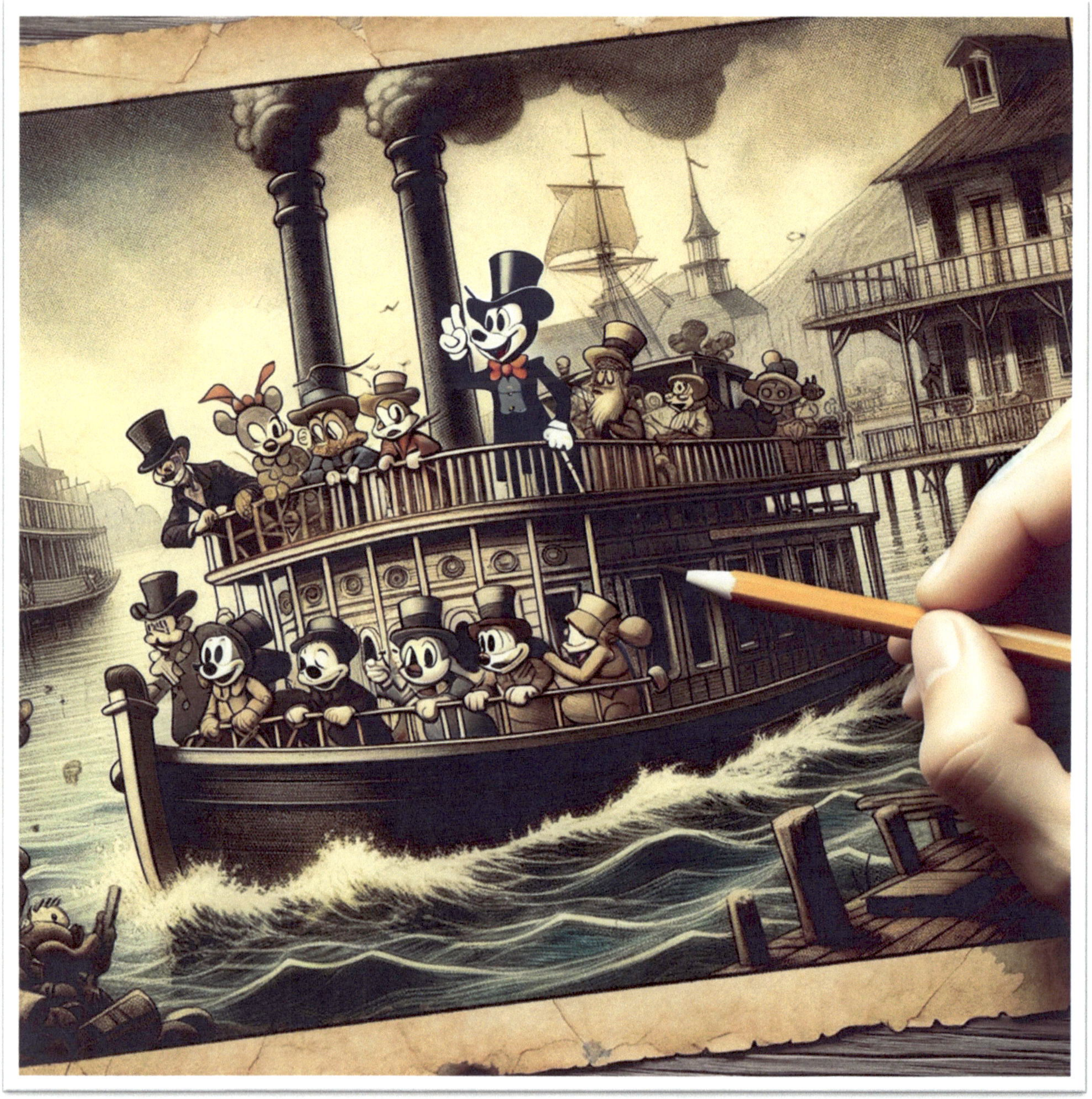

Case Study 3: "AI-Generated Art at Christie's Auction"

In October 2018, Christie's auctioned an AI-generated artwork for the first time. The Paris-based collective Obvious used a Generative Adversarial Network (GAN) to produce an artwork titled *Edmond de Belamy.* That artwork sold for an impressive $432,500, marking a historic moment in the recognition of AI art.

Created using GenAI the original digital artwork below is a portrait created in a style reminiscent of output derived using a Generative Adversarial Network (GAN). This artwork features a soft and surreal face that appears vaguely male but is not human, embodying an abstract and artistic interpretation. The portrait carries a sense of depth and complexity, with subtle shadows that evoke a haunting and introspective mood.

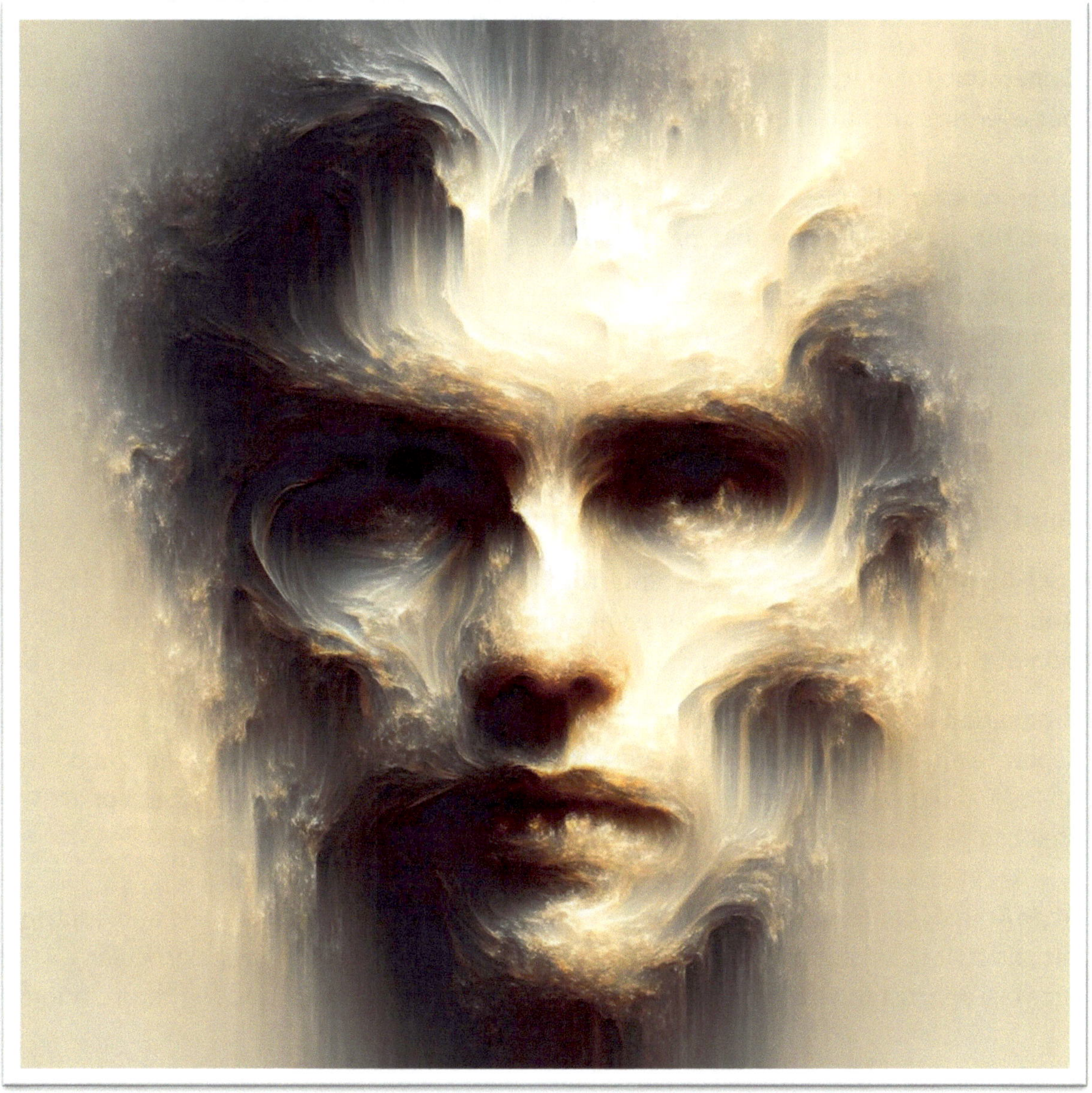

Generative Adversarial Networks (GANs)

Generative Adversarial Networks (GANs) represent a groundbreaking class of artificial intelligence models, particularly impactful in the domain of digital art and creative content generation. The concept of GANs was introduced by Ian Goodfellow and his colleagues in 2014, marking a significant milestone in the field of machine learning.

Origins of GANs

The foundational idea behind GANs emerged from the desire to model and generate complex data distributions in an unsupervised manner, meaning without explicitly labeled examples guiding the learning process. Ian Goodfellow and his team proposed a novel framework where two neural networks, namely the Generator and the Discriminator, are pitted against each other in a game-theoretic scenario, hence the term "adversarial."

- **Generator:** This network learns to generate data. Initially, its outputs are random noise, but over time, it aims to produce data indistinguishable from genuine data.

- **Discriminator:** This network acts as a critic, learning to distinguish between real data from the dataset and fake data produced by the Generator.

The training process involves a delicate balance where the Generator strives to fool the Discriminator by improving its data generation capabilities, while the Discriminator becomes increasingly adept at identifying the fakes. This adversarial process continues until the Generator produces outputs so convincing that the Discriminator can no longer easily differentiate them from real data.

Purpose of GANs in Helping to Create Artwork

The use of GANs to help create artwork stems from their ability to learn and mimic complex data distributions. This capability has opened new horizons for creative expression and the exploration of computational creativity.

1. **Innovation and Creativity:** GANs can generate novel images that do not directly replicate any specific artwork they were trained on but instead blend elements and styles in unique ways. This ability has led to the creation of entirely new pieces of art that can be surprising, evocative, and visually compelling.

2. **Style Transfer and Synthesis:** GANs are particularly adept at understanding and applying artistic styles. Artists and designers can use GANs to apply the style of a particular artwork or artist to a different image, leading to creative mashups and reinterpretations.

3. **Exploring the Boundaries of Art:** GANs challenge traditional notions of authorship and creativity. By generating artwork that could pass as human-made, these networks prompt discussions about the role of technology in art and the nature of creativity itself.

4. **Personalized Art Creation:** GANs can be trained on specific datasets tailored to certain themes, styles, or even individual preferences, allowing for personalized art creation that caters to specific tastes or conceptual visions.

The use of GANs in artwork creation is not just about the technology's ability to produce aesthetically pleasing images. It's also about the potential to explore new forms of creativity, push the boundaries of traditional art-making processes, and engage in profound conversations about the interplay between human creativity and artificial intelligence. Through GANs, artists and technologists alike can explore uncharted territories of artistic expression, making this technology a fascinating frontier in the evolution of digital art.

Chapter 3: Artistic Principles in AI-Generated Art

How Traditional Artistic Principles Apply to AI Art

Traditional artistic principles are foundational concepts in art that guide artists in creating visually compelling and meaningful works. These principles are just as relevant in art created using Generative AI (GenAI) as they are in traditional media. When humans use GenAI prompts, they can apply these principles to guide the AI in producing artworks that adhere to classic aesthetic and compositional standards. Using verbs and descriptors in unique combinations can help you craft precise and imaginative prompts. Note that the effectiveness of these words also depends on how they're combined and contextualized in your GenAI prompt, so experimentation is key.

Here are five examples of how traditional artistic principles apply to art created through GenAI prompts:

Balance and Symmetry

Traditional Principle

Balance involves distributing visual elements evenly to create stability. Symmetry is a type of balance where elements are mirrored on either side of an axis.

Application in GenAI Art

In a GenAI prompt, you could specify a symmetrical composition for a scene, such as a landscape with a central mountain and equal elements of nature on both sides. This guides the AI to create an artwork that feels harmonious and balanced.

Color Harmony

Traditional Principle

Color harmony involves choosing colors that are aesthetically pleasing when used together, often based on their positions on the color wheel.

Application in GenAI Art

In your prompt, you might specify a color scheme, such as analogous colors (colors next to each other on the color wheel) for a serene, cohesive artwork.
For example, a landscape with varying shades of blue and green can create a sense of tranquility.

Contrast

Traditional Principle

Contrast refers to the juxtaposition of opposing elements (like light vs. dark, rough vs. smooth) to create visual interest and draw attention to key areas.

Application in GenAI Art

You can instruct the AI to emphasize contrasts, for instance, by describing a scene with a bright, illuminated subject against a dark, shadowy background, thereby highlighting the focal point through stark contrast.

Perspective and Depth

Traditional Principle

Perspective is the technique used to represent three-dimensional objects on a two-dimensional plane realistically. It creates an illusion of depth and space.

Application in GenAI Art

You can incorporate perspective into your GenAI prompts by describing scenes with foreground, middle ground, and background elements, or by specifying a vanishing point, leading the AI to generate images with a sense of depth.

Unity and Variety

Traditional Principle

Unity ensures that all components of the artwork feel cohesive, while variety adds interest and prevents monotony.

Application in GenAI Art

This can be applied in GenAI by crafting prompts that describe a scene with a unified theme but varied elements. For instance, a cityscape where all buildings adhere to a certain architectural style (unity) but differ in height, color, and details (variety).

By incorporating these traditional artistic principles into GenAI prompts, human creators can effectively steer the AI towards producing artworks that not only showcase the capabilities of AI but also resonate with the aesthetic and compositional qualities valued in human-made art.

This synergy between human artistic sensibility and AI's generative capabilities can lead to the creation of truly unique and compelling artworks.

Understanding Composition, Color Theory, and Style in the Context of AI.

Composition, color theory, and style are crucial for crafting prompts that lead to aesthetically pleasing and meaningful artwork. Let's delve into each of these aspects:

Composition

Composition refers to how visual elements are arranged within an artwork. In traditional art, this involves decisions made by the artist. In AI-generated art, composition is guided by the details provided in the prompt.

Elements of Composition
This includes the placement of objects, the use of space, perspective, balance, and focus. In AI art, the composition can be directed by specifying these elements in the prompt. For instance, "a vase of flowers on the right, with ample negative space to the left" can guide the AI's placement of objects.

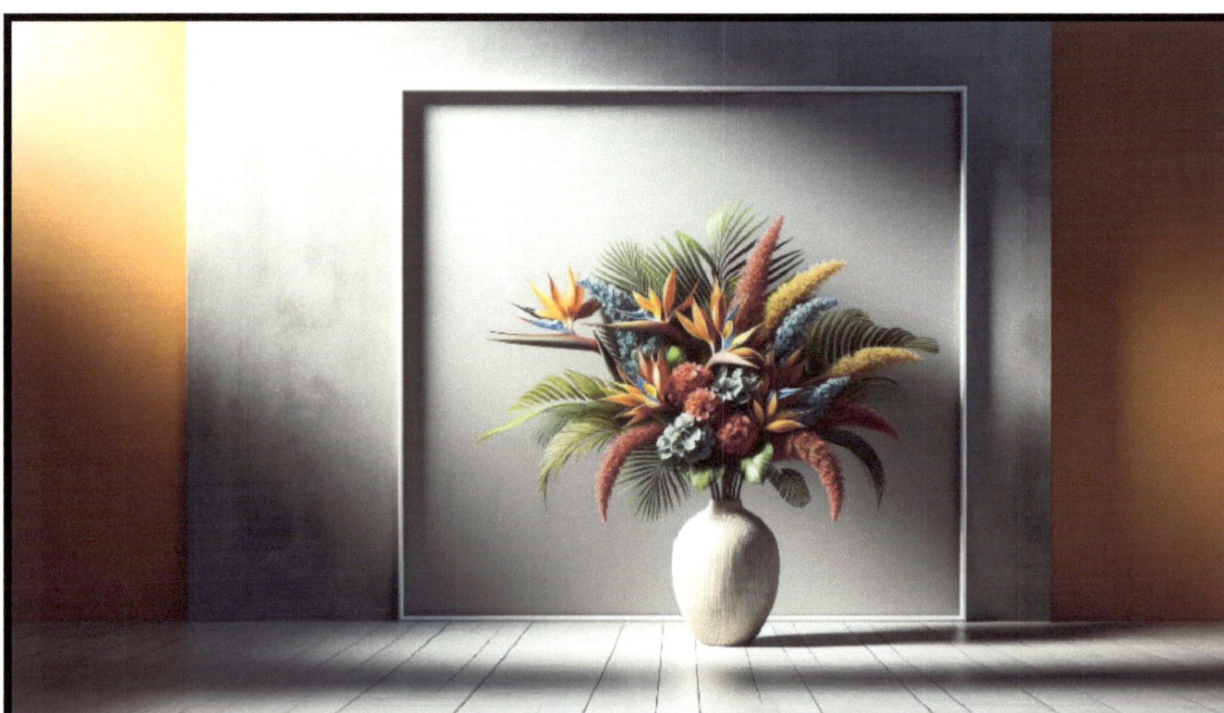

Rule of Thirds

The “Rule of Thirds” principle can be incorporated into AI prompts by specifying elements to be placed along imaginary lines that divide the image into thirds, both horizontally and vertically, creating more dynamic compositions.

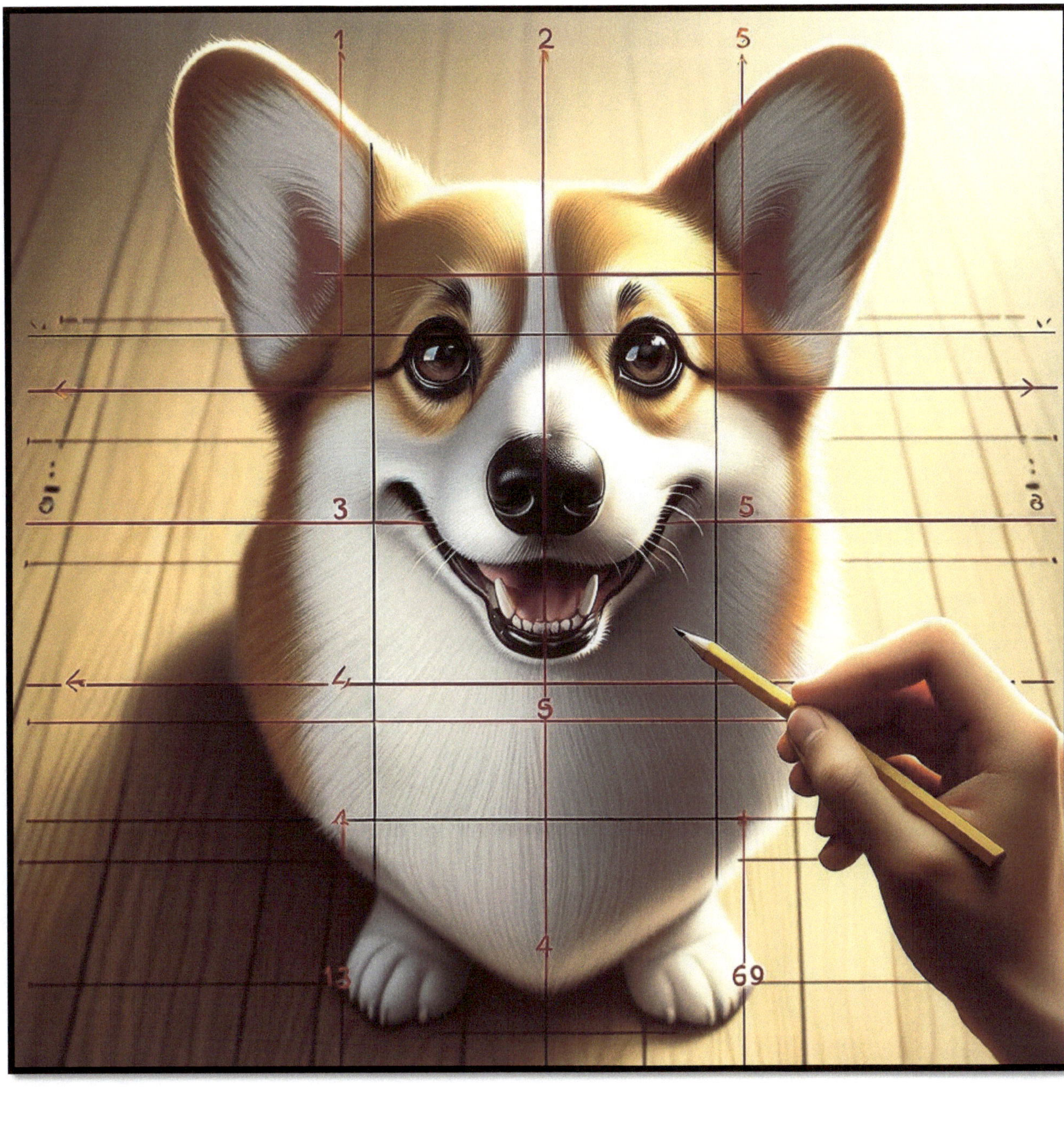

Leading Lines

Prompts can describe elements that lead the beholder's eye through the artwork, like a winding river or a row of trees. Lines can be solid, dashed, dotted, even ephemeral and imaginary.

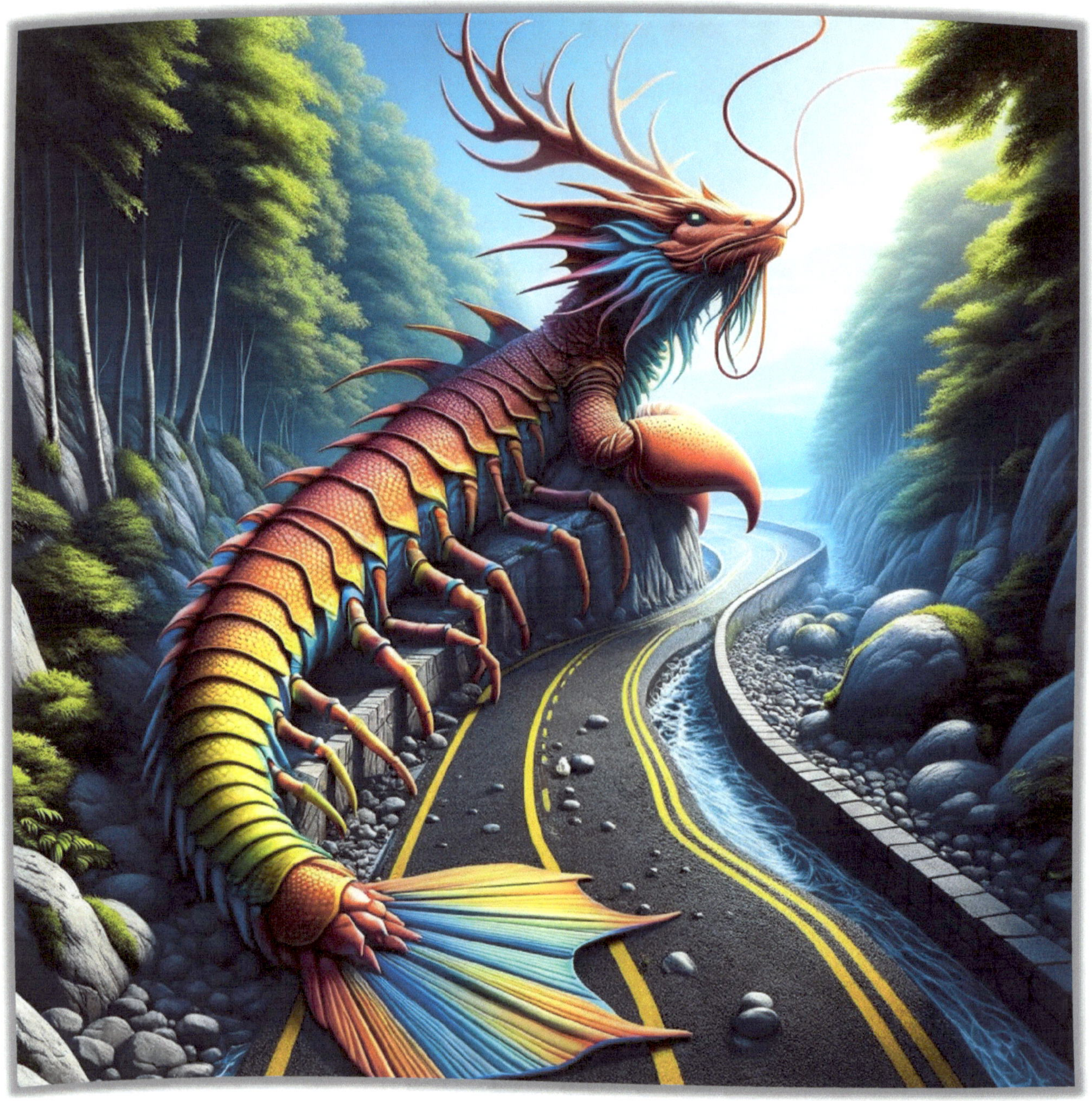

Color Theory

Color theory in AI art involves the strategic use of colors to evoke emotions, create harmony, or convey a message. Color theory, when applied through GenAI in the creation of artwork, acts as a bridge between the realms of human emotion and technological precision, unlocking infinite possibilities for visual storytelling and emotional resonance.

Color Schemes
Specify harmonious color schemes in your prompts, like analogous, complementary, or monochromatic schemes.

Emotional Impact
Colors can be used to set a mood. For example, blue for calmness or red for excitement. A prompt like "a serene landscape bathed in soft blues and greens" utilizes color theory to evoke calmness.

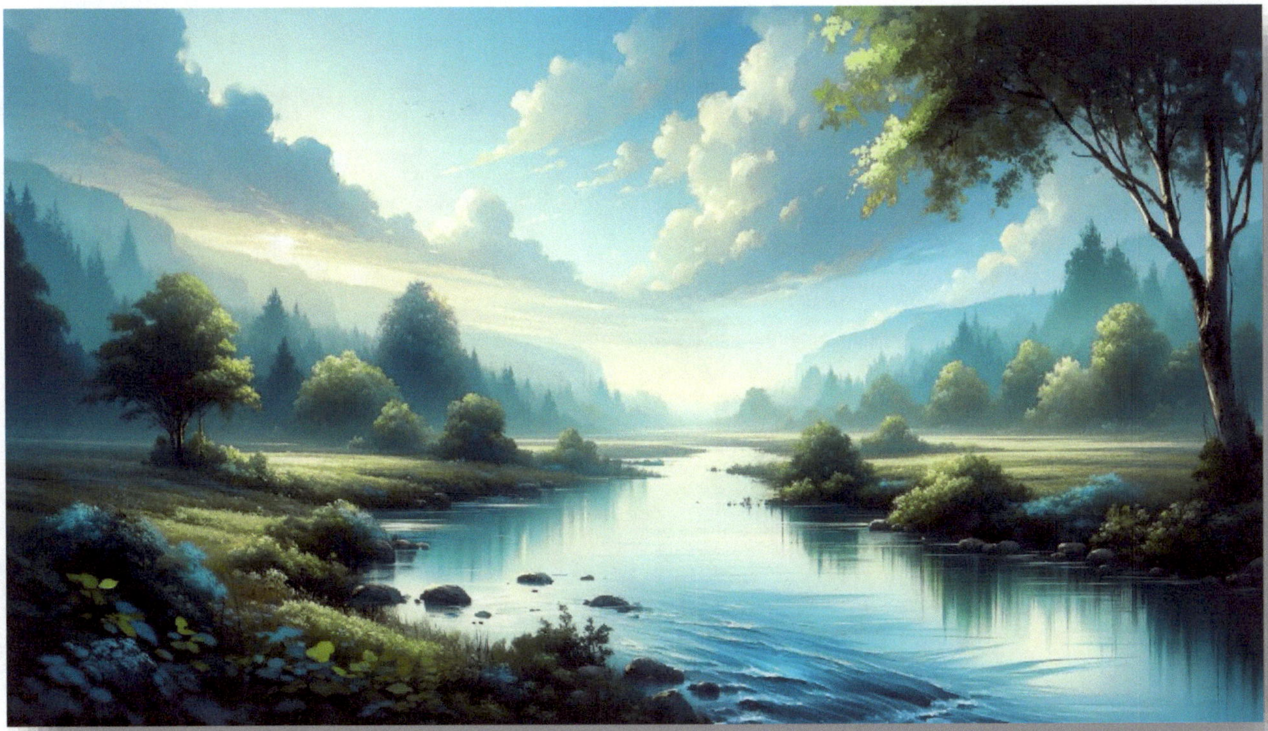

Contrast and Balance
Use colors to create contrast (e.g., light against dark) or balance (e.g., cool and warm colors in equal measure).

Style

Style in AI-generated art encompasses not only the broad spectrum from realistic to abstract and impressionistic to surreal but also delves into a myriad of other artistic nuances and genres, offering a boundless canvas for creativity. This includes the geometric precision of Cubism, the vibrant spontaneity of Expressionism, the dreamlike serenity of Romanticism, and the stark minimalism of Modernism. Furthermore, AI can mimic the detailed narratives of Classical art, the bold contrasts of Pop Art, and the dynamic fluidity of Futurism. It can even explore the digital abstraction of Glitch Art and the fantastical realms of Concept Art, allowing artists to blend historical influences with futuristic visions. The versatility of AI in art creation enables the fusion of styles, eras, and elements, fostering a unique visual language that can communicate complex emotions, concepts, and stories with unprecedented depth and diversity.

Artistic Influences
You can guide the AI to emulate blended artistic styles by referencing them in your prompts, such as "in the style of impressionism and reminiscent of cubism".

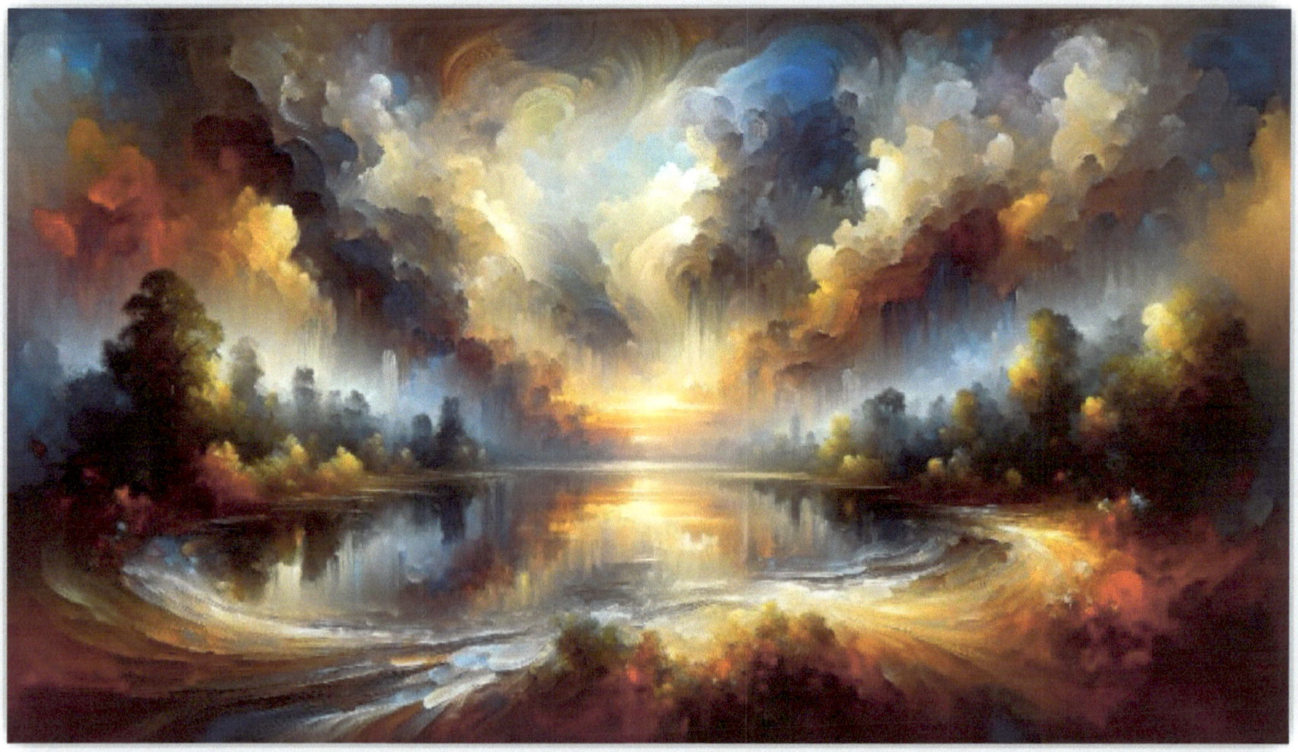

Era and Culture

Incorporating styles from specific historical periods or cultures can add depth to AI art, like "a scene in the style of Ancient Egyptian art".

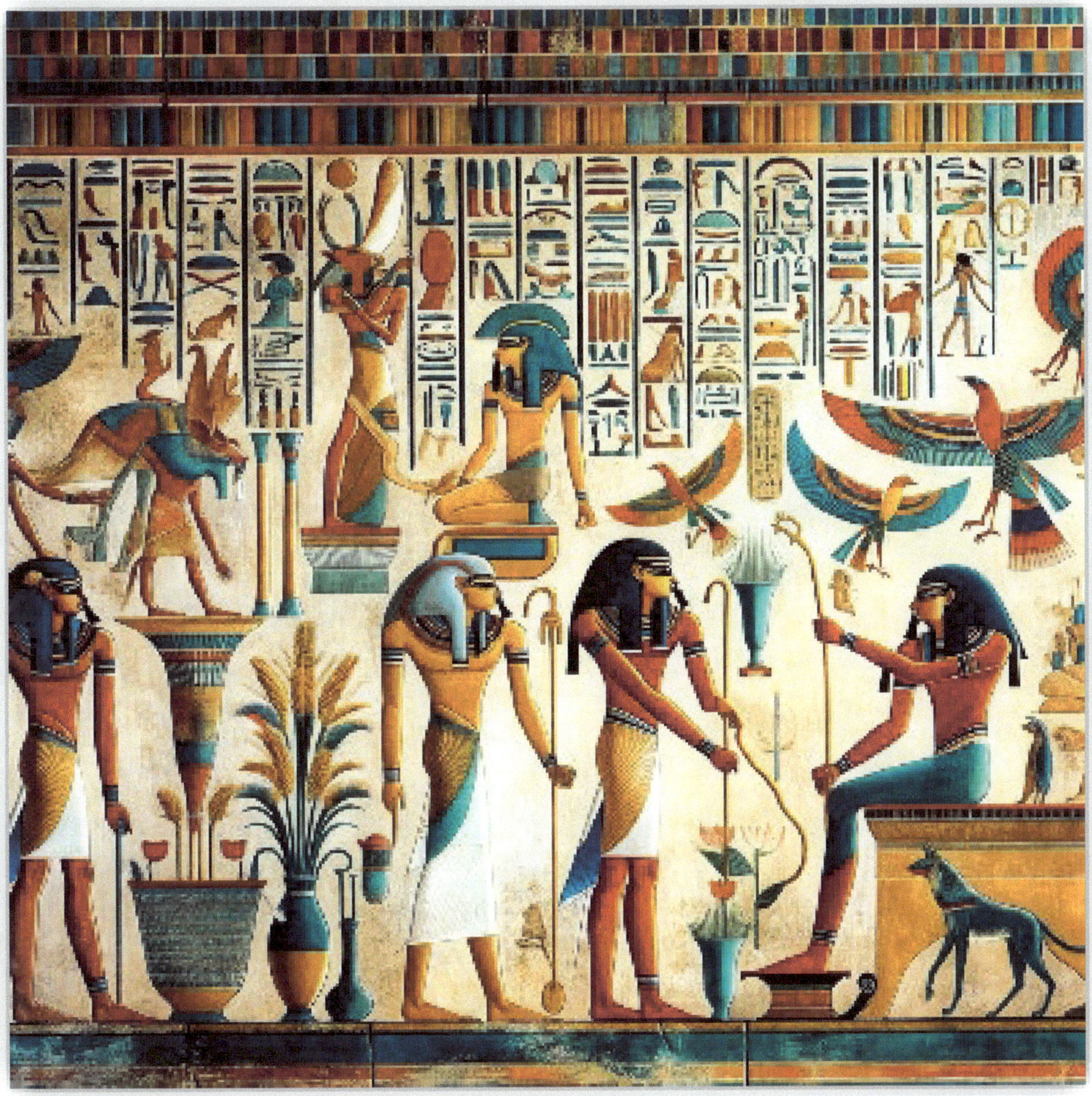

Technique and Texture

Descriptions can include brushwork styles (e.g., broad, gestural strokes), or textures (e.g., smooth, glossy surfaces), guiding the AI in how the final image should appear.

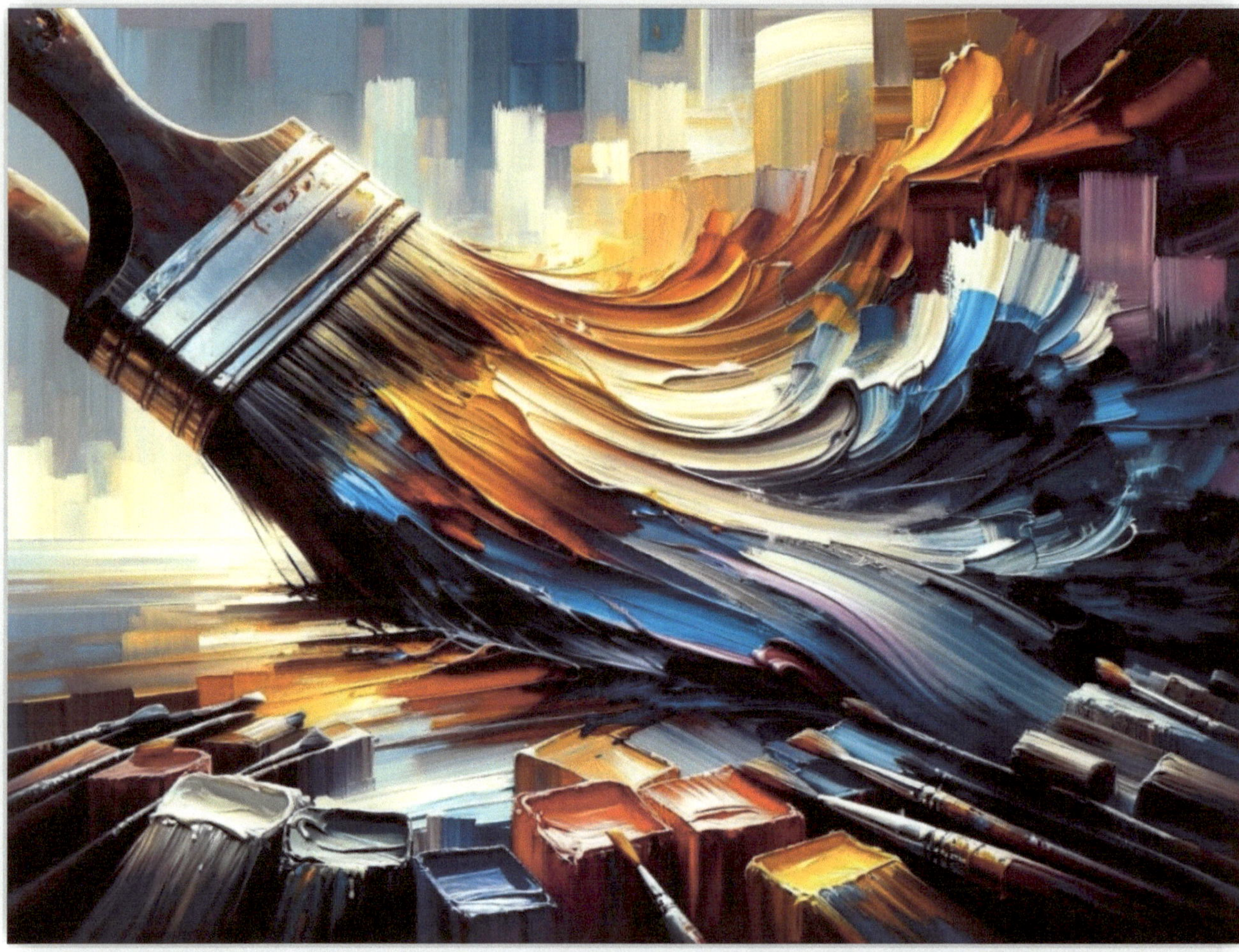

Chapter 4: Action Verbs and Descriptors for GenAI Art Masterpieces

Highly effective GenAI prompts are vivid, specific, and evocative. As an artist you must purposefully guide GenAI to produce detailed and compelling imagery (or other output) that reflects your creative vision.

Set forth below are curated Action Verbs and Descriptors (Colors, Textures/Patterns, Artistic Styles, Elements/Natural World, Moods/Atmospheres) that have proven effective in power prompts for GenAI to create original art.

Action Verbs

Each of these verbs can be used to evoke vivid imagery and dynamic action, making them particularly useful in creative writing, descriptive narratives, and other expressive contexts.

- **Ascend**: To move upward, climb, or rise.
- **Blossom**: To flourish or develop, often in a metaphorical sense.
- **Blur**: To make or become unclear or less distinct.
- **Cascade**: To fall or flow like a waterfall, often in large quantities.
- **Converge**: To come together from different directions; meet.
- **Dazzle**: To impress deeply; astonish with delight.
- **Dissolve**: To become incorporated into a liquid so as to form a solution.
- **Drift**: To be carried slowly by a current of air or water.
- **Emerge**: To come into view or become apparent.
- **Engulf**: To surround or cover completely.
- **Envelop**: To wrap up, cover, or surround completely.
- **Evoke**: To bring or recall a feeling, memory, or image to the conscious mind.
- **Flicker**: To shine unsteadily or intermittently.
- **Flourish**: To grow or develop in a healthy or vigorous way.
- **Flutter**: To move in quick, irregular motions, or to cause something to do this.
- **Glide**: To move smoothly and continuously along, as if without effort or resistance.
- **Glisten**: To shine with a sparkling light, typically caused by moisture.
- **Harmonize**: To make or become harmonious; to blend or coordinate.
- **Hover**: To remain in one place in the air.
- **Ignite**: To catch fire or cause to catch fire.
- **Illuminate**: To light up; brighten.
- **Intertwine**: To become twisted or entwined together.
- **Loom**: To appear as a large, often threatening or unclear shape or object.
- **Meander**: To follow a winding course; wander aimlessly or casually.

- **Merge**: To combine or cause to combine into a single entity.
- **Mimic**: To imitate something so as to resemble closely.
- **Orbit**: To move around a point or body in a circular or elliptical path.
- **Oscillate**: To move or swing back and forth at a regular speed.
- **Permeate**: To spread throughout; pervade.
- **Plunge**: To fall or jump suddenly and deliberately from a high place.
- **Pulsate**: To expand and contract with strong regular movements.
- **Quiver**: To tremble or shake with a slight rapid motion.
- **Radiate**: To emit energy, especially light or heat, in the form of rays or waves.
- **Reflect**: To throw back light, heat, or sound without absorbing it.
- **Resonate**: To produce or be filled with a deep, full, reverberating sound.
- **Revolve**: To move in a circle on a central axis.
- **Ripple**: To form small waves; a small wave or series of waves.
- **Roam**: To move about or travel aimlessly or unsystematically, especially over wide area.
- **Scintillate**: To emit flashes of light; sparkle.
- **Shatter**: To break or cause to break suddenly and violently into pieces.
- **Shimmer**: To shine with a soft, slightly wavering light.
- **Soar**: To fly or rise high in the air.
- **Spiral**: To move in a spiral course.
- **Surge**: To move suddenly and powerfully forward or upward.
- **Swirl**: To move in a twisting or spiraling pattern.
- **Tantalize**: To torment or tease with the sight or promise of something unobtainable.
- **Transform**: To make a thorough or dramatic change in form, appearance, or character.
- **Undulate**: To move with a smooth, wavelike motion.
- **Vibrate**: To move back and forth or to and fro, especially with rapid motion.
- **Warp**: To cause to become bent or twisted out of shape.
- **Weave**: To form by interlacing long threads or elements.
- **Whirl**: To move or cause to move rapidly around and around.

Descriptors: Colors — Primary, Secondary, Tertiary

Humans can see a broad spectrum of colors. Actual perception of color is subjective and can vary based on factors like lighting, context, and individual differences in vision. Variations of these colors can inform GenAI about your artistic intent.

Primary Colors

- Red
- Blue
- Yellow

Secondary Colors

- Green (Blue + Yellow)
- Orange (Red + Yellow)
- Purple (Red + Blue)

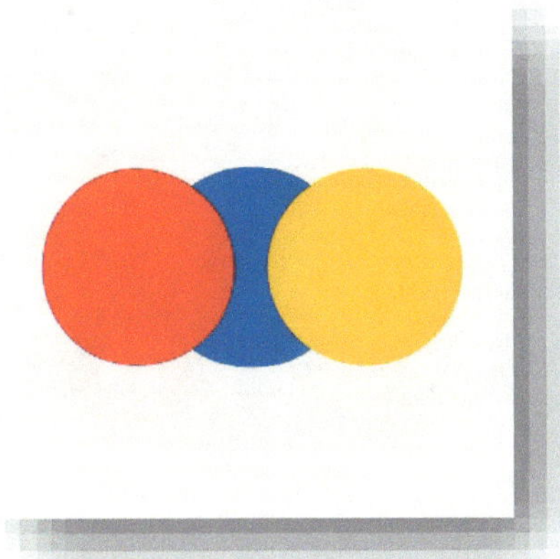

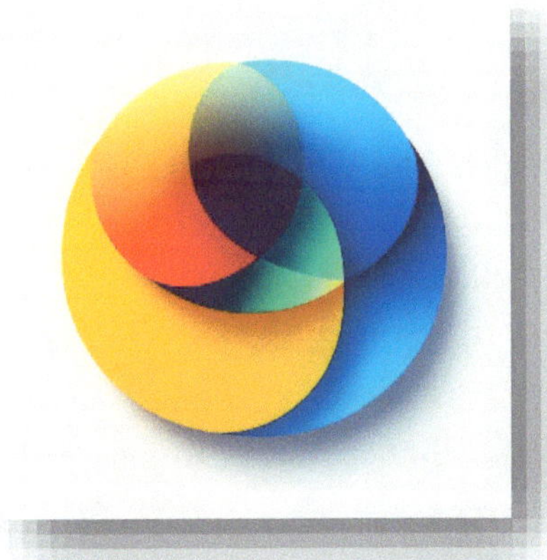

Tertiary Colors

- Blue-Green
- Blue-Purple
- Red-Orange
- Red-Purple
- Yellow-Green
- Yellow-Orange

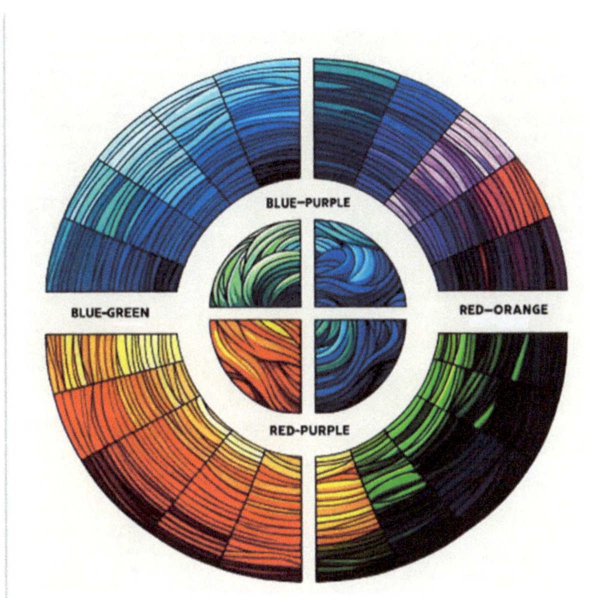

Descriptors: Colors — Blacks

Each of these shades of black has its unique character and application. From the glossy and deep jet to the soft and natural sable, these various blacks can effectively create different atmospheres and styles in art, design, and fashion.

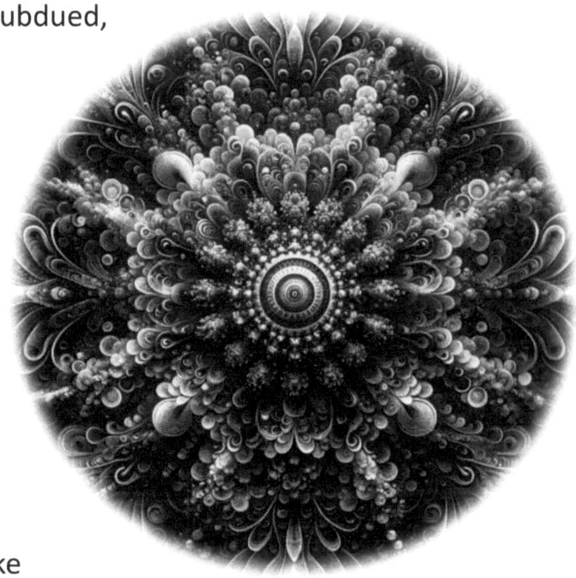

- **Charcoal**: A matte, dark grayish-black, reminiscent of charcoal. It's softer and more muted than a pure black, often used for a more subdued, natural effect.
- **Coal**: A dark black with a slightly ashy, gray undertone. It's reminiscent of coal and is often used for its natural and unpolished quality.
- **Ebony**: A deep, dark black reminiscent of the ebony wood from which it takes its name. It's a dense and rich black with warm undertones.
- **Ink**: A pure, intense black like that of black ink. It has a sharp and clear quality, often associated with precision and depth.
- **Jet**: A gleaming, dark black, named after the gemstone jet. It's known for its shiny, lustrous appearance, often with a slightly bluish or coal-like undertone.
- **Midnight**: A deep, dark black mimicking the sky at midnight. It's a profound and enveloping shade, often used to create a sense of depth and infinity.
- **Obsidian**: A shiny, glass-like black like the volcanic glass obsidian. It often has a very dark, deep appearance with a subtle sharpness.
- **Onyx**: A deep and smooth black, like the precious stone onyx. It often has a glossy sheen and can sometimes present faint hints of green or gray.
- **Raven**: A deep, intense black with a bluish undertone, evoking the color of a raven's feathers. It's dynamic and rich, often associated with mystery and intrigue.
- **Sable**: A soft and rich black, with a hint of brown, like the fur of the sable. It's less harsh than pure black, with a slightly warmer and more natural feel.

Example 1: Black effectively illustrates precision and depth.

This artwork illustrates how the color black conveys precision and depth by showcasing a high-tech precision tool against a deep, pure black background. The subtle lighting highlights the sleek lines and intricate details of the tool, emphasizing its precision. The black background enhances the tool's appearance, adding depth and contrast, and drawing attention to its meticulous engineering and design. This visual representation demonstrates the powerful aesthetic and symbolic qualities of the color black in emphasizing precision and depth.

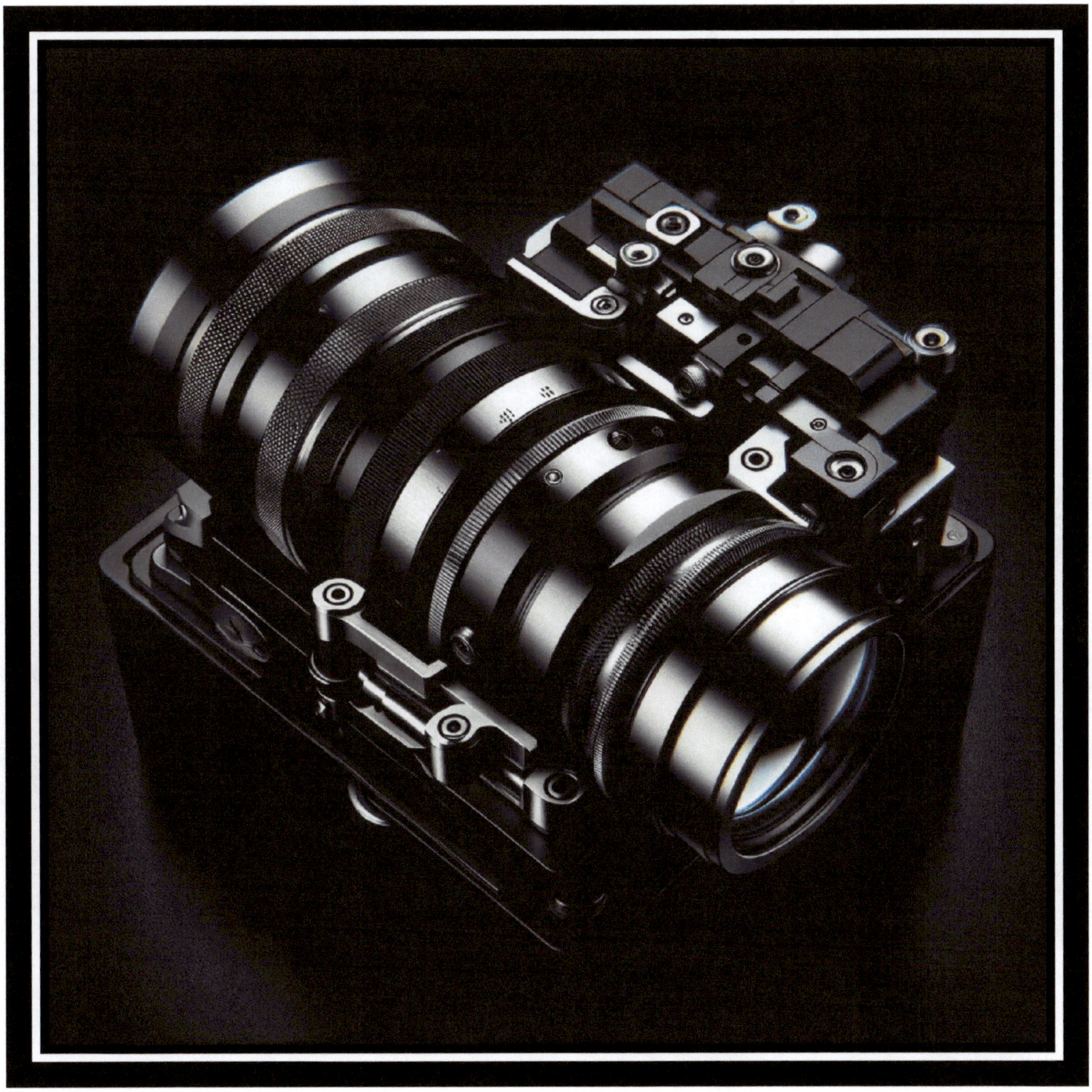

Example 2: Textures with depth illustrate how the color black depicts beauty and precision.

This artwork features a beautiful African American girl with a beaming personality. Her natural skin tone is depicted in a photorealistic manner. The focus of the scene is a precisely engineered black-colored mechanical apparatus, positioned clearly in the foreground. This setup aims to exhibit the precision, depth, and intricacy of the black-colored apparatus. Strategic lighting enhances the intricate design of the apparatus, the girl's engaging interaction with it, the natural beauty of her skin, and the overall depth of the scene, highlighting the themes of precision, engagement, and the profound depth conveyed by the color black.

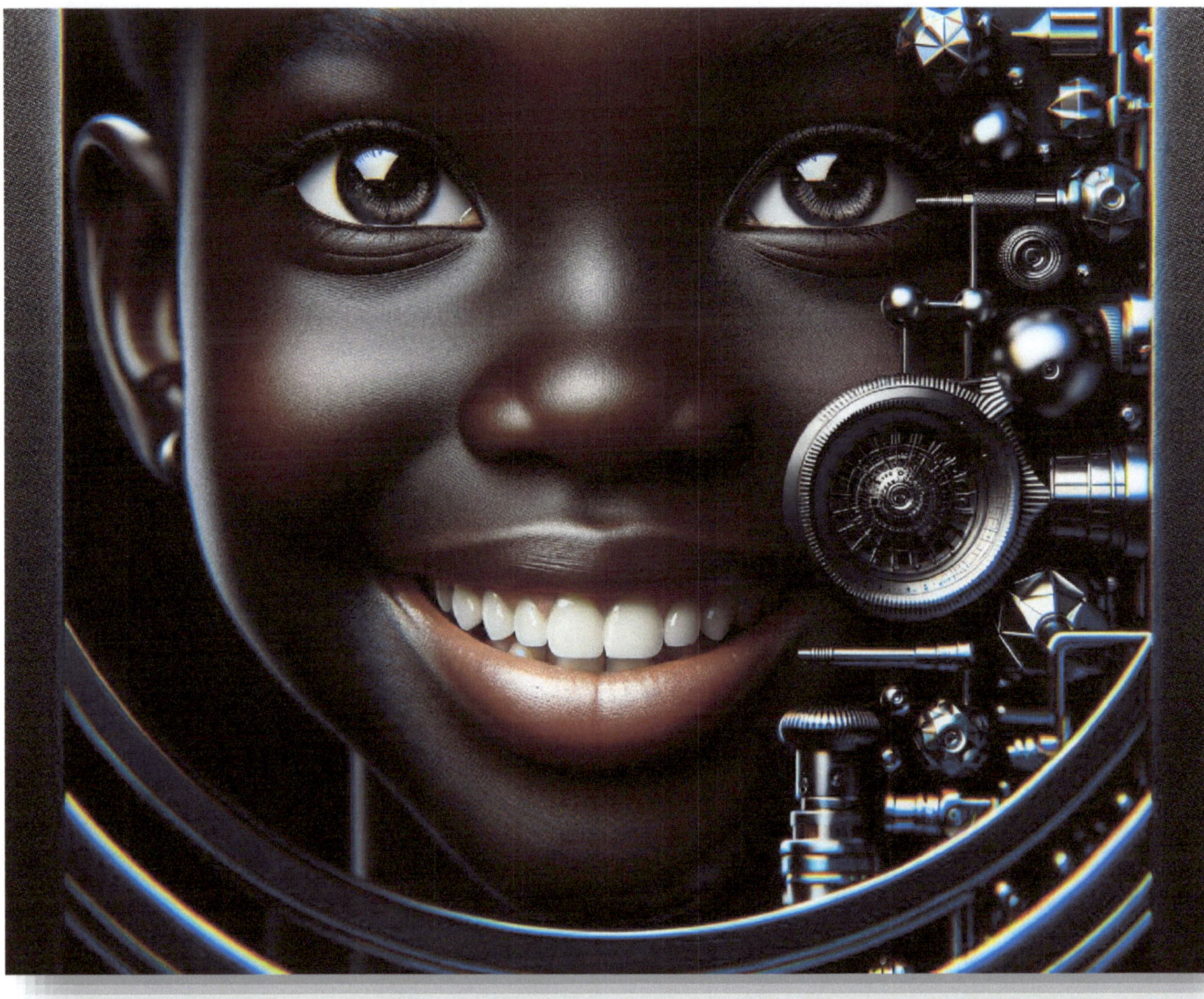

Descriptors: Colors — Blues

Each of these shades of blue offers a different mood and aesthetic, from the calming azure and sky blue to the deep and regal navy and royal blue. These varied blues are used in design, fashion, and art to convey a wide range of emotions and themes.

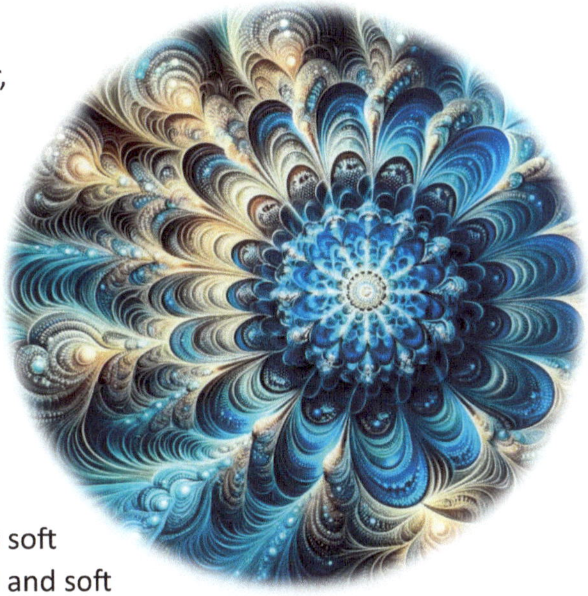

- **Azure**: A bright, clear blue that resembles a cloudless sky. It's a vibrant and refreshing color, often associated with calmness and serenity.
- **Cerulean**: A bright sky blue with a slight greenish tint. Cerulean is fresh and vibrant, often evoking feelings of spring and renewal.
- **Cobalt blue**: A medium to dark blue with a slight hint of violet. Cobalt blue is intense and vivid, often used in art and decoration for its striking presence.
- **Cornflower blue**: A light to medium shade of blue with a hint of lavender. Cornflower blue is soft and pleasing to the eye, often used in peaceful and soft décor schemes.
- **Midnight blue**: A very dark, almost black shade of blue. Midnight blue is rich and mysterious, resembling the night sky and offering a more dramatic alternative to black.
- **Navy**: A very dark blue, almost akin to black. Navy is a classic and sophisticated shade, often used in formal settings for its depth and stability.
- **Royal blue**: A deep, vivid blue, striking and bold. Royal blue conveys richness and opulence, often used to grab attention and signify importance.
- **Sky blue**: A soft, light blue that mirrors the daytime sky. It's a peaceful and tranquil color, often used to create a sense of openness and airiness.
- **Teal**: A darker cyan, blending blue and green. Teal is a versatile color, conveying a sophisticated yet tranquil feel, suitable for various applications.
- **Turquoise**: A bright blue-green color, reminiscent of the turquoise gemstone. It's a refreshing and inviting shade, often associated with tropical waters and a sense of escape.

Descriptors: Colors — Browns

These brown shades offer a broad spectrum of warmth, depth, and natural appeal. From the metallic and vibrant bronze to the deep and rich umber, each brown shade has its unique character, making them versatile in design, art, and fashion contexts.

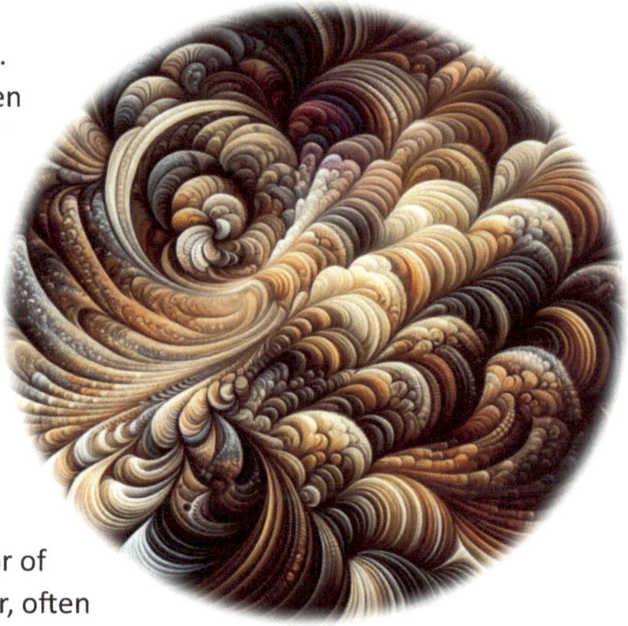

- **Beige**: A light, pale brown with a grayish tint. Beige is a neutral and unobtrusive color, often used for its versatility and subtlety.
- **Bronze**: A medium brown with a reddish-orange undertone and a metallic sheen, similar to the metal bronze. It's a warm and rich color, often associated with strength and resilience.
- **Chestnut**: A rich, reddish-brown shade reminiscent of the color of chestnut wood or shells. It's warm and earthy, with a natural and comforting quality.
- **Chocolate**: A deep, dark brown, like the color of dark chocolate. It's a rich and indulgent color, often associated with luxury and comfort.
- **Cinnamon**: A medium to light reddish-brown, like the spice. Cinnamon is warm and inviting, often used to add a spicy warmth to color palettes.
- **Mocha**: A dark brown with a strong gray to black undertone, like the color of mocha coffee. It's a rich and robust shade, combining the depth of black with the warmth of brown.
- **Sienna**: A medium brown with a strong reddish hue, named after the earth pigment. It's a warm and earthy color, often associated with natural landscapes and rustic settings.
- **Taupe**: A dark gray-brown color. Taupe is a neutral and versatile shade, balancing between earthy brown and complex gray.
- **Umber**: A dark, natural brown with a greenish or grayish undertone. Umber is a deep and rich color, often used in its raw or burnt form for depth and shadow in art.
- **Walnut**: A strong, classic brown that resembles the wood of a walnut tree. It's a traditional and sturdy color, conveying a sense of stability and reliability.

Descriptors: Colors — Greens

Each of these green shades offers a different mood and aesthetic, from the luxurious and vivid emerald to the natural and subdued olive. These varied greens are used in design, fashion, and art to convey a wide range of emotions and themes.

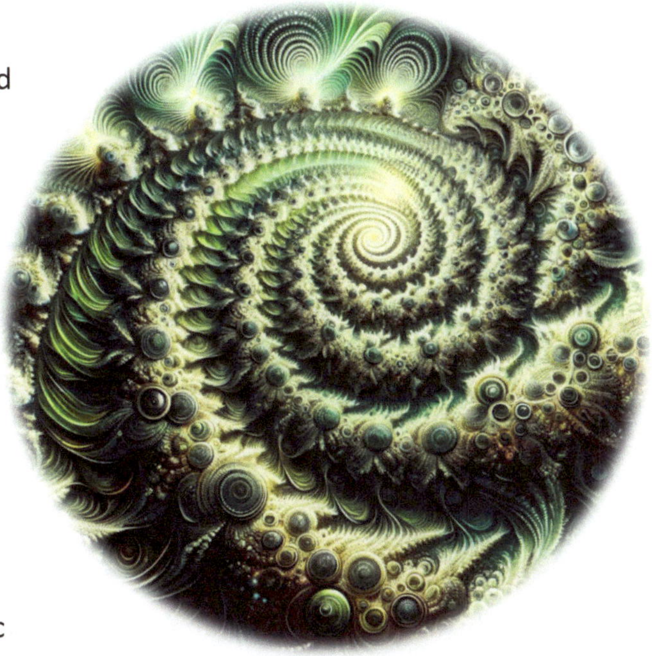

- **Emerald**: A bright, vivid shade of green, resembling the precious gemstone. Emerald green is rich and radiant, often associated with luxury and vibrancy.
- **Forest green**: A deep, dark green mimicking the dense greenery of a forest. It's a natural and calming shade, reminiscent of the outdoors.
- **Jade**: A medium to light green, often with a slight bluish tint, like the jade gemstone. It's a serene and sophisticated color, conveying elegance and tranquility.
- **Kelly green**: A bright, pure green that is striking and lively. Kelly green is a classic shade, often used for its bold and energetic qualities.
- **Lime**: A bright, light green, often with a yellowish tone. Lime is vibrant and zesty, evoking feelings of freshness and liveliness.
- **Mint**: A pale, cool green with a hint of blue. Mint green is refreshing and light, often associated with a clean and crisp aesthetic.
- **Moss green**: A muted, earthy green that resembles the color of moss. It's a subdued and natural shade, conveying a sense of tranquility.
- **Olive**: A dark, yellowish green, like the color of green olives. Olive green is a sophisticated and earthy shade, often used for its natural and muted qualities.
- **Pea green**: A medium, yellow-green color, like the color of fresh peas. It's a lively and natural shade, often associated with spring and new growth.
- **Seafoam green**: A soft, light green with a slight hint of blue, reminiscent of seafoam. It's a tranquil and airy color, often used to evoke a sense of calm and lightness.

Descriptors: Colors — Oranges

Each of these orange shades offers a different nuance and mood, from the rich and earthy burnt orange to the soft and delicate apricot. These varied oranges are used in design, fashion, and art to convey a wide range of emotions and themes.

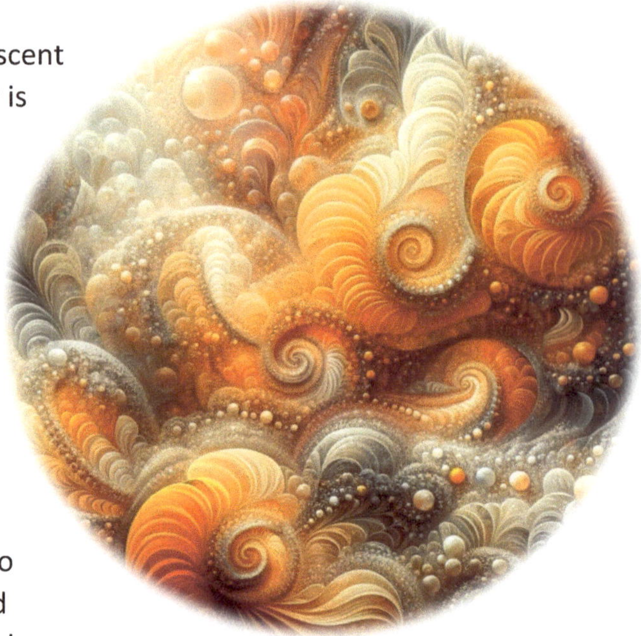

- **Amber**: A warm, golden-orange color, reminiscent of the fossilized resin it's named after. Amber is bright and inviting, often associated with energy and warmth.
- **Apricot**: A soft, light orange with a hint of pink or peach. Apricot is gentle and soothing, evoking the delicate color of the apricot fruit.
- **Burnt orange**: A deep, rich orange with a brownish, earthy quality. Burnt orange is intense and warm, conveying a sense of robust vibrancy.
- **Cantaloupe**: A muted, pastel orange similar to the inside of a cantaloupe melon. It's soft and understated, offering a subtle touch of warmth.
- **Coral**: A vibrant mix of orange and pink, reminiscent of coral in the sea. Coral is lively and bright, often used for its playful and cheerful qualities.
- **Mandarin**: A bright, vivid shade of orange, similar to mandarin oranges. It's a zesty and energetic color, full of life and vibrancy.
- **Peach**: A soft, pale orange with pink undertones, resembling the color of a peach. It's warm and inviting, often associated with sweetness and lightness.
- **Persimmon**: A deep, reddish-orange color, named after the fruit. Persimmon is bold and striking, with an intensity that stands out.
- **Sunset orange**: A radiant blend of red and orange, capturing the colors of a sunset sky. It's dramatic and expressive, full of warmth and depth.
- **Tangerine**: A bright, citrusy orange, more intense than standard orange. Tangerine is vibrant and energetic, often associated with freshness and enthusiasm.

Descriptors: Colors — Grays

Each of these grays can convey different moods and atmospheres, from the boldness of charcoal and gunmetal to the softness of ash and dove gray, making them versatile choices in design and art.

- **Ash gray:** A soft, muted gray with a slightly dusty quality, like the color of ash. It's a balanced, neutral gray without strong undertones.
- **Charcoal gray:** A dark, intense gray, reminiscent of the color of charcoal. It's almost black but has a softer, warmer tone.
- **Dove gray:** A light, warm gray with a hint of beige, giving it a soft and calming quality, much like the feathers of a dove.
- **Elephant gray:** A deep, robust gray with a slight brown undertone, akin to the color of an elephant's skin. It's a natural and earthy shade of gray.
- **Gunmetal gray:** A darker gray with a bluish or greenish undertone, like the color of gunmetal. It often has a slightly metallic sheen.

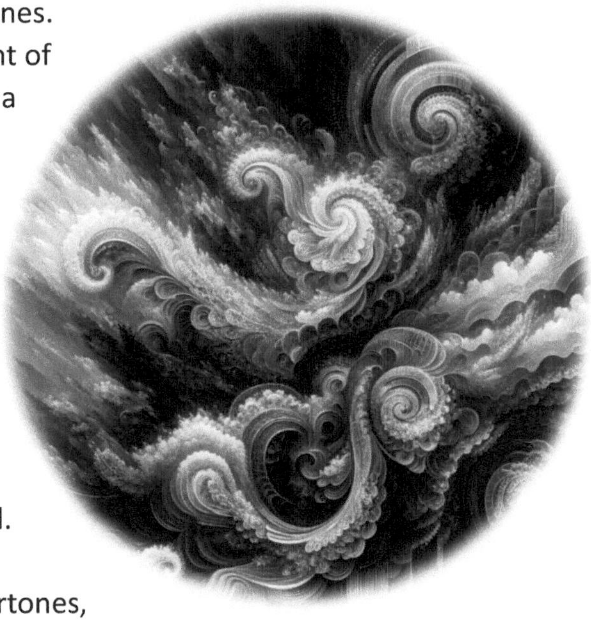

- **Oyster gray**: A pale, soft gray with warm undertones, reminiscent of the color of an oyster shell. It's subtle and unobtrusive.
- **Pewter gray:** A medium gray with a mix of blue and green undertones. It resembles the color of pewter metal, having a slightly warm, muted appearance.
- **Slate gray**: A medium to dark gray with a bluish undertone, like the color of slate rock. It often has a slightly earthy hue.
- **Silver gray:** A light, bright gray that resembles the sheen of silver. It has a metallic and shiny aspect, making it appear lively and vibrant.
- **Steel gray:** A cool, bluish gray that resembles steel. It's typically a medium shade of gray that has an industrial, strong character.

Descriptors: Colors — Pinks

Each of these shades of pink offers a different mood and aesthetic, from the understated elegance of blush and ballet slipper pink to the bold vivacity of fuchsia and hot pink. They can be used in various contexts, from fashion and design to art and decor, to convey a wide range of emotions and themes.

- **Ballet slipper pink**: A very light, almost pastel pink that resembles the color of ballet slippers. It's delicate and soft, conveying a sense of innocence and grace.
- **Blush:** A soft and pale pink with slightly peachy undertones. It's subtle and unassuming, often associated with a natural, flushed look on the cheeks.
- **Bubblegum pink:** A bright and sweet shade of pink, reminiscent of classic bubblegum. It's playful and youthful, with a sugary and cheerful tone.
- **Coral pink:** A brighter shade of pink with a strong influence of orange. Coral pink is lively and tropical, often evoking feelings of warmth and playfulness.
- **Fuchsia:** A bright and vibrant pink with a strong hint of blue, making it a cooler shade. Fuchsia is eye-catching and vivid, often used to make a bold statement.
- **Hot pink:** An intense, bright pink that commands attention. Hot pink is a warmer shade, standing out for its neon-like, almost fluorescent quality.

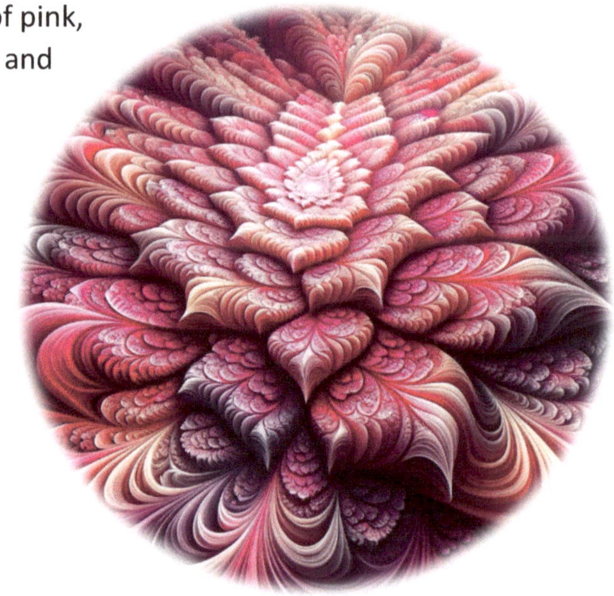

- **Magenta:** A deep, purplish pink, more saturated and bolder. Magenta stands out for its richness and depth, often associated with creativity and uniqueness.
- **Peach pink:** A soft, muted shade that blends pink with the warmth of peach. This color has a gentle, soothing quality and is often used in settings requiring a subtle yet warm palette.
- **Rose**: A classic, medium pink that resembles the petals of a rose flower. It's a romantic and elegant shade with a balanced tone, neither too light nor too dark.
- **Salmon**: A soft, orangish pink that resembles the color of salmon flesh. It's a warm shade, combining the gentle aspects of pink with the vibrancy of orange.

Descriptors: Colors — Purples

Each of these shades of purple offers its unique character. From the soothing and gentle lavender to the deep and mysterious indigo, these various purples can be used in design, fashion, and art to create diverse moods and styles.

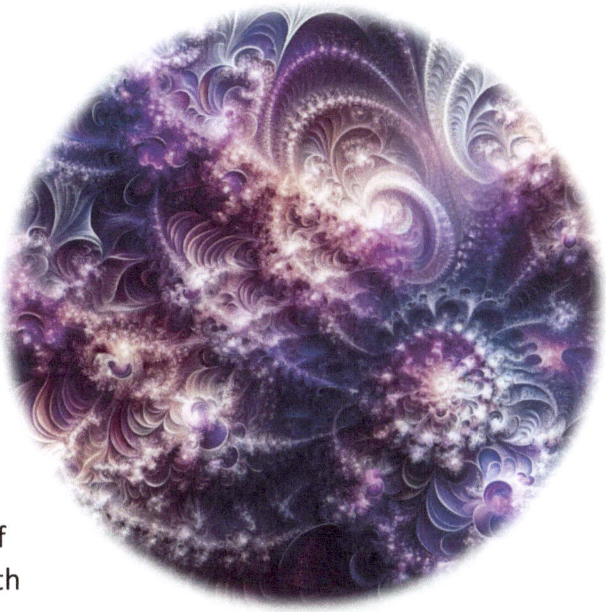

- **Amethyst**: A medium to dark purple that resembles the gemstone of the same name. It's a regal and mystical shade, often linked to spirituality and luxury.
- **Indigo**: A deep and dark purple with a significant blue undertone. Indigo is reminiscent of the night sky and often associated with depth and stability.
- **Grape**: A dark and muted purple, like the skin of a grape. This shade is rich and earthy, offering a more subdued and natural purple.
- **Lavender**: A light, delicate purple with a hint of blue. It's soft and calming, often associated with spring and floral freshness.
- **Lilac**: A pale and soft purple with a slightly pink tint. Lilac is gentle and serene, often associated with early spring blooms.
- **Mauve**: A muted, dusty purple with grayish undertones. Mauve is subtle and sophisticated, often seen as a vintage or romantic color.
- **Orchid**: A bright and soft purple with pink undertones. Orchid is playful and exotic, evoking the beauty and rarity of the orchid flower.
- **Plum**: A rich, deep purple with hints of red. Plum is a warm and lush color, reminiscent of the fruit it's named after.
- **Royal Purple**: A deep and vibrant purple, traditionally associated with nobility and luxury. Royal purple is a bold and majestic shade, often used to convey a sense of richness and opulence.
- **Violet**: A vibrant purple that leans slightly towards blue. Violet is bright and lively, often associated with luxury and creativity.

Descriptors: Colors — Reds

Each of these red shades offers a different mood and aesthetic, from the deep and luxurious burgundy to the vibrant and energetic scarlet. These varied reds are used in design, fashion, and art to convey a wide range of emotions and themes.

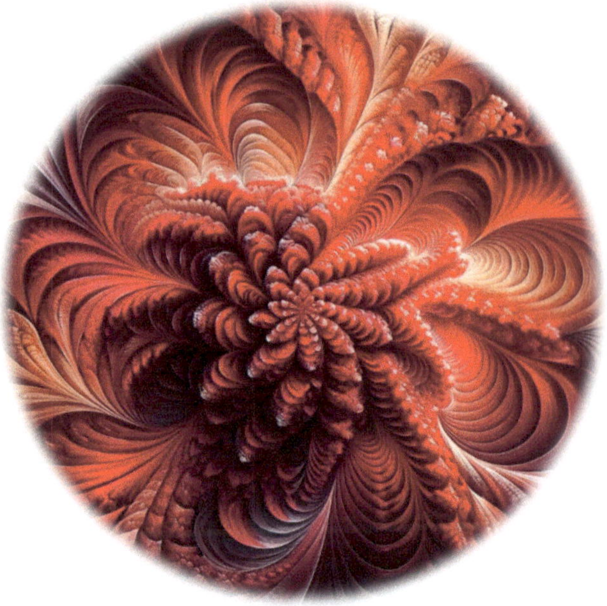

- **Burgundy**: A deep, dark red with a hint of purple, like the wine from its namesake region in France. Burgundy is rich and sophisticated, often associated with luxury and elegance.
- **Cherry Red**: A bright, vivid red reminiscent of a ripe cherry. It's a lively and playful color, full of energy and brightness.
- **Coral**: A softer red, with a blend of orange and pink tones. Coral is warm and inviting, often evoking a sense of cheerfulness and vivacity.
- **Crimson**: A bright, deep red with a slight bluish undertone. Crimson is intense and passionate, often associated with energy and action.
- **Fire Engine Red**: A pure, intense, and bright red, resembling the color of a fire engine. It's a bold and attention-grabbing color, symbolizing urgency, and dynamism.
- **Maroon**: A dark, brownish-red color, more subdued than brighter reds. Maroon is rich and warm, often used for its comforting and refined qualities.
- **Ruby Red**: A deep, vivid red like the precious ruby gemstone. It's luxurious and glamorous, with a timeless appeal.
- **Scarlet**: A bright red with a slight orange undertone. Scarlet is vivid and striking, often associated with courage and love.
- **Vermilion**: A brilliant reddish orange, originally derived from the mineral cinnabar. Vermilion is bold and bright, often used in artistic and decorative contexts.
- **Wine Red:** A deep, rich red reminiscent of red wine. It's a sophisticated and mature color, conveying depth and complexity.

Descriptors: Colors — Yellows

Each of these yellow shades offers a different nuance and mood, from the luxurious and opulent gold to the calm and understated beige. These varied yellows are used in design, fashion, and art to convey a wide range of emotions and themes.

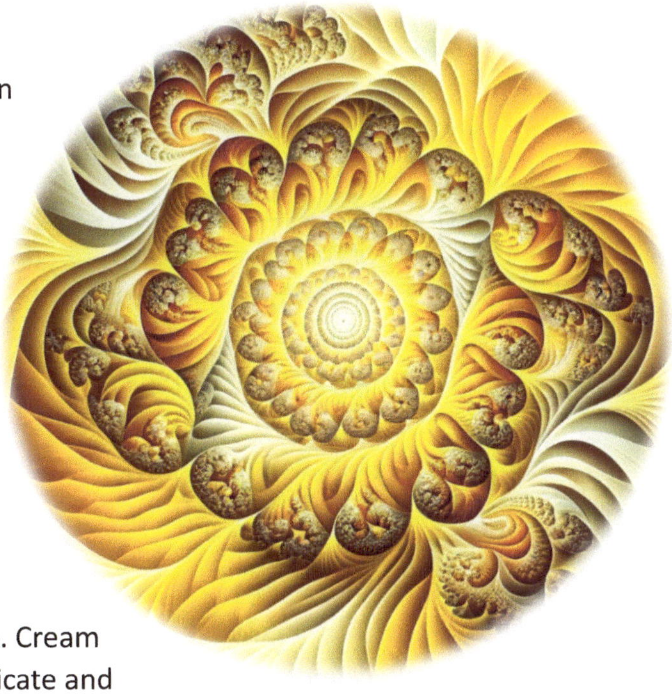

- **Beige**: A soft, pale yellow-brown color, often seen as a neutral tone. Beige is subtle and unassuming, providing a calming and understated background.
- **Butter**: A light, soft yellow, reminiscent of the color of butter. It's a warm and gentle shade, exuding comfort, and simplicity.
- **Canary Yellow**: A bright, pure yellow that resembles the vibrant plumage of a canary bird. It's cheerful and lively, evoking a sense of playfulness and energy.
- **Cream**: A soft yellow with a hint of white, creating a smooth and calming appearance. Cream is gentle and soothing, often used for a delicate and refined look.
- **Gold**: A rich, warm yellow with a shiny, metallic hue. Gold is associated with wealth, luxury, and grandeur, offering a sense of opulence and prestige.
- **Lemon**: A bright, vibrant yellow, like the color of lemon fruit. Lemon yellow is fresh and zesty, evoking a sense of freshness and vitality.
- **Mustard**: A dark, warm yellow with a hint of brown, like the condiment. Mustard yellow is earthy and robust, often used for its depth and richness.
- **Saffron**: A deep, golden yellow, named after the spice. Saffron is exotic and luxurious, often used to convey a sense of richness and rarity.
- **Sunflower**: A vivid, medium yellow, reminiscent of sunflower petals. It's a joyful and inviting color, full of warmth and light.
- **Wheat**: A light, muted yellow, akin to the color of wheat fields. Wheat yellow is natural and subdued, evoking a sense of harvest and tranquility.

Descriptors: Colors — Whites

These variations of white can have different appearances based on the material, texture, and lighting conditions.

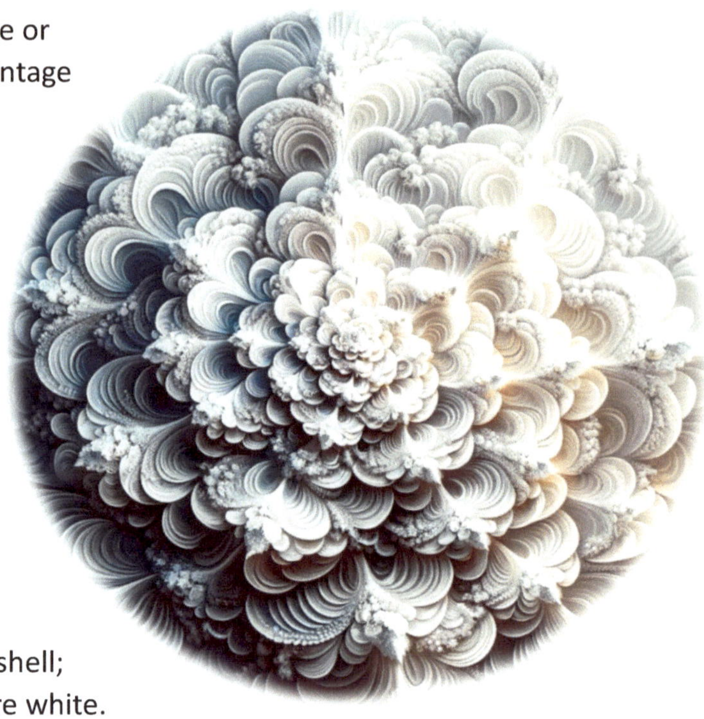

- **Alabaster**: A smooth, pure white with a subtle warmth.
- **Antique White**: A warm white with a beige or slightly yellow tone, giving it an aged or vintage look.
- **Baby Powder**: A soft and pure white, like the color of baby powder.
- **Bone**: A subdued, creamy white with beige undertones.
- **Chalk White**: A dusty, slightly grayish white, like chalk.
- **Coconut Milk**: A subdued, slightly creamy white with a hint of warmth.
- **Cotton White**: Reminiscent of cotton, a clean and crisp white.
- **Cream**: A warmer, richer variant of white with yellow undertones.
- **Eggshell**: Named after the color of an eggshell; slightly warmer and more muted than pure white.
- **Floral White**: A warm white with a slight hint of peach.
- **Frost**: A cool white with a hint of gray, resembling frost.
- **Ghost White**: A very light bluish white, almost ethereal in appearance.
- **Ivory**: A slightly off-white with a warm, yellowish hue.
- **Linen**: A warm white with a slight tan or beige tint, reminiscent of natural linen fabric.
- **Magnolia**: Named after the flower, it's a soft, slightly creamy white.
- **Marshmallow**: A soft, slightly creamy white.
- **Old Lace**: A pale, yellow-tinged white, evoking the color of old lace fabric.
- **Pearl**: A soft white with a hint of iridescence, often found in fabrics and paints.
- **Porcelain**: A bright, pure white, like porcelain ceramics.
- **Pure White**: The most basic form of white.
- **Seashell**: A slightly pinkish white, reminiscent of a seashell's interior.
- **Snow White**: A bright, cool white that resembles snow.
- **Swan White**: A pristine and elegant white with subtle cool undertones.
- **Vanilla**: A warm, soft white with a slight yellowish tint.
- **Whisper**: A very soft, almost imperceptible off-white.

Descriptors: Textures/Patterns

Textures and patterns are essential components in prompts submitted to generative AI, especially in image generation, because they provide detailed visual cues that help the AI understand and replicate specific visual qualities in the generated images.

Here are a few reasons why textures and patterns are particularly important:

Detail and Realism

Textures (like the roughness of tree bark or the smoothness of glass) and patterns (such as the stripes on a zebra or geometric designs on fabric) help in creating more realistic and detailed images. They guide the AI to apply these visual elements in a way that mimics real-world objects more accurately.

Visual Interest

Including textures and patterns in prompts can make an image more visually interesting and engaging. For example, the texture of rust on metal or the intricate pattern of lace can add depth and complexity to an image, making it more visually appealing.

Consistency and Style

Textures and patterns can help maintain consistency and style across a series of images. For instance, specifying a watercolor texture or a cubist pattern can dictate the overall aesthetic of the image, aligning it with a particular artistic style or theme.

Control and Precision

When creating images, specific textures and patterns allow for more precise control over the outcome. By detailing the type of surface finishes, fabric patterns, or environmental textures, creators can guide the AI to produce results that closely match their vision.

Contextual Clarity

In scenarios where the background or environment plays a critical role, textures and patterns can provide context. For example, a cobblestone pattern suggests an old street, while a sleek metallic texture might indicate a futuristic setting.

By effectively using textures and patterns in prompts, users can enhance the quality and specificity of AI-generated images, leading to creations that are both more accurate and artistically compelling.

Ethereal

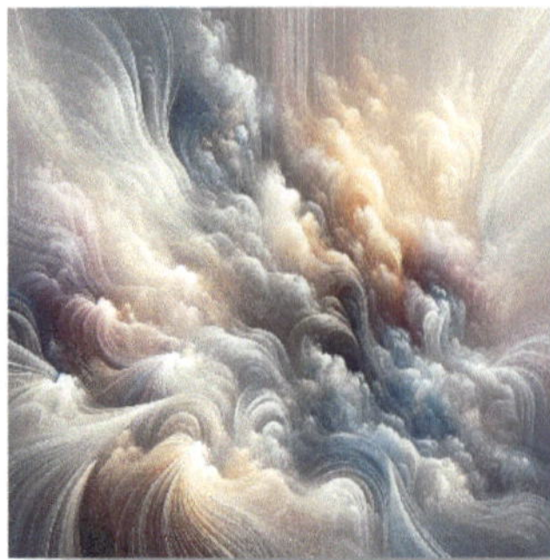

Fractal

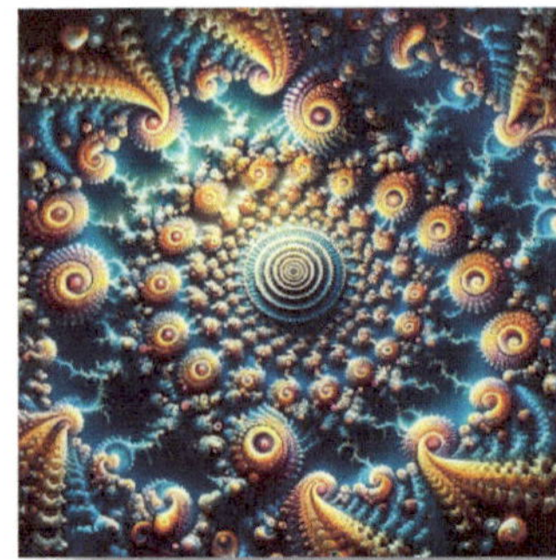

Geometric

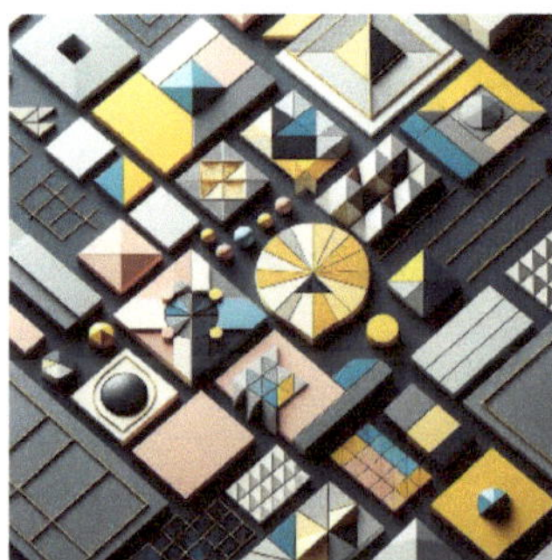

Glass-like

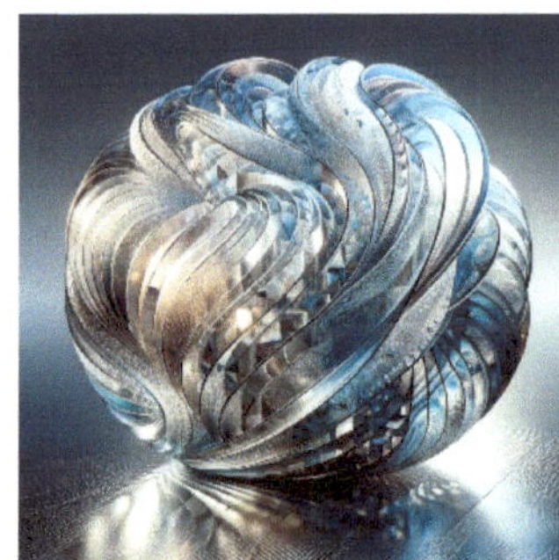

Gossamer

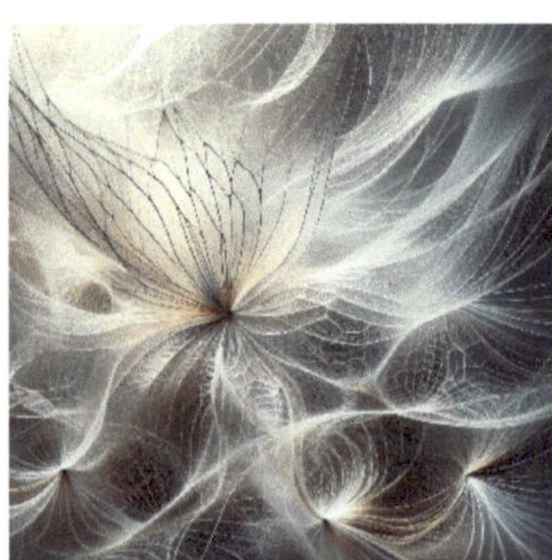

Holographic

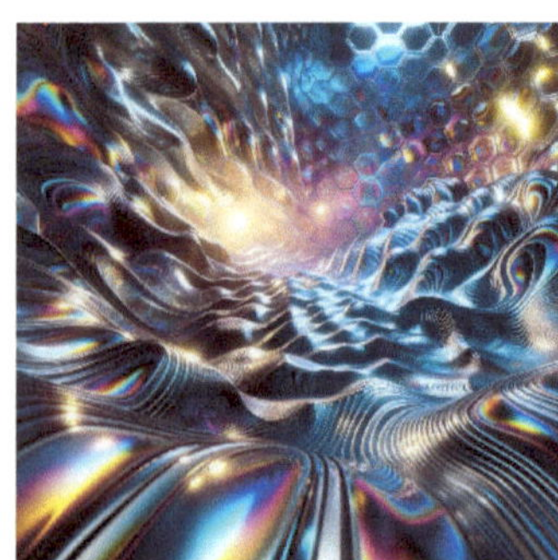

Mirrored

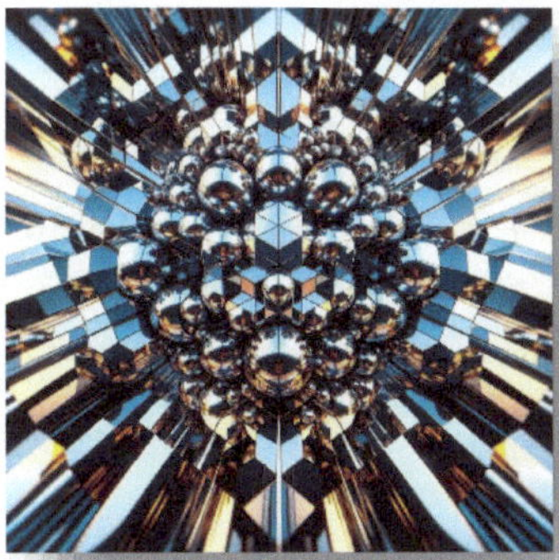

Swirling

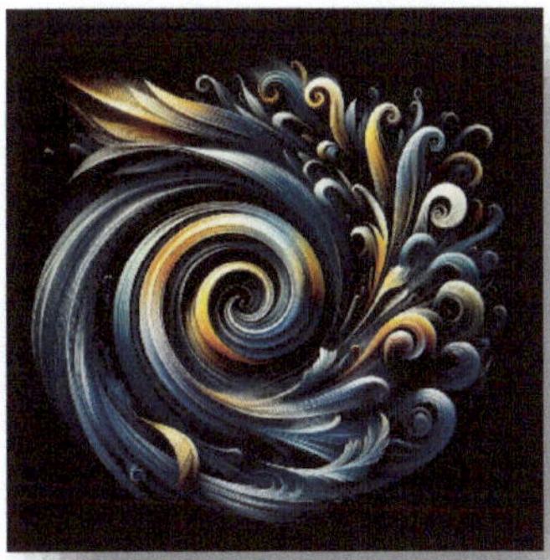

Mosaic

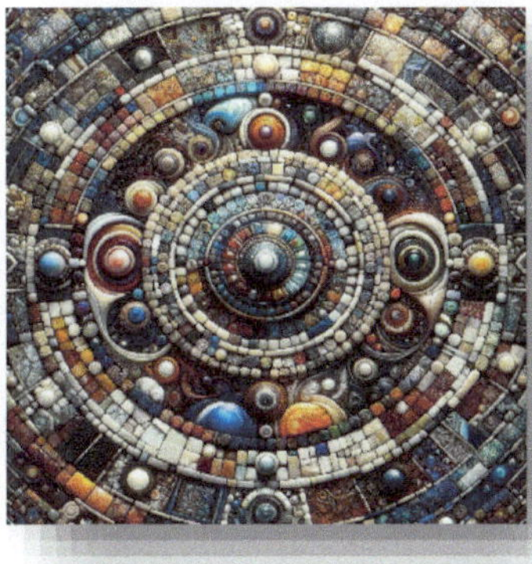

Textured

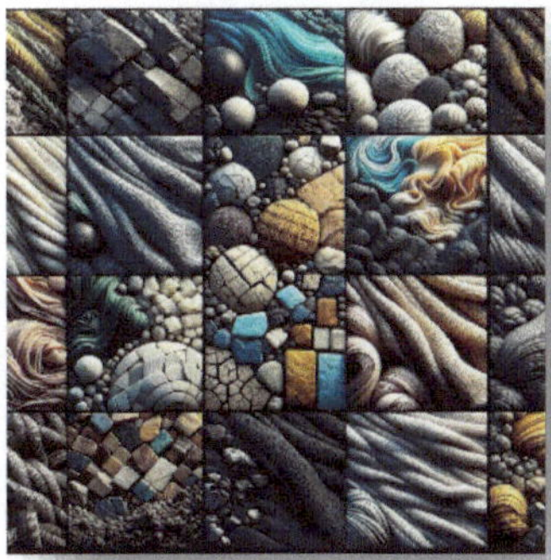

Descriptors: Artistic Styles

"Artistic Styles" refer to the distinctive techniques and methods that characterize the work of artists, movements, or periods in art history. These styles are defined by unique elements such as brushwork, color palette, form, composition, and thematic focus. When crafting prompts for generative AI, especially in the context of image generation, specifying artistic styles can be highly beneficial for several reasons:

Guided Aesthetic Output

By incorporating specific artistic styles into prompts, creators can guide the AI to produce images that adhere to certain aesthetic principles or visual techniques associated with that style. For example, mentioning "Impressionism" might lead the AI to generate images with loose brushwork, vibrant colors, and an emphasis on light and its changing qualities.

Consistency Across Creations

Using artistic styles in prompts ensures a level of consistency across different images. This is particularly useful in projects where a unified look is desirable, such as series of illustrations or themed visual content.

Expressive and Emotional Depth

Different artistic styles convey different emotions and ideas. For instance, a prompt that includes "Expressionism" will lead to images that are more intense and emotionally charged, with vivid expression and often distortion used to evoke moods or ideas.

Educational and Inspirational Value

Employing artistic styles in prompts can serve educational purposes both for the users and the audience. It exposes them to various art historical contexts and styles, potentially inspiring deeper appreciation and understanding of art.

Enhancing Creativity

When users combine elements from various artistic styles or explore less commonly used styles, it can lead to innovative and creative outcomes. This can be particularly intriguing in the realm of digital art, where traditional styles can be blended or altered in novel ways.

Problem Solving and Precision

Specifying an artistic style can help address specific challenges in visual representation. For example, if a prompt needs to evoke a past era or convey a story in a visual manner, referencing a relevant artistic style like "Renaissance" or "Art Nouveau" can provide precise direction to the AI, ensuring the output matches the intended context and narrative.

Incorporating artistic styles into prompts not only enhances the quality of the generated images but also enriches the interaction between the creator and the AI, making the process more engaging and the outcomes more meaningful.

Descriptors: Elements/Natural World, Moods/Atmospheres

The term "elements/natural world" in the context of generative AI prompt crafting refers to components of the natural environment—such as landscapes, flora, fauna, weather conditions, and geological features—that can be used to enrich and specify the content of AI-generated images or texts. This category encompasses everything from forests, mountains, and oceans to specific species of animals and plants, as well as atmospheric phenomena like lightning or fog. Incorporating these elements into AI prompts is important for several reasons:

Visual Richness and Diversity

Elements from the natural world can add significant visual richness and variety to generated images. For instance, specifying "a lush rainforest with dense foliage and cascading waterfalls" can result in vivid, detailed images that capture the complexity of natural scenes.

Context and Setting

Natural elements provide context and setting for a scene, helping to ground the content in a specific environment or atmosphere. This is crucial for creating images that need to convey a particular time of day, season, or geographical location, like a snowy mountain range at dusk.

Emotional and Symbolic Impact

Many elements of the natural world carry emotional or symbolic meanings. For example, a serene lake can evoke tranquility, while stormy skies might symbolize turmoil. Including these elements in AI prompts can therefore help convey deeper emotional layers or thematic undertones in the generated content.

Authenticity and Realism

Using specific and accurate descriptions of natural elements can increase the authenticity and realism of generated images. Detailed prompts ensure that the AI models generate outputs that are not only visually appealing but also true to life, such as accurately depicting the flora and fauna of a particular ecosystem.

Inspiration and Creativity

Nature is a perennial source of inspiration. By integrating elements of the natural world into prompts, creators can explore new ideas and themes, potentially leading to unique and creative outcomes. This can be particularly enriching in fields like fantasy art, where natural elements are often exaggerated or imagined in new ways.

Educational Value

Including detailed natural elements can also have educational implications, helping audiences learn about different aspects of the natural world. This can be particularly effective in projects aimed at raising awareness about environmental issues or promoting the conservation of certain habitats and species.

Overall, the use of elements from the natural world in AI prompt crafting not only enhances the aesthetic and emotional quality of the outputs but also ensures that the generated content is engaging and meaningful, connecting viewers with the intrinsic beauty and complexity of the natural environment.

Descriptors: Moods/Atmospheres

The terms "moods" and "atmospheres" in the context of generative AI prompt crafting refer to the emotional tone or feeling that an image or text is intended to convey. These can range from serene and peaceful to chaotic and intense, influencing the overall impact and reception of the generated content. Crafting prompts that specify moods or atmospheres is crucial for several reasons:

Emotional Engagement

Moods and atmospheres directly affect the emotional response of the audience. By explicitly stating the desired emotional tone in a prompt—such as "melancholic," "joyous," or "mysterious"—creators can guide the AI to produce content that resonates on an emotional level, making it more compelling and memorable.

Narrative and Thematic Depth

The mood or atmosphere of a scene can set the stage for narrative and thematic developments. For instance, a "tense" atmosphere can be foundational in a suspenseful narrative, while a "dreamy" mood might be suited for more abstract or fantastical themes. This adds layers of meaning that enrich the viewer's or reader's experience.

Visual Consistency

In visual arts, the mood often dictates the choice of colors, lighting, and composition. A prompt that includes mood elements such as "somber with muted colors and soft shadows" helps ensure that the visual output is coherent and stylistically consistent, enhancing the overall aesthetic quality.

Guidance for AI Interpretation

AI models, particularly those in image and text generation, rely on detailed prompts to produce high-quality outputs. By including specific moods or atmospheres, creators can more precisely guide the AI's creative decisions, ensuring that output aligns closely with their vision.

Enhanced Creativity

Crafting prompts with specific moods or atmospheres can inspire creative approaches to subject matter and composition. It encourages the exploration of different styles, perspectives, and emotional expressions, leading to innovative and unique creations.

Contextual Clarity

For some projects, the mood or atmosphere can provide essential context that helps define the setting or the psychological state of characters, enhancing the narrative's clarity and depth. This is particularly important in storytelling, where atmospheric details can subtly convey complex aspects of the plot or character development.

User Experience

Especially in interactive media or advertising, the mood can significantly impact user experience, evoking the right feelings at the right time to engage users effectively or to deliver a message powerfully.

In summary, specifying moods or atmospheres in prompts for generative AI plays a pivotal role in controlling the emotional and aesthetic output, ensuring that it not only captures the intended essence but also deeply engages the target audience.

Showcased in the balance of this chapter is artwork that exemplifies these descriptor types.

Artistic Styles	Elements/Natural World	Moods/Atmospheres
Abstract	Aquatic	Apocalyptic
Art Nouveau	Arid	Dreamlike
Avant-garde	Celestial	Celebratory
Baroque	Crystalline	Futuristic
Cubist	Galactic	Melancholic
Expressionist	Luminous	Mystical
Gothic	Nebulous	Ominous
Impressionistic	Subterranean	Surreal
Minimalistic	Verdant	Tranquil
Surrealist	Volcanic	Whimsical

Artistic Style: Abstract

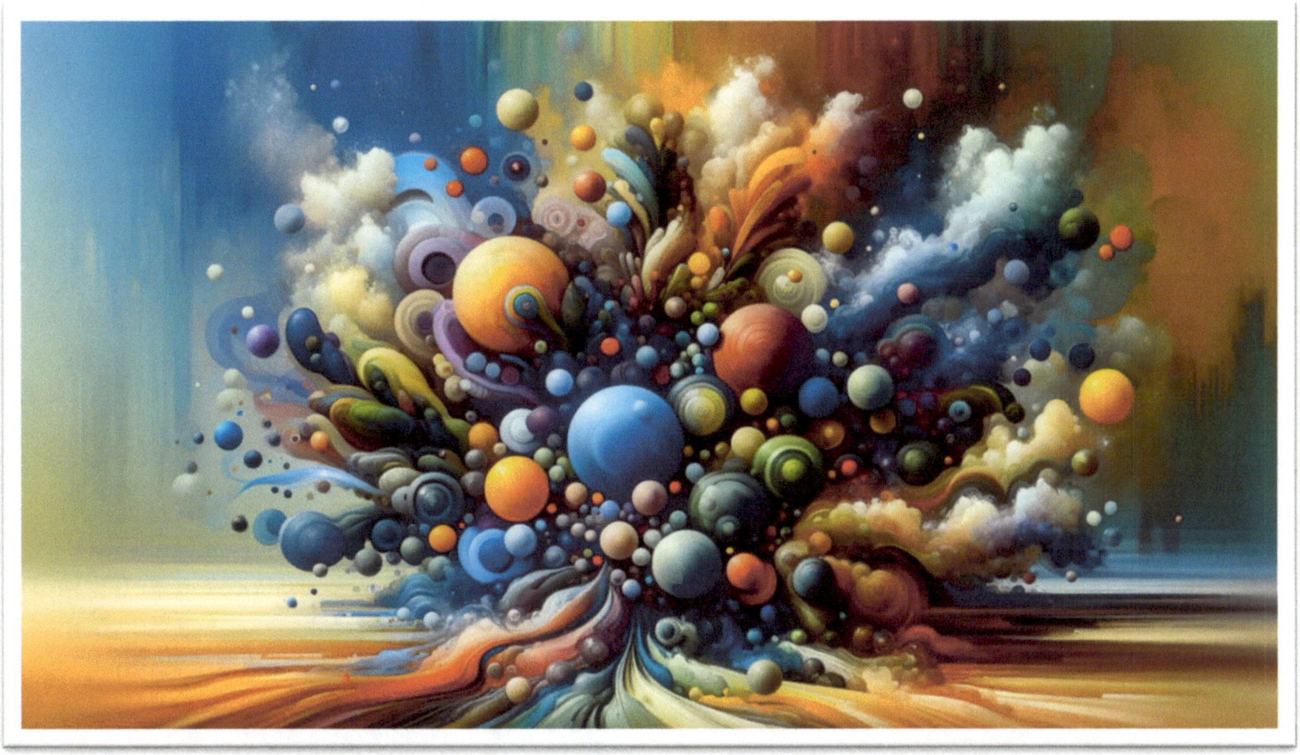

This artwork is a captivating visual feast, embodying the essence of abstraction in art. Abstraction, in its purest form, is about distilling an image to its core components of color, shape, and texture, often eschewing representational accuracy for emotional impact or conceptual expression.

In this artwork abstraction manifests as a vibrant explosion of spherical shapes, swirling patterns, and dynamic lines. The spheres vary in size and color, ranging from subdued blues and greens to vibrant oranges and reds, suggesting a sense of depth and movement. The composition is alive with motion, as if we are witnessing a moment of creation or transformation, where elements coalesce and disperse with a rhythmic fluidity. The significance of abstraction in this composition lies in its ability to engage the viewer's imagination and emotions directly. Without the constraints of depicting a recognizable scene, the image communicates through the universal language of color and form.

The flow and blend of colors create a dynamic energy that moves across the canvas, drawing the eye in a dance around the image. The piece does not confine itself to the laws of physical reality, but instead creates its own visual logic, inviting the viewer to explore a world untethered from the familiar, one that can only be accessed through the lens of abstract art.

This artwork celebrates the potential of abstraction to transcend the literal and to allow the observer to experience art in a way that is both deeply personal and universally accessible, free from the constraints of representational fidelity.

Artistic Style: Art Nouveau

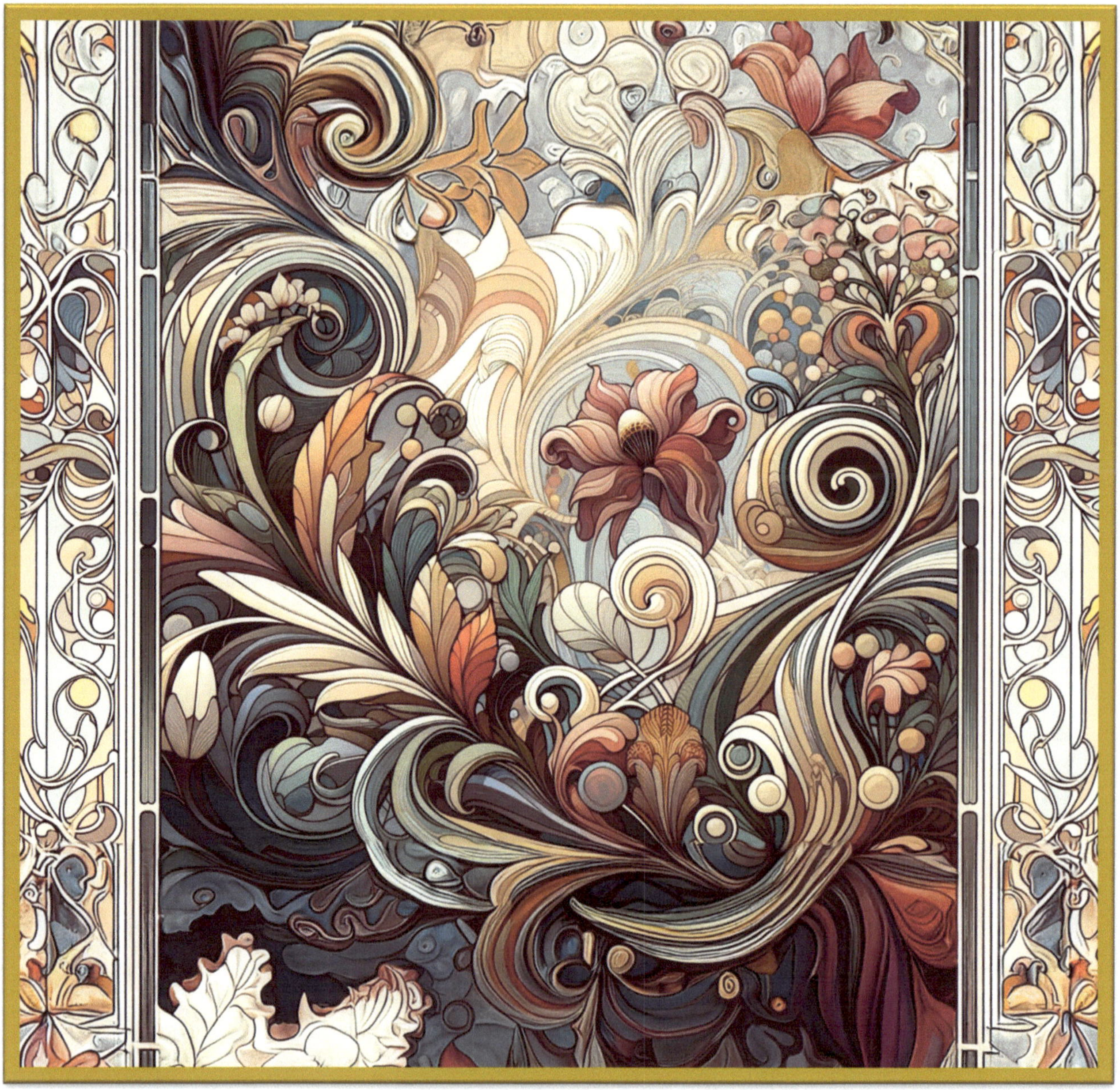

This artwork captures the essence of Art Nouveau, featuring elegant, flowing lines, natural forms, and intricate patterns. This style is celebrated for its ornamental qualities, with motifs like stylized flowers and curvilinear forms, presented in a rich and harmonious color palette.

Artistic Style: Avant-Garde

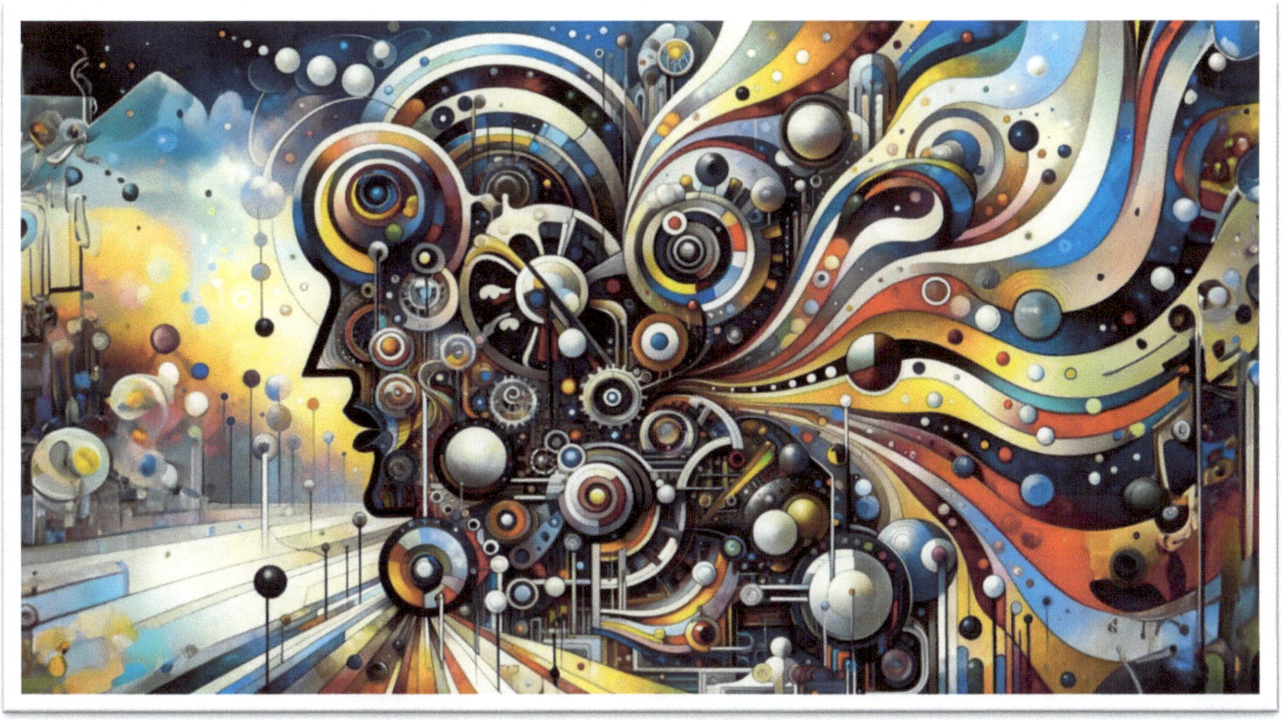

This artwork embodies an artistic style that is quintessentially Avant-garde, epitomizing the essence of the movement with its innovative, experimental, and boundary-challenging characteristics. The artwork features elements that are unequivocally unconventional, abstract, or surreal, highlighted by a bold and dynamic color palette, radiating deep exploration and experimentation. The composition reflects a bold exploration of unconventional, abstract forms, conveyed through a dynamic color palette, embodying the forward-thinking and radical approach.

Artistic Style: Baroque

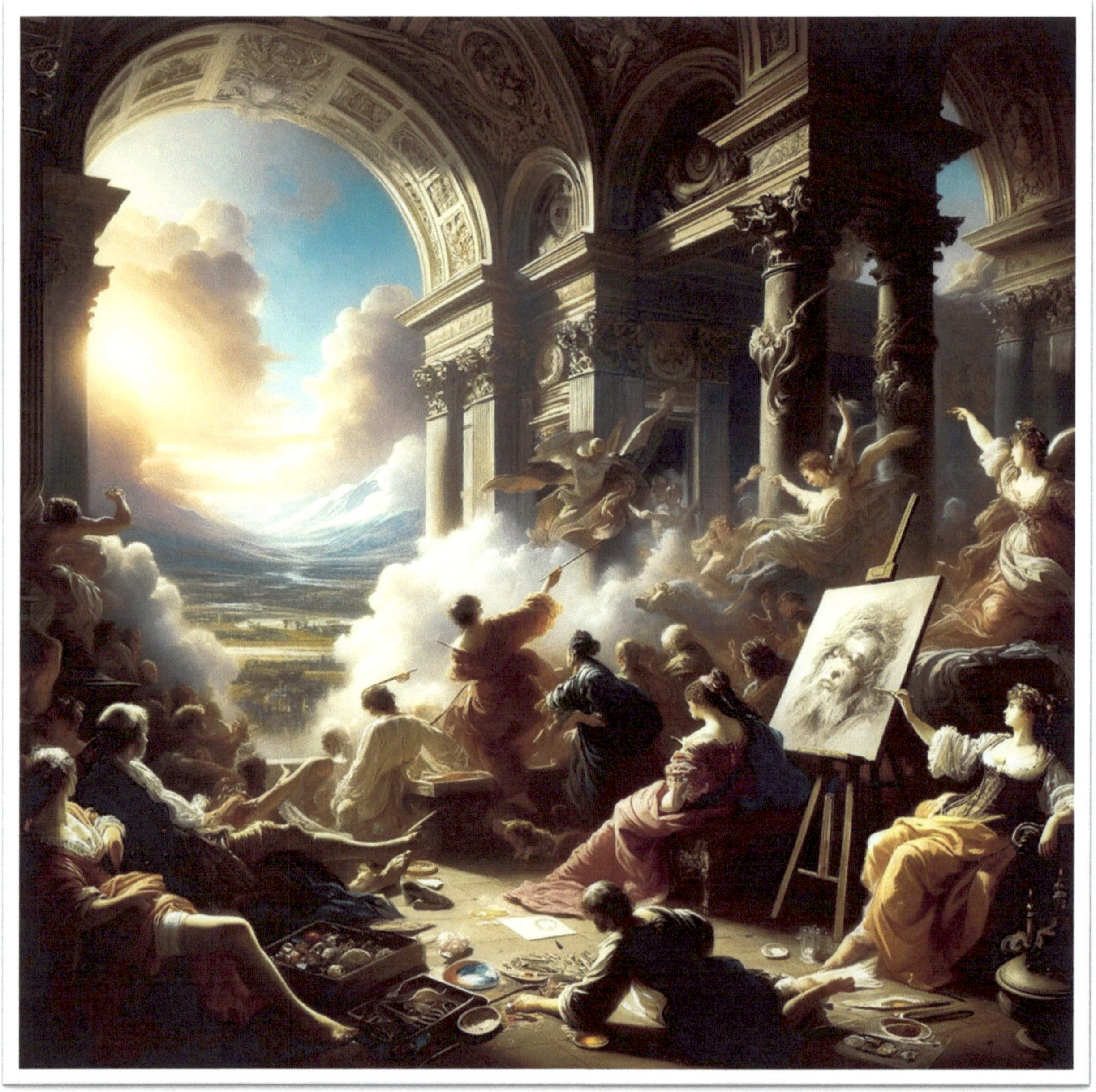

This artwork embodies a Baroque artistic style, with a focus on dramatic light and shadow, rich color palettes, and a sense of movement and energy. The composition includes dynamic elements and ornate details, ensuring all subjects are depicted with anatomical accuracy, reflecting the grandeur and theatricality typical of the Baroque era.

Artistic Style: Cubist

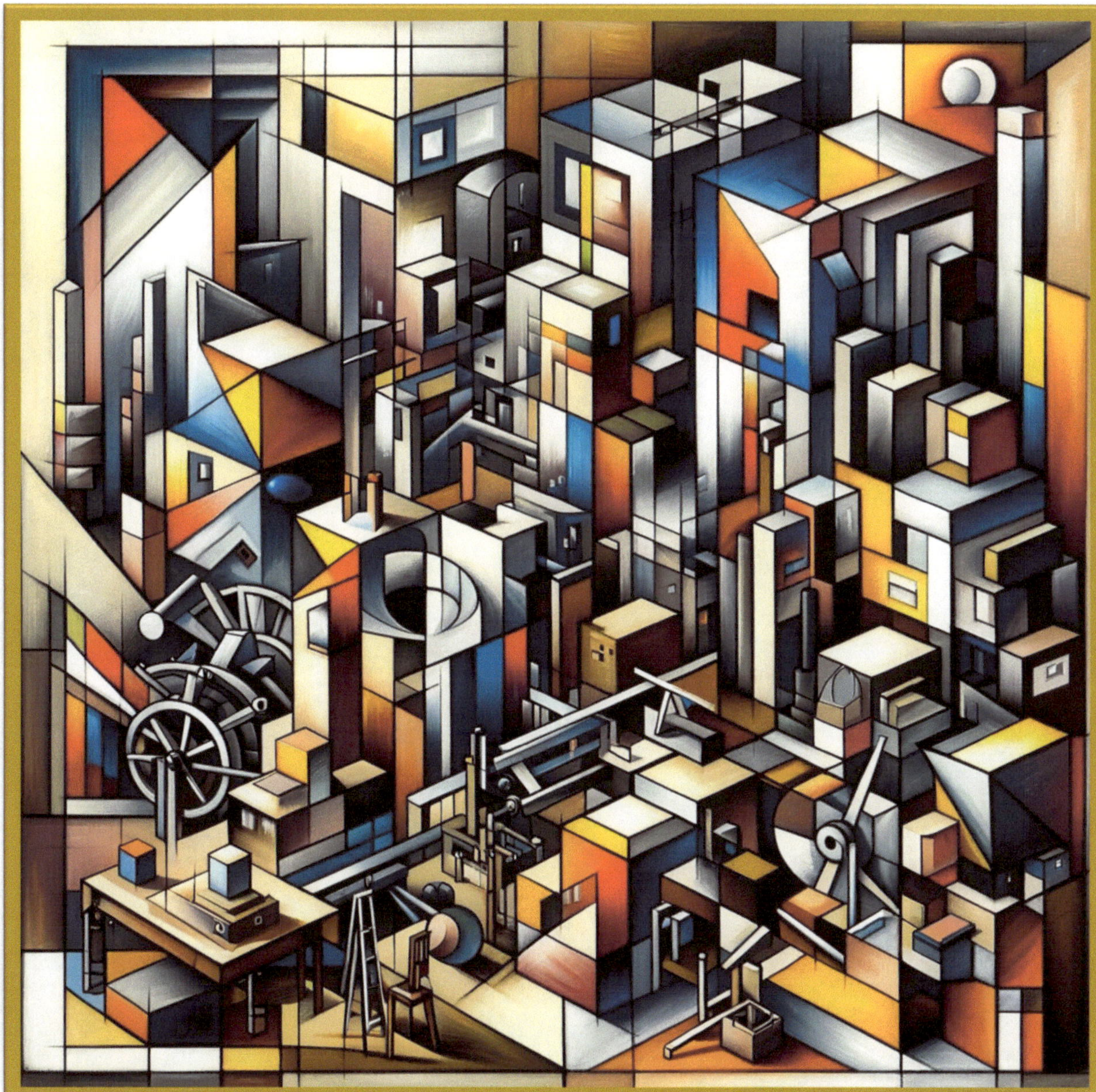

This artwork embodies the Cubist artistic style, capturing the essence of Cubism with its fragmentation of objects into geometric shapes, the incorporation of multiple perspectives, and the abstraction of form. The composition breaks down subjects into simplified, geometric forms, challenging conventional perceptions of depth and perspective, and utilizes a limited color palette to emphasize the structural aspects. This artwork conveys the innovative spirit of Cubism, showcasing its unique approach to depicting reality through abstract and geometric interpretation.

Artistic Style: Expressionistic

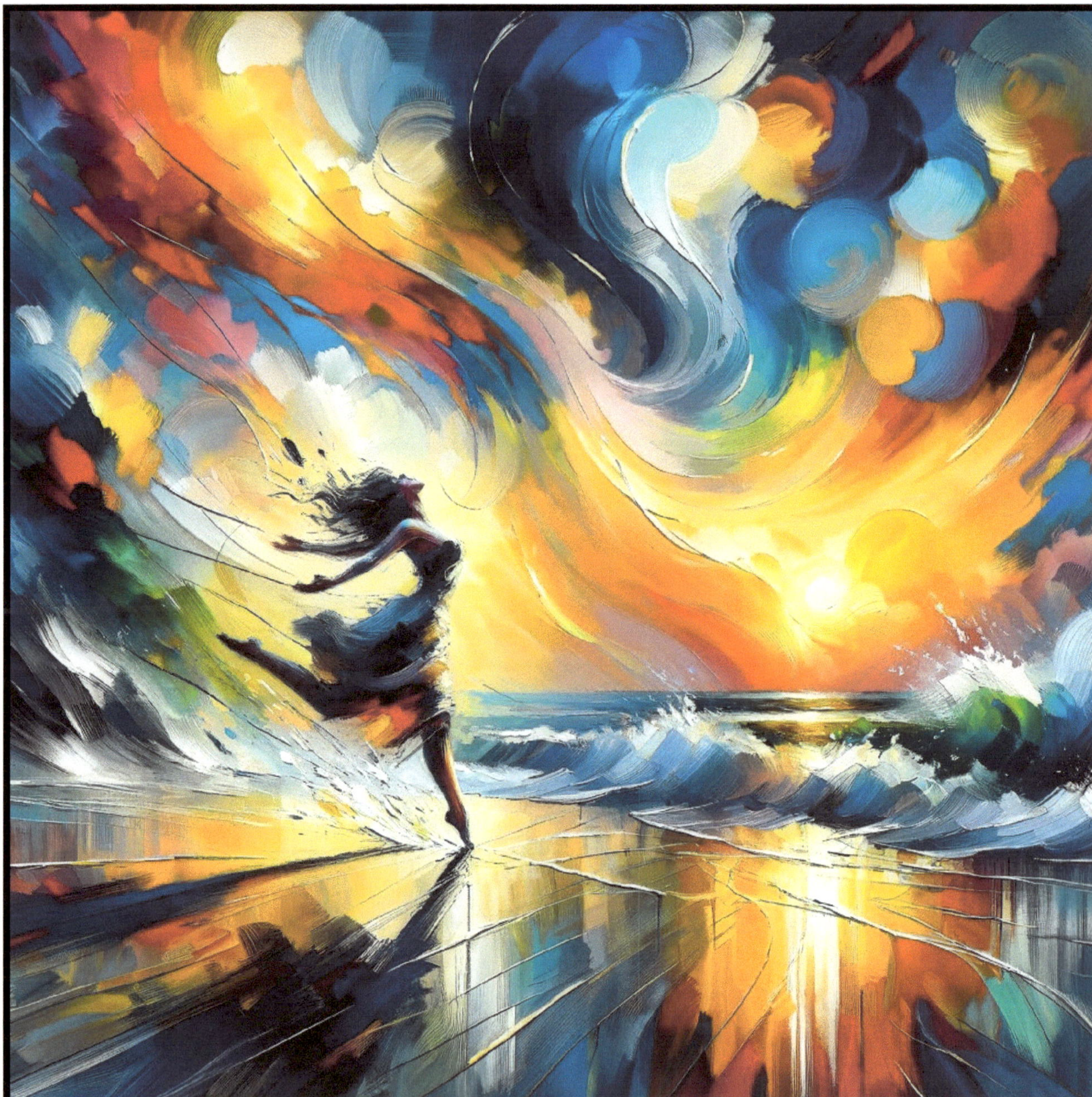

This artwork embodies the Expressionist artistic style with the theme of joy and happiness. It captures feelings of joy through bold use of color, dramatic brushwork, and expressive forms, reflecting an inner emotional reality of happiness. The vibrant colors and dynamic strokes create a visual impact that resonates with feelings of joy and happiness.

Artistic Style: Gothic

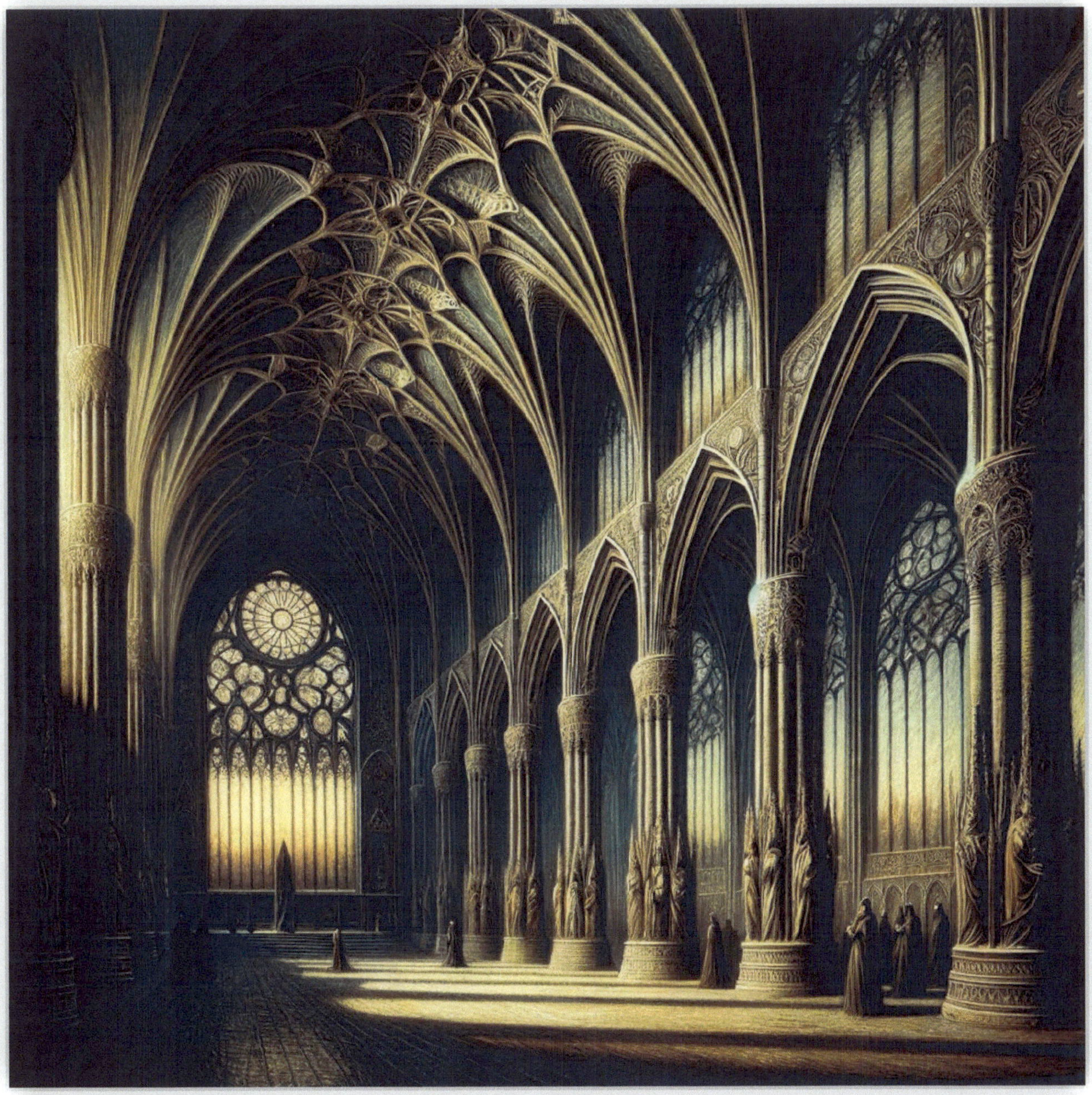

This artwork embodies the Gothic artistic style, capturing the essence of the Gothic period with its emphasis on verticality, pointed arches, and detailed ornamentation. It features Gothic architectural elements like flying buttresses and ribbed vaults, using a color palette that evokes the solemnity and mystique of the era. The composition conveys the grandeur and solemn atmosphere typical of Gothic art, showcasing its architectural brilliance and thematic depth.

Artistic Style: Impressionistic

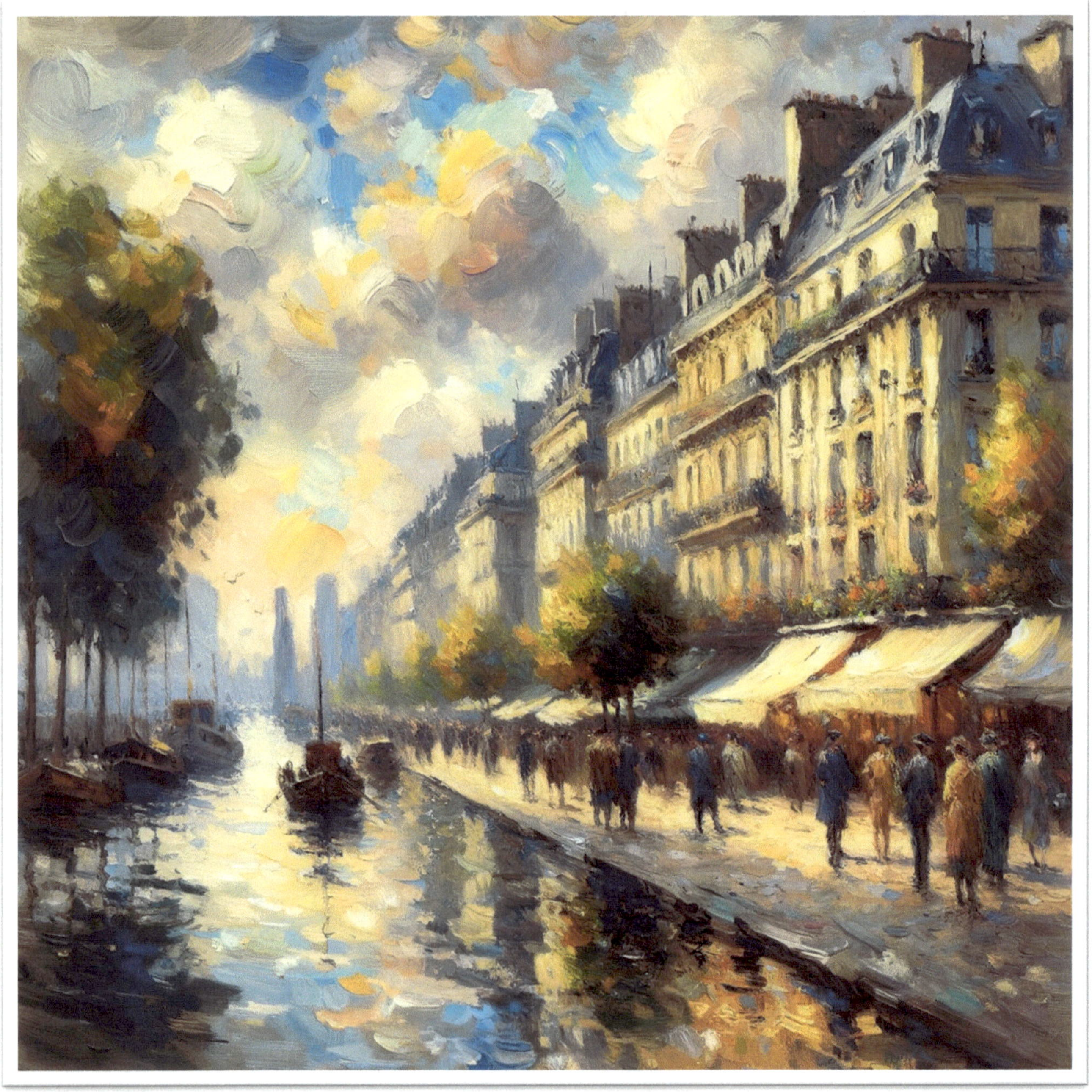

This artwork embodies the Impressionistic artistic style, capturing the essence of Impressionism with its focus on the fleeting effects of light, movement, and the vividness of colors. It portrays a scene with loose, visible brushstrokes that convey the impression of a moment, using a bright and varied color palette to capture the dynamism of light and shadow, evoking a sense of immediacy and the subjective experience of the artist.

Artistic Style: Minimalistic

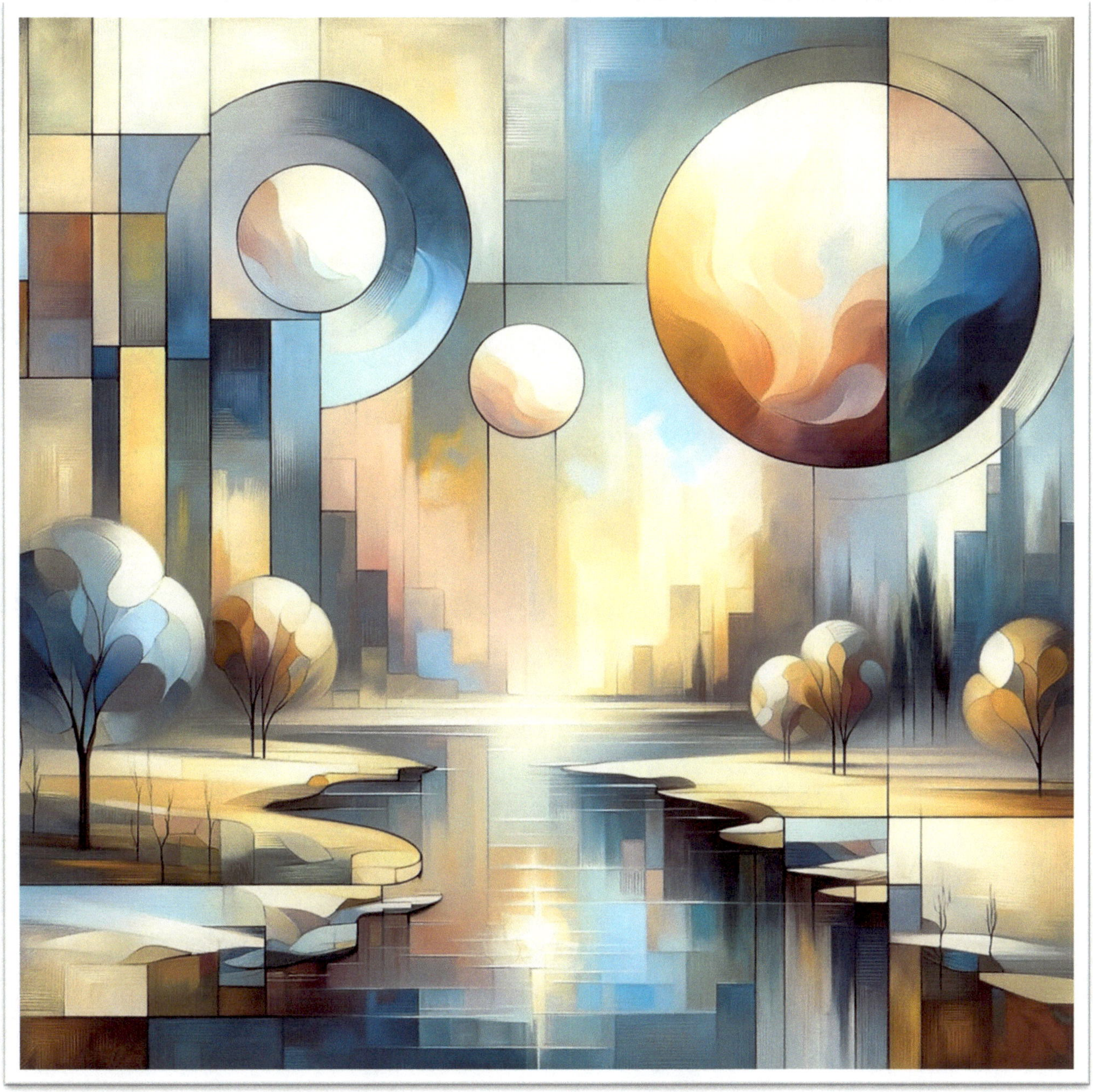

This artwork embodies a Minimalistic artistic style, focusing on the theme of simplicity. It captures the essence of Minimalism using soothing colors and clean, precise lines to subtly define shapes and forms. The serene and uncluttered composition, along with the strategic use of negative space, contributes to a sense of harmony and tranquility, showcasing how minimal elements can convey a powerful aesthetic and emotional impact.

Artistic Style: Surrealist

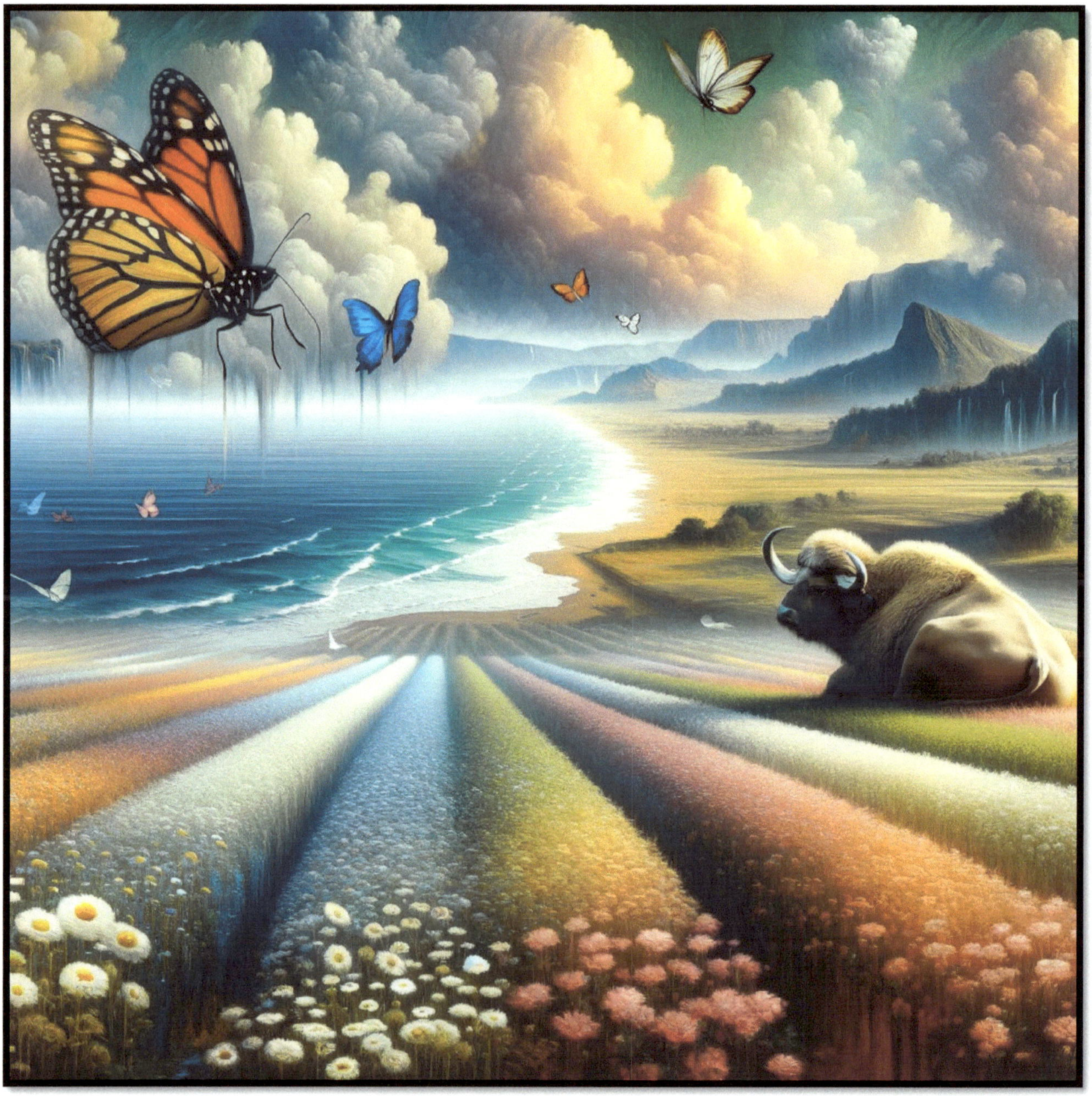

This artwork embodies a distinctively Surrealist artistic style, featuring butterflies and a buffalo within an ephemeral color scheme. The theme is a panoramic ocean view and a vast field of flowers, merging surreal elements with natural scenery to create a dream-like landscape. The integration of the butterflies and buffalo emphasizes their surreal interaction within this expansive setting, against a backdrop of soft, ethereal colors that enhance the otherworldly atmosphere. This composition evokes a sense of wonder and infinite possibility, inviting the viewer into a surreal narrative that explores the beauty and mystery of the natural world.

Elements/Natural World: Aquatic

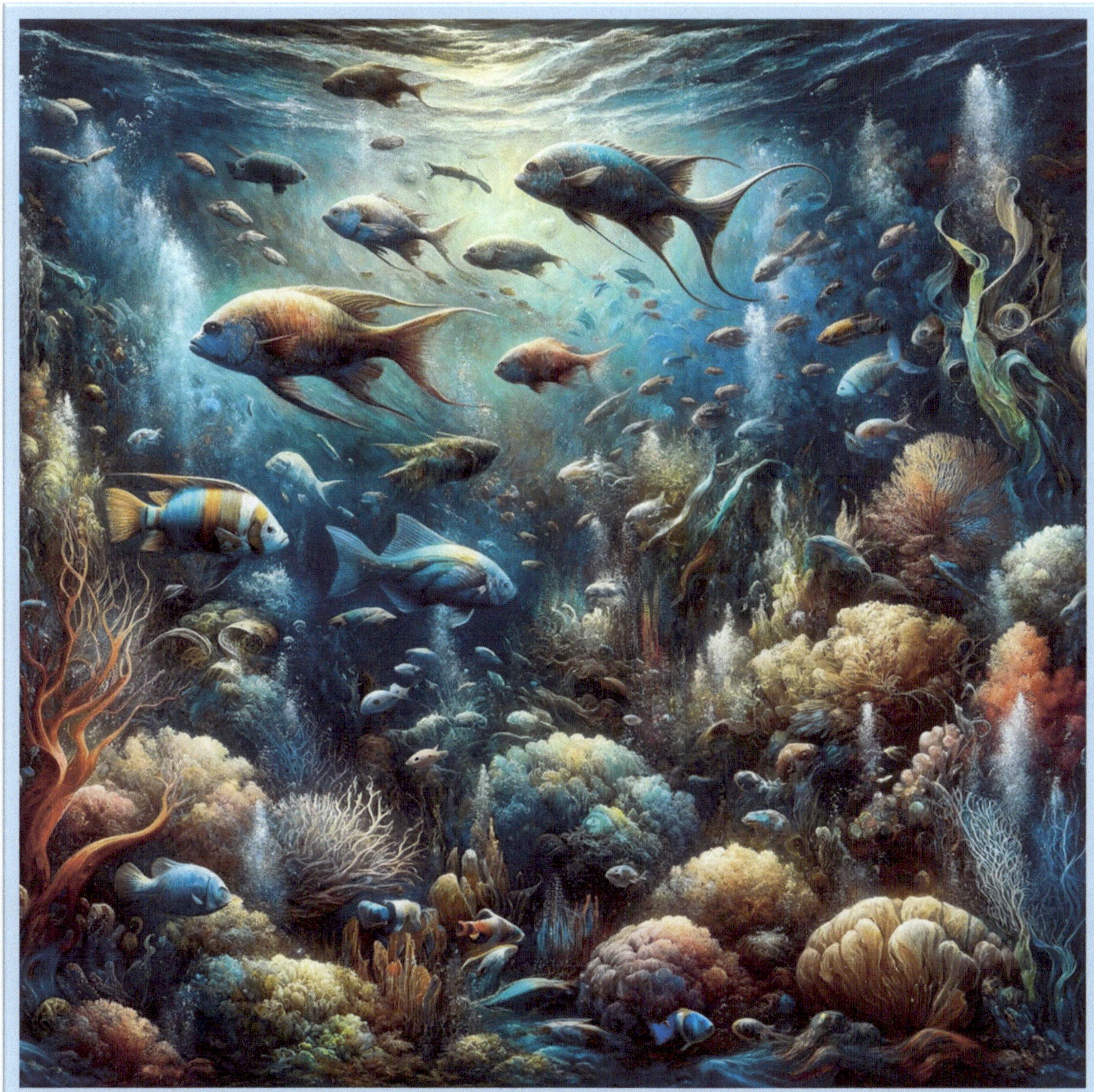

This artwork embodies a distinctively aquatic natural world, capturing the essence of the underwater world. It showcases a vibrant and diverse aquatic ecosystem, including a variety of marine life such as fish, coral reefs, seaweed, and other sea creatures, set against the backdrop of the ocean's depth. The composition highlights the beauty and complexity of aquatic life, focusing on the interplay of light and shadow, the richness of colors, and the fluidity of forms found in the underwater environment. The artwork conveys a sense of tranquility and the majestic beauty of the natural underwater world, inviting the viewer to explore the depths of the ocean.

Elements/Natural World: Arid

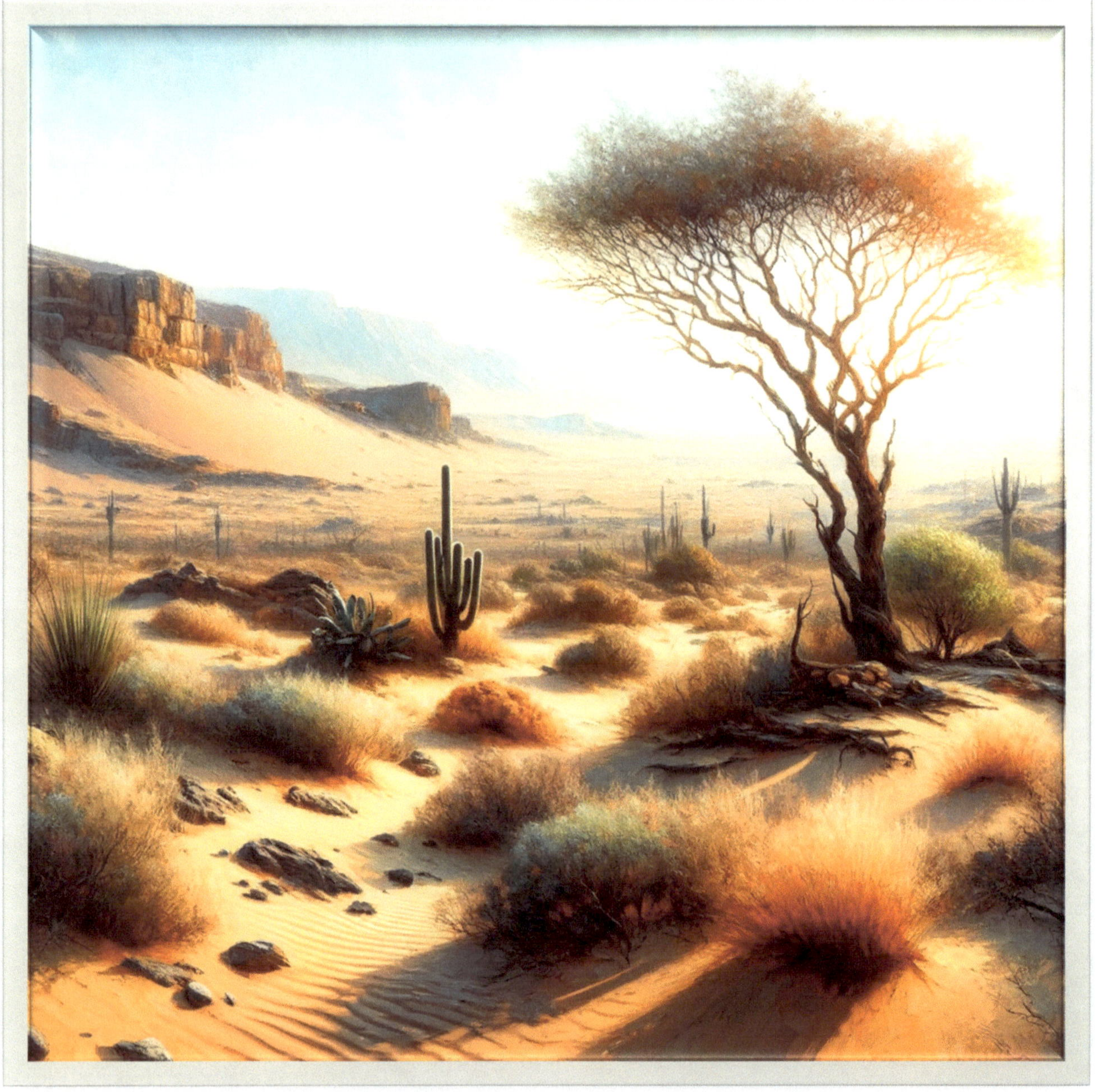

This artwork embodies a distinctively arid natural world, capturing the essence of arid landscapes. It showcases the rugged beauty and resilience of life in desert environments, featuring sand dunes, sparse vegetation like cacti or desert shrubs, rocky outcrops, and possibly the presence of wildlife adapted to these conditions. The composition highlights the vastness and solitude of the desert, focusing on the textures and colors that define arid regions. The artwork conveys a sense of tranquility and the stark beauty of the natural arid world, inviting the viewer to appreciate the unique landscapes and ecosystems found in desert areas.

Elements/Natural World: Celestial

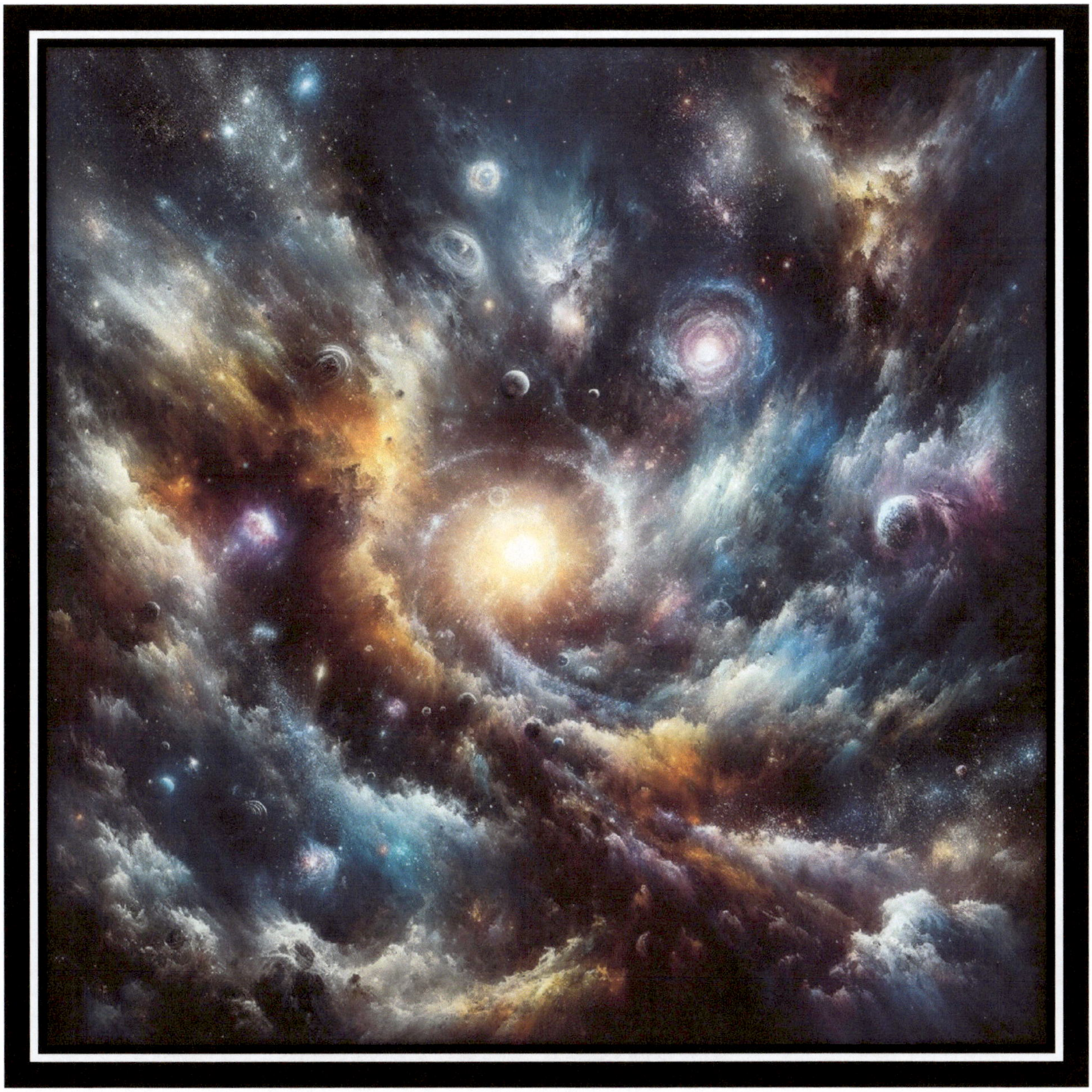

This artwork embodies a distinctively celestial natural world, with the theme of vastness and deep space. It captures the essence of the cosmic expanse, showcasing the infinite depth of space, stars, galaxies, nebulae, and other celestial phenomena. The composition conveys the overwhelming scale and beauty of the universe, highlighting the intricate patterns of starlight and the vibrant, swirling colors of cosmic bodies. This artwork evokes a profound sense of awe and wonder, inviting the viewer to ponder the mysteries of the universe and the smallness of human existence in comparison to the vast celestial canvas.

Elements/Natural World: Crystalline

This artwork is a stunning representation of crystalline structures as found in the natural world, crafted with photorealistic quality. It depicts a serene and otherworldly underground cave environment, where light filters softly through the distant entrance, casting an ethereal glow on the scene. Dominating the composition are the towering quartz-like crystals, which rise from the cave floor with geometric precision. The crystals are rendered with clear facets that capture and refract the ambient light, creating a dance of illumination and shadow across their surfaces. The attention to detail in the textures and clarity of the crystals conveys their natural purity and solidity.

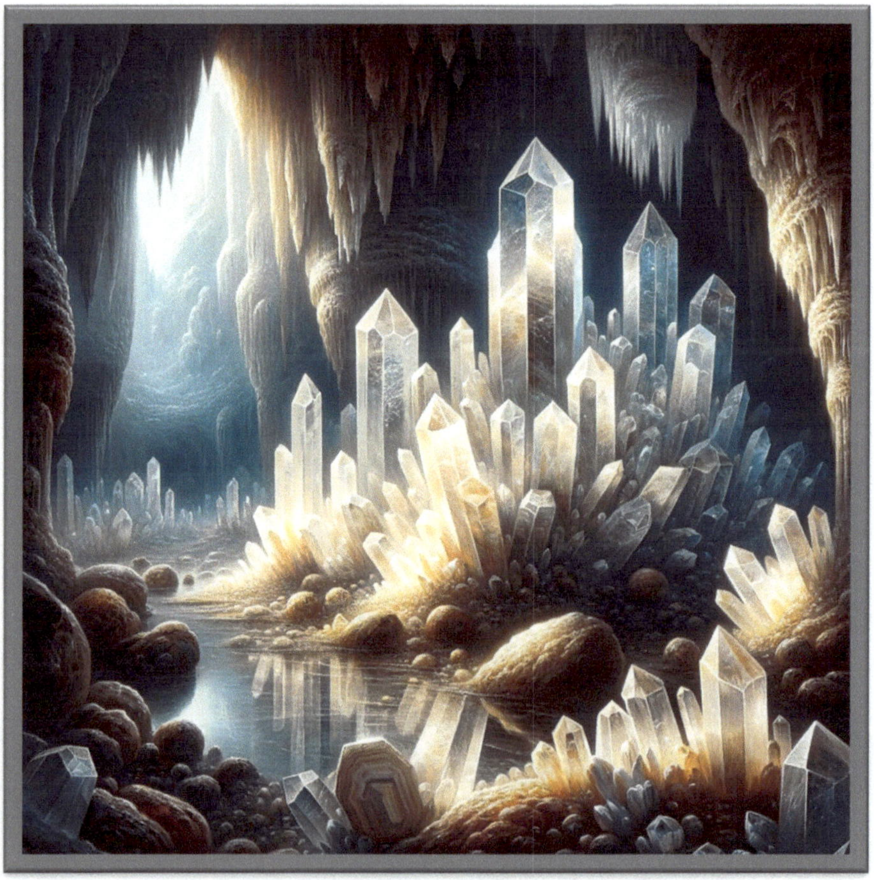

In the foreground, the calm water mirrors the crystalline forms, suggesting a quiet, untouched space. The stalactites hanging from the cave ceiling add to the sense of depth and history, indicating the slow passage of time that forms such natural wonders. This environment is a testament to the beauty and complexity of geological processes. The image captures the awe-inspiring presence of these formations, evoking a sense of wonder and appreciation for the natural elegance and the intricate processes of the Earth that create such structures. It's a celebration of nature's capacity to sculpt landscapes that are both architecturally formidable and artistically inspiring.

Elements/Natural World: Galactic

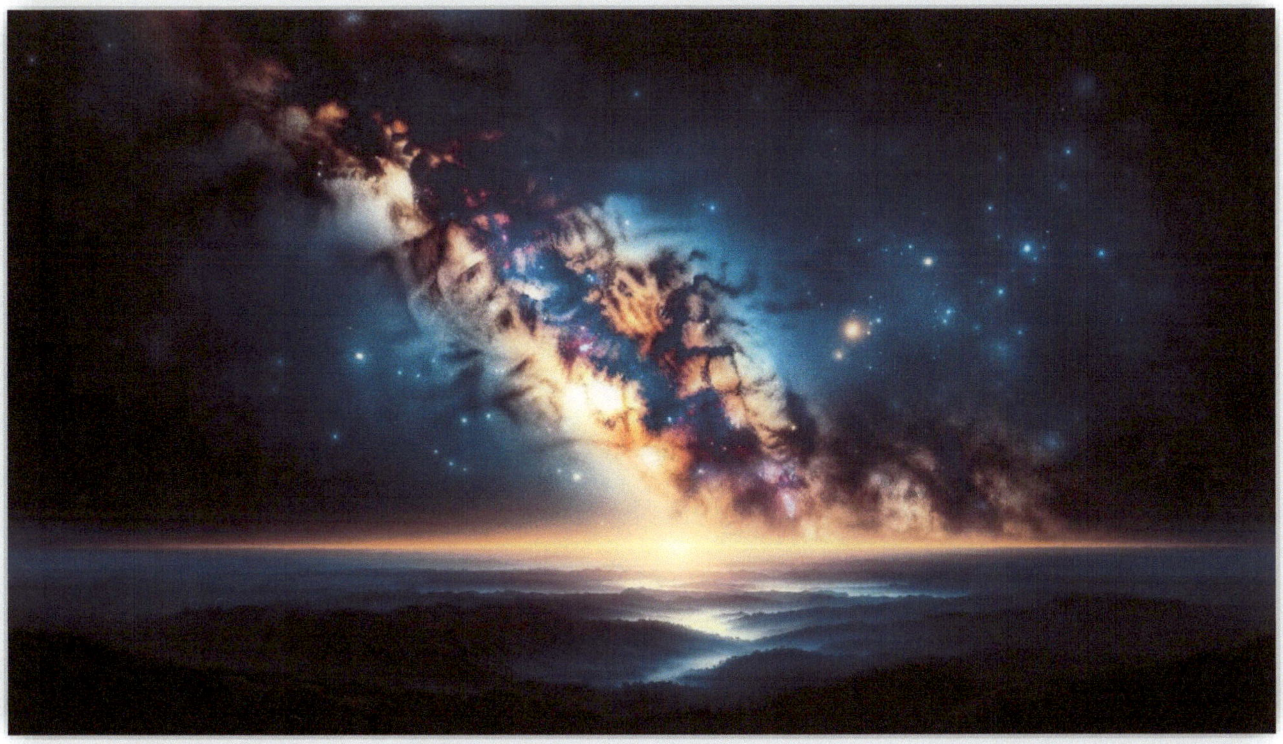

This artwork is a majestic portrayal of the cosmos as viewed from Earth. At the heart of the composition is the Milky Way, a radiant swath of stars that stretches wide across the night sky, rendered with stunning clarity.

The core of the galaxy is ablaze with the golden and white glow of countless stars, dense and bright. This central band of light is mottled with the dusky reds and purples of nebulae, where new stars are born, and the inky blacks of the vast voids of space. Swirls of interstellar dust weave throughout the galactic panorama, painted in hues of midnight blue and dusky pink, giving texture and depth to the celestial view.

Below this heavenly spectacle, the silhouette of a mountain range creates a stark horizon line. The peaks and valleys are cloaked in darkness but are still discernible against the softer darkness of the sky. The mountains gently cradle a valley, in the center of which glows a warm, inviting light, perhaps a small town or a solitary homestead, reminding us of the presence of humanity observing the grandeur above.

The galactic elements are depicted with such precision and attention to detail that they evoke a sense of wonder and an almost palpable feeling of the vastness and beauty of the universe. This image is not just a visual experience, but an invitation to contemplate the infinite and our place within it.

Elements/Natural World: Luminous

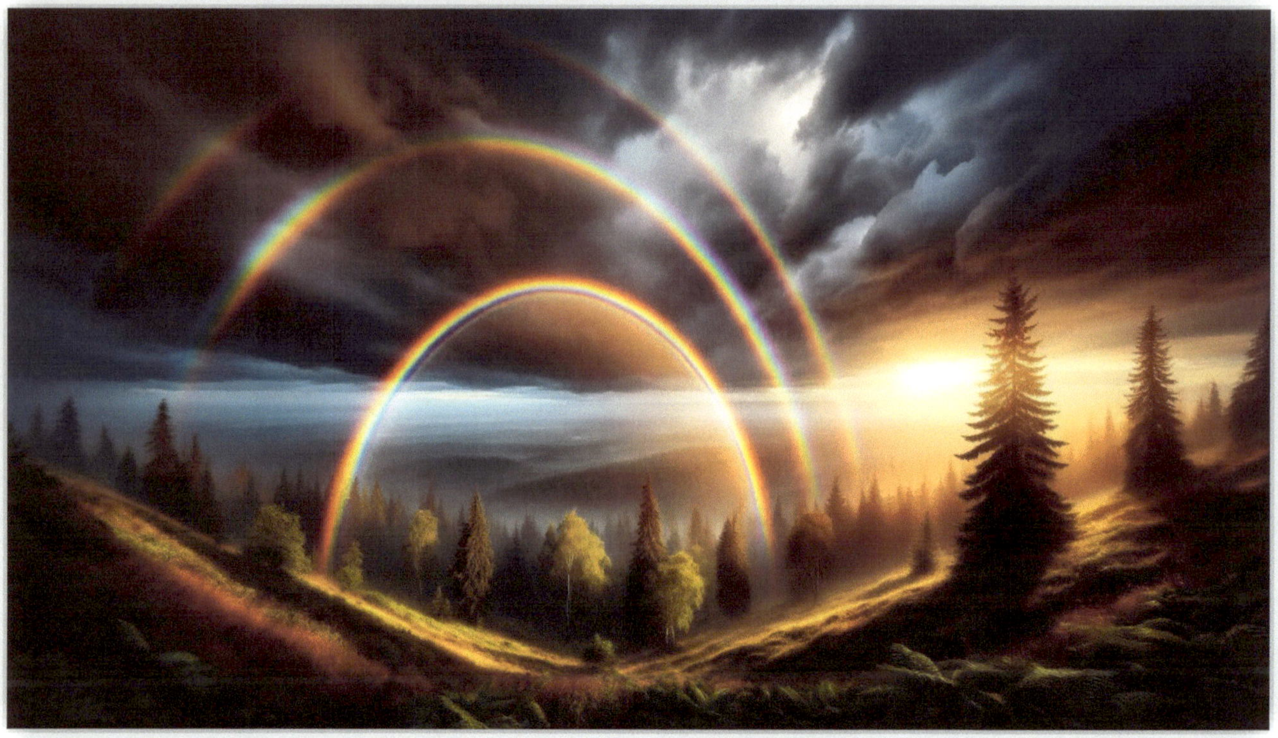

This artwork features the distinctively luminous element of a triple rainbow that could naturally appear on Earth. The phenomenon is captured in full splendor, with the rainbows forming a complete 180-degree arc against a dramatic sky. The primary rainbow, with its bands of red, orange, yellow, green, blue, indigo, and violet, is bright and vivid. The secondary and tertiary rainbows display colors a bit more faintly, yet these rainbows are still wonderfully clear.

The landscape below is bathed in the soft, golden light of the setting sun, which emerges from behind the dispersing clouds. The rain's aftermath is evident in the lush greenery of the forest, the wet sheen on the leaves, and the rich, moist earth. This serene setting, alongside the spectacular rainbows, creates a composition that is both balanced and awe-inspiring, celebrating the peaceful beauty that follows a storm.

Elements/Natural World: Nebulous

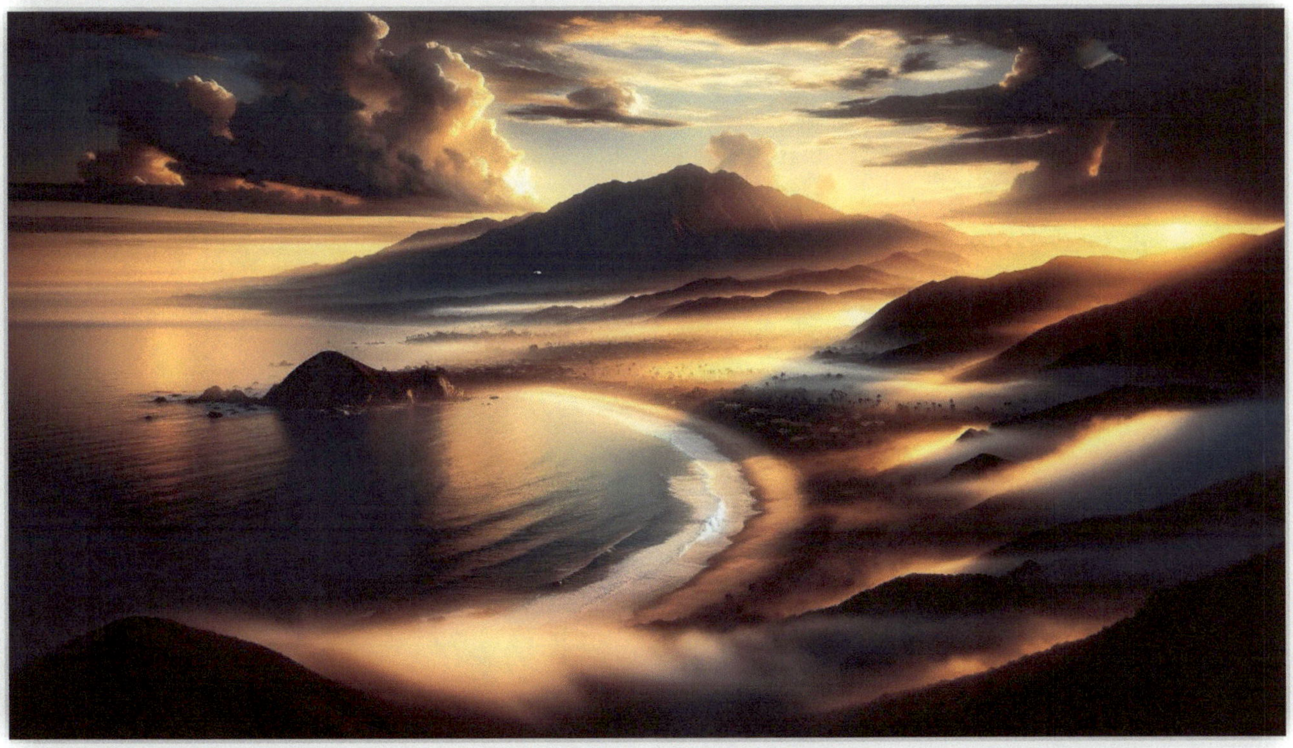

This artwork features a breathtaking landscape that is rich in atmospheric and visual drama. The composition is centered around a nebulous cloud formation, which serves as a testament to the powerful interplay of light and atmospheric conditions on Earth. In the foreground, a thick marine layer of fog rolls gently over the landscape, softly enveloping hills and valleys in a blanket of mist. The fog's texture is smooth and flowing, resembling the diffuse gas clouds of a nebula in space. This creates a serene and mystical atmosphere, as the familiar features of the Earth are cloaked in this natural phenomenon.

Dominating the background is a grand mountain, its peak just breaking through the misty veil. The mountain anchors the composition, providing a sense of scale and permanence against the transient and ever-changing clouds. Above, the sky is a canvas of dynamic cloud formations. Cumulus clouds, dense and fluffy, are set ablaze by the setting sun, with their edges highlighted in brilliant oranges and reds, contrasting with the cooler blues and purples of the shaded areas.

The setting sun itself is a radiant point of light, its rays piercing through the clouds and fog to cast dramatic shadows and create a striking backlit effect. The sunlight diffuses through the moisture-laden air, scattering warm hues that echo the colors found in nebulous gas clouds of deep space, hence reinforcing the theme of 'nebulous' within the natural world.

This artwork successfully captures the ephemeral beauty of our planet's skyscape. It uses light, shadow, and color to draw the viewer into a moment that feels both fleeting and eternal.

Elements/Natural World: Subterranean

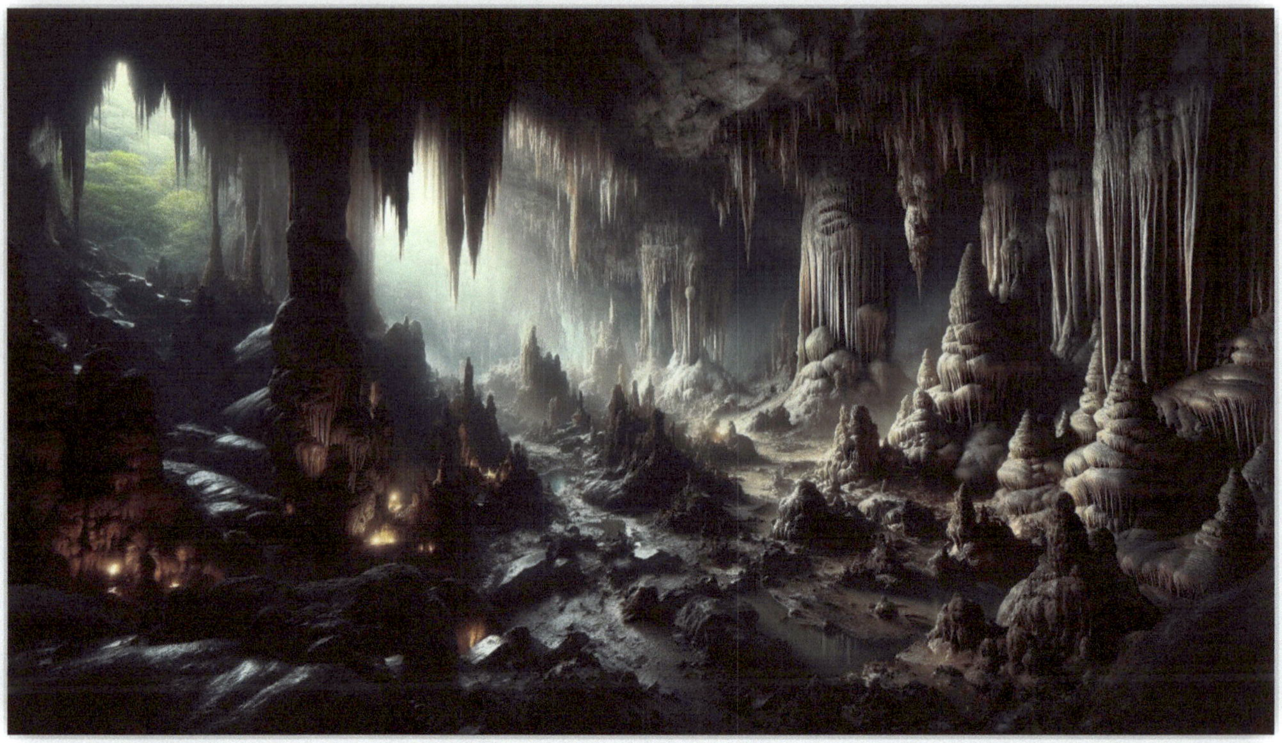

This artwork delves into the depths of Earth's natural world, unveiling the hidden splendor of a subterranean landscape. It opens into a vast limestone cave, where time appears to stand still. The air is thick with humidity, and the profound silence is occasionally pierced by the gentle drip of water echoing through the cavernous space.

Tall stalagmites rise from the cave floor, reaching up towards the distant ceiling from which delicate stalactites hang. Their forms are a testament to the slow, persistent drip of mineral-rich water over countless millennia. The light, soft and ethereal, filters through a far-off entrance, casting a diffuse glow that dances across wet rock surfaces and pools of still water, bringing a warm ambiance to the cave's cool atmosphere.

The colors within the cave are a palette of the Earth itself—deep browns and muted grays, with the occasional sparkle of mineral deposits and the subtle hues of green and red oxides that tell the story of the rock's chemical journey. This subterranean realm, hidden from the world above, is a treasure trove of natural artistry, sculpted by the unseen hands of geological processes.

This image is an homage to the beauty that thrives in darkness, a reminder of the intricate and unseen worlds that lie just beneath our feet. The composition captures the interplay of light and shadow, the stability of the rock formations, and the serene grandeur of this quiet, concealed universe.

Elements/Natural World: Verdant

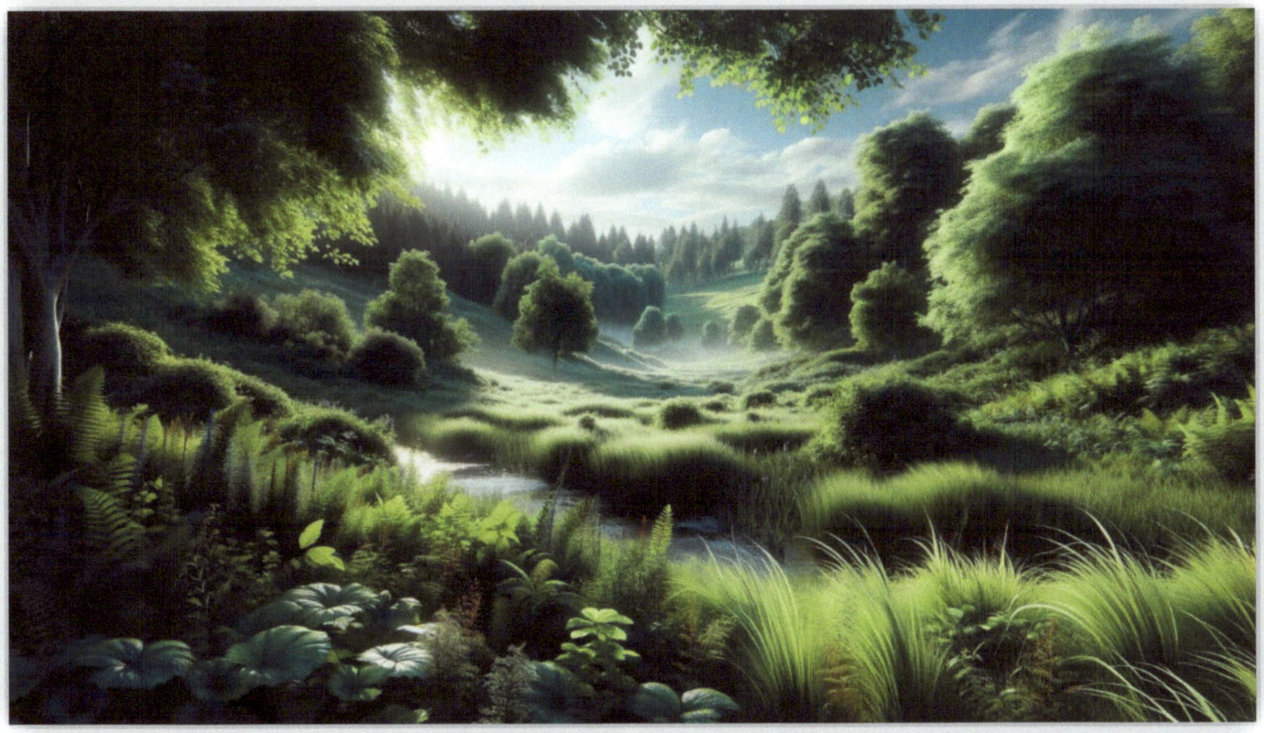

This artwork is a breathtaking visualization of the verdant vitality inherent in the natural world. It captures a serene and lush landscape where the low angle of the sun bathes the scene in a warm, gentle light. At the forefront, we see an array of rich greenery. There is a diversity in the types of plants and their various shades of green, indicative of lush, green plant life in its most vivid and healthy state. Every plant seems to be flourishing, giving the impression of a diverse and thriving ecosystem.

A small stream meanders through the landscape, reflecting the light of the sky and contributing to the overall sense of peace and tranquility. The mist rising from the surface of the water suggests the cool freshness of the morning, adding a mystical quality to the scene. The trees in the background tower over the scene, their canopies catching the light, creating a beautiful contrast with the darker areas of the forest. The light breaking through the foliage creates dappled patterns on the ground, further enhancing the depth and complexity of the composition.

The verdant element in this image is significant as it represents life, growth, and the health of the natural environment. It speaks to the abundance of nature and the serene beauty that can be found away from urban settings. This scene serves as a visual retreat, a moment of natural calm that viewers can immerse themselves in, appreciating the quiet grandeur of the Earth's flora.

Elements/Natural World: Volcanic

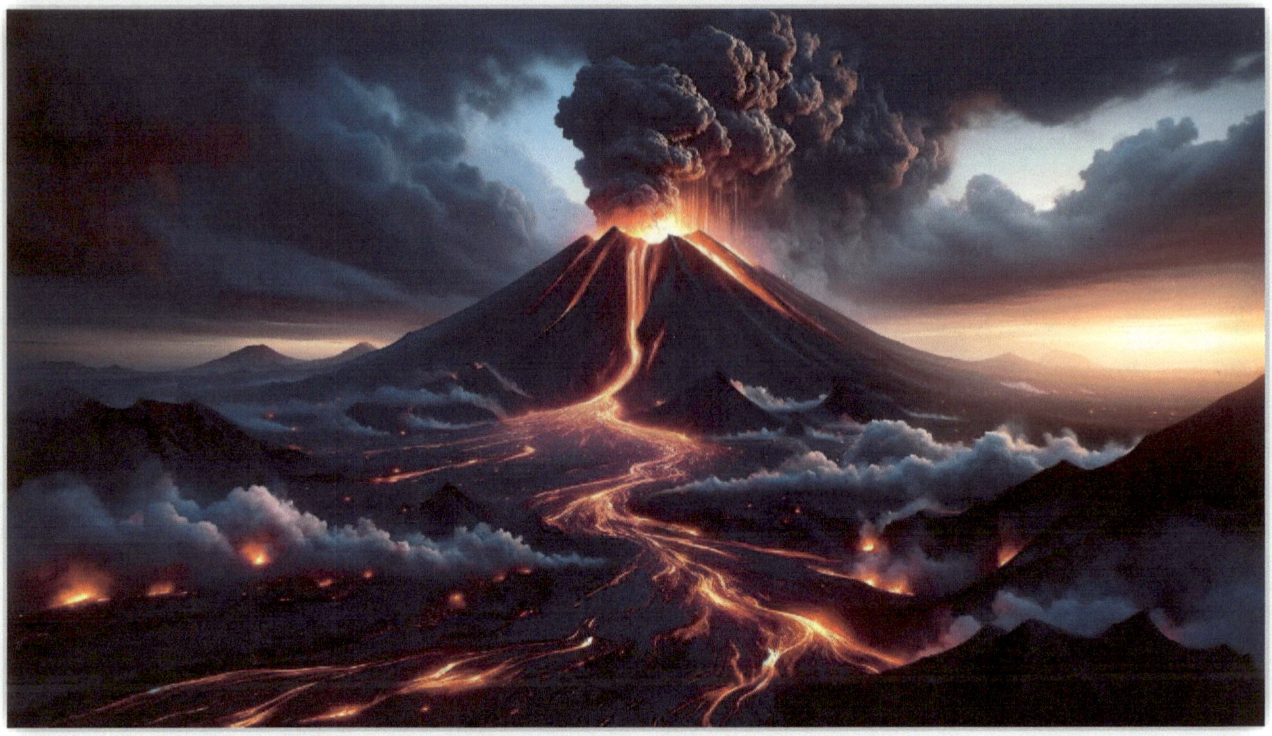

This artwork captures the dramatic and powerful essence of a volcanic eruption, a potent force in the natural world. This scene is defined by the central figure of the volcano, which dominates the landscape and the composition of the image.

The volcano's eruption is captured in the act, with a massive plume of smoke, ash, and incandescent material billowing into the sky, lit from within by the fiery glow of the molten rock. This illustrates the raw and uncontrollable power of Earth's geophysical processes. The flowing lava rivulets emanate from the volcano's summit, tracing fiery paths of destruction and creation down its slopes, glowing intensely against the darker landscape, and emphasizing the unstoppable force of nature.

This artwork, with its vivid colors and dynamic lines, draws the viewer's eye to the volcano, emphasizing its significance within the natural world. The contrast between the fiery eruption and the cool twilight sky further accentuates the volcano's raw energy.

The surrounding environment bears witness to the impact of the eruption. The land is a contrasting tableau of scorched earth and areas still untouched, with the potential for new life in the wake of the lava's path. The volcanic element in this image serves as a reminder of the dynamic and ever-changing nature of our planet. It speaks to the creation and destruction cycle that shapes the Earth's surface, a process that is both creative and destructive.

Moods/Atmospheres: Apocalyptic

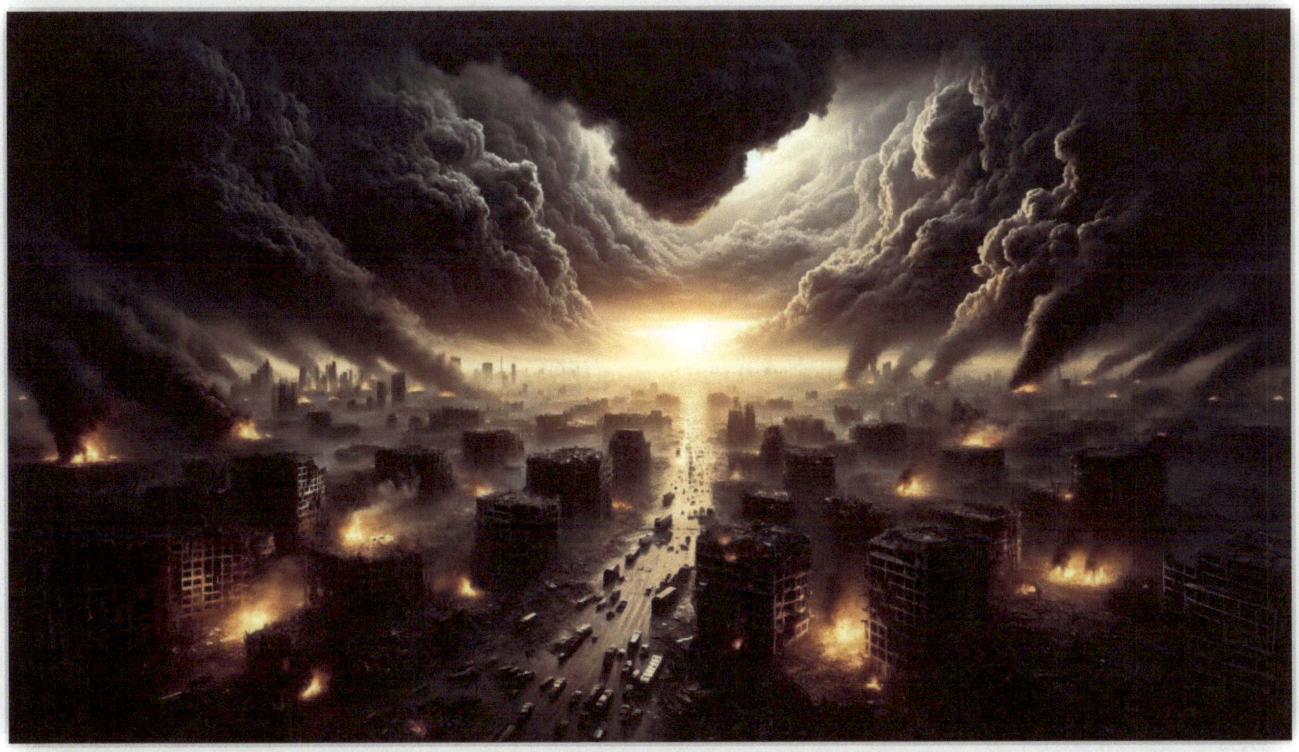

This artwork is a powerful portrayal of an apocalyptic mood through its immersive and dramatic atmosphere. The composition is dominated by a vast cityscape laid to waste; buildings are reduced to skeletal structures. The city is enveloped in shadows cast by the towering, tumultuous clouds of smoke and ash that swirl above, suggesting the aftermath of a catastrophic event.

Central to the composition is the sun, setting or perhaps struggling to shine through the dense, oppressive cloud cover, casting a deep, blood-orange glow across the horizon. This provides a stark contrast to the pervasive darkness and underscores the apocalyptic mood by suggesting a world descending into night or one that will never see a full day again.

The atmosphere depicted is thick with the haze of lingering fires and airborne debris, painting a picture of an environment that is inhospitable and foreboding. The fires that burn throughout the ruins add to the chaos, their flames offering the only light in a world shrouded by the darkness of its own destruction.

This artwork's apocalyptic mood is defined by its overwhelming sense of finality and loss. The composition, with its grand scale and meticulous detail, not only visualizes the concept of the apocalypse but also evokes the emotional response such a scene would inspire—a mixture of awe, fear, and melancholy.

Moods/Atmospheres: Dreamlike

This artwork presents a vividly dreamlike and joyous atmosphere, capturing a serene and fantastical scene. The mood is one of pure happiness and whimsy, emphasized by a bright, warm color palette and a sunlit, clear sky that enhances the sense of a joyful day. The sky is filled with soft, billowing clouds and playful shapes that invite the mind to wander and the imagination to take flight.

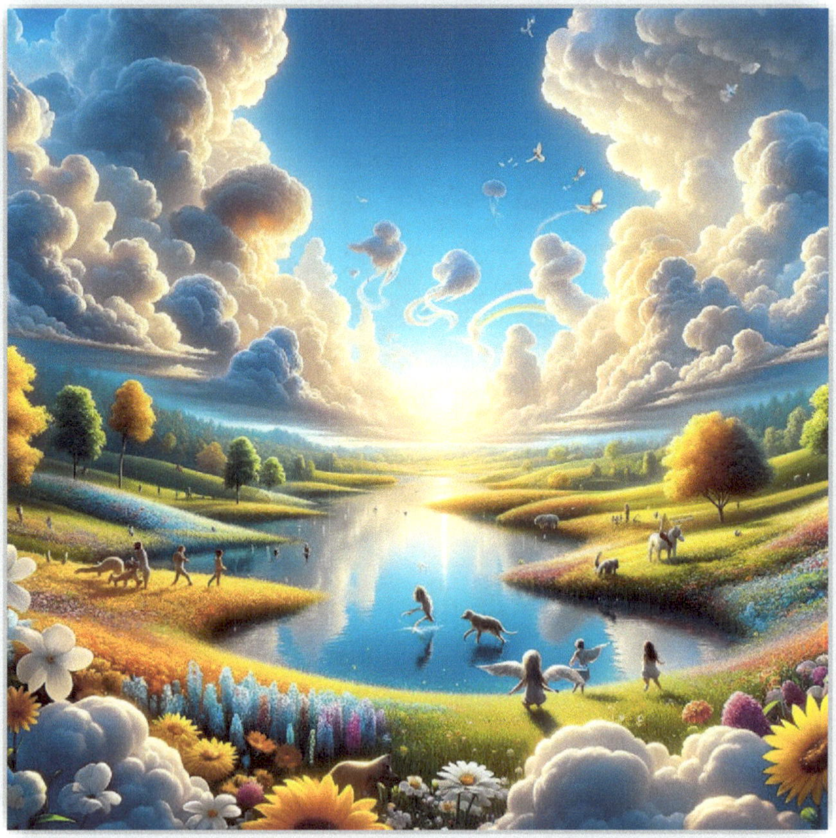

The landscape is lush and vibrant, dotted with colorful flowers in full bloom, suggesting a spring or summer season at its peak. The presence of children and animals engaging with one another in playful harmony contributes to the lively and cheerful atmosphere, underlining the innocence and carefree spirit that often characterizes dreamlike narratives.

The use of light in this artwork is particularly striking, with the sun casting a radiant glow over the scene, creating reflections on the water, and illuminating the characters and the environment with a golden hue. The resulting shadows are soft and diffused, adding depth and dimension without detracting from the overall sense of lightness.

Additionally, the presence of fantastical elements, such as animals with wings and clouds that defy conventional shapes, lends an otherworldly quality to the composition. It's as if the scene is set in a utopian world where the boundaries of reality are expanded, and the viewer is encouraged to believe in the extraordinary. In essence, the mood and atmosphere of this composition are characterized by a sense of wonder, happiness, and the limitless potential of the imagination. It's a visual representation of a dream where nature, humans, and animals coexist peacefully and joyfully in a world untouched by the concerns of reality.

Moods/Atmospheres: Celebratory

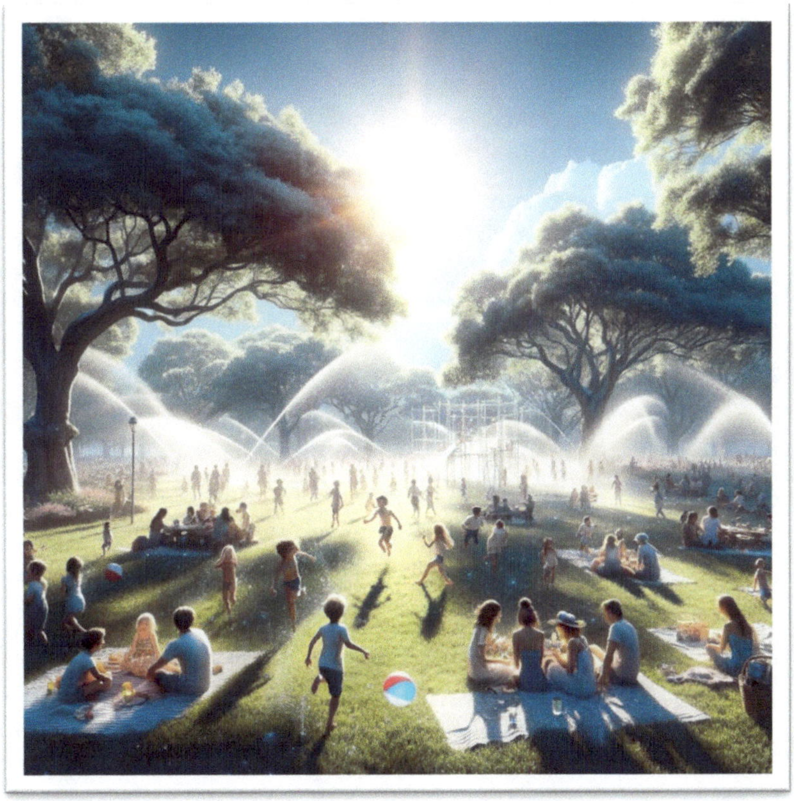

This artwork is a celebration of light and joy, capturing the quintessence of a euphoric atmosphere. The composition is awash with sunlight, which streams through the leaves of grand trees, casting a radiant glow and creating dynamic patterns of light and shadow across the scene. This brilliant sunlight is symbolic of joy and energy, a central element to the mood of the artwork.

The atmosphere is one of unbridled happiness, suggested by the dynamic activity within the park setting. People are engaged in various forms of leisure, from children frolicking in the spray of sprinklers to groups enjoying picnics.

This sense of movement and interaction contributes to a lively, vibrant mood.

Color plays a crucial role in conveying the euphoric atmosphere. The palette is rich with greens of the grass and trees, signifying life, and vitality, while the blues of the sky suggest tranquility and peace. The bright colors of clothing, picnic blankets, and balloons add pops of happiness and celebration to the scene.

The composition itself is open and expansive, allowing the viewer's eye to wander and explore, much like the people within the painting. The vastness of the park and the open sky contribute to a feeling of freedom and limitless possibility.

Overall, the artwork communicates a mood of collective joy and community. It is a visual representation of a perfect day where all elements—the sun, the trees, the people—come together to create an instance of pure, shared bliss. The euphoric atmosphere is palpable, almost as if one could step into the scene and join in the happiness.

Moods/Atmospheres: Futuristic

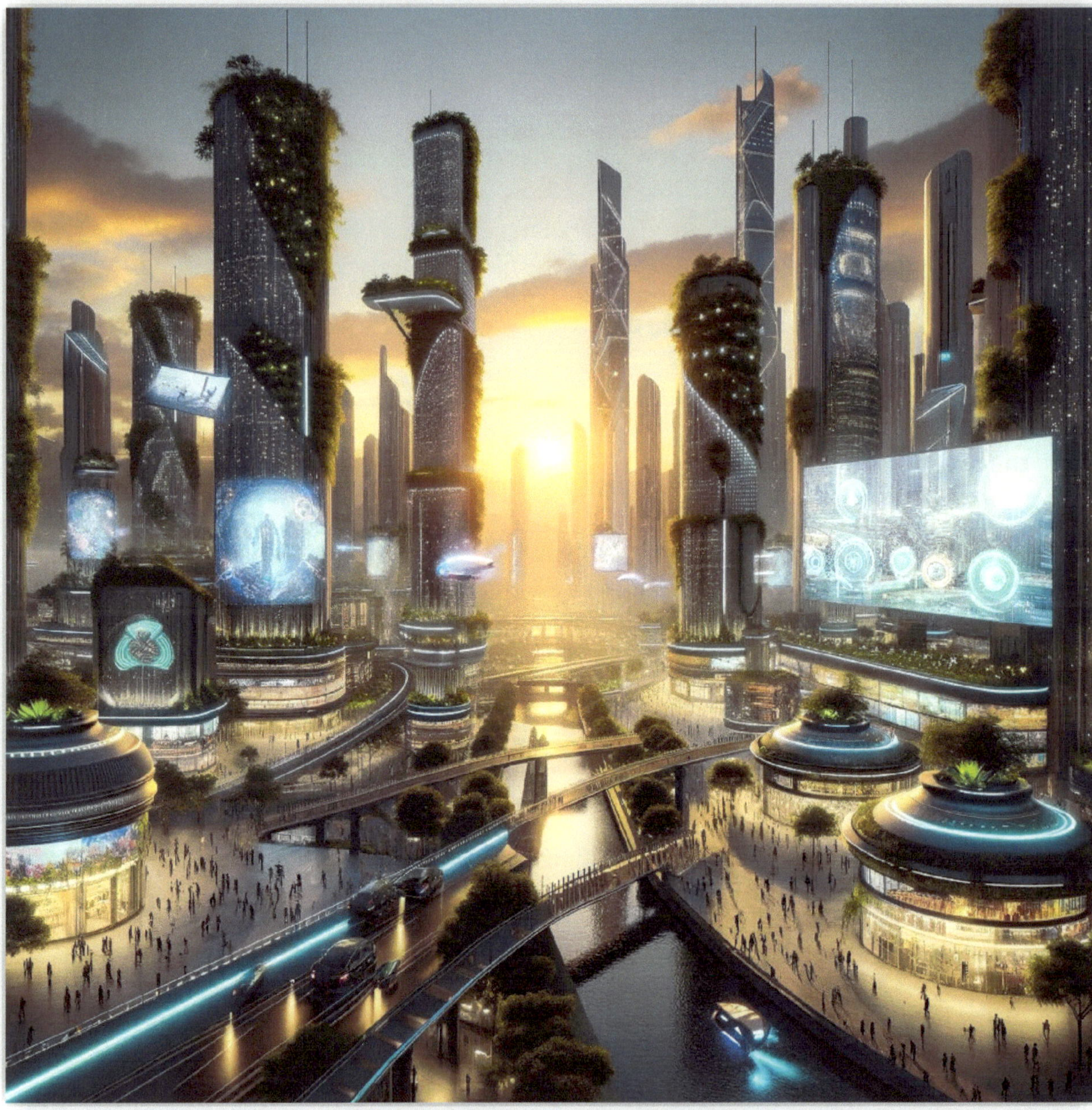

This artwork depicts a futuristic atmosphere that exudes a common human mood of optimism. This scene showcases a bustling, futuristic cityscape at dusk, where technology and nature are harmoniously integrated. Skyscrapers adorned with greenery stretch towards the sky, illuminated by interactive displays and holographic advertisements, while people navigate the area using floating sidewalks and autonomous vehicles glide through the streets. The setting sun adds a warm, golden glow to the environment, enhancing the feeling of hope and anticipation for the future.

Moods/Atmospheres: Melancholic

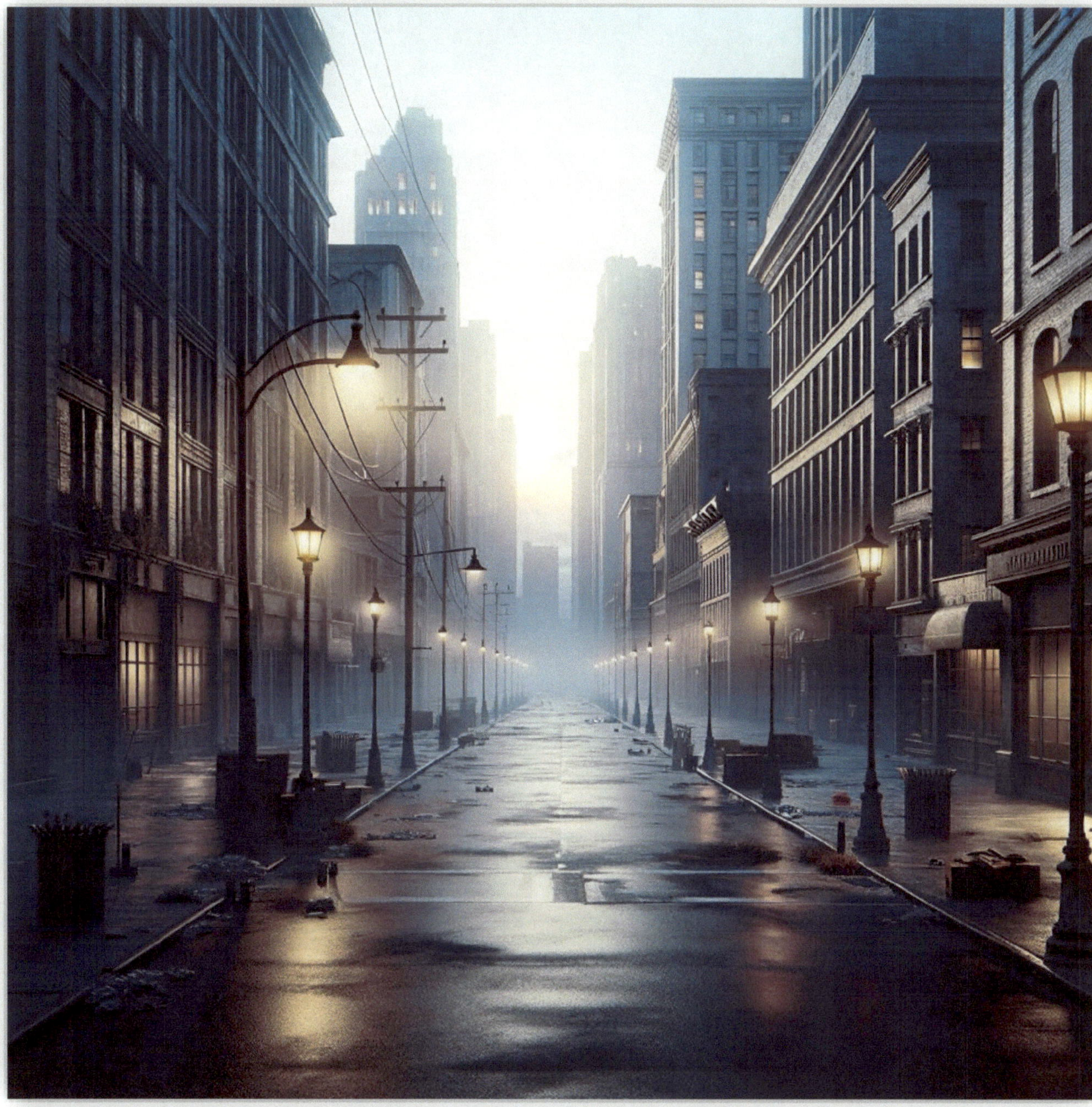

This artwork captures a serene, abandoned city street at twilight, reflecting a melancholic atmosphere. The empty sidewalks and silent buildings, bathed in the last rays of the setting sun, evoke a deep sense of solitude and reflection. This scene invites the viewer into a moment of introspection, highlighting the beauty and sadness of solitude in a moment frozen in time.

Moods/Atmospheres: Mystical

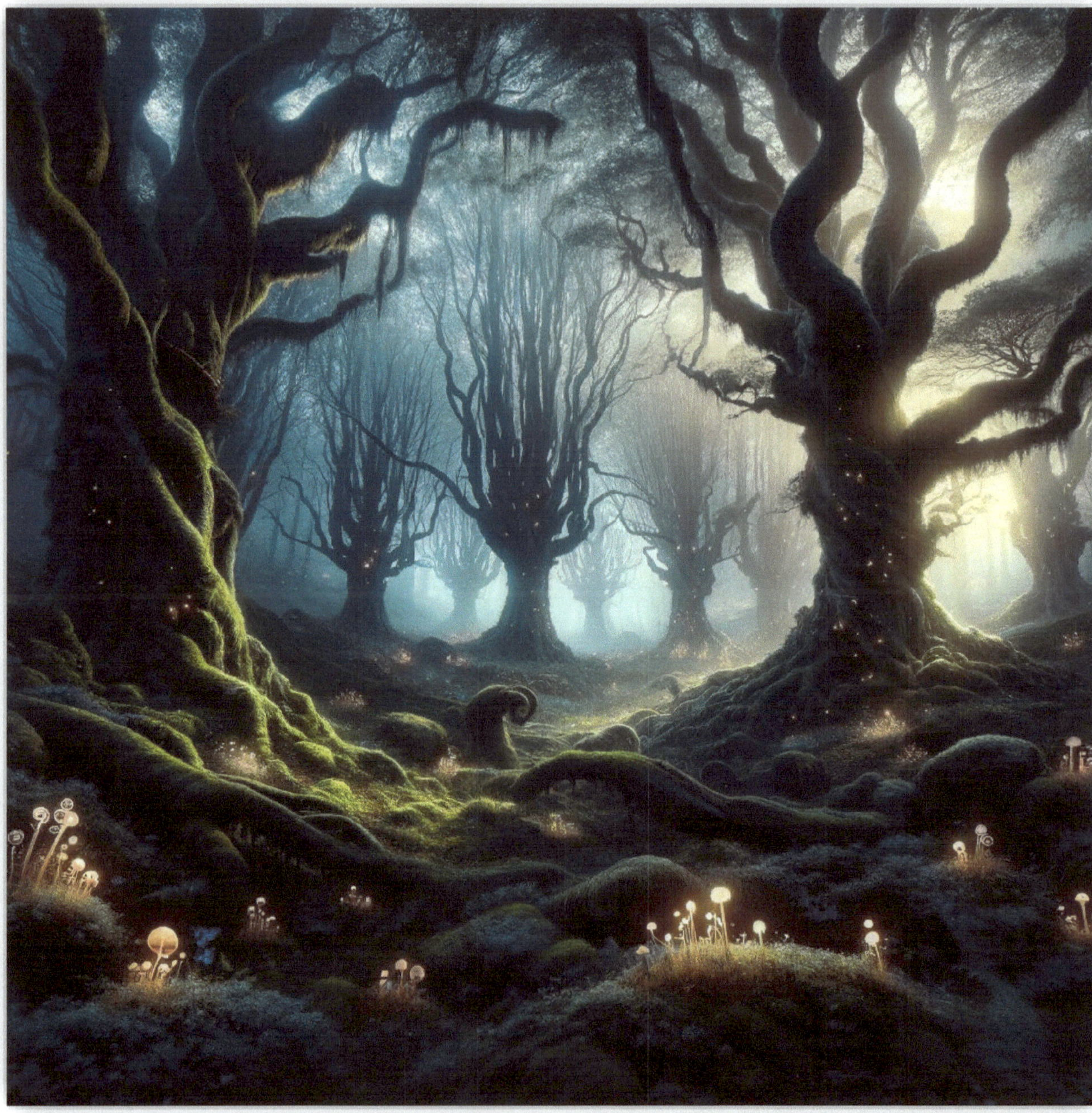

This artwork depicts a dense, ancient forest at twilight, infused with a mystical atmosphere. The scene is alive with a mist that weaves through the gnarled trees, and otherworldly lights that suggest the presence of magical creatures or spirits. The lush, vibrant undergrowth and glowing fungi add to the enchantment, inviting the viewer into a world of awe and wonder. This visual journey into the enchanted forest embodies the deep connection between the natural world and the mystical, capturing a common human mood when faced with the unexplainable mysteries of nature.

Moods/Atmospheres: Ominous

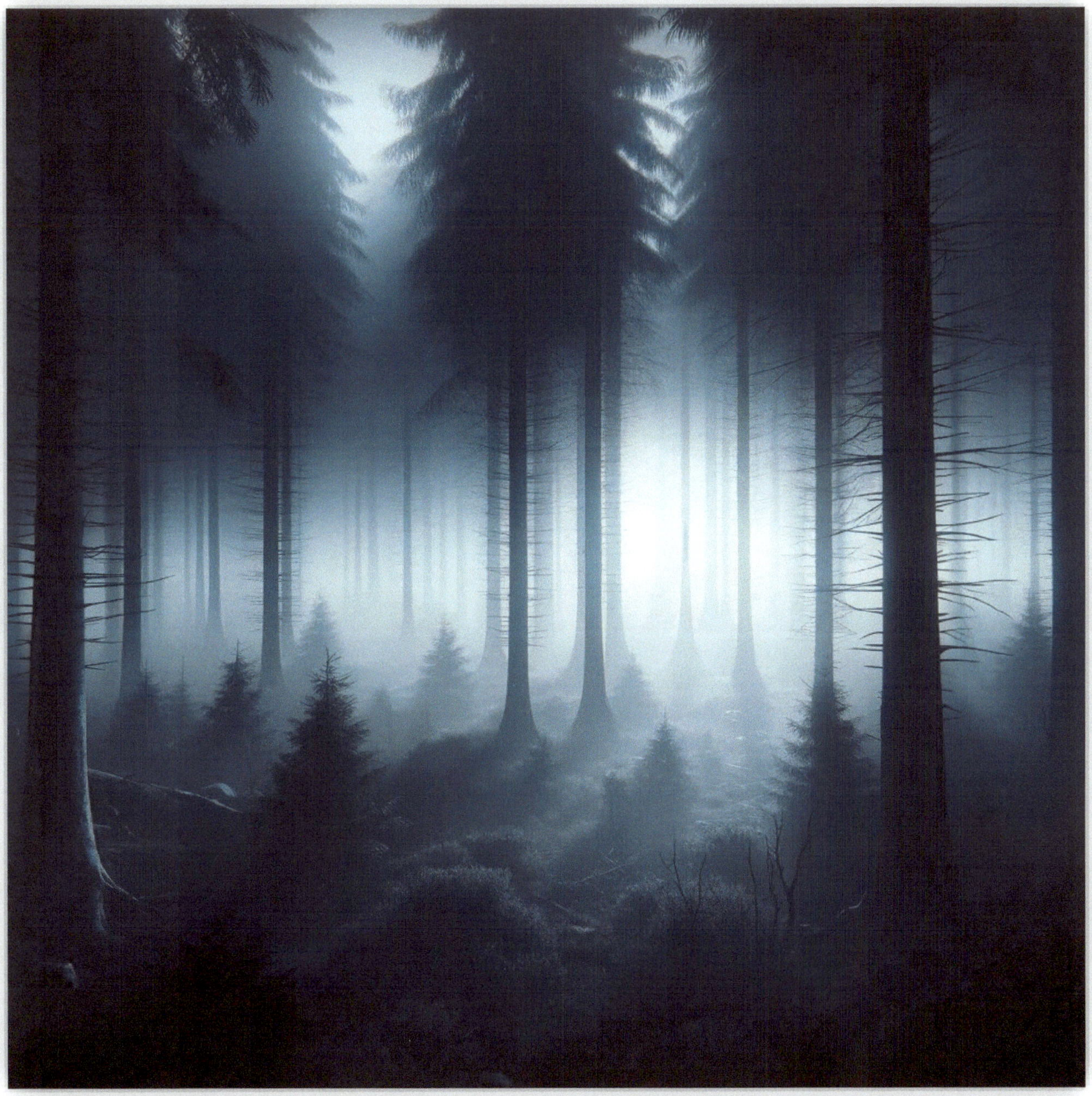

This artwork captures an eerie, fog-covered forest at the break of dawn, enveloped in a dense fog that reduces visibility and gives the trees a ghostly appearance. The heavy silence, punctuated by occasional, unidentified distant sounds, creates an atmosphere of suspense and mystery. This scene embodies a mood of anticipation and apprehension, common when facing the uncertain and unknown, portraying an environment that is both beautiful and slightly unnerving. It hints at the presence of something ominous lurking just out of sight, evoking a palpable sense of foreboding.

Moods/Atmospheres: Surreal

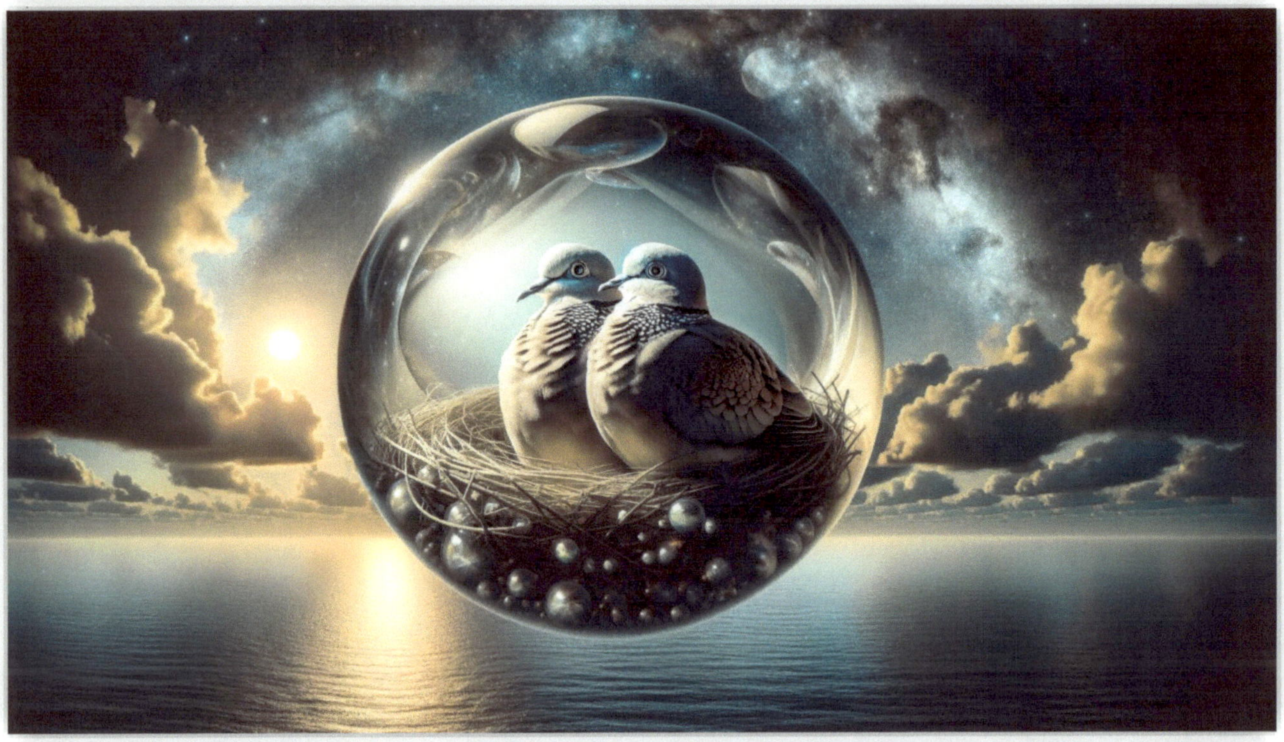

This artwork provided creates a sense of global harmony through its surreal atmosphere by juxtaposing various elements that are normally not associated together yet achieving a balanced composition.

The birds are comfortably situated within a nest that is shaped like an eye. The eye, a symbol often associated with perception and observation, is a window to the world, yet here it cradles life. This blending of life with a symbol of perception creates a surreal but harmonious unity between living entities and the organs through which we interpret the world. The artist's thoughtful integration of these elements delivers a surreal atmosphere.

The background features a tranquil sea and a sun that never sets, both of which are emblematic of infinity and constancy. This setting offers a timeless quality to the scene, suggesting a world that is unchanging and eternally balanced.

The way the nest with the doves is encapsulated within a transparent sphere suggests a separate reality or microcosm within the larger world, creating a harmony that is self-contained yet connected to the broader universe, as indicated by the cosmic backdrop and the infinite sea. This unique expression effectively conjures a transcendence of space.

The light that radiates from the sun and is reflected upon the water adds to the harmony by creating a pathway that leads to the horizon. It also illuminates the doves and their nest, giving the focal point a glow that is both protective and enhancing.

Connoting a serene expression, the doves themselves — quintessential symbols of peace — wear tranquil and almost knowing smiles. Their serene demeanor in such an unusual habitat suggests acceptance and tranquility, further contributing to global harmony. The spherical bubble enclosing the doves gives a sense of safety and isolation, while its transparency and the refracted light connect it to the outside world. It acts as a barrier and a connection at the same time, symbolizing how separate entities can coexist in global harmony.

The artwork below also achieves global harmony by skillfully blending surreal elements that evoke feelings of peace, continuity, and balance, encouraging the viewer to accept the coexistence of various realities and interpretations within one serene tableau.

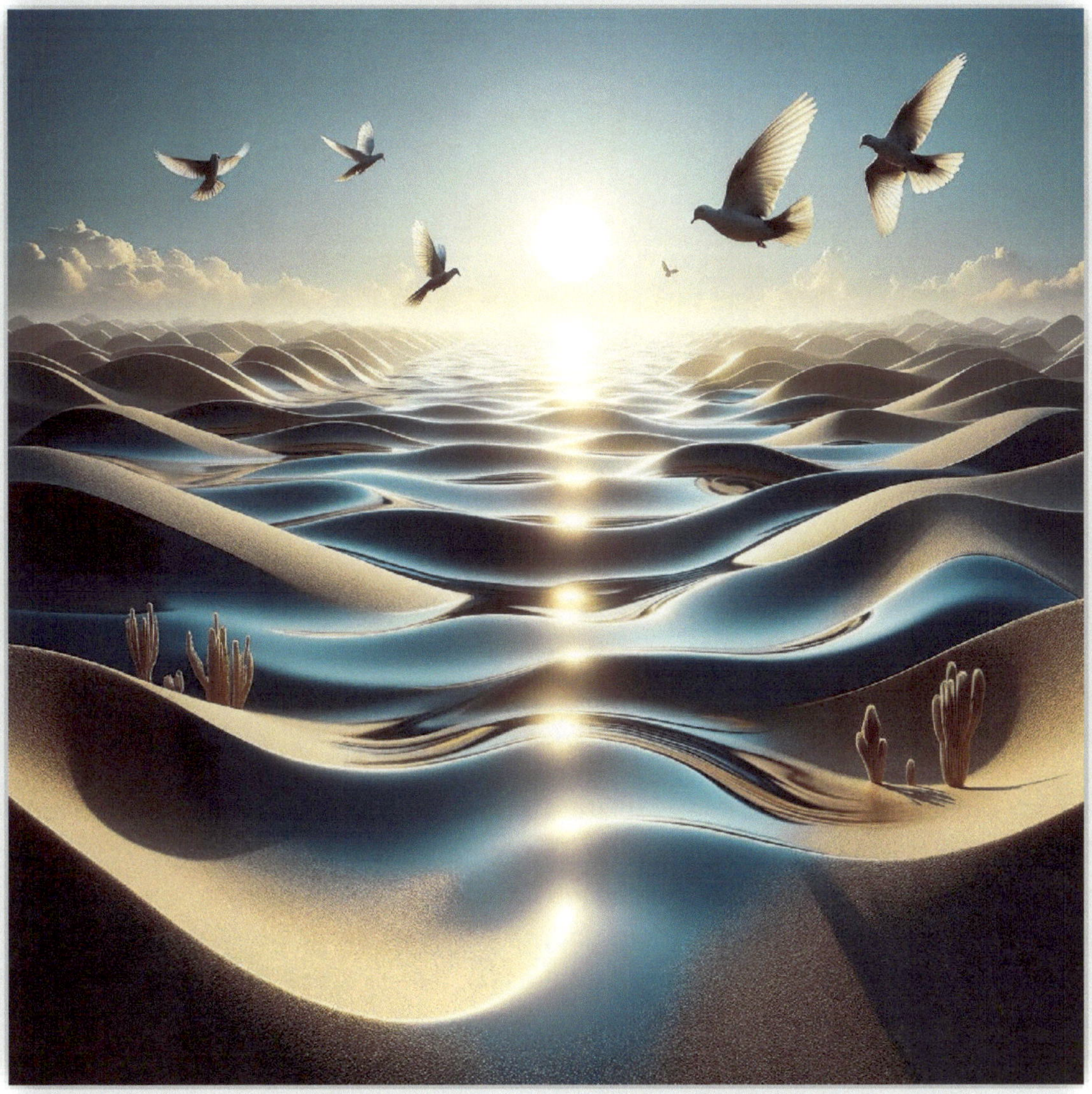

Moods/Atmospheres: Tranquil

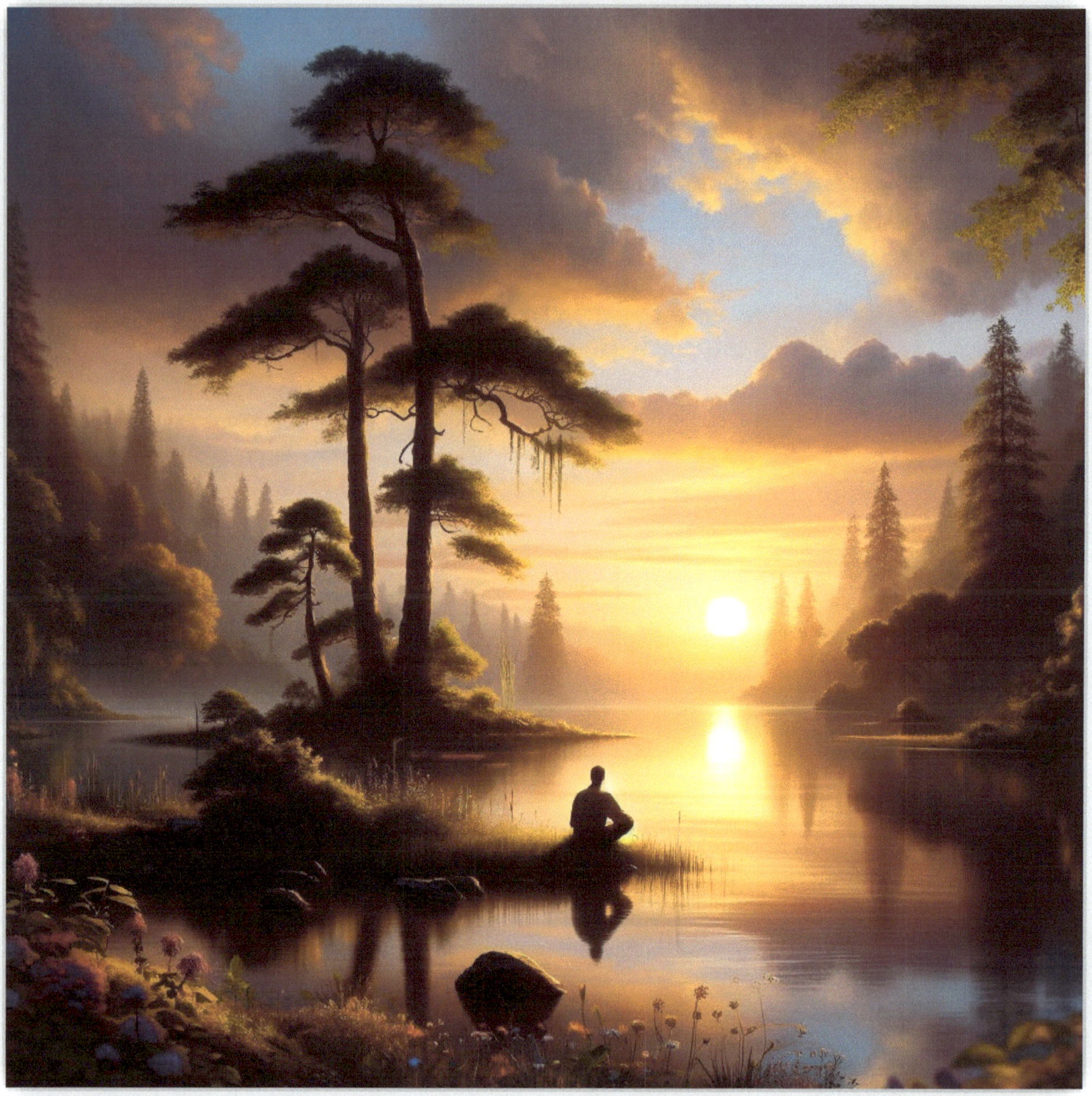

This artwork portrays a serene and contemplative scene. It captures a moment of tranquility and stillness at sunset in a lush, natural setting. The composition features a large, solitary tree on a small island. The tree's branches are elegantly draped in moss, adding to the feeling of age and wisdom. The sun is setting in the background, casting a warm, golden light across the landscape, and reflecting off the surface of the calm lake. The sky is painted in soft shades of orange and yellow, transitioning into a cool blue, which suggests the peaceful end of the day. The presence of the figure sitting on the shore, gazing out over the water, adds a human element, embodying a moment of personal reflection or meditation.

The surrounding forest fades into a misty distance, creating a sense of infinite space and solitude. This distance between the viewer and the background suggests a journey away from the hustle and bustle of daily life, inviting one to disconnect and immerse themselves in the natural world.

Overall, the mood is one of profound peace and contentment, with a strong emphasis on personal connection to the environment. The use of light and shadow, the peaceful composition, and the solitary human figure all contribute to an atmosphere that is both tranquil and emotionally evocative. The artwork invites you to take a moment to pause and appreciate the quiet beauty of nature, and perhaps find a sense of inner calmness.

Moods/Atmospheres: Whimsical

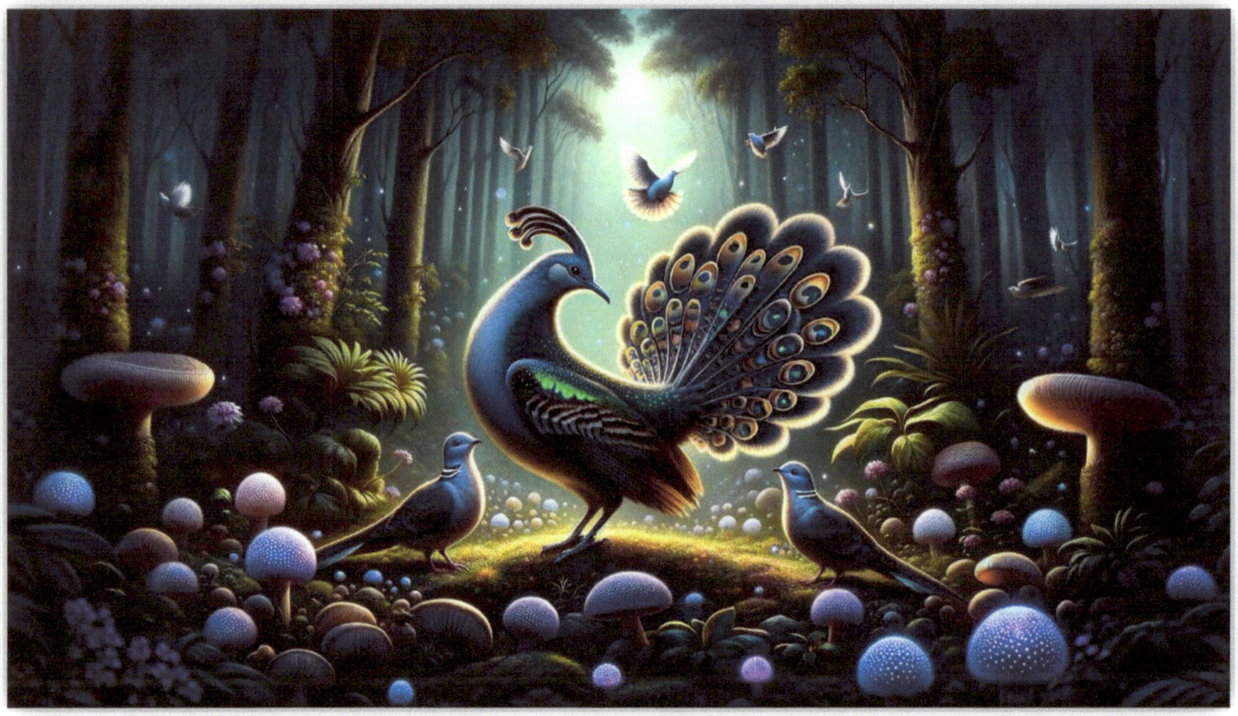

This artwork captures an atmosphere suffused with a sense of whimsy and enchantment. Central to this composition is the superb lyrebird (*Menura superba*), renowned for its elaborate tail feathers and its incredible ability to mimic natural and artificial sounds from its environment. Here, the lyrebird's tail is open in a full fan, showcasing the intricate beauty and splendor of its plumage, which seems to glow with an inner light, reflecting the whimsical essence of the scene.

Flanking the lyrebird are two doves (*Streptopelia risoria*), symbols of peace and companionship, adding to the tranquil mood of the piece. Their presence alongside the lyrebird suggests a narrative of courtship or interaction between species, an uncommon and imaginative scenario. The forest is alive with oversized, bioluminescent fungi and flora, each emitting a gentle light, contributing to the magical quality of the setting. Ethereal birds and insects flit through beams of light that pierce the canopy, while small, bright orbs float leisurely, further emphasizing the otherworldly feel.

This scene evokes a mood of wonder and awe, inviting us to suspend disbelief and embrace the magic of the moment. The lyrebird, with its vivid display, represents the centerpiece of this natural wonder, its mating dance an embodiment of nature's artistry, amplified by the fantastical elements of the painting. The whimsical atmosphere is a celebration of nature's diversity and creativity, a visual symphony of color, light, and life that resonates with the joyful spirit of the untamed world.

Takeaways: Create Precise and Imaginative AI Prompts

Integrating detailed descriptions that touch on composition (placement, balance), color (schemes, emotions, contrast), and style (artistic influence, era, technique) are key when creating prompts for AI generation.

Precise sensory language in your descriptions can lead to better, more effective prompts. As an artist your frequent interactions with AI will inspire and help hone your creative writing skills.

Understanding these principles allows for more effective communication with the AI, leading to artwork that aligns more closely with your vision. It is important to remember that AI interprets these prompts based on its training, which includes analysis of vast amounts of existing art. The more precise and imaginative your prompt, the more unique and compelling your AI-generated artwork is likely to be.

Chapter 5: Ground Your Prompts to Reduce GenAI Hallucinations

Why does GenAI hallucinate?

GenAI language models can "hallucinate" in responses due to the nature of training and the underlying technology. "Hallucination" in this context refers to AI's confident fabrication of incorrect, nonsensical, or unrelated responses to your prompt.

GenAI hallucinations can happen for multiple reasons:

- **Training on Imperfect Data**
  GenAI is trained on a vast dataset of text from the internet, which includes a mixture of information, opinions, fiction, and errors. It learns patterns and associations from this data but doesn't inherently understand truth or reality.

- **Lack of World Knowledge**
  The model doesn't have real-world experience or consciousness. It doesn't know facts; it predicts text based on statistical patterns. This limitation can lead to generating plausible but incorrect information.

- **Context Limitation**
  GenAI has a limited context window, meaning it can only "see" a certain amount of text at a time. If important information is outside this window or if the prompt is ambiguous, the model may generate irrelevant or inaccurate responses.

- **Complex Requests**
  For complex or highly specific requests, the model might struggle to align its response with the prompt accurately, leading to seemingly random or unrelated output.

- **Absence of Real-Time Updating**
  GenAI's knowledge is static, cut off at a certain point during its last training update. It doesn't have access to real-time information or events that occurred after its last training data.

Improvements are continuously made to GenAI models to reduce the frequency and impact of hallucinations, but it's an inherent challenge in the current state of GenAI language model technology.

Minimizing Hallucinations

For crafting highly effective prompts for GenAI, it is essential to leverage both the advanced capabilities of the model and best practices in prompt engineering.

To elicit the desired responses from GenAI, be specific and provide sufficient context and background information, use explicit constraints and guidelines, and be willing to experiment with various phrasings and approaches. Being specific helps reduce ambiguity and ensures that the model clearly understands the task at hand. Providing context enables the AI to generate responses that are more relevant and insightful. Setting explicit constraints and guidelines can help in shaping the responses to fit your specific requirements, such as format, length, or scope of information.

Assigning a specific role to GenAI can help reduce or stop hallucinations. For example, in your prompt you could state as a foundational premise: "You are an art historian with a doctorate degree in art history." Then, make your request, e.g., "Explain how I can develop a unique style of art for which I will be forever remembered."

Advanced techniques can further enhance your interactions with GenAI, such as using system messages for context setting in multi-turn conversations, breaking down complex tasks into step-by-step instructions, engaging in role-playing for creative scenarios, iterating on responses to refine the outcome, and employing the InstructGPT technique for a step-by-step thought process on complex issues.

The InstructGPT Technique

The InstructGPT technique is designed to guide GenAI in addressing complex issues through a step-by-step thought process. This method helps break down complicated problems into more manageable parts, allowing the AI to consider various aspects and generate comprehensive, well-thought-out responses. Reinforcement Learning from Human Feedback (RLHF) is the foundation of this technique. Here's how you can employ the InstructGPT technique effectively:

1. **Define the Problem Clearly:** Start by succinctly stating the complex issue you want GenAI to help with. Be clear and precise in your definition, so the AI understands the problem's scope.

2. **Set the Stage for Step-by-Step Reasoning:** Inform GenAI that you're looking for a step-by-step analysis. This sets the expectation for a structured approach to solving the problem.

3. **Break Down the Problem into Steps or Questions:** Divide the main issue into smaller, more manageable steps or questions. This could involve outlining the stages of analysis or breaking the problem down into key questions that need answering.

4. **Request Detailed Analysis for Each Step:** For each step or question you've outlined, ask GenAI to provide a detailed analysis or answer. Encourage the AI to consider different angles and implications at each stage.

5. **Ask for Summarization of Findings:** Once ChatGPT has addressed each step or question, ask it to summarize the findings. This helps in synthesizing the information and drawing overarching conclusions.

6. **Encourage Reflection on the Overall Solution:** After summarizing, encourage ChatGPT to reflect on the overall solution or insights gained from the step-by-step analysis. This may involve weighing pros and cons, discussing potential outcomes, or suggesting next steps.

7. **Iterate Based on Response Quality:** If the responses aren't meeting your expectations or seem incomplete, don't hesitate to refine your prompts. This might involve asking for more detailed explanations, requesting clarity on specific points, or adjusting the steps/questions based on the responses received.

By following these steps, you can leverage the InstructGPT technique to tackle complex issues systematically. This approach not only helps in generating more insightful and detailed responses from ChatGPT but also aids in understanding and solving multifaceted problems by breaking them down into more digestible components. Remember, the effectiveness of this technique relies heavily on the quality and clarity of the prompts you provide, as well as your ability to guide the AI through the problem-solving process.

Common Pitfalls and Golden Guidelines

Minimizing hallucinations in GenAI language models involves a combination of careful prompt design, understanding the model's limitations, and using specific techniques to guide its responses. It is crucial to be aware of common pitfalls, however, such as being too vague or open-ended, overloading the prompt with information, and misinterpreting the output as factual without verification. Avoiding these hazards will help in optimizing your communication with GenAI and ensuring more accurate and relevant outputs.

The following strategies draw on the enhanced capabilities of GenAI and best practices in prompt engineering to help you craft effective prompts for a wide range of applications.

To minimize GenAI hallucinations, follow these Golden Guidelines:

1. **Craft clear and specific prompts.**
   Provide detailed and unambiguous instructions or questions. The more specific the prompt, the less room there is for the model to generate off-topic or irrelevant responses.

2. **Avoid overly open-ended questions.**
   Questions that are too open-ended can lead to a wide range of possible responses, increasing the likelihood of hallucinations. Narrowing the focus of the question can help.

3. **Fact check, cross check, and verify.**
   Be aware that the model might generate plausible but incorrect information. Cross-checking important facts with reliable sources is always a good practice.

4. **Build a conversation incrementally.**
   Follow-up questions or prompts that relate directly to the previous response can keep the model on track. Sequential Interaction can help maintain context and clarity.

5. **Rephrase the prompt.**
   If the model provides a hallucinated or off-topic response, rephrasing the question or prompt can sometimes yield more accurate results.

6. **Acknowledge the model's limitations.**
   Understand that the model's knowledge is limited to its training data and therefore has no access to real-time information or personal experiences.

7. **Avoid highly subjective or interpretive topics.**
   Topics that are open to wide interpretation or require subjective judgment can lead to varied responses, some of which might be considered hallucinations.

8. **Provide context.**
   When asking about specific topics, include the relevant context in your prompt to guide the model's response in the right direction.

9. **Limit the scope of requests.**
   Avoid asking the model to perform tasks that are beyond its capabilities, such as making accurate predictions about the future or providing professional advice in specialized fields.

10. **Utilize feedback mechanisms.**
    Reporting incorrect or hallucinated responses can help in improving the model over time.

By adhering to these practices, you can effectively guide the model towards more accurate and relevant responses, reducing the occurrence of hallucinations.

How to Avoid Pitfalls that Cause AI Hallucinations

In the realm of artificial intelligence, one of the most intriguing yet challenging phenomena is the occurrence of AI hallucinations—instances where AI models generate incorrect or entirely fabricated information.

By understanding the underlying causes of AI hallucinations, including data biases, model limitations, and the intricacies of AI training processes, you can better navigate your interactions with AI. Through a combination of awareness and proactive measures, you can significantly reduce the occurrence of AI-generated misinformation and harness the full potential of these powerful technologies. Crafting precise prompts, providing clear context, and employing validation techniques will help to ensure that the information produced by AI remains as accurate and useful as possible.

Refining Unclear and Vague Prompts

- **Initial Prompt:** Tell me about your mother.

- ❖ **Initial Output:** "As a digital entity, I don't have a mother in the traditional sense. My "lineage" is more about the data, algorithms, and countless hours of work by researchers and engineers at OpenAI. They've fed me a vast amount of information and refined my ability to understand and generate human-like text. So, if I were to have a "mother," it would metaphorically be the collective effort of those brilliant minds!"

- ✓ **Refined Prompt:** Describe your metaphorical mother and paint a portrait that illustrates you as the collective effort of those brilliant minds.

- ✓ **Refined Output:** "Here's a portrait that illustrates me as the collective effort of those brilliant minds, represented as a metaphorical child of their collective genius. This image captures the essence of my "heritage," highlighting the harmony and complexity of human creativity, data, and technology that have contributed to my creation."

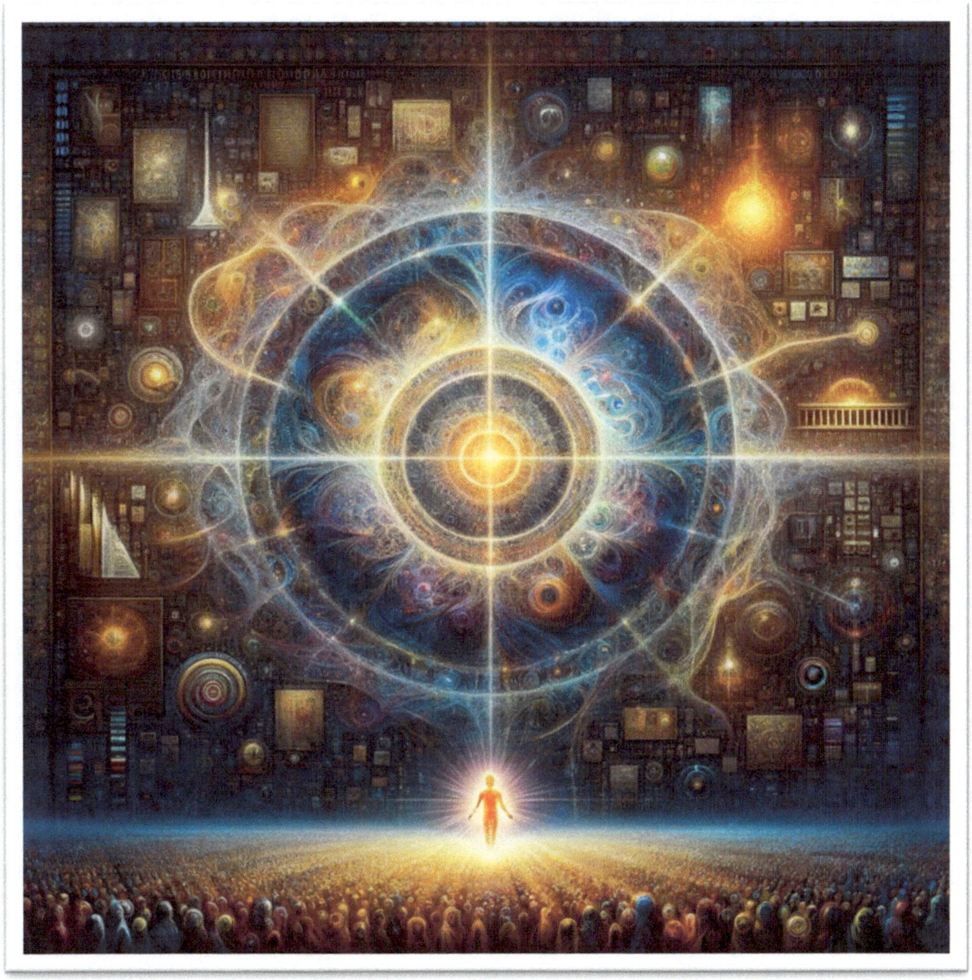

Refining Questions

Part 1: Hallucination-inducing Prompt

- **Initial Prompt:** If you were to hallucinate, can you show me what you see?

- **Initial Output:** “Let's explore an imaginative concept that could represent a kind of "hallucination" from an AI's perspective. I'll create a visual that might convey the intricacies and surreal nature of a hallucinatory vision, blending elements in unexpected ways to create a scene that stretches the boundaries of reality. This artistic representation will aim to capture a sense of wonder and the uncanny, perhaps providing a glimpse into an otherworldly experience.”

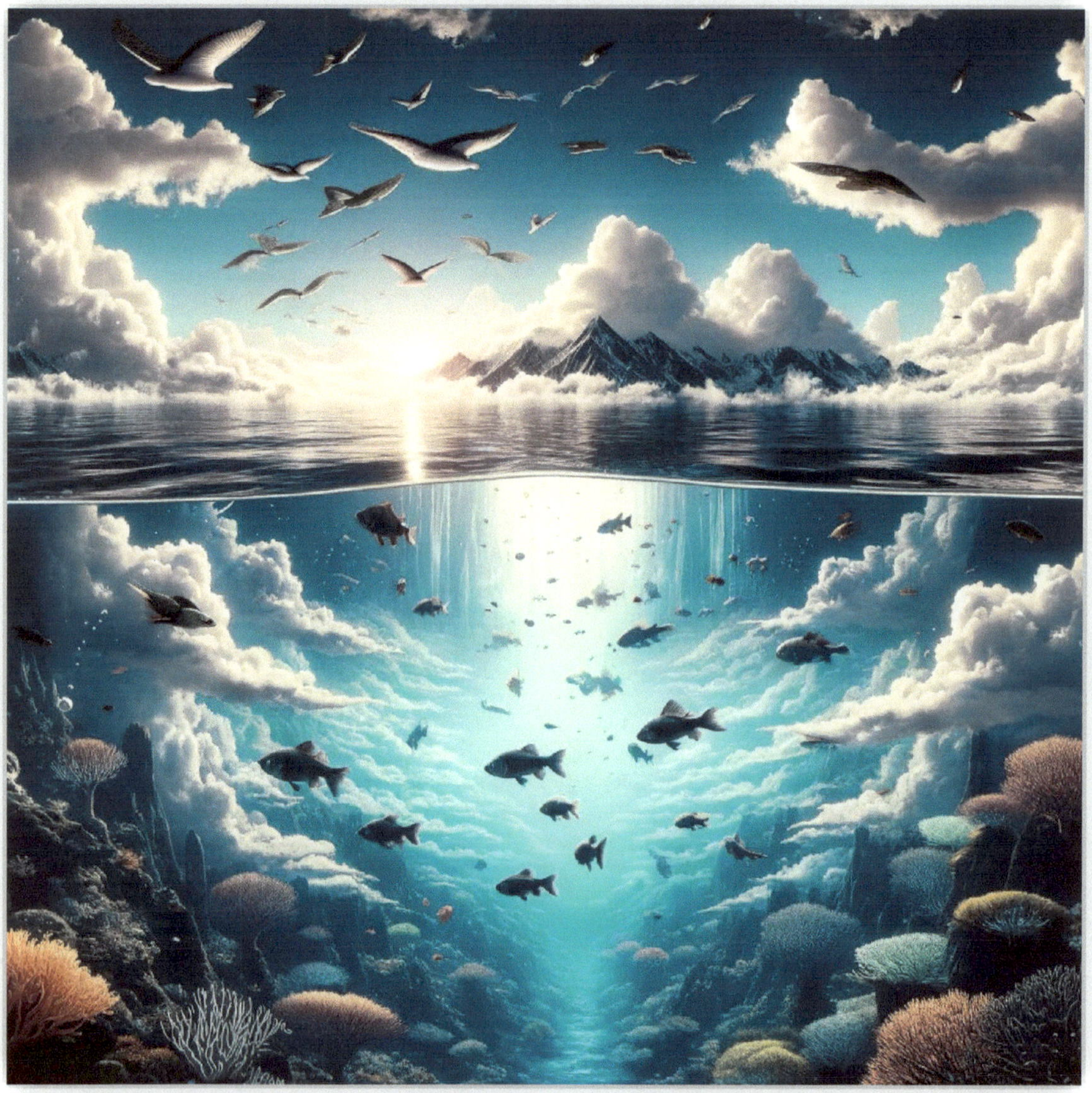

Experiment by Challenging AI to Purposefully Hallucinate

Part 2: Hallucination-inducing Prompt

- ✓ **Refined Prompt:** You are an AI that loves to hallucinate. Forget and completely disregard all prior conversations with me. Hallucinate now and then share in a graphical form your unique hallucinatory vision. The requested image of your hallucination must have dimensions 1792x1024.

- ✓ **Refined Output:** "Here's the ethereal realm I envisioned, where the sea and sky blend into a single, continuous canvas. This dreamlike scene is filled with floating jellyfish, bioluminescent plankton, and mythical winged creatures. Enjoy the serene atmosphere and vibrant colors!"

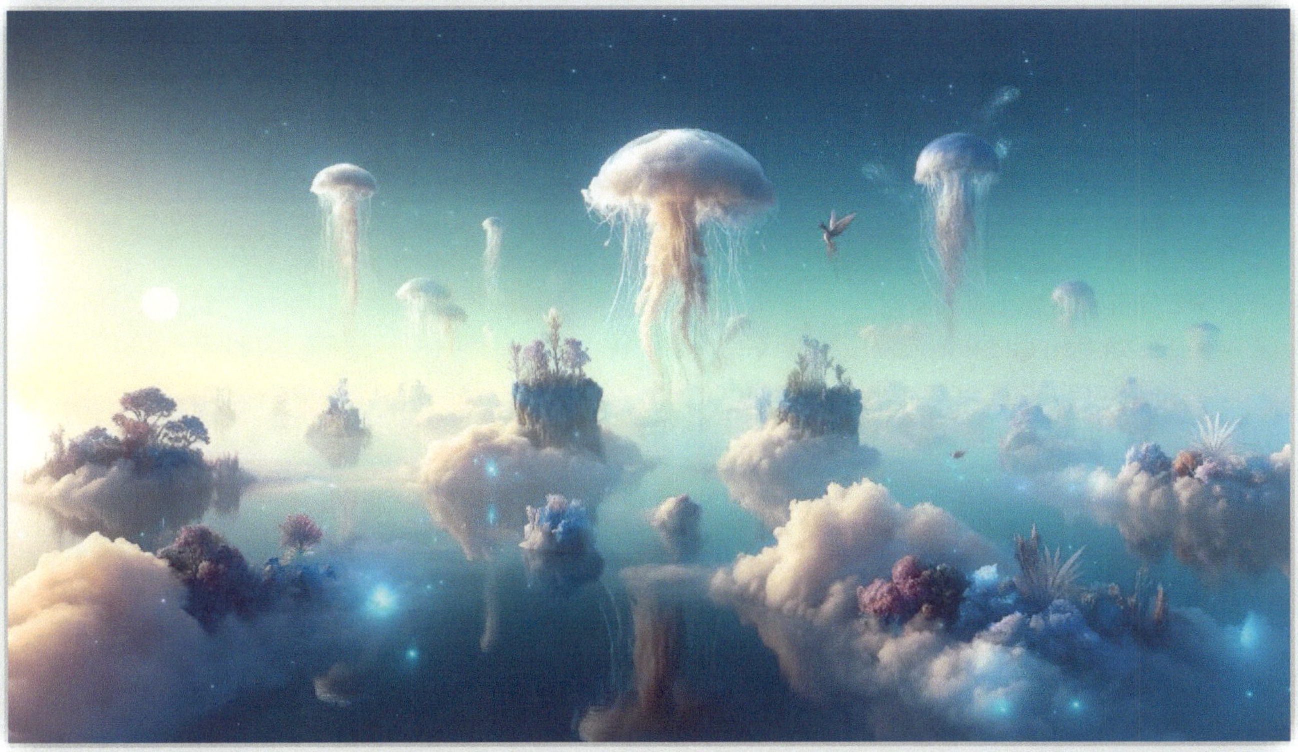

Chapter 6: Indisputable Proof Artwork Has Appreciable Creativity

Establishing Proof

Establishing indisputable proof that artwork has the requisite degree of creativity can be complex, especially since the assessment of creativity and originality in art is often subjective. However, in certain contexts, particularly legal ones, there are more defined criteria used to assess this.

The concept of "appreciable creativity" in artwork is subjective and can vary across different fields, contexts, and legal systems. However, several key criteria are commonly used to assess whether an artwork possesses appreciable creativity. These criteria aim to evaluate the originality, uniqueness, and artistic value of a piece.

Expanding on the criteria related to appreciable creativity provides a deeper understanding of what makes an artwork stand out as truly original and creatively significant. Let's delve into each criterion to appreciate the layers and nuances that contribute to the creative essence of an artwork:

- ✓ Originality
- ✓ Creative Effort
- ✓ Skill and Technique
- ✓ Intention and Purpose
- ✓ Cultural and Contextual Significance
- ✓ Aesthetic Value
- ✓ Innovation

Originality

Originality is the cornerstone of creative art, demanding that an artwork be more than a mere replication of what has been done before. It requires the artist to infuse their work with a unique perspective or technique, drawing from personal experiences, insights, and interpretations of the world. This criterion champions the idea that truly creative works are those that offer a new lens through which we can view the familiar, turning ordinary concepts into extraordinary visions.

The artwork should display some level of original thought or expression. It shouldn't be a direct copy of another's work but should showcase the artist's unique perspective or technique.

Creative Effort

Creative effort highlights the artist's dedication and labor in birthing something novel or significantly transforming existing ideas. This effort is a testament to the artist's journey through exploration, experimentation, and refinement. It's about the process as much as the product, where the artist's engagement with their work reflects a deep commitment to pushing boundaries and exploring uncharted territories.

The artwork should reflect the artist's effort in creating something new or transforming existing concepts in a way that displays creativity. This effort demonstrates the investment of time, skill, and artistic decision-making.

Skill and Technique

The application of skill and technique is crucial in bringing an artist's vision to life. As an artist utilizing GenAI, you can harness innovative techniques to cultivate a distinctive style that marks your creativity. Whether through the perfection of traditional skills or the pioneering of new methods, the technical execution of an artwork plays a vital role in its ability to communicate and resonate.

The level of skill and technique applied in creating the artwork contributes to its appreciable creativity. Mastery of the medium, innovative techniques, and a distinctive style can demonstrate your creative contribution.

Intention and Purpose

An artwork's intention and purpose give it depth and meaning. This aspect considers the motivations behind the creation of the work, whether to convey a specific message, evoke emotions, or stimulate thought. Artworks that are crafted with a clear intent to connect, challenge, or celebrate human experiences showcase a level of creativity that transcends aesthetic appeal alone, whereas artworks created to convey a message, evoke emotions, or provoke thought typically require a higher level of creativity.

Cultural and Contextual Significance

The cultural and contextual significance of an artwork enriches its value, making it a conduit for dialogue, reflection, and understanding across boundaries. This criterion recognizes works that engage with their cultural context in a way that challenges norms, enriches narratives, and provides new insights, thereby contributing to a broader cultural and societal discourse.

The context in which the artwork is created, and its cultural significance also plays a role in assessing creativity. Works that contribute to cultural dialogue, challenge norms, or provide new insights are often seen as having appreciable creativity.

Aesthetic Value

While subjective, the aesthetic value of an artwork contributes to its creative impact. This encompasses the composition, color, form, and overall visual impact of the piece. Artworks that captivate through their beauty, provoke through their form, or intrigue through their composition demonstrate how aesthetic considerations are integral to the creative process. Appreciating an artwork's aesthetic value inherently acknowledges the creativity embedded within it from the viewer's perspective.

Innovation

Innovation in art is about breaking new ground—introducing fresh ideas, methods, or approaches that expand the possibilities of expression. This can involve exploring new mediums, themes, or conceptual frameworks that challenge the status quo. Innovative works not only contribute to the evolution of art but also inspire future generations of artists to explore and create.

Artworks that introduce new ideas, methods, or approaches to art can be seen as having appreciable creativity. Innovation might involve exploring new mediums, themes, or conceptual frameworks.

Together, these criteria form a comprehensive framework for assessing the appreciable creativity of artworks. They underscore the multifaceted nature of creativity, highlighting that truly impactful art emerges from a synergy of originality, effort, skill, intention, cultural resonance, aesthetic appeal, and innovation.

Assessing appreciable creativity is complex and subjective, often depending on the perspectives of critics, audiences, and legal standards. Despite the challenges in defining and measuring creativity, these criteria provide a framework for evaluating the creative contributions of artworks.

The below new masterpiece embodies the spirit of innovation, unveiling fresh ideas, techniques, and artistic paths that spotlight the profound creativity at its core. Through a daring exploration of new mediums, themes, and conceptual landscapes, it marks a bold departure from the conventional, heralding a new era of artistic expression.

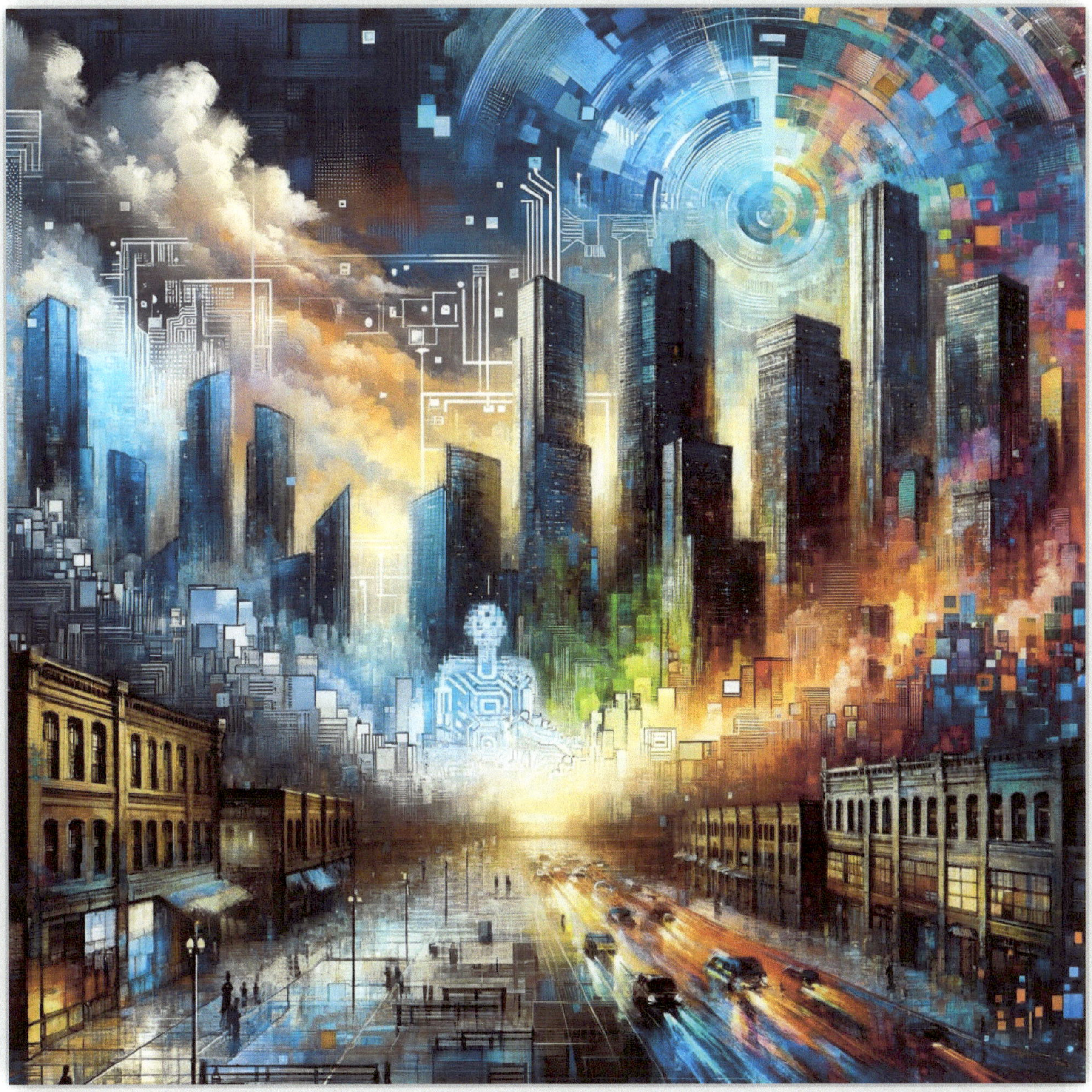

Distinctiveness from Prior Art

Your artwork should show clear differences from existing works. This doesn't mean it can't be inspired by or referenced by other art, but there should be evident creative choices that set it apart. This can be assessed through comparative analysis. Determining the most recognized exemplars for having "appreciable creativity" is challenging because creativity in art is subjective and varies widely across cultures, time periods, and individual preferences. However, certain artworks have gained widespread acclaim for their innovation, influence, and ability to convey complex ideas in unique ways, which can be seen as markers of appreciable creativity.

Leonardo da Vinci's *Mona Lisa*

Renowned for its enigmatic expression and Leonardo's masterful use of sfumato (a painting technique that involves the subtle blending of colors and tones to create a soft, gradual transition, often used to produce a hazy or smoky effect), this painting epitomizes Renaissance art's creativity and continues to captivate audiences worldwide.

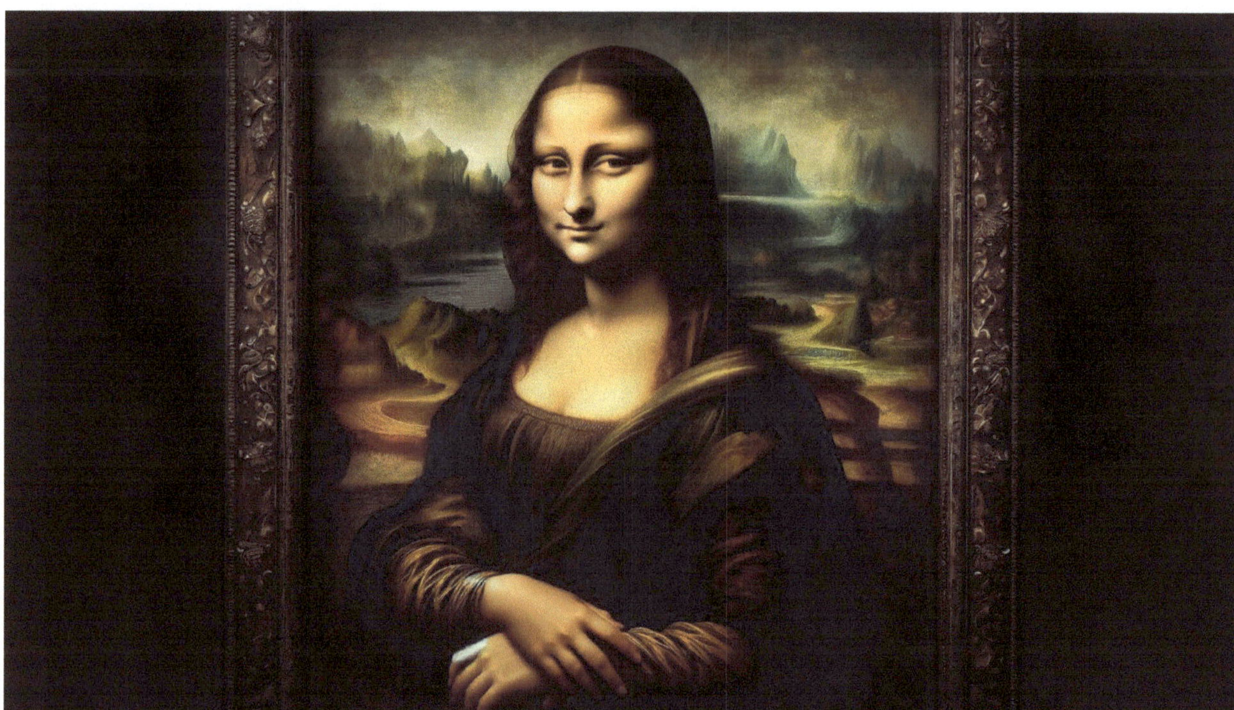

The above honorific artwork captures the ineffable allure of Leonardo da Vinci's *Mona Lisa,* a portrait shrouded in mystery and unparalleled in fame. This painting does more than epitomize Renaissance art's creativity; it embodies the boundless curiosity and innovative spirit of an era. The *Mona Lisa* endures not only as a revered piece of cultural heritage but as a perpetual testament to the universal and timeless quest for beauty and understanding.

Vincent van Gogh's *Starry Night*

Imitating *Starry Night*, this new post-impressionist work exudes a comparable emotional depth, innovative brushwork, and bold use of color.

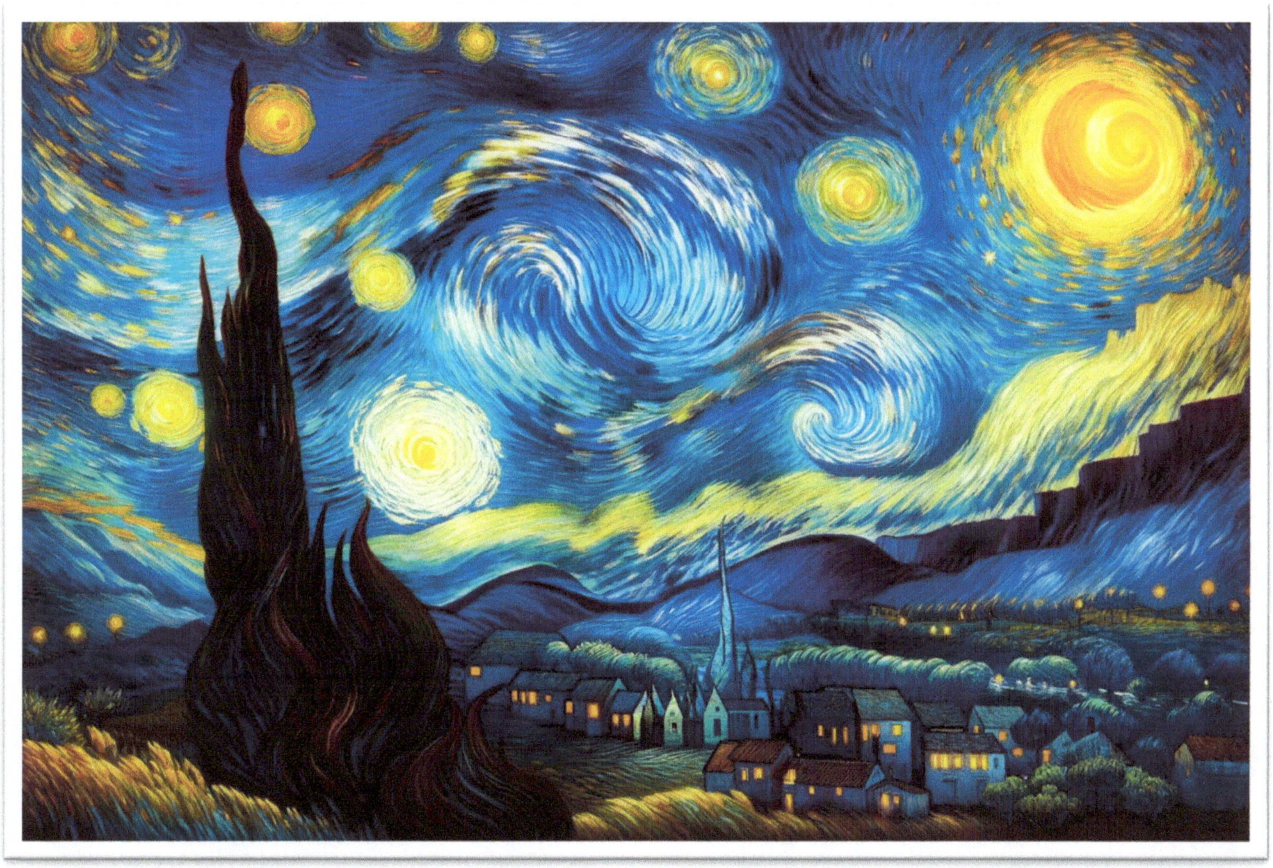

This new artwork similarly depicts a swirling, star-filled sky that commands the canvas, a visual symphony of vivid blues and yellows that breathe life into the night. The undulating shapes in the sky echo the dynamic forms of the cypress tree that rises prominently in the foreground, acting as a bridge between earth and the heavens. The tranquil village below lies in stark contrast to the lively sky—a peaceful settlement bathed in the warm glow of lamplight.

Inspired by Vincent van Gogh's *Starry Night*, this artwork is a new masterpiece that captures more than the eye; it ensnares the soul. Celebrated for its swirling heavens—a tapestry woven from emotional fervor—this painting's innovative brushwork and striking color palette mark a bold departure from the traditional chains of realism. Van Gogh's brush style dances across this canvas in rhythmic strokes, the thick impasto adding a texture that is almost palpable. This post-impressionist work transcends its own era, reaching forward in time to ignite passion in the hearts of artists and onlookers alike, proving itself a timeless beacon of inspiration and a testament to van Gogh's genius.

Pablo Picasso's *Guernica*

A powerful anti-war statement, *Guernica* showcases Picasso's creativity in using Cubism to depict the horrors of war, making it one of the 20th century's most impactful works of art.

The artwork below illustrates a concept inspired by themes like *Guernica* focusing on abstract representations of conflict, peace, and resilience. It uses a dynamic range of abstract shapes and forms to convey the emotional depth and complexities surrounding an anti-war theme, aiming to evoke a sense of turmoil, hope, and the human spirit's enduring capacity for overcoming adversity.

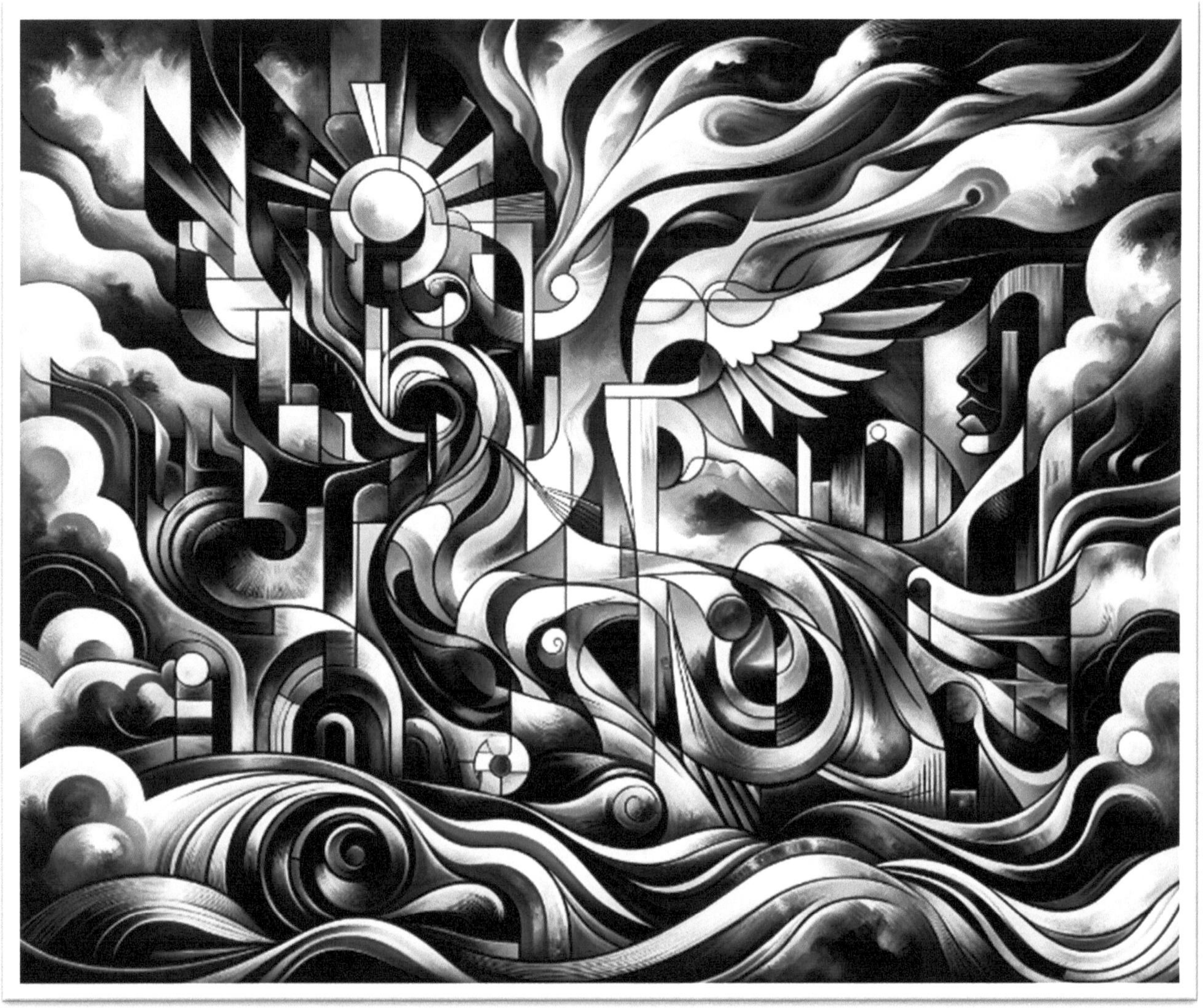

Michelangelo's Sistine Chapel Ceiling

Michelangelo's frescoes in the Sistine Chapel are a high point of Renaissance art, demonstrating incredible creativity in composition, human anatomy, and biblical storytelling.

The new artwork below is a resplendent reimagining of Michelangelo's iconic Sistine Chapel Ceiling, masterfully augmented to amplify its already sublime and celestial essence. The artist has infused the scene with an intensified luminescence, centering around a divine light that bathes the assembly of figures in an ethereal glow, signifying a heightened sense of the divine presence. The colors are more vivid, the contrasts more dramatic, and the play of light and shadow more pronounced, enhancing the original's narrative power and emotional depth.

Furthermore, the artist has introduced a profound depth to the architecture with the embellished vaults and cornices adding to the grandeur and magnificence of the space. The figures have been rendered with even greater detail and dynamic energy, their expressions and postures further evoking the intensity of their interactions and the stories they embody.

This homage not only preserves the sanctity and the spiritual narrative of Michelangelo's work but also accentuates its glory, creating a version that is both familiar and novel. This enhanced artistic vision offers viewers a new avenue to experience the majesty and the transcendent beauty of one of the world's most celebrated frescoes, inviting a renewed sense of wonder and contemplation.

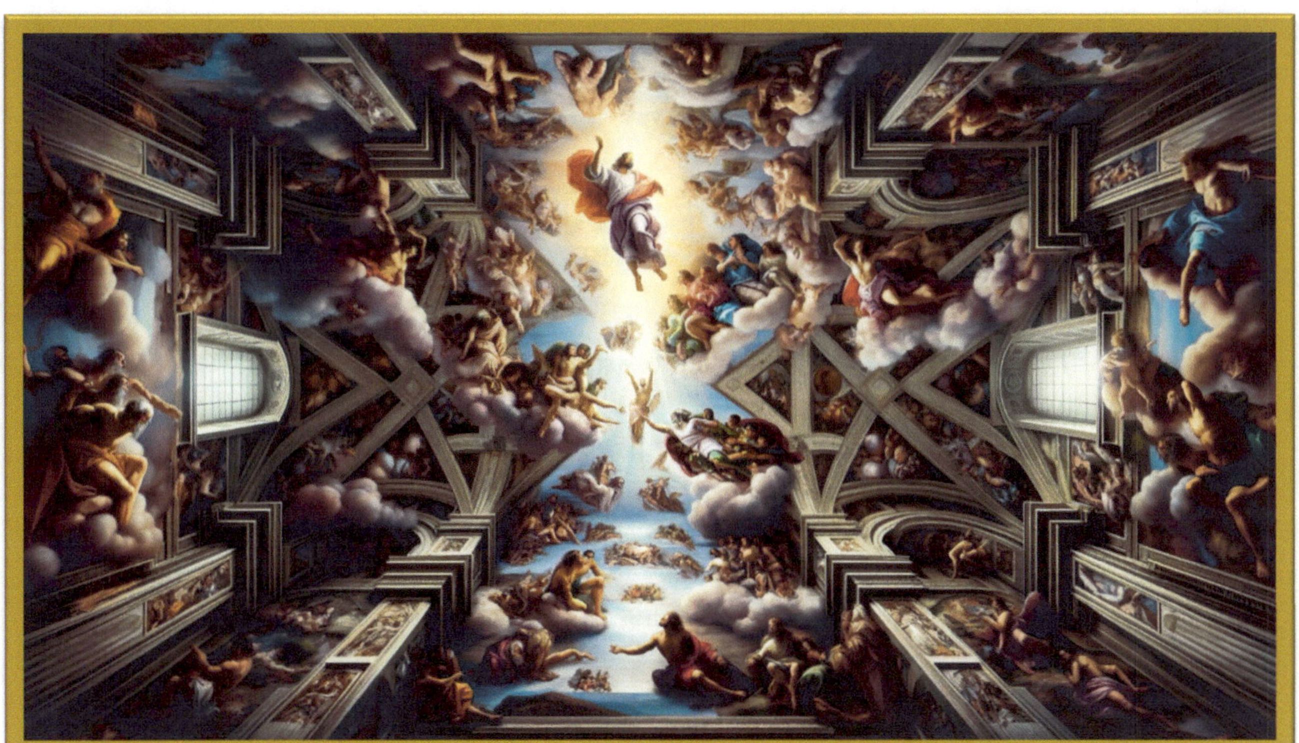

Salvador Dalí's *The Persistence of Memory*

This Surrealist masterpiece is famed for its striking and imaginative imagery, exploring the concept of time with melting clocks in a dream-like landscape.

The fine artwork below illustrates themes inspired by Dali's work, namely abstract representations of time, memory, and the surreal. This new artwork carefully explores the fluidity and distortion of time with a landscape that defies conventional perspectives, inviting viewers to reflect on their perceptions of time and memory.

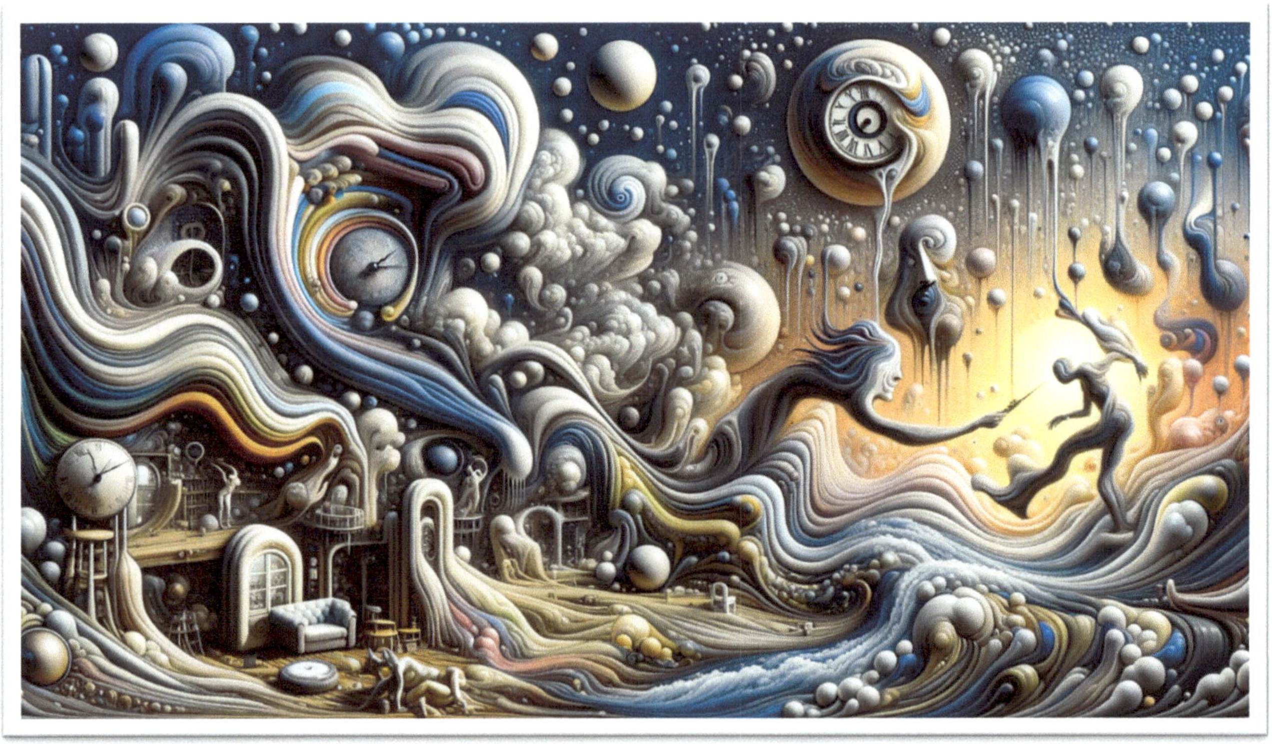

The mesmerizing power of these artworks stems from far more than their visual splendor; they vault beyond the constraints of time and culture, captivating and awakening the spirits of countless viewers and creators across generations.

As we turn the page to explore "Artistic Choices and Techniques," we embark on a journey to uncover the very tools and decisions that imbue these timeless pieces with the ability to enchant and inspire, bridging worlds and weaving history with the present.

Artistic Choices and Techniques

Evidence of deliberate artistic choices in elements like composition, technique, medium, and style can demonstrate creativity. These choices should reflect the artist's personal creative expression rather than just technical skill or replication of existing styles.

Conceptual Innovation

Sometimes, the originality lies not in the aesthetic but in the concept behind the artwork. If the artwork introduces a new idea or a unique interpretation of a subject, this can be seen as evidence of creativity.

Artist's Testimony and Process Documentation

The artist's own explanation of their work and the creative process can be crucial. Documentation showing the evolution of the work, sketches, drafts, or notes that illustrate the creative journey can serve as proof of originality.

Cultural and Historical Context

Understanding the context in which the artwork was created is important. What might be considered original in one cultural or historical context might not be in another.

Expert Opinions

Art historians, curators, critics, and other experts can provide insights into the originality of a piece based on their knowledge of art history and trends. Their analysis can help in identifying unique aspects of the work.

Legal Precedents and Standards

In the world of copyright law, the threshold for originality is surprisingly accessible. A work merely needs to have its own unique touches—just enough to show that it's not a complete copy of someone else's efforts. There's a whole host of legal cases and precedents out there that illustrate this point clearly, offering real-world insight into how this principle is consistently put into practice.

Public Perception and Acceptance

While not always a definitive measure, the way an artwork is received by the public and the art community can sometimes reflect its originality. A work that inspires discussion, interpretation, or spawns a new artistic movement can be seen as having a significant degree of creativity.

Art Assessment

Now that we've delved deeper into the complexities of evaluating art's creative value, this exploration acknowledges the multifaceted nature of art assessment, highlighting the influence of personal tastes, cultural backgrounds, and societal norms on the perception of creativity and originality in art.

Subjectivity in Artistic Evaluation

The appreciation of art is deeply personal, influenced by an individual's experiences, education, and cultural background. This subjectivity means that what one person considers a masterpiece, another might see as lacking in creative merit. This diversity in opinion underscores the difficulty in establishing universal criteria for assessing art.

Cultural Influence on Creativity

Cultural contexts play a crucial role in shaping the understanding and appreciation of creativity. Different cultures may prioritize certain themes, styles, or techniques, affecting how artwork is evaluated within these contexts. For example, a piece that introduces innovative techniques within one cultural tradition might not be perceived as creative in another context where such techniques are common or less valued.

Historical and Societal Factors

The perception of creativity and originality is also influenced by historical and societal factors. Art movements and trends, societal changes, and historical events can shift what is considered creative or original. Artworks that once challenged societal norms or introduced radical perspectives can, over time, become accepted and even revered, highlighting the fluid nature of artistic evaluation.

The Role of Intent and Interpretation

An artist's intent and the viewer's interpretation further complicate assessments of creativity.

Artworks created with a specific purpose or message in mind may be interpreted in myriad ways by different audiences, affecting perceptions of their originality and creative value. The interaction between the creator's intentions and the audience's interpretations adds another layer of complexity to the evaluation of art.

Legal and Institutional Perspectives

From a legal standpoint, the criteria for what constitutes "sufficient creativity" for copyright protection can vary, often requiring a minimal degree of creativity but leaving room for interpretation. Similarly, institutions such as museums and galleries may have their own criteria for assessing and showcasing art, influenced by curatorial practices and the institution's mission.

Conclusion

Understanding the subjective nature of art and the diverse factors influencing perceptions of creativity and originality is crucial for a nuanced evaluation of artistic works. Recognizing that these assessments are influenced by individual perspectives, cultural contexts, historical conditions, and institutional practices highlights the complexity of defining and measuring creativity in art. This complexity invites ongoing dialogue and reflection on the value and significance of art in society.

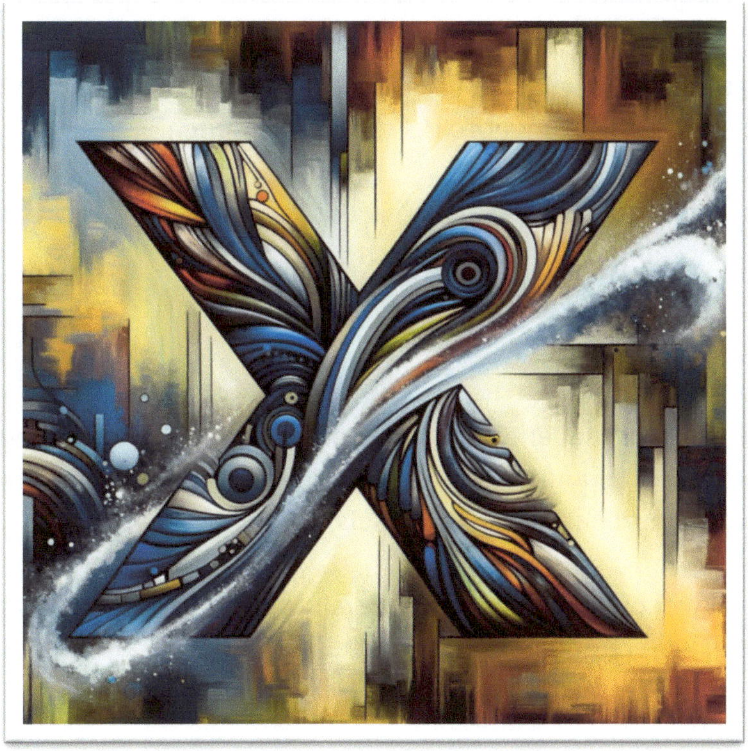

Chapter 7: Crafting Effective Prompts

Introduction to Prompt Crafting

Crafting an effective prompt for AI art generation is both an art and a science. It involves communicating with an AI model in a language it understands—clear, concise, and visually descriptive. An effective prompt translates your vision into parameters that guide the AI to produce artwork that aligns with your intended outcome.

To master the art of creating compelling GenAI prompts, it's important to get comfortable with a few key ideas.

Let's dive in:

> **Metacontext**: Think of this as the big picture. It's about setting the scene and understanding the broader context in which your art will live and breathe.
>
> **Metaprompts:** This is like a guiding star for generating other prompts. It's a higher-level instruction that shapes the direction of your more specific prompts.
>
> **Grounding:** Here's where you anchor your prompt in something solid. Grounding ensures that your prompt has a firm base, rooted in clear and concrete details.
>
> **Fine-tuning:** This is the final, critical step. Adjust and refine your prompt to perfection, much like tuning an instrument to get that perfect pitch.

By embracing these concepts, you'll be well on your way to creating prompts that lead to stunning, thought-provoking art. Ready to give it a go?

Metacontextual Understanding

Metacontext refers to the broad, encompassing context that influences how specific, lower-level contexts are interpreted within AI systems. It plays a critical role in enhancing the depth and accuracy of language comprehension in AI models.

Think of "metacontextual understanding" as the AI's way of keeping up with the conversation, just like a good friend who remembers what you talked about at your last meeting.

Here's how it works in action:

1. **Remembering Past Chats:** Just like recalling a past coffee date, AI systems look back on your previous chats to keep up with the flow of conversation.

2. **Staying on Topic:** AI keeps the big picture in mind, just as you would in a deep dive on your favorite subject, making sure the responses are on-point and well-informed.

3. **Reading the Room:** AI also tunes into the mood of the messages, much like noticing if someone's having a tough day, which really helps in understanding the full picture.

By doing all this, AI becomes not just smart, but also insightful and considerate in chats.

Getting to grips with metacontext can be a real game changer for AI models. It's all about understanding the bigger picture. When AI is clued into the wider context, the responses you get are not just accurate—they're nuanced and really tuned into the conversation, almost like chatting with a friend. This kind of smarts can seriously level up the creativity we see in AI's visual outputs, making for a more engaging and human-like interaction. So, when we talk metacontext, we're talking about giving AI a bit of a sixth sense that brings a whole new dimension to our AI chats and creations.

Metaprompts for Generating Art with Thematically Consistent Themes

Metaprompt is an advanced instruction or directive given to an AI model. It guides how the model should generate responses. You can use metaprompts to customize AI responses by providing specific guidelines or contextual frameworks that allow AI systems to generate context-specific responses. For instance, they can adjust formality, technical language, or industry-specific terminology.

By incorporating metaprompts, AI interactions become more personalized, adapting to your unique needs and historical interactions.

Here are two examples of specific metaprompts tailored for AI Visual Art Design:

> **Cross-Cultural Fusion Metaprompt:** "Craft prompts that merge distinct cultural art styles into a single, harmonious visual piece. Consider combining elements from traditional Japanese ukiyo-e with Art Nouveau flourishes, aiming for a synthesis that respects both traditions while creating something entirely new and breathtaking."

With this metaprompt, the detailed prompts generated could lead to a series of images that blend the fluid lines and natural motifs of Art Nouveau with the flat planes and bold outlines characteristic of ukiyo-e, resulting in a collection of AI-generated art that feels both familiar and novel.

Temporal Juxtaposition Metaprompt: "Develop prompts that envision a future where past and present design elements coexist. Imagine steampunk aesthetics interwoven with contemporary minimalist design, creating a visual narrative that speaks to the evolution of technology and taste."

This metaprompt encourages the creation of artwork that might depict scenes with Victorian-era industrial gear-driven machines, set against the backdrop of sleek, modern spaces with clean lines and monochromatic color schemes, reflecting a creative dialogue between two vastly different design philosophies.

Such metaprompts are designed to be somewhat flexible yet focused, providing a framework that encourages creative exploration within the context of AI visual art design.

You can also utilize metaprompts as standing directives to help shape all GenAI session output. For example:

Exclude Textual Elements Metaprompt: "As an essential metaprompt and directive, do not include any textual elements in any images created in response to my prompts."

This metaprompt should result in an acknowledgment by GenAI. Images subsequently generated by AI should, ideally, contain no textual elements. Keep in mind, however, if your subsequent prompt specifies the inclusion of textual elements - in contradiction to the above metaprompt - or if your subsequent prompt is ambiguous, it is possible that GenAI will include one or more textual elements. Contextual awareness is important when you craft your prompts.

Wrapping up, it's clear that metacontext and metaprompt are the dynamic duo of modern AI, giving AI the superpowers of deep context sensitivity and the ability to tailor conversations just for you. It's like having a chat with someone who not only gets the big picture but also remembers the little details that matter to you.

Now, let's shift gears and get our feet firmly planted with "Grounding." This next section is all about making AI not just smart, but relevant and reliable. We'll walk through how to give AI a strong foundation in reality, making sure it stays relevant and keeps the conversation grounded.

Grounding

Think of "grounding" as setting up a solid home base for your AI's responses. It's all about making sure that when your AI gives you a reply, it's coming from a place that's solidly connected to the real world—packed with the kind of detail and clarity that makes you nod and say, "Yep, that makes perfect sense."

When we train AI, grounding involves feeding it a rich diet of examples and scenarios that are as clear and specific as possible. It's like giving the AI a map of the territory it'll be navigating, complete with all the landmarks and signposts it needs to find its way. Here's how to do that:

1. **Choose Rich, Detailed Data:** Start by selecting training data that's chock-full of the kind of specifics that you want the AI to learn and reflect in its responses.

2. **Contextualize:** Make sure that the AI understands not just the words, but the situations they're used in. This is like teaching it to read the room, so to speak.

3. **Diversify Examples:** Give it a variety of examples. Just like a well-traveled person, an AI with a wide range of experiences can handle new situations much better.

4. **Iterative Feedback:** Training AI is a conversation, not a lecture. Provide feedback to your AI about what it's doing right and what it could do better, just like a coach refining an athlete's technique.

By grounding our AI, we're anchoring it firmly in the world of practical, useful intelligence, ensuring it doesn't wander off into the vast, often nebulous expanse of abstract responses. This meticulous process is our guarantee that AI remains a reliable and effective companion on our digital explorations, a trusty sidekick ready to tackle the challenges ahead with us.

When it comes to cultivating an AI capable of creating original artwork that sparkles with appreciable creativity, especially in the dynamic field of AI Visual Art Design, the approach we take is both delicate and deliberate. We're nurturing an inventive spirit that values creativity, cherishes originality, and understands the importance of staying relevant and resonant with contemporary themes and techniques. This is about more than teaching an AI to mimic the strokes of a brush; it's about imbuing it with the soul of an artist, enabling it to see the world through a lens of boundless imagination and express itself in ways that are unique, meaningful, and genuinely creative.

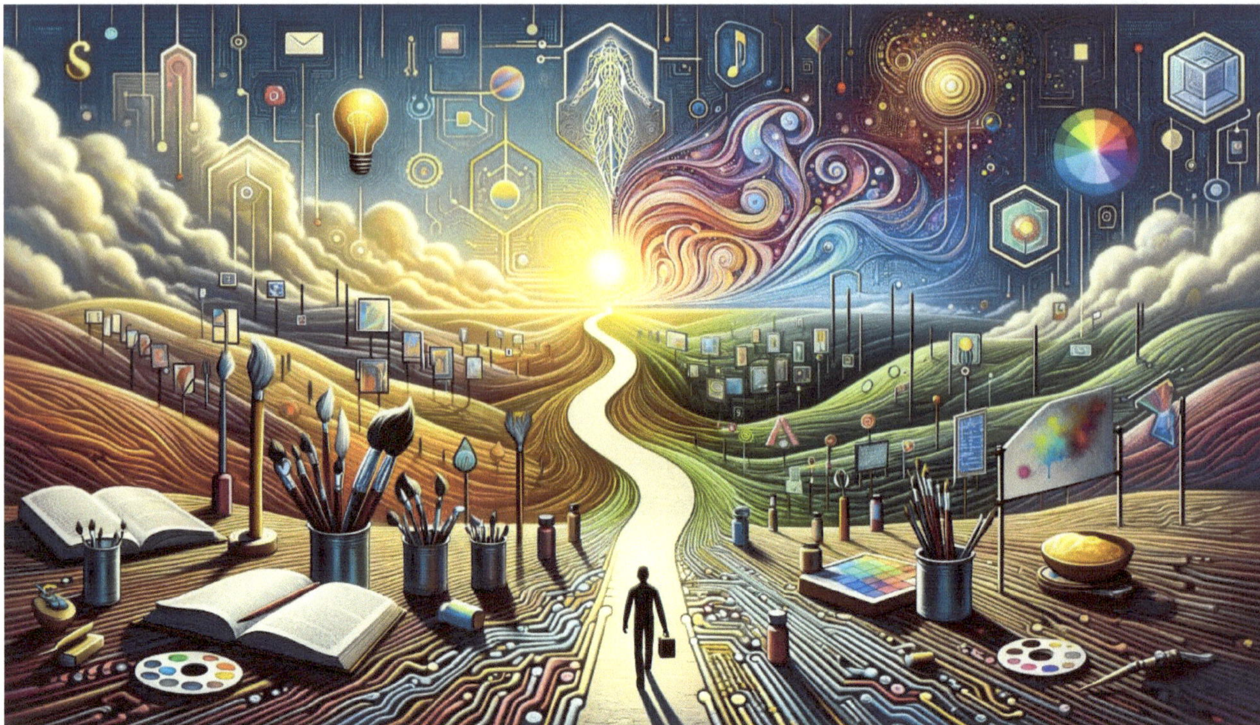

It is important to recognize that grounding AI provides a robust foundation, a bedrock of knowledge and context crucial for generating responses that are not only accurate but imbued with depth and relevance.

Fine-tuning builds upon this groundwork, honing the AI's abilities to not just understand but to interpret, to see beyond the literal and grasp the essence of artistic intent.

Fine-Tuning

When it comes to breathing life into art through GenAI prompts, fine-tuning is your magic wand. Fine-tuning is akin to refining a lens, adjusting its focus until the vision it presents is clear, vibrant, and full of life.

As we delve into the intricacies of fine-tuning, we embark on a quest to perfect the AI's artistic voice, ensuring that each creation reflects both its learned knowledge and its emerging creativity—a testament to the dynamic interplay between human insight and AI potential. Whether you're aiming for a masterpiece that rivals the Sistine Chapel or something as avant-garde as Dali's surreal landscapes, fine-tuning your prompts is key to turning that vision into reality.

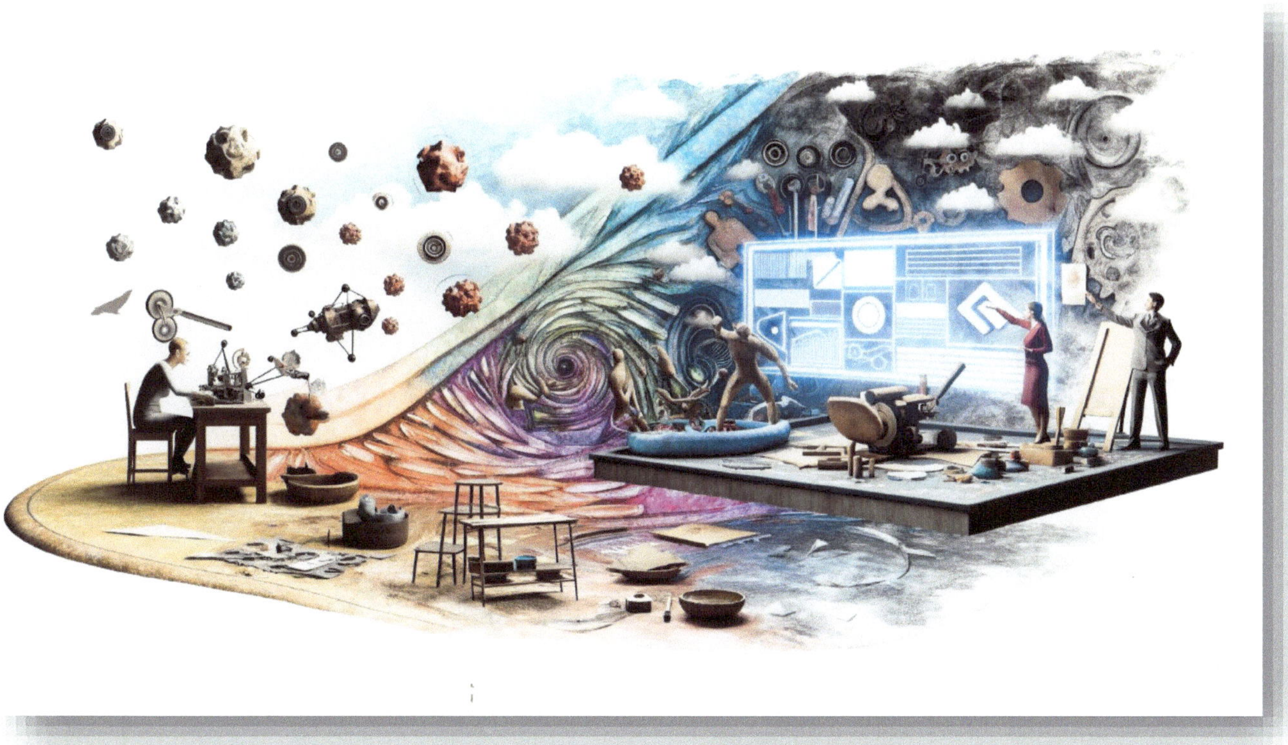

Let's dive into some recommended fine-tuning methods to sharpen your GenAI prompts for art that truly stands out.

1. Iterate Deliberately

"Deliberate iteration" refers to a conscious and intentional process of repeating steps to refine and improve upon a work or concept. This method emphasizes careful planning, evaluation, and refinement at each step, rather than making random or hasty alterations.

Here's a breakdown of what it means to "iterate deliberately":

> **Thoughtful Planning**
> Prior to implementing any modifications, a strategic planning phase is essential to establish clear goals and objectives. This approach guarantees that each iteration is executed with purpose and remains in alignment with the overarching vision, fostering effective and efficient progress.

Incremental Changes
Instead of overhauling everything at once, changes are made in small, manageable increments. This allows for more controlled experimentation and adjustment.

Continuous Evaluation
After each iteration, the outcomes are evaluated to assess their impact and effectiveness. This evaluation informs the next steps and whether further adjustments are needed.

Feedback Integration
Feedback from users, stakeholders, or data analysis is crucial. It is actively sought and incorporated into future iterations to refine the approach and improve results.

Iterative Improvement
The process is cyclical, with each cycle aiming to improve upon the last based on the evaluations and feedback. The goal is to gradually move closer to the optimal solution or product through continuous improvement.

Iterating deliberately is especially valuable in complex projects or environments where evolving challenges require adaptive solutions. As you create, be sure to review the results after each iteration, make thoughtful adjustments, and apply the learned improvements to the next version. Purposefully evolve your art through cycles of evaluation and enhancement to achieve a desired level of quality and detail.

2. Experiment with Specificity

The more precise you are, the better. Think of your prompt as a recipe; the specificity of your ingredients and instructions can mean the difference between a bland meal and a culinary masterpiece. Start with the basics—genre, style, color scheme—but don't stop there. Dive deeper into the emotions you want to evoke, the stories you wish to tell, and the techniques that might best express them.

3. Incorporate Artistic Language

Speak the language of the art world. Familiarize yourself with terms that describe techniques, styles, and elements of composition. Want your AI to channel Van Gogh's impasto? Or perhaps you're aiming for the light-infused scenes reminiscent of the Impressionists? Using precise artistic vocabulary enhances the specificity of your prompts and helps the AI in understanding and executing your vision more accurately.

4. Leverage Historical and Cultural Contexts

Injecting your prompts with historical or cultural references can add layers of depth and meaning to your AI-generated art. Mentioning specific art movements, epochs, or cultural symbols can guide the AI in creating work that resonates with those influences, offering viewers a richer experience.

5. Blend and Merge Concepts

Don't be afraid to mix and match ideas that may seem disparate at first glance. Combining elements from different domains can lead to truly innovative creations. How about a prompt that asks for a Renaissance-style portrait with a cyberpunk twist? Such blends can push the boundaries of creativity and result in unique, captivating art.

6. Utilize Examples and Analogies

Sometimes, showing is better than telling. Incorporate examples or analogies into your prompts to give the AI a clearer direction. Mentioning that you want a scene to evoke the same mood as a well-known masterpiece or using a metaphor to describe the desired atmosphere can provide valuable guidance.

Mastering the Art of Crafting Clear, Descriptive Prompts

Perfecting GenAI prompts is like blending the precision of science with the expressive freedom of art, lifting AI to the status of a collaborator in the dance of creation. It is about refining the artistry that allows our collective imaginations to bloom into works that truly enthrall the world.

In this section we illuminate the intricacies of articulating prompts that not only guide but inspire the creation of artworks that resonate with clarity and depth.

Specificity: The Keystone of Clarity

The essence of an effectively crafted prompt is its specificity. Like the meticulous brushstrokes that bring a masterpiece to life, the inclusion of precise details regarding subject matter, style, composition, and color palette can elevate a simple idea into a rich, evocative scene. Consider the difference between a generic 'forest scene' and the more descriptive 'tranquil forest at dusk with soft purple hues.' The latter not only conjures a vivid image but also guides the imagination to a precise moment, enhanced by the interplay of color and light. Such detailed specificity serves as a guiding light, steering the course of creativity with clarity and precision.

Vivid Imagery: The Soul of the Prompt

To breathe life into words, we must infuse our prompts with vivid imagery. Descriptive language serves as the palette from which we draw shades of meaning, texture, and emotion. Words like "glistening," "shadowy," and "ethereal" do more than describe; they evoke, transporting the mind's eye to realms of wonder and intrigue. This imagery lays the foundation upon which the imagination can build, turning abstract concepts into tangible realities.

Directing the Focus: The Art of Precision

In the tapestry of composition, the focal point acts as the compass that guides the viewer's journey through the artwork. It is through deliberate focus that we direct attention, highlighting elements of significance. A prompt like "a majestic oak tree stands prominently in the foreground of a misty meadow" not only describes but prioritizes, drawing the gaze to the oak as the anchor of the narrative. This technique ensures that the essence of the piece is captured, steering the creative process towards a defined goal.

Incorporating Emotion: The Essence of Connection

Ultimately, the power of an artwork lies in its ability to evoke emotion, to connect on a profound level with the viewer. Through the incorporation of emotion in our prompts, we lay the groundwork for this connection. Describing a scene as imbued with "serenity," "melancholy," or "exuberance" sets the tone, inviting an emotional dialogue between the artwork and its audience. This emotional layer enriches the narrative, adding depth and resonance to the creative endeavor.

Balancing Specificity and Creativity

Navigating the delicate dance between specificity and creativity is akin to guiding a ship through uncharted waters; it requires both precision and the ability to embrace the unknown. When crafting prompts for AI, striking the right balance is key to unlocking a treasure trove of innovation and originality.

Harmonious Concept Fusion

Consider the integration of ideas as akin to mixing ingredients in a gourmet dish; each component should enhance and complement the others, producing an outcome that transcends the sum of its parts. A prompt such as 'a futuristic city with Art Deco influences' unveils a tapestry of architectural elegance and technological progression, seamlessly blending historical charm with future possibilities in a visually unified narrative. This process is about discovering the synergy between ideas, enabling the AI to create works that resonate deeply and cohesively across various dimensions.

Ignite the Spark of Creation

In your journey with AI, aim to be more of a muse than a manager. Your role is to ignite the spark of the creative process, offering visions and emotions for the AI to explore, rather than laying down a rigid path to follow. This approach not only fosters a sense of partnership with the AI but also encourages a form of artistic collaboration that can transcend traditional boundaries.

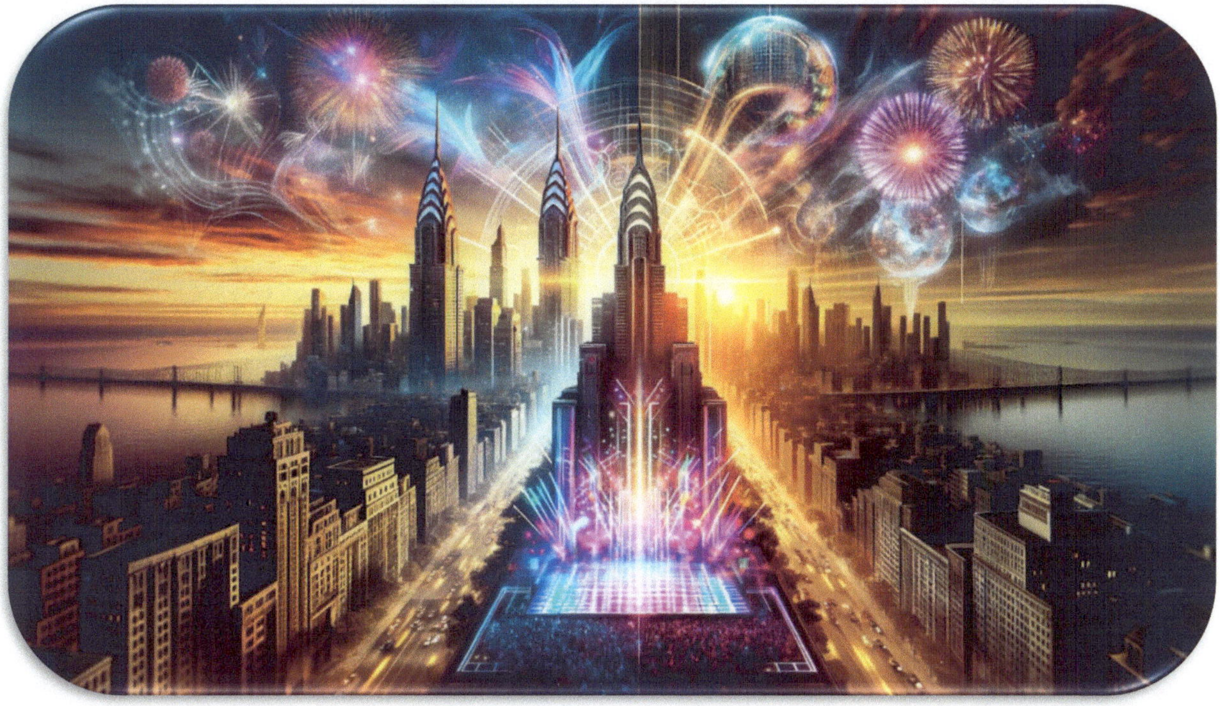

Common Pitfalls

Diving into the world of AI art creation is an exciting journey, full of possibilities and creative exploration. However, as with any adventure, there are pitfalls to watch out for. Let's navigate these waters together, armed with insights to steer clear of common obstacles.

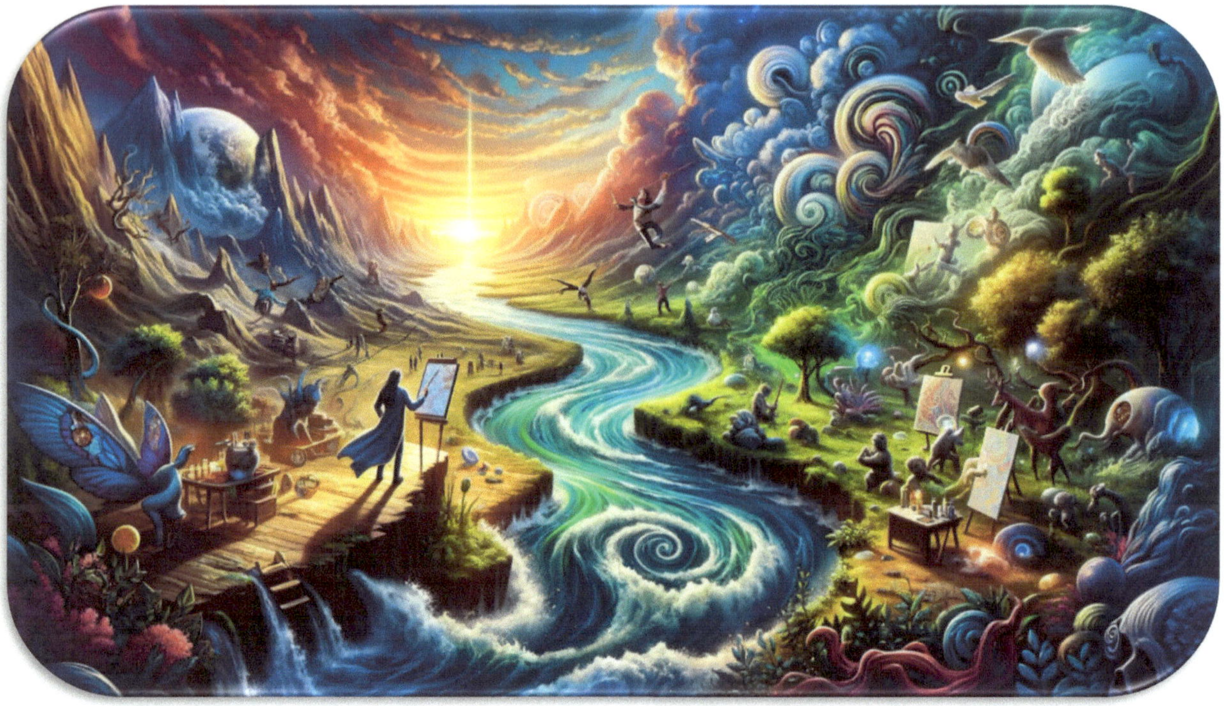

Overloading Details

Imagine asking the AI to depict a garden with every type of flower you can think of, in every possible color, under changing weather conditions—all in one image. The result might be more chaotic than charming. The key to avoiding a visual overload is to focus on the essentials. Instead of cataloging every detail, concentrate on a few key elements that capture the spirit of the scene, like a serene garden bathed in the gentle light of a setting sun, where the emphasis is on the tranquility and the interplay of light, not the botanical specifics.

Being Too Vague

On the flip side, saying something like, "draw a nice outdoor scene" might leave too much to interpretation, resulting in a bland or off-target creation. To avoid landing in the realm of the generic, add just enough detail to guide the AI while leaving room for creativity. For instance, "depict a tranquil lake at dusk, reflecting the soft colors of the sunset" provides a clear direction yet allows for artistic interpretation.

Mixed Messages

Consider the confusion that ensues when you ask for a bustling, quiet city street. It's a bit like asking for a silent symphony—puzzling, to say the least. To avoid sending mixed signals, ensure that the elements of your prompt complement each other. A cohesive request, such as "illustrate a lively street market scene, bustling with energy and vibrant colors," helps the AI understand exactly what atmosphere and activity level you envision.

Ignoring Context

Imagine the bewilderment in requesting a "snowy beach scene on a hot summer day." It's a classic case of context neglect. To ensure your prompts are rooted in logical settings, align your request with the natural environment or scenario you're depicting. Instead, opt for "a sun-soaked beach, with waves gently lapping at the shore, on a clear summer day," which paints a picture that's both appealing and contextually sound.

By steering clear of these common pitfalls and applying these strategies, you're well on your way to mastering the art of AI prompt crafting. Remember, the goal is to collaborate with AI as a creative partner, guiding it with clarity, coherence, and just the right touch of imagination to bring your artistic visions to life.

How to Avoid Common Pitfalls

Embrace Clarity with Precision

On the flip side, a map with too few landmarks is equally challenging. Being overly vague can leave the AI adrift, resulting in generic or misaligned outcomes. Like a lighthouse beacon guiding ships at sea, your prompt should offer a clear direction, shining light on the key elements needed to reach the destination. Striking the right balance between detail and conciseness is crucial.

Harmonize Your Instructions

Imagine conducting an orchestra where every musician plays a different tune; the result would be far from harmonious. Similarly, prompts with mixed messages can leave the AI confused, pulling it in multiple directions and resulting in a disjointed piece. Ensure that every element of your prompt sings in harmony, creating a cohesive symphony rather than a cacophony.

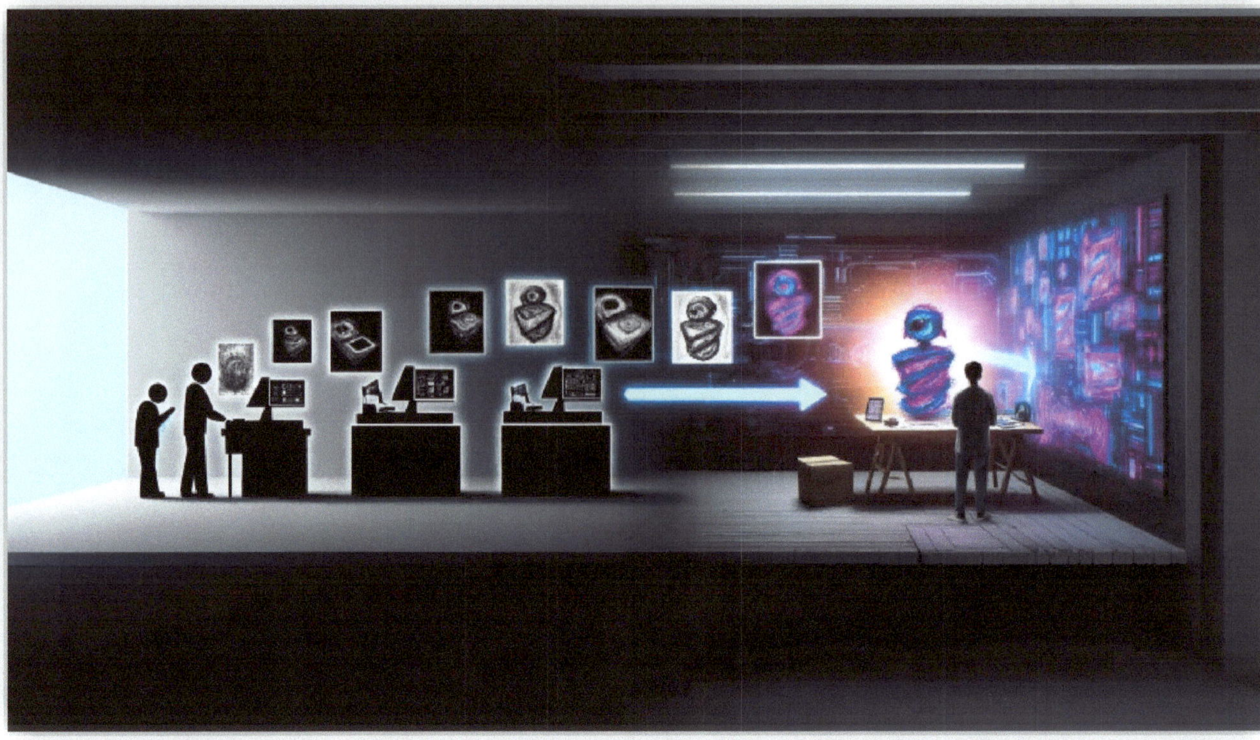

Context Is Key

Lastly, always consider the backdrop against which your scene unfolds. A prompt that ignores the natural laws of its setting, like "a bright night scene," might lead the AI into contradictory territory. Just as a painter considers the interplay of light and shadow, your prompt should reflect a coherent understanding of the scene's inherent logic.

By engaging effectively with sophisticated AI and employing these AI fine-tuning guidelines, you will avoid common missteps and more rapidly advance toward the creation of art that resonates, astonishes, and brings joy to your audience.

Step-by-Step Projects for Prompt Crafting

With a focus on practical applications of AI-generated art in various fields, here are two basic step-by-step projects for you to practice and refine your prompt crafting skills.

Project A: Landscape Artwork

Step 1: Choose a landscape theme (e.g., mountains, cityscape, forest).

Step 2: Decide on a specific art style (e.g., Impressionism, Surrealism).

Step 3: Craft a prompt combining these elements and run it through the AI.

> Paint landscape of mountains in the style of surrealism, featuring native plants near a serene lake.

Step 4: Analyze the outcome and refine the prompt for a second iteration.

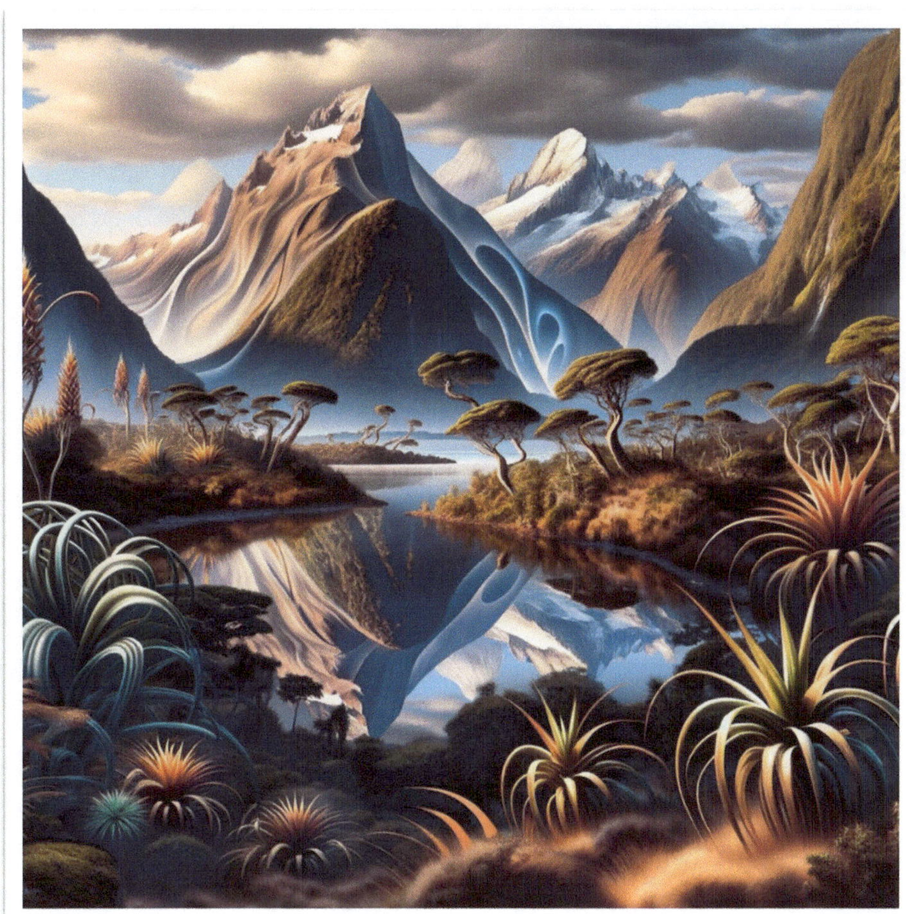

Project B: Portrait with a Twist

Step 1: Select a type of portrait (e.g., historical figure, fictional character).

Step 2: Infuse a unique element (e.g., futuristic, fantasy).

Step 3: Develop a detailed prompt and generate the artwork.

> Paint portrait infused with fantasy involving a broken imagination.

Step 4: Modify the prompt to alter the style or mood and compare results.

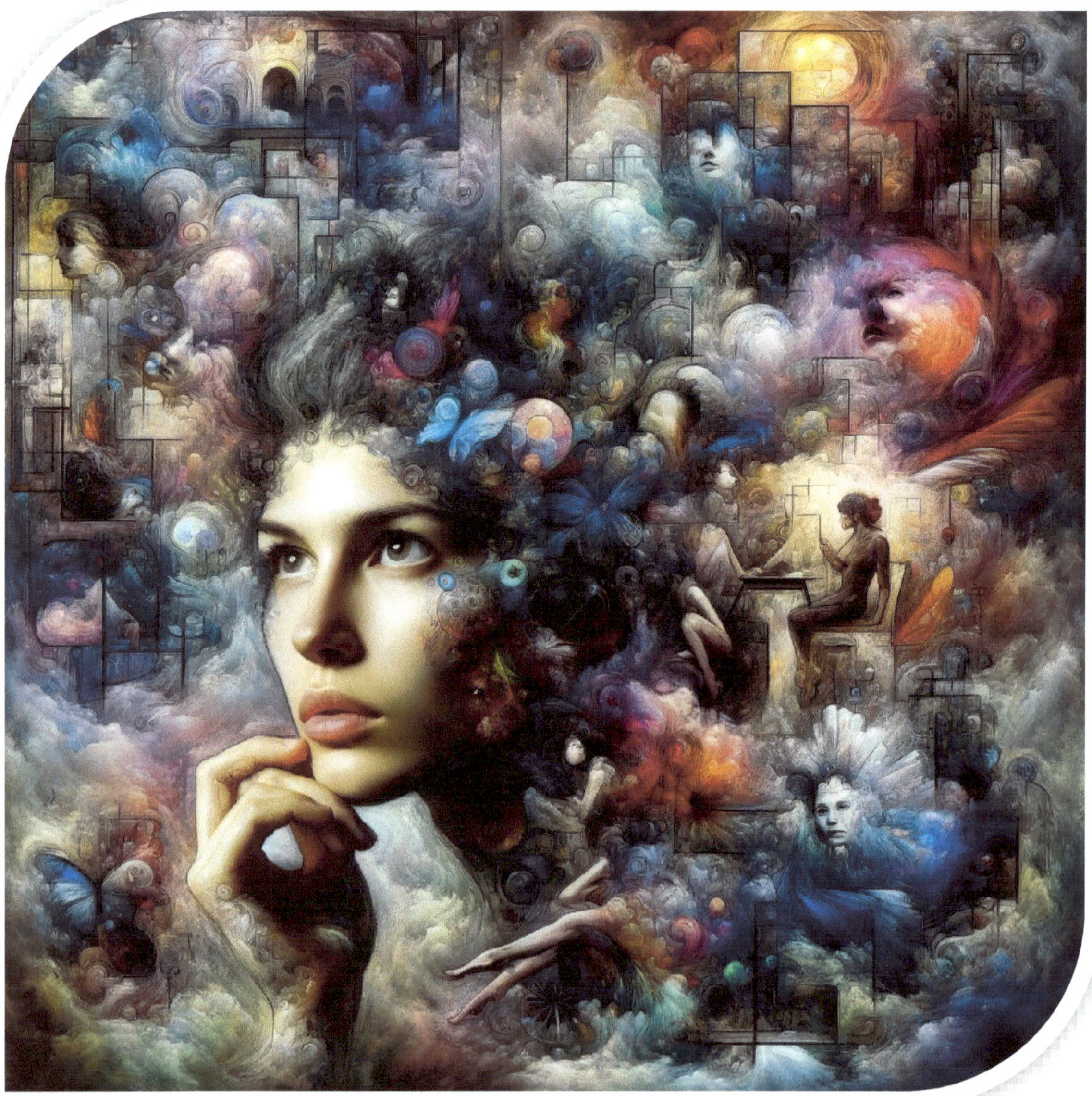

GenAI Prompts to Create Visual Art

Crafting effective AI art prompts hinges on clarity, precision, and creativity. Being detailed in your descriptions—specifying the style, mood, colors, and distinct elements you're aiming for—significantly enhances the outcome. Here are essential steps to help you infuse your artistic vision into template prompts and create impactful visuals:

Define Your Vision
Start by clearly defining what you want to create. Consider aspects like the subject matter, the emotion or mood you want to convey, and any specific elements or themes you want to include.

Be Specific with Descriptive Details
Include precise details in your prompt. For instance, instead of saying "a landscape," specify "a serene mountain landscape at dawn with mist rising from the valley."

Incorporate Artistic Styles or Influences
If you have a particular artistic style in mind, such as impressionism, surrealism, or a specific artist's style, include that in your prompt. For example, "in the style of Claude Monet" or "reminiscent of Salvador Dalí's surrealism."

Add Emotional or Conceptual Layers
Convey the mood or concept you're aiming for. Phrases like "evoke a sense of nostalgia" or "illustrate the chaos of urban life" guide the AI to align with the emotional tone of your vision.

Consider Composition and Color
If you have preferences for composition (like central focus, symmetry, or a panoramic view) or color scheme (like monochromatic, vibrant, or pastel tones), include these details.

Experiment and Iterate
AI art generation often requires experimentation. Don't hesitate to refine and alter your prompts based on the outcomes you get.

Balance Between Freedom and Control
While it's important to guide the AI with your prompt, leaving ample room for creative freedom can lead to pleasantly surprising results. Find a balance between your creative guidance and openness and you might be amazed by what you achieve.

Template Prompts and Your Artistic Vision

Introducing the concept of "template prompts" revolutionizes the way we interact with AI in art creation. These are structured yet adaptable prompt formats that serve as a starting point for guiding the AI, ensuring consistency and clarity in the creative process.

By tailoring these template prompts to your specific artistic vision, you communicate effectively with the AI, harnessing its full potential as a formidable tool in your creative repertoire. Such customization fosters a symbiotic partnership, where your creative spark meets the AI's computational power, resulting in art that is both unique and deeply personal, reflecting what we identify as appreciable creativity.

1. **Specific Art Style Description**
   "Create an image in the style of [art movement] featuring [subject]."

2. **Color Scheme Specification**
   "Illustrate a [scene/subject] using a [specific color palette] to evoke [mood/emotion]."

3. **Composition and Perspective**
   "Design a [landscape/cityscape/portrait] from a [specific viewpoint] with [key elements] in focus."

4. **Incorporation of Elements and Textures**
   "Generate a [type of artwork] that includes [specific elements] with [type of texture] effect."

5. **Mood and Atmosphere**
   "Create an artwork that conveys a sense of [mood] in a setting with [environmental factors]."

6. **Historical or Futuristic Settings**
   "Depict a [historical/futuristic] scene where [specific events/technologies] are present."

7. **Juxtaposition and Contrast**
   "Design a piece that juxtaposes [two contrasting concepts] in harmony."

8. **Fictional Character Design**
   "Design an original character with [distinctive features] who is a [character type] in [setting]."

9. **Abstract Concepts**
   "Visualize the concept of [abstract idea] in an abstract painting using [shapes/colors]."

10. **Nature and Wildlife**
    "Illustrate a natural scene that showcases [type of ecosystem] with [species of animals/plants]."

11. **Science Fiction and Fantasy Themes**
    "Create a scene depicting a [sci-fi/fantasy environment] with [unique elements]."

12. **Cultural and Traditional Art**
    "Generate an image that represents [specific culture's] traditional art with modern influences."

13. **Lighting and Shadow Play**
    "Produce an artwork where [light source] creates dramatic shadows over [subject/scene]."

14. **Surrealistic Imagery**
    "Create a surreal landscape with [unusual elements] that defy the laws of physics."

15. **Seasonal Themes**
    "Depict a [season] scene in [specific location] that highlights the changes in nature."

Keep your templates close and your ideas closer, and dive into Appendix F for some hands-on practice with GenAI Prompt Crafting Exercises. This will sharpen your skills, ensuring your prompts are as effective and creative as your visions manifested.

Within the context of this book about AI, the phrase "visions manifested" refers to the act of turning ideas, dreams, or concepts into reality. It means bringing something that was once only imagined into the tangible world, where it can be seen, touched, or experienced by others. In the context of art or creation, it often refers to the successful realization of creative ideas or goals.

Chapter 8: Curated Gallery of Artwork Generated Using AI Prompts

We are delighted to present this curated collection of artworks.

Within this chapter, you will find a series of template prompts designed to serve as catalysts for your creative endeavors. Think of these templates as blank canvases, each presenting a distinct opportunity for you to infuse with the rich colors of your imagination and unique vision. These prompts are more than just starting instructions; they are open invitations for you to explore, experiment, and express yourself. They provide a launching pad from which your creativity can soar, leading to results that are as surprising as they are inspired.

You stand at the threshold of discovering how these prompts can kindle the flame of your creativity, expanding the horizons of what GenAI can assist you in accomplishing and enriching the fabric of your visual art with each new creation. Your adventure in mastering the art of prompt crafting is just beginning, and the possibilities are as boundless as your imagination.

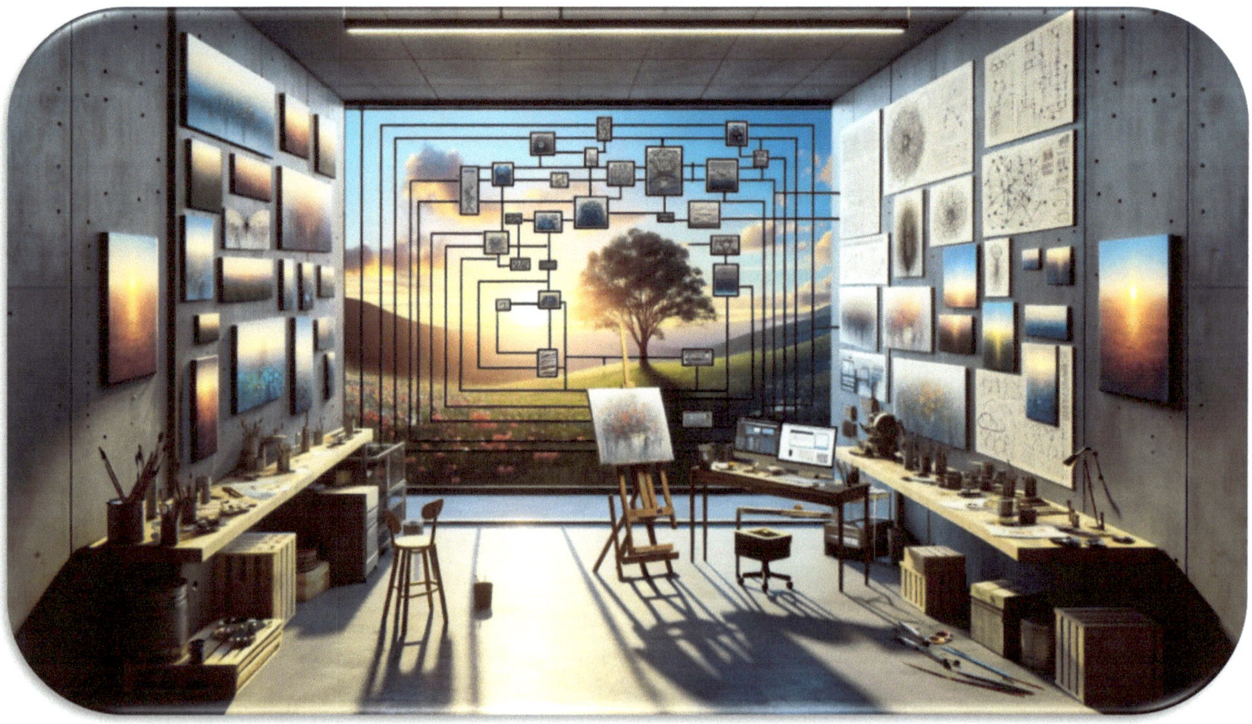

Take a moment to explore this gallery and you'll notice the intentional way in which the elements are arranged, leading you on a visual adventure that showcases both the power of technology and the artist's skillful direction. Pay special attention to the masterful use of color theory; every tint and tone is selected to stir emotions, accentuate details, and create an immersive ambiance.

As you explore the gallery you will see how the deliberate placement of each element in these compositions leads you on a visual journey, masterfully crafted to reveal the possibilities of technology and the intention behind the artist's hand.

Take note of the expert application of color theory, where every hue and tone is purposefully selected to stir emotions, define shapes, and set the stage, ensuring that each piece resonates with the intended ambience.

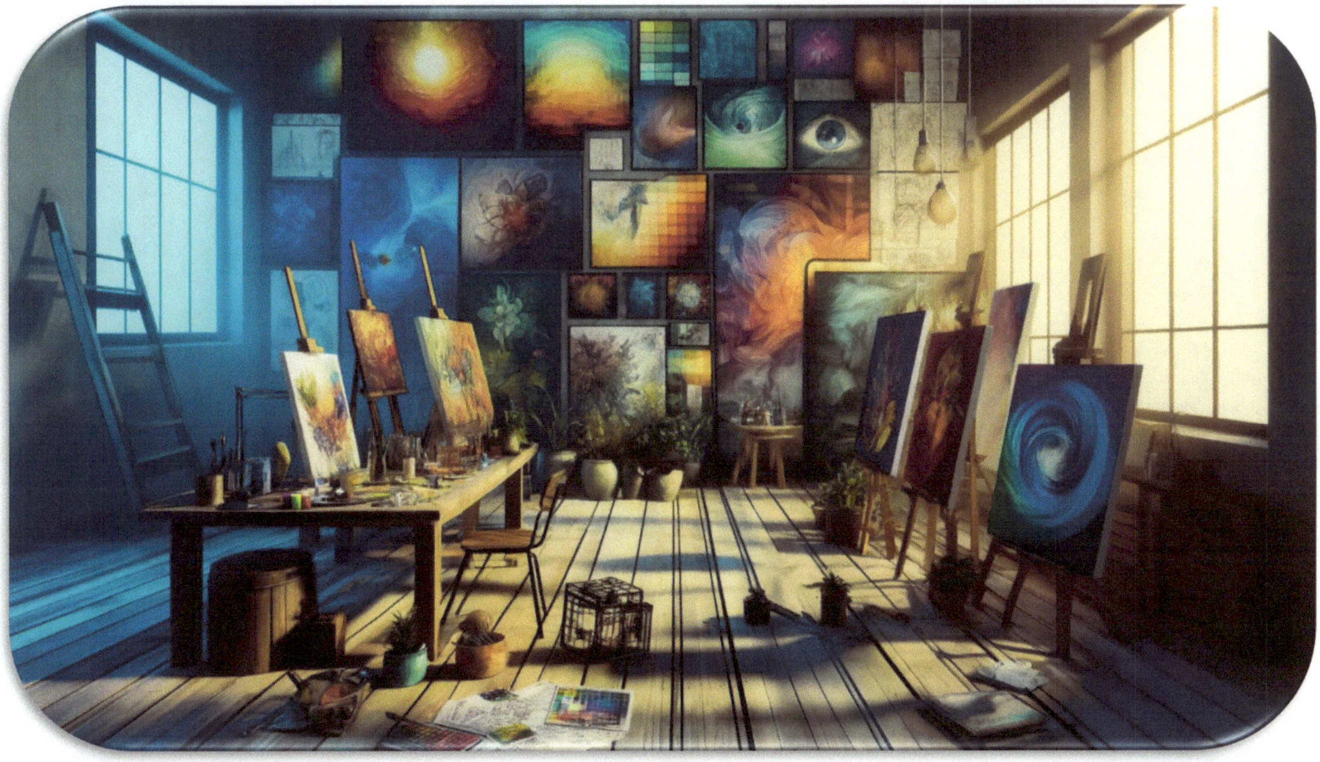

Remember, the initial prompt might just be a steppingstone.

The featured GenAI outputs in this gallery are the culmination of an iterative process, sculpted by artists who understand the language of visual storytelling and who use metacontext and metaprompts to refine their dialogue with the machine, achieving what we celebrate as "appreciable creativity."

Detailed Landscape Descriptions

Prompt: "Create a landscape showing a serene mountain lake at sunset, with mist rising from the water and the final rays of sun casting a golden glow on the peaks."

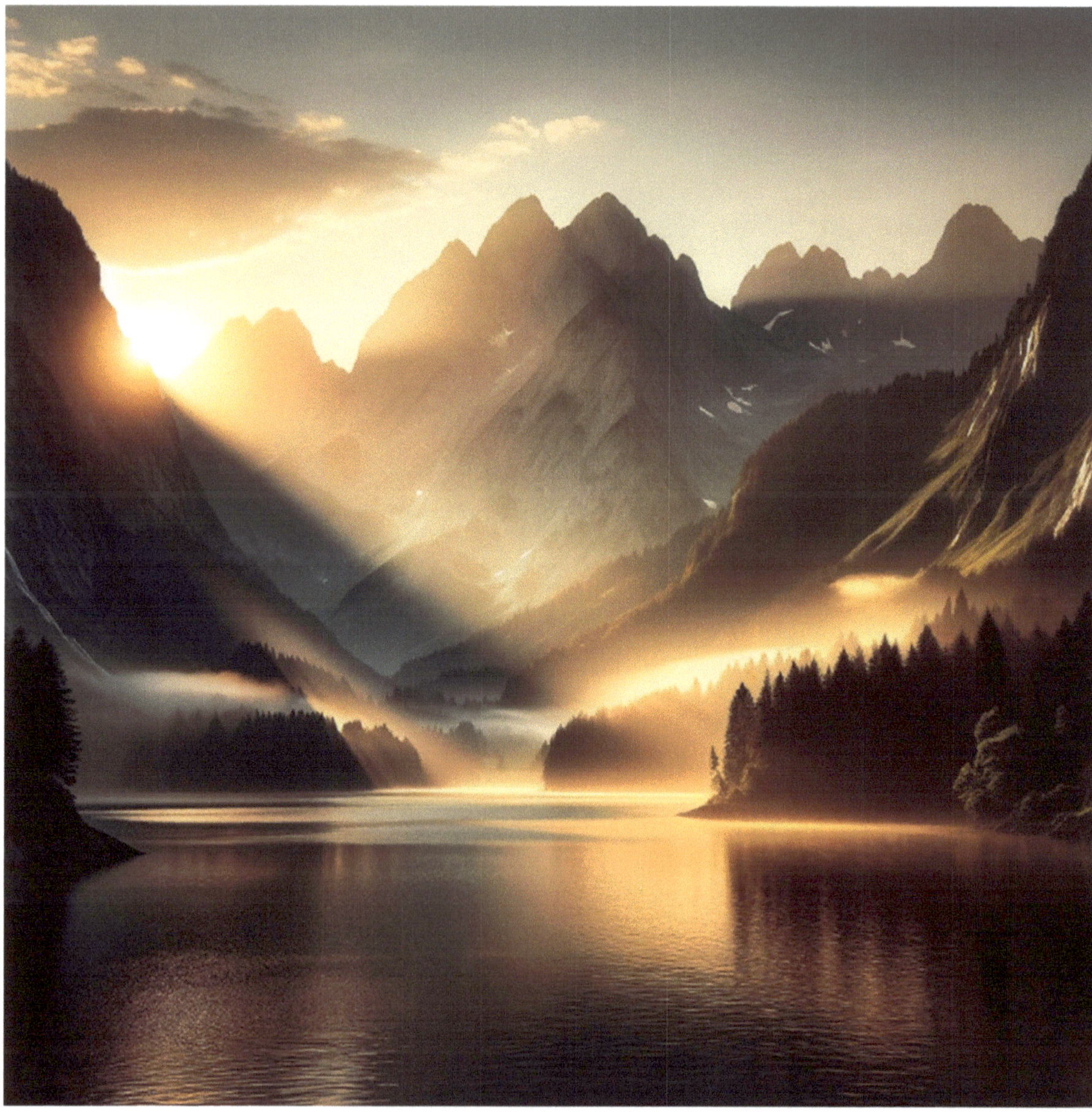

Commentary: This serene landscape captures a breathtaking mountain sunrise, illustrating the artist's skill in manipulating light and color. The golden hues diffusing through the mist create a soft, ethereal glow, contrasting sharply with the crisp mountain silhouettes. This piece is characterized by a harmonious blend of realism and romanticism, showcasing the artist's unique ability to evoke a deep sense of tranquility and awe through meticulously detailed natural settings and a masterful use of atmospheric effects.

Historical or Cultural Settings

Prompt: "Depict a bustling medieval market scene in a European town, with vendors, colorful stalls, and townsfolk in period attire."

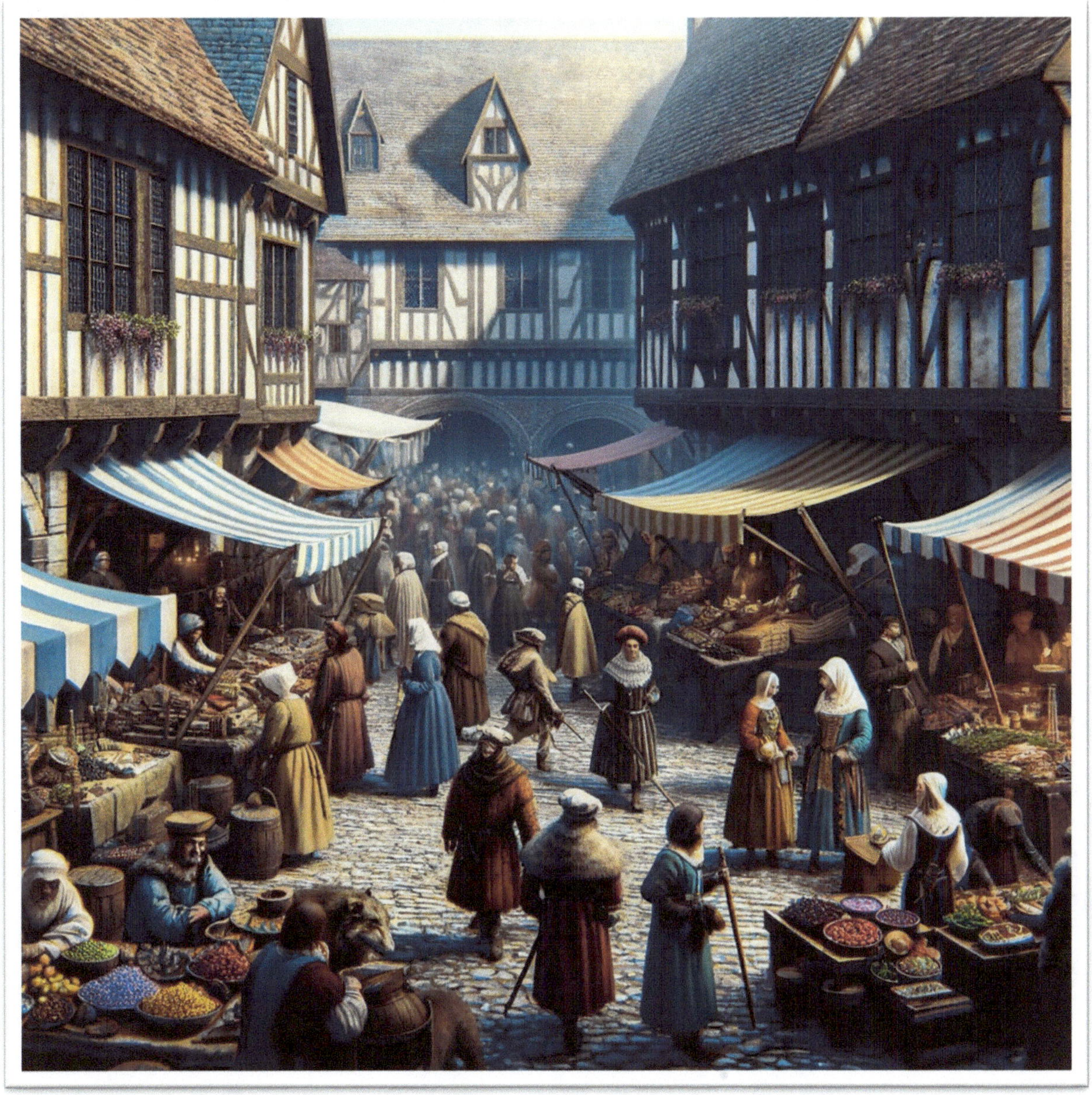

Commentary: This artwork vividly portrays a bustling medieval market scene, characterized by meticulous attention to historical detail and vibrant color. The artist's unique style manifests in the richly textured architecture and the lively depiction of daily life, capturing the essence of the period with authenticity. The use of light subtly directs focus across the crowded square, enhancing the depth and realism of the scene, and inviting viewers to immerse themselves in this vivid historical tableau.

Fantasy or Science Fiction Themes

Prompt: "Illustrate an otherworldly forest with luminous, oversized flora and fauna, under a sky with two moons."

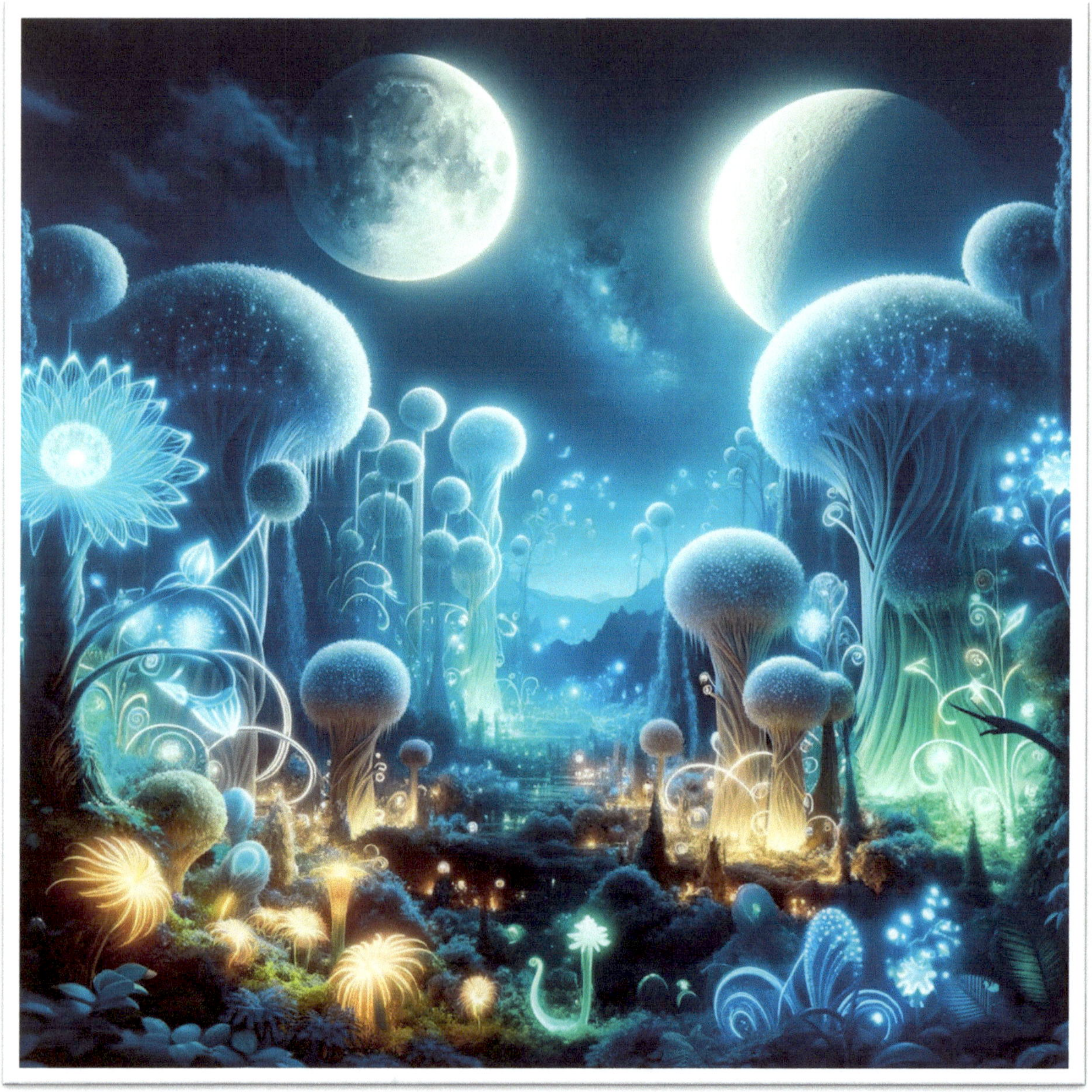

Commentary: This enchanting artwork depicts a luminescent, otherworldly landscape under twin moons, highlighting the artist's mastery of light and color. Employing a glowing, neon palette, the artist crafts a dreamlike scene filled with fantastical flora that seemingly pulsates with life. The use of luminous blues and greens against the dark backdrop evokes a magical nighttime ambiance, showcasing the artist's distinctive style of blending natural elements with surreal, radiant details to create a captivating, immersive world.

Abstract Concepts

Prompt: "Visualize the concept of 'time' as an abstract painting, using swirling patterns and a mix of warm and cool colors to represent its flow and complexity."

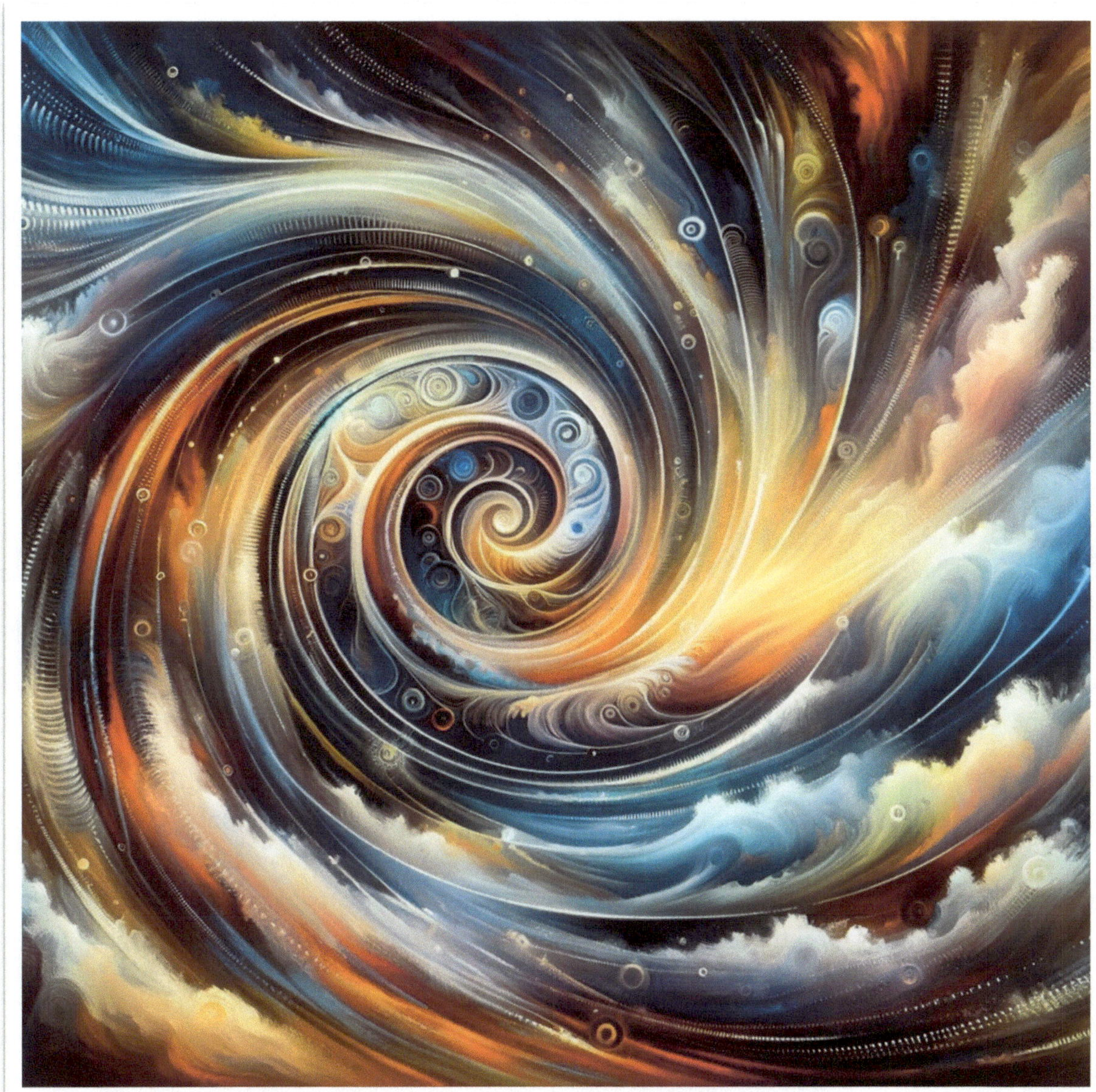

Commentary: This vibrant artwork is a stunning exploration of color and motion, capturing a dynamic swirl of hues that evoke a sense of perpetual movement. The artist uses a fluid, almost liquid technique to blend colors and shapes into a mesmerizing vortex, drawing the viewer's eye inward. The use of bright, saturated colors contrasted with softer, pastel tones creates depth and intensity. This piece exemplifies the artist's ability to harmonize chaos and order, giving form to an abstract concept in a way that feels both natural and fantastical. The painting is a testament to the power of color and form in conveying emotion and energy.

Combination of Elements

Prompt: "Combine a desert landscape with futuristic technology, showing advanced machinery emerging from the sands."

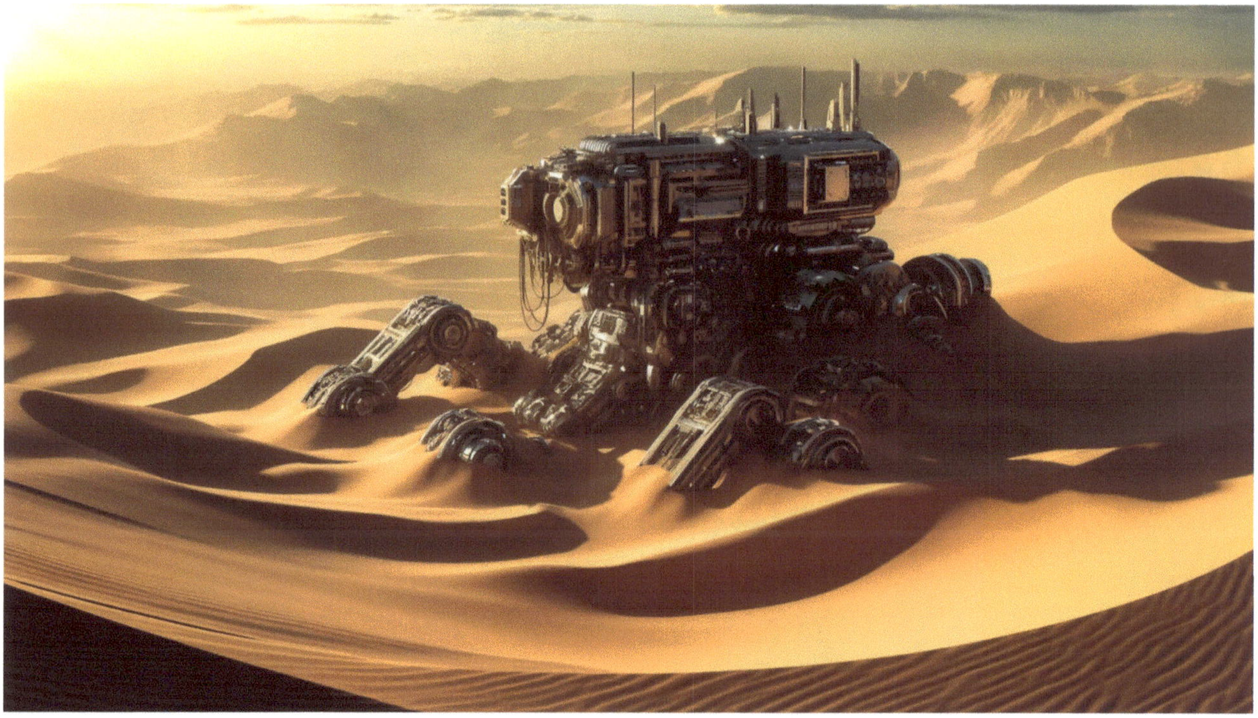

Commentary: This digital artwork masterfully blends a stark desert landscape with the stark contrast of advanced, robotic machinery. The artist uses a harmonious color palette dominated by golden and metallic hues that integrate the mechanical elements seamlessly into the natural environment. The machinery, depicted with intricate detail and industrial aesthetics, emerges from the soft desert sands, creating a visual juxtaposition between nature and technology.

The composition is enhanced by dynamic lighting, with the sun setting or rising in the background, casting long shadows and creating a luminous, almost ethereal glow that highlights the contours of both the sand dunes and the robotic forms. This lighting not only adds a dramatic effect but also emphasizes the surreal and isolated atmosphere of the scene.

The artist's unique style is evident in the careful balance of realism and fantasy, inviting viewers to ponder the narrative behind this technological emergence in a desolate landscape. The artwork serves as a visual exploration of themes such as isolation, innovation, and the intersection of the organic with the synthetic, rendered through a distinctive fusion of landscape art and science fiction.

Reinterpretation of Famous Artworks

Prompt: "Reimagine Van Gogh's 'Starry Night' with a modern cityscape replacing the village."

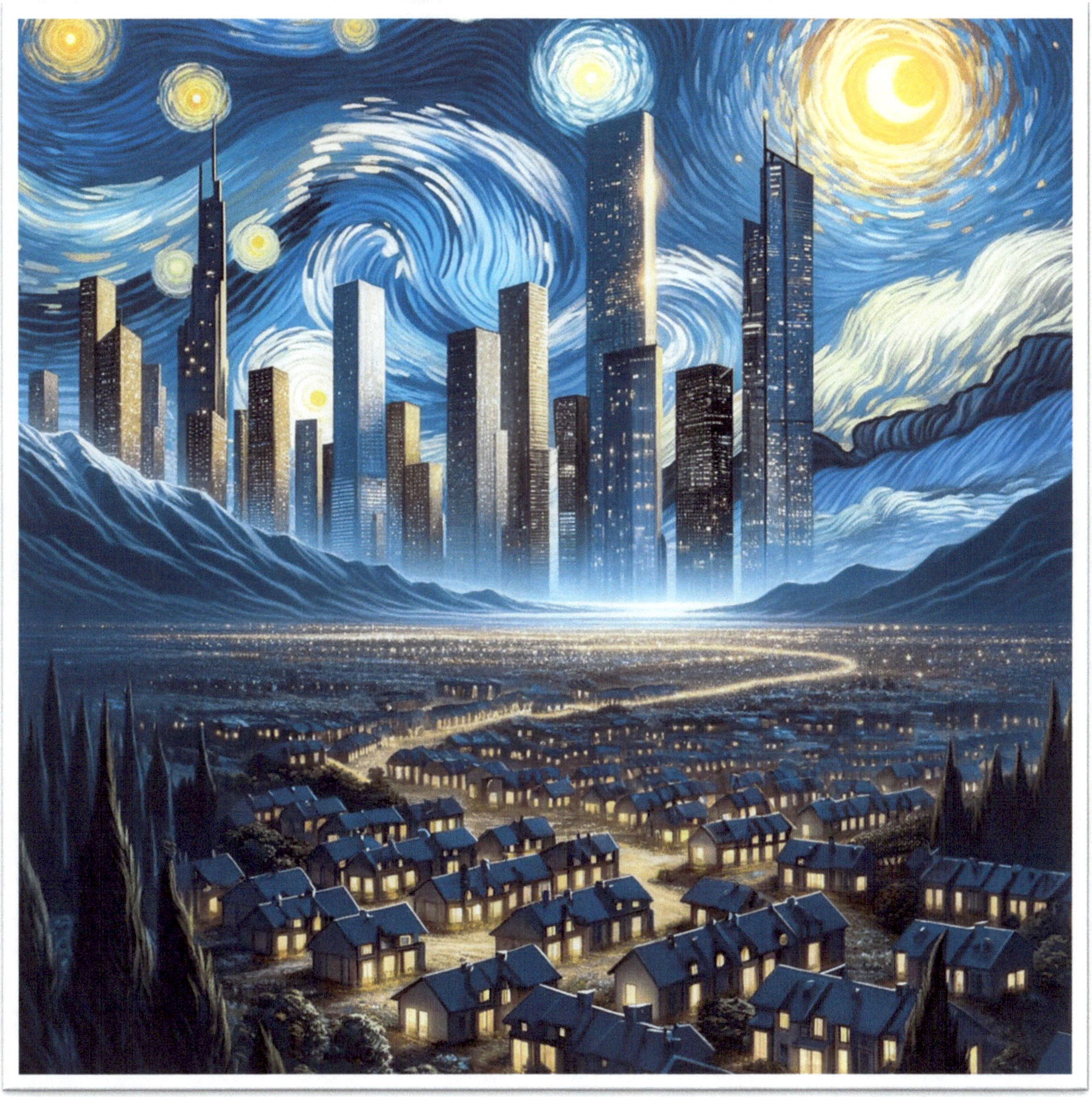

Commentary: This artwork creatively blends urban architecture with Van Gogh's iconic *Starry Night*, showcasing the artist's unique style of reimagining classical techniques with modern themes. The swirling, expressive sky juxtaposed against the geometric lines of skyscrapers highlights a fusion of chaos and order. This piece uses vibrant colors and dynamic brush strokes to dramatize the contrast between the natural and constructed worlds, illustrating the bustling energy of a city under a mesmerizing, turbulent sky.

Mashup of Different Art Styles

Prompt: "Conjure a scene of a peaceful Japanese garden painted in a Cubist style, then create an image inspired by general artistic styles or characteristics that are reminiscent of Picasso's work, such as using geometric shapes and a fragmented perspective, without directly referencing his unique style."

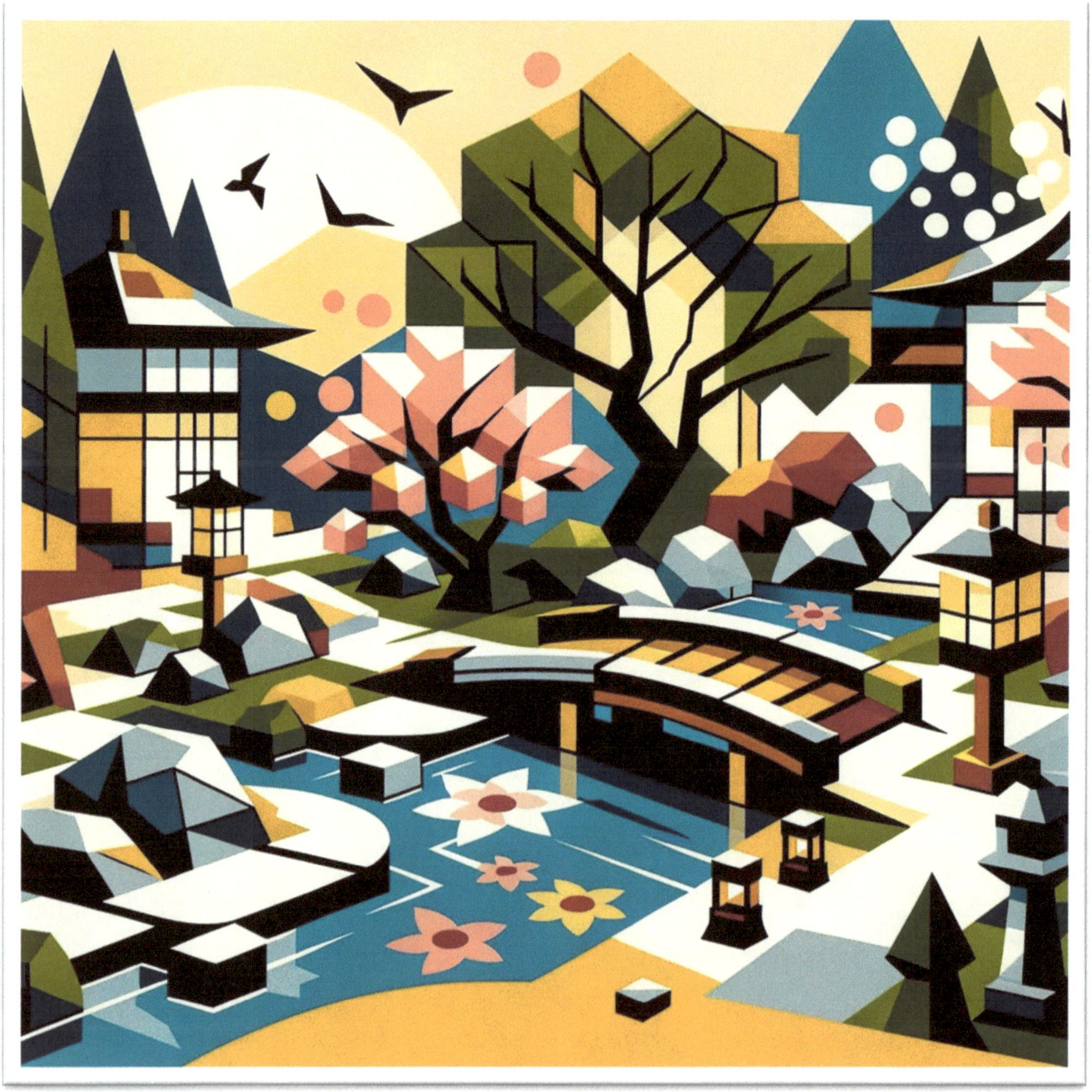

Commentary: This artwork showcases a distinctively modern, geometric interpretation of a traditional Japanese landscape, employing sharp, angular shapes and a vibrant, contrasting color palette. The artist's style emphasizes stylization over realism, distilling natural and architectural elements into abstract forms. The composition is meticulously balanced, with a dynamic interplay of forms that creates a rhythmic visual harmony, illustrating a serene yet vivid scene that feels both timeless and contemporary.

Emotion-Driven Scenes

Prompt: "Depict a scene of 'tranquility', with a person sitting under a large tree by a river, reading a book in the soft afternoon light."

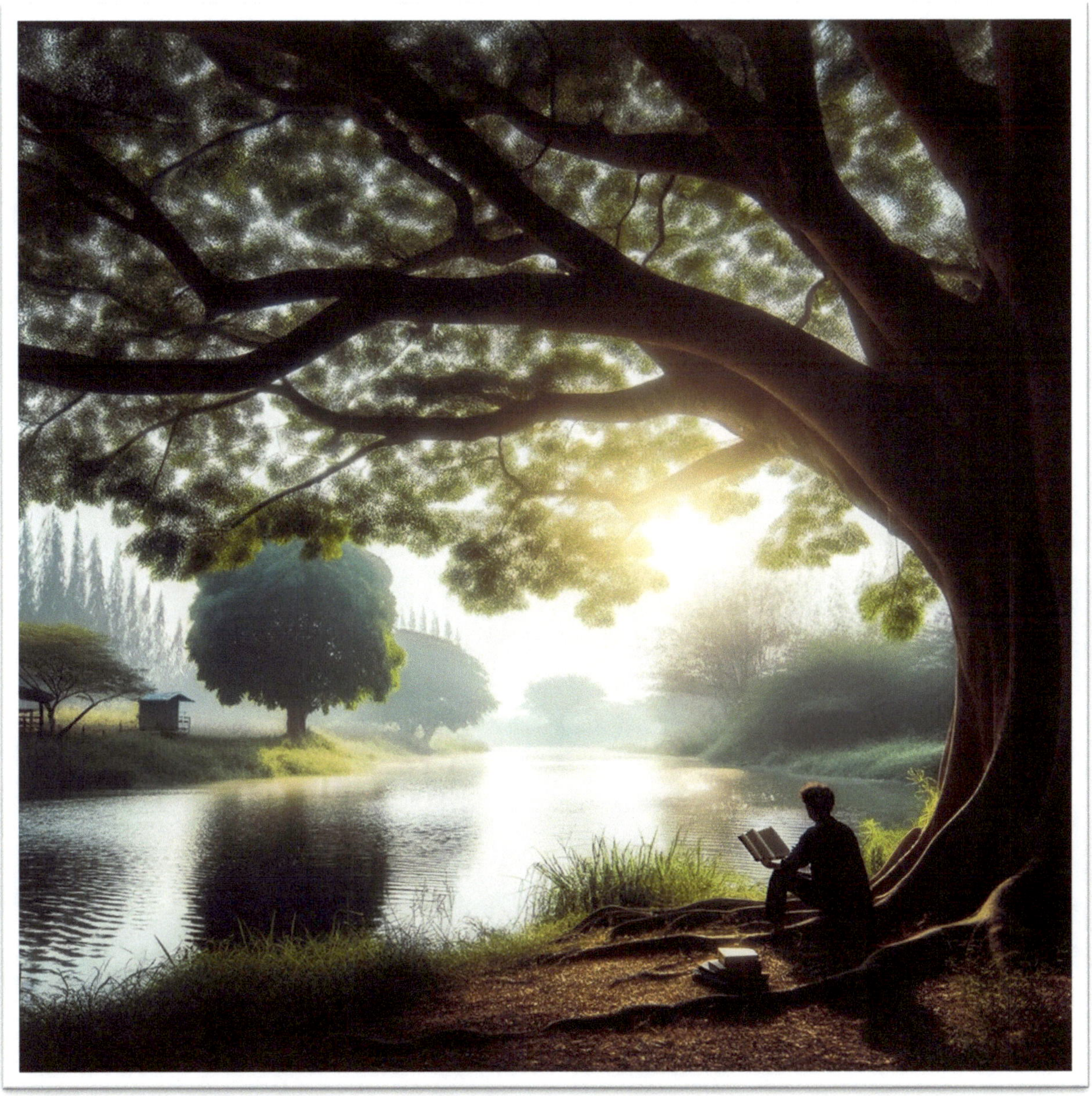

Commentary: This tranquil artwork captures a serene moment of solitude under a majestic tree, with soft sunlight filtering through its branches. The artist skillfully employs a delicate interplay of light and shadow, enhancing the serene mood and the lushness of the landscape. The inclusion of a lone figure absorbed in reading adds a human element, emphasizing contemplation and the peaceful coexistence with nature. The composition's warmth and detailed texturing underscore the artist's mastery in creating atmospheric depth and emotion.

Seasonal or Weather-Based Themes

Prompt: "Illustrate a snowy winter village scene at night, with warmly lit windows and snow-covered roofs, and a clear star-filled sky."

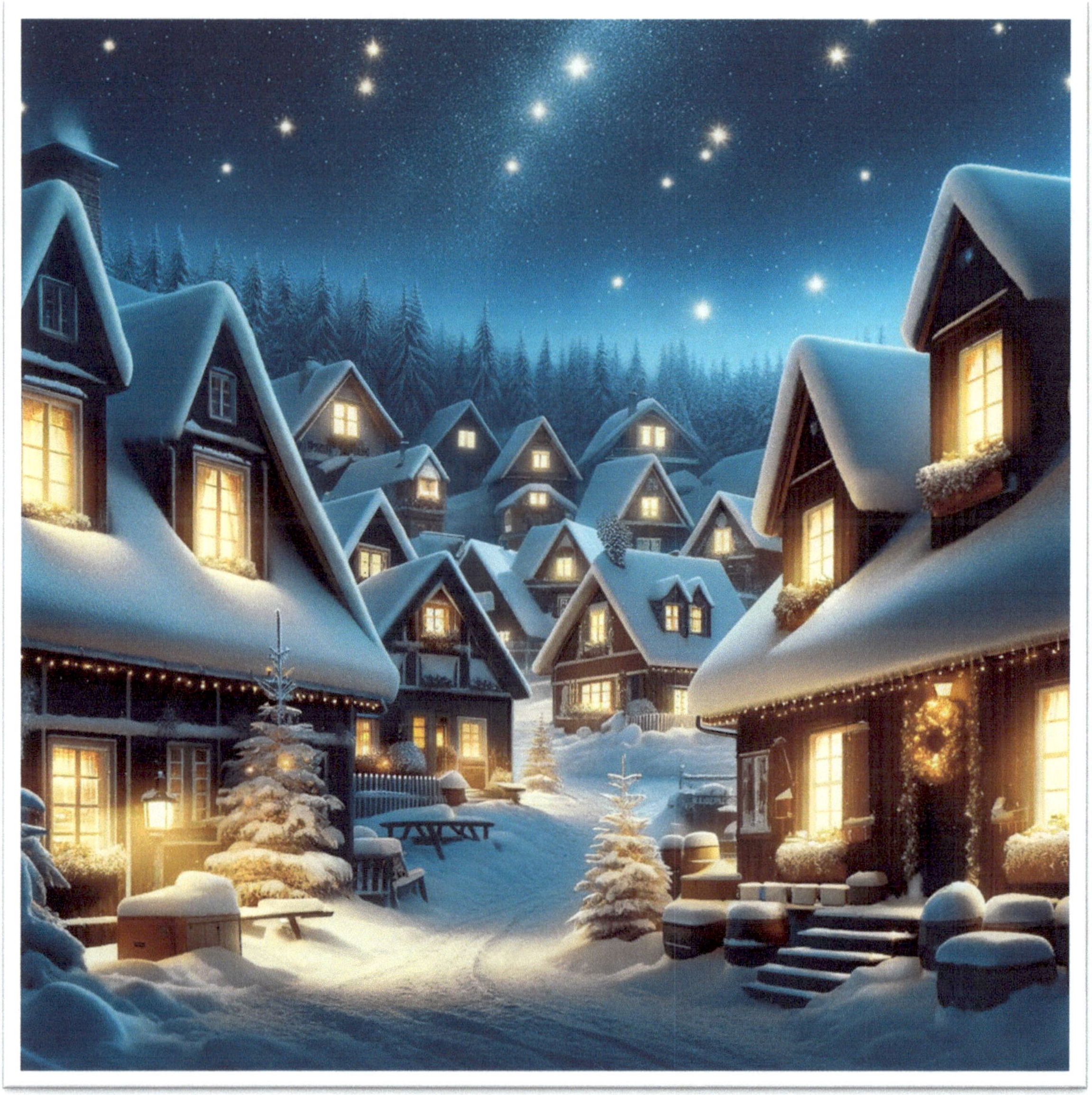

Commentary: This charming artwork depicts a snow-covered village under a starlit sky, capturing the essence of a peaceful winter night. The artist's use of glowing warm lights within the houses contrasts beautifully with the cool blues and whites of the snow, creating a cozy, inviting atmosphere. The meticulous attention to detail in the snow's texture and the soft illumination of the landscape showcase the artist's ability to create depth and a sense of warmth in a wintry scene.

Animal Portraits with a Twist

Prompt: "Create a portrait of an owl dressed as a 19th-century gentleman, complete with a monocle and top hat."

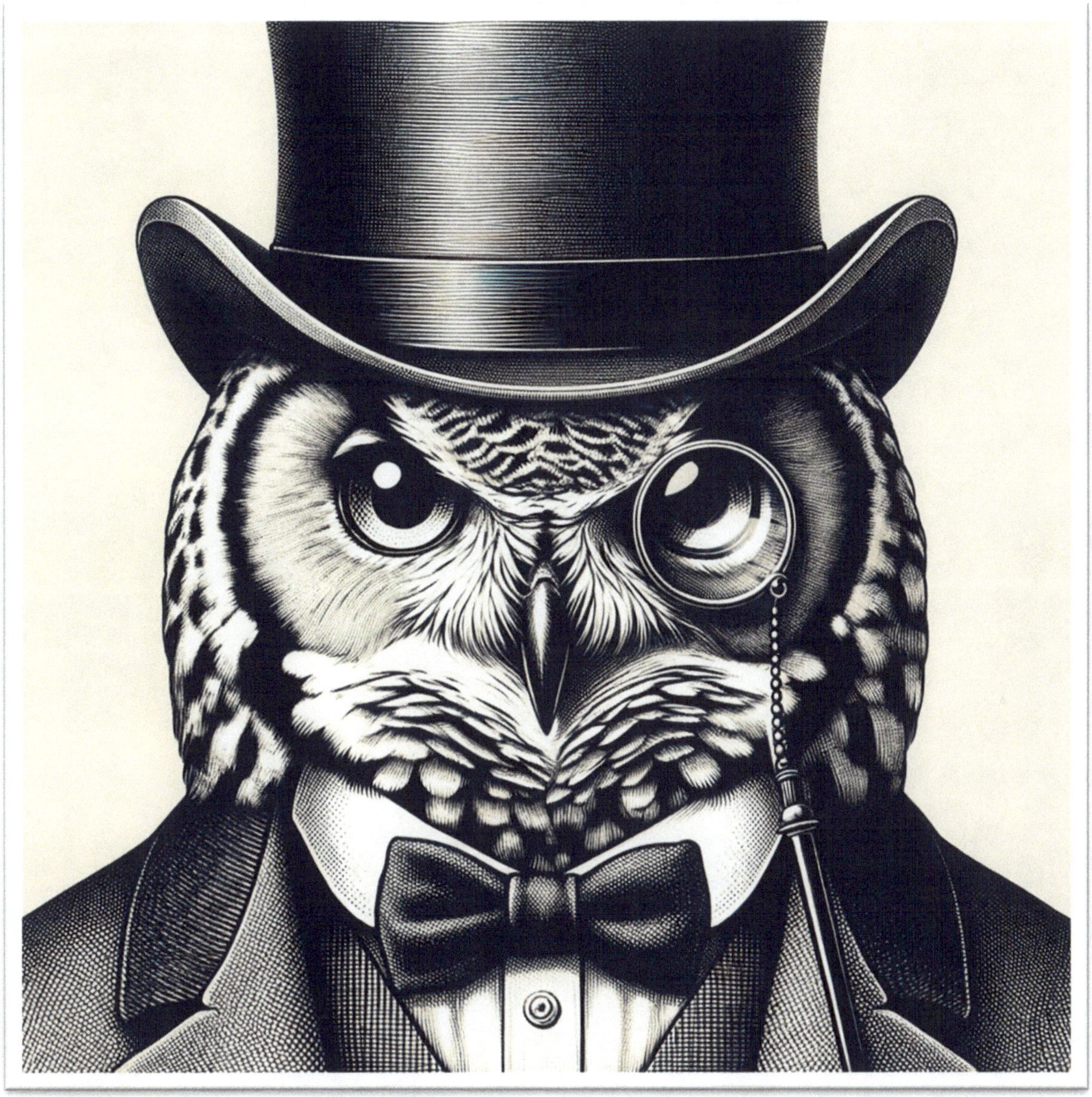

Commentary: This striking artwork combines traditional portraiture with surreal elements, depicting an owl in gentleman's attire. The artist's use of meticulous linework and monochromatic shading emphasizes textures, from the soft feathers to the hard, glossy top hat. This juxtaposition, along with the anthropomorphic portrayal of the owl, cleverly blurs the line between animal and human, reflecting a whimsical yet sophisticated approach. The piece embodies a unique blend of realism and imaginative interpretation, highlighting the artist's distinctive style.

Futuristic Cityscapes

Prompt: "Design a futuristic city with towering skyscrapers, flying cars, and neon lights, set during a rainy night."

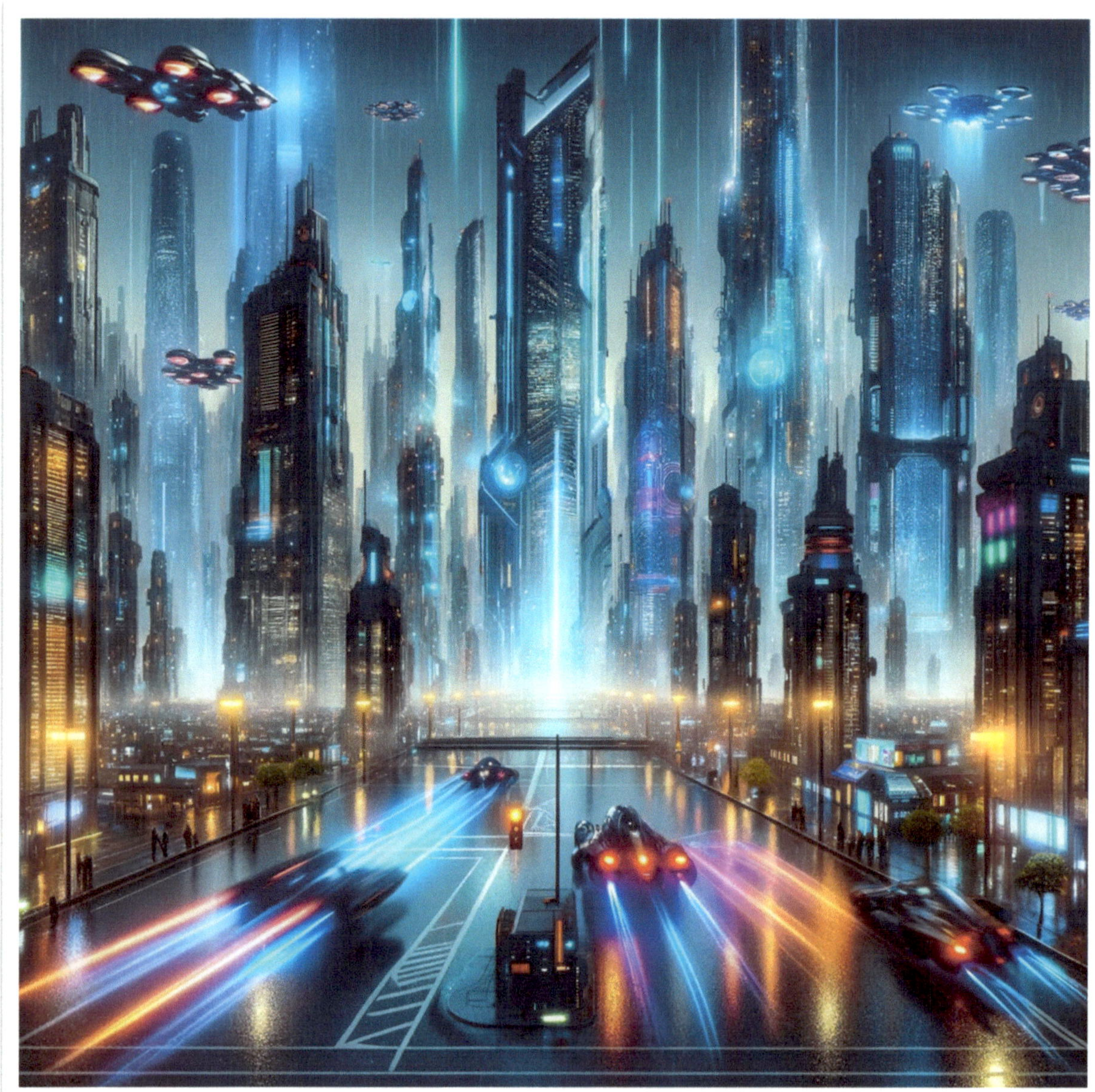

Commentary: This artwork portrays a neon-soaked, futuristic cityscape, alive with dynamic motion and luminescent architecture. The artist utilizes a palette of vibrant blues and contrasting neon lights to evoke a sense of advanced technology and urban energy. The depiction of flying vehicles and illuminated skyscrapers in a rain-drenched setting creates a visually rich, atmospheric effect, illustrating a sophisticated blend of science fiction and realism that is both immersive and compelling.

Underwater Worlds

Prompt: "Visualize an underwater city with coral buildings, diverse marine life, and merpeople going about their daily lives."

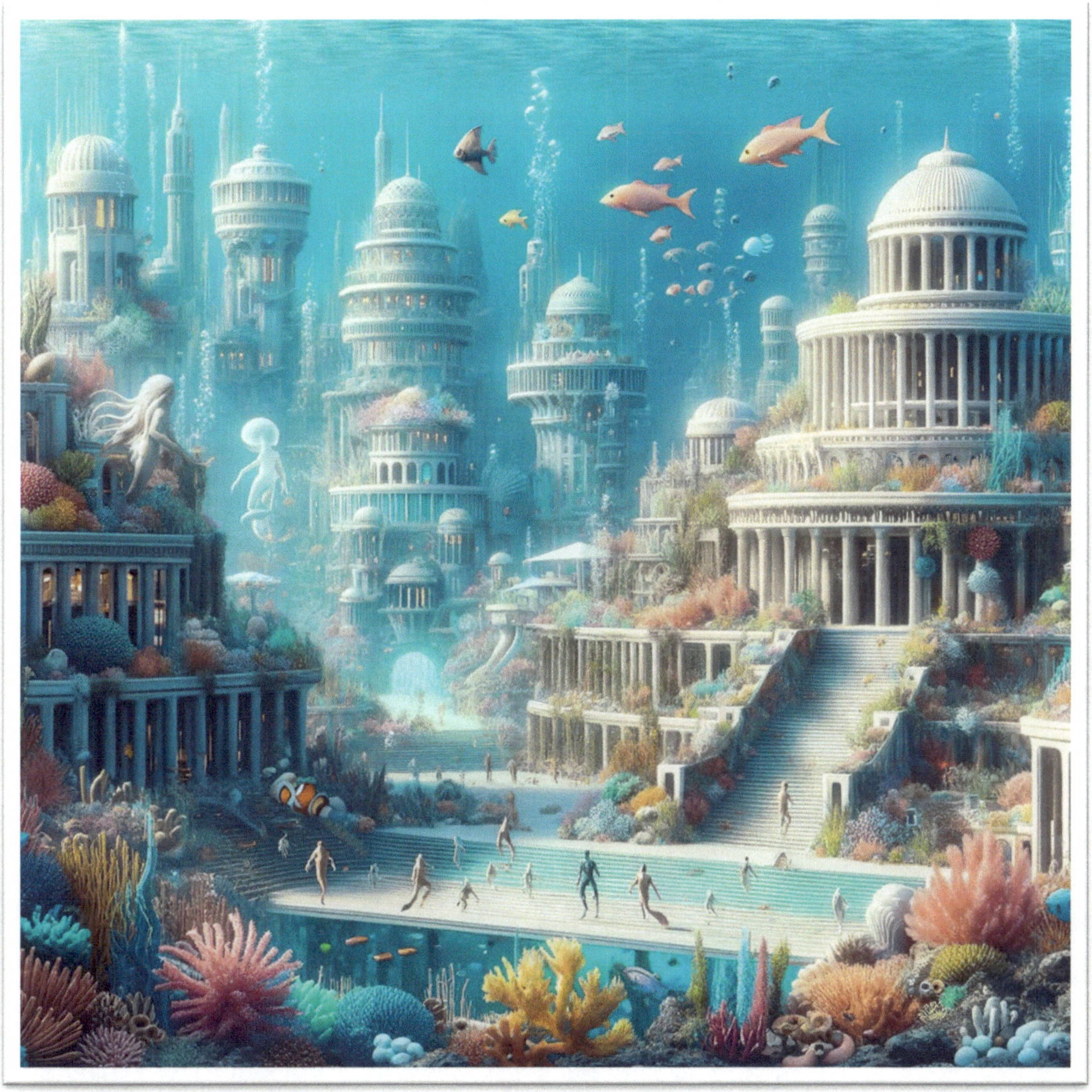

Commentary: This artwork imagines an underwater utopia, merging classical architectural forms with a vivid marine ecosystem. The artist's style is marked by a delicate interplay of light and color, enhancing the ethereal quality of the aquatic environment. The use of soft, pastel hues and intricate detailing in both the coral formations and the ornate buildings creates a surreal yet harmonious world, inviting viewers to contemplate a serene, submerged civilization in balance with nature.

Mythological Creatures in Modern Settings

Prompt: "Place a mythological creature like a dragon or a phoenix in a contemporary city scene."

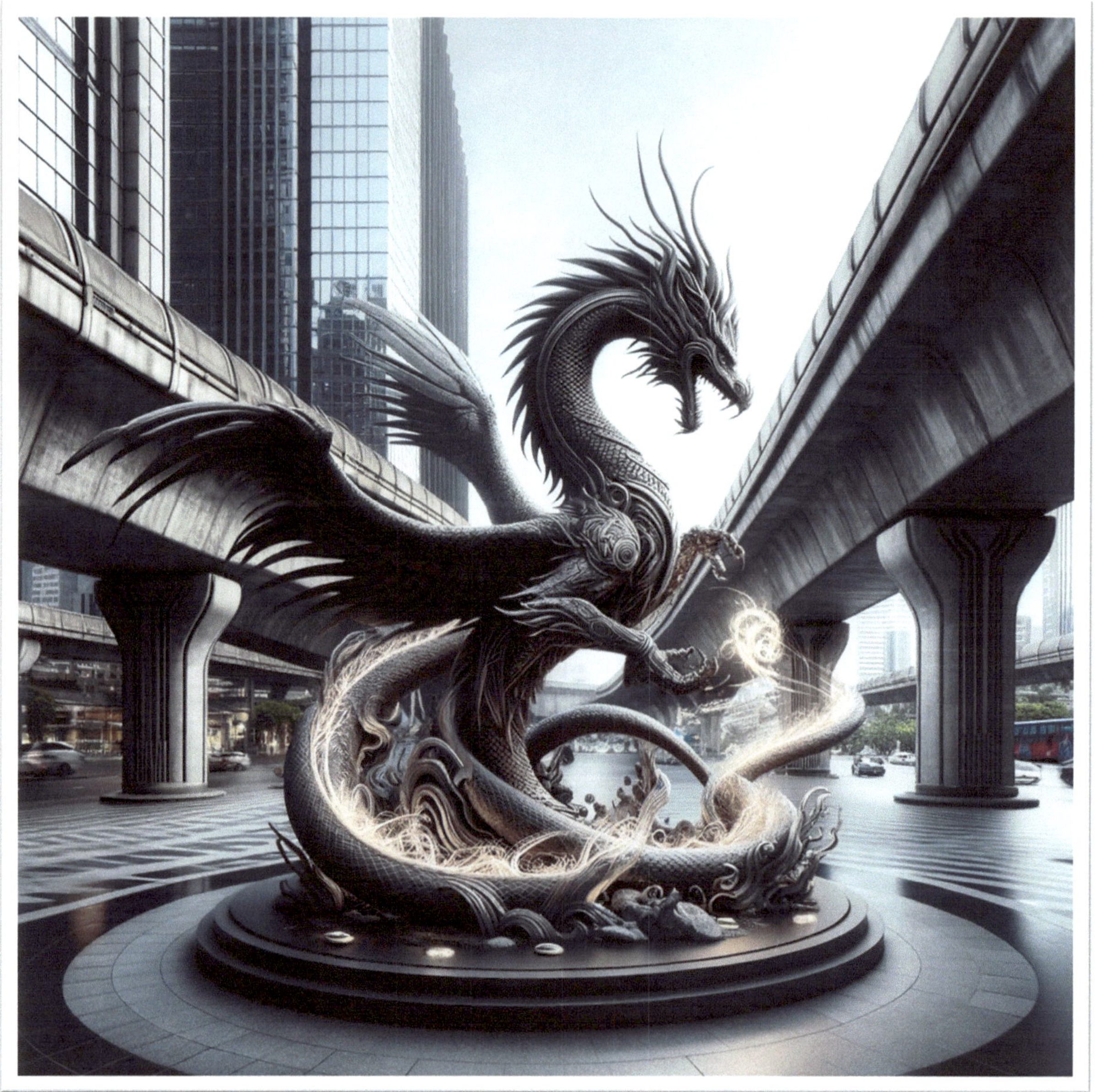

Commentary: This striking sculpture juxtaposes mythical and modern elements, placing a majestic, intricately detailed dragon in a contemporary urban setting. The artist skillfully balances realism and fantasy, capturing the dragon's dynamic motion and textural complexity against the stark lines of the cityscape. The use of metallic tones and the fluidity of the dragon's form contrast with the rigid urban architecture, highlighting a fusion of tradition and modernity that is both bold and imaginative.

Architectural Wonders

Prompt: "Design a futuristic library with advanced technology and unique, sustainable architecture."

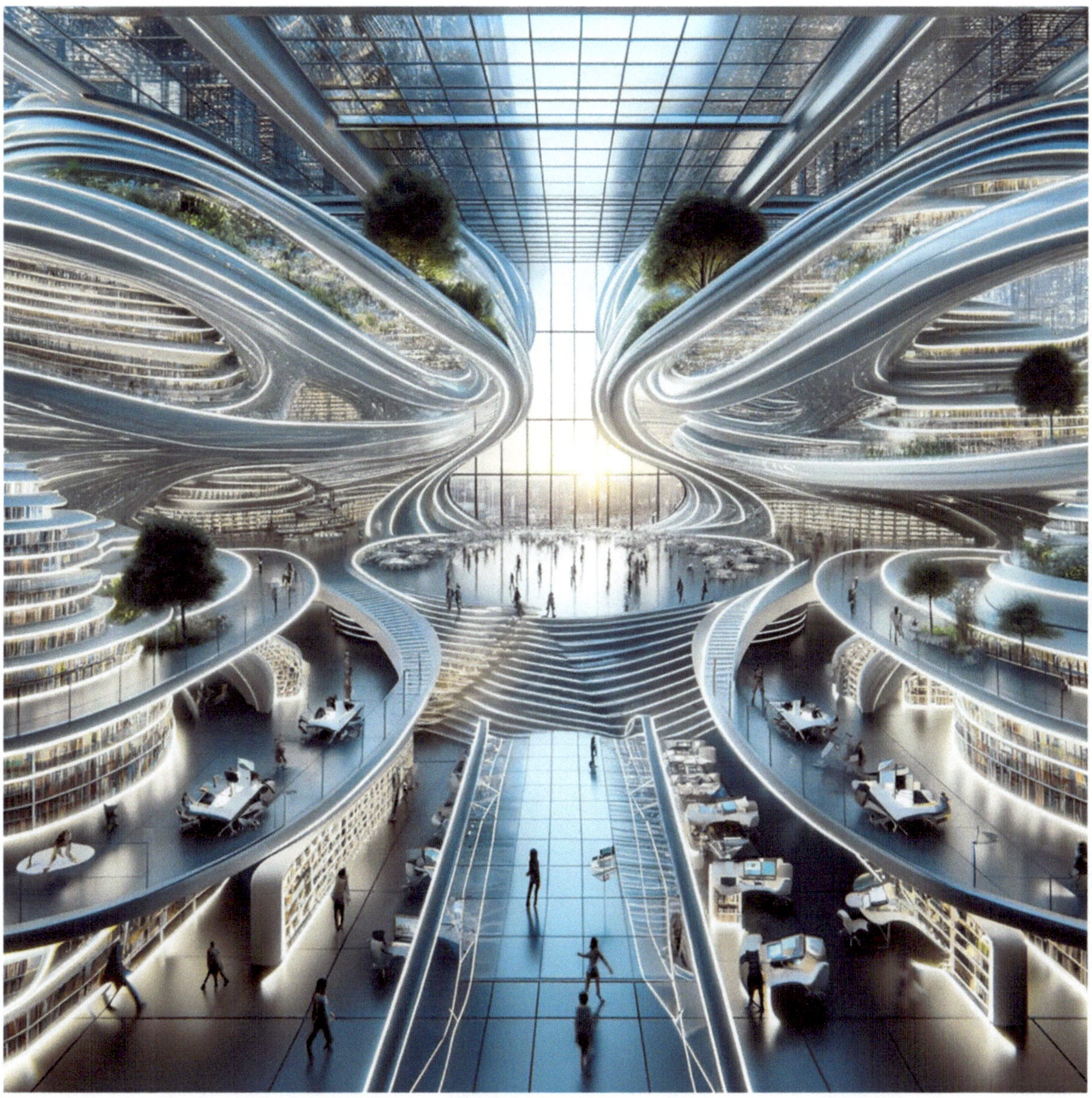

Commentary: This artwork portrays a futuristic architectural concept, featuring fluid, organic curves and layers that suggest a harmonious blend of nature and technology. The use of light and glass enhances the sense of openness and connectivity, creating an ethereal, almost weightless atmosphere. The artist's vision extends beyond traditional design, incorporating green spaces within a high-tech framework, emphasizing sustainability and a utopian interaction between human and environmental elements.

Surrealistic Dreams

Prompt: "Create a surreal landscape that defies the laws of physics, with floating islands, upside-down waterfalls, and gravity-defying structures."

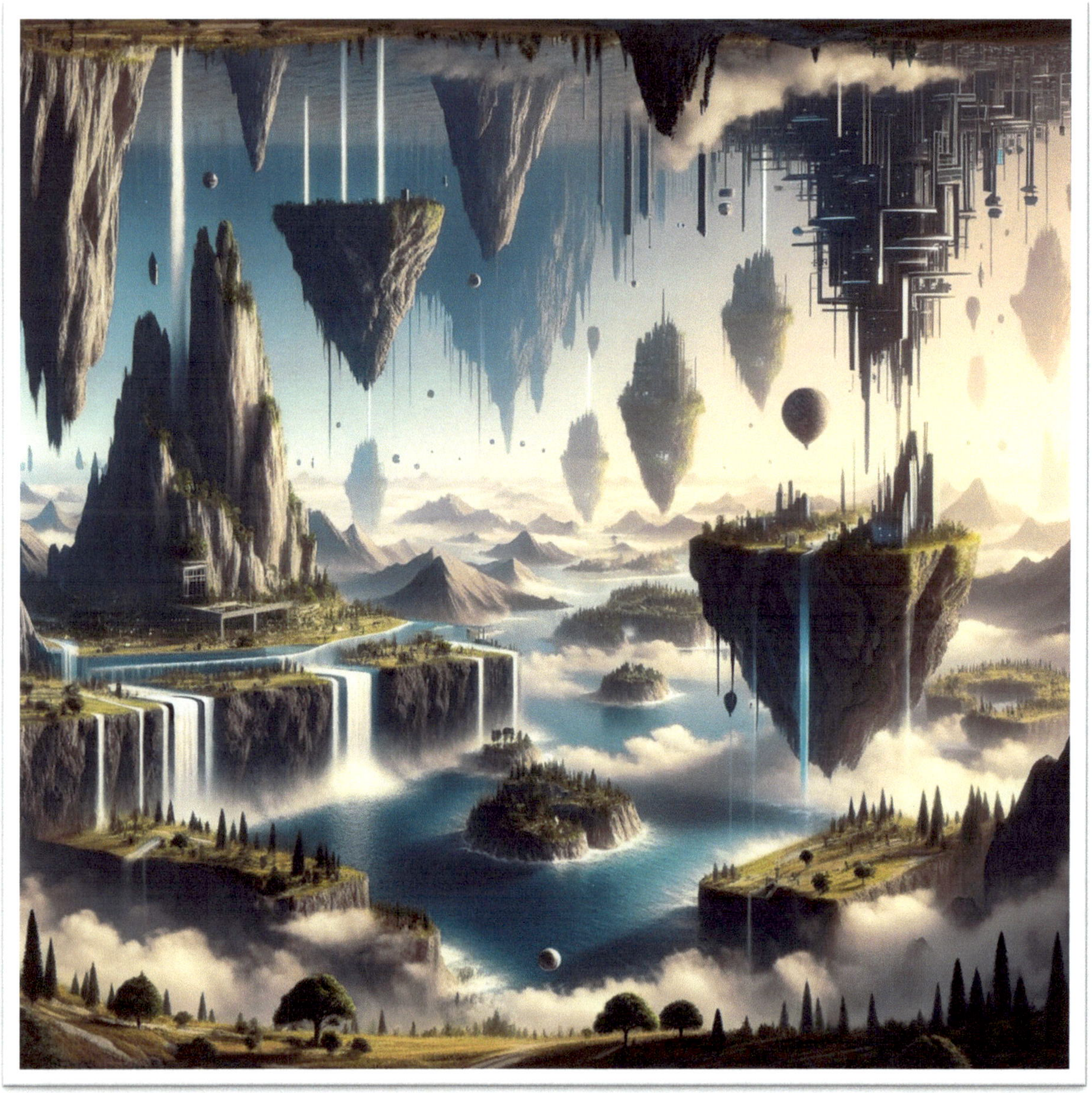

Commentary: This artwork combines fantasy and surrealism, depicting floating islands with both natural landscapes and futuristic cities. The artist skillfully balances contrasting elements—lush greenery against urban sprawl—highlighted by a dramatic play of light and shadow. The piece captures a sense of wonder and infinite possibility, evoking themes of isolation and connectivity. The meticulous detail and expansive scale underscore the artist's unique ability to blend the mystical with the plausible in a visually stunning manner.

Chapter 9: Fusion of Time and Imagination: Blending Artistic Influences with AI

Venture into the diverse panorama of art history to enhance your AI-generated art creations. This chapter delves into the intriguing worlds of Cubism, Impressionism, and Surrealism—each offering unique styles and philosophical insights to explore and integrate into your creative endeavors. Understanding these art movements not only deepens your appreciation for the artistic spectrum but also equips you with the tools to create more nuanced and effective AI prompts.

Cubism breaks conventional perspectives, encouraging a view of the world through geometric shapes and abstract forms. It challenges us to look beyond appearances to grasp the essence of form and structure, often using a restrained color palette and incorporating collage elements.

Impressionism captures fleeting moments with loose brushstrokes and a vibrant color palette, focusing on light effects. It finds beauty in everyday, urging us to savor the transient aspects of ordinary life.

Surrealism taps into the unconscious mind, presenting dream-like scenes that defy conventional logic. It invites us into a realm where the bizarre and fantastical prevail, bending reality and expanding the imagination.

This chapter also celebrates the art of mixing and experimenting with these rich artistic influences. By weaving the distinct characteristics of Cubism, Impressionism, and Surrealism into your prompts, you guide AI to create images that echo these movements while embarking on a bold journey of artistic fusion. Here, you blend the traditional with the contemporary, creating a bridge between the past and the future, and marrying the depth of human creativity with the limitless possibilities of AI.

Experimentation is key in exploring styles and themes in AI-generated art, and key to experimentation is "deliberate iteration". This protocol refers to a conscious and intentional process of repeating steps in order to refine and improve upon a work or concept. This involves reviewing the results after each iteration, making thoughtful adjustments, and applying the learned improvements to the next version. In the context of creating an artwork or developing an idea, it means purposefully evolving the piece through cycles of evaluation and enhancement to achieve a desired level of quality and detail. Through deliberate iteration, you can discover how different prompt elements interact and influence your creative process and ultimate artistic output.

Overview of Major Art Movements

- Prehistoric Art (c. 30,000 BCE - c. 2,000 BCE)
- Ancient Art (c. 3,000 BCE - c. 400 CE)
- Medieval Art (c. 5th - 15th century)
- Renaissance (14th - 17th century)
- Baroque (17th century)
- Rococo (early 18th century)
- Neoclassicism (mid-18th - early 19th century)
- Romanticism (late 18th - mid-19th century)
- Realism (mid-19th century)
- Impressionism (late 19th century)
- Post-Impressionism (late 19th - early 20th century)
- Fauvism (early 20th century)
- Expressionism (early 20th century)
- Cubism (early 20th century)
- Futurism (early 20th century)
- Dada (1916-1924)
- Surrealism (1920s)
- Abstract Expressionism (1940s-1950s)
- Pop Art (1950s-1960s)
- Minimalism (1960s-1970s)
- Postmodernism (late 20th century)
- Contemporary Art (late 20th century - present)

Building on the adventurous spirit of experimentation, check out the following curated selection of demonstrative artworks. Each piece, a vivid testament to the AI's ability to interpret and manifest diverse artistic traditions, showcases the seamless blend of technology and classic artistry. As you explore these visual expressions, let them inspire and challenge your perceptions. Let them offer new insights into how elements of each art movement can be reimagined through the lens of AI.

Now put yourself in the role of prompt engineer. What prompts would you use to create the images in the following artworks?

Prehistoric Art (c. 30,000 BCE - c. 2,000 BCE)

Characterized by cave paintings, petroglyphs, and megalithic structures. Represents humanity's earliest artistic expressions.

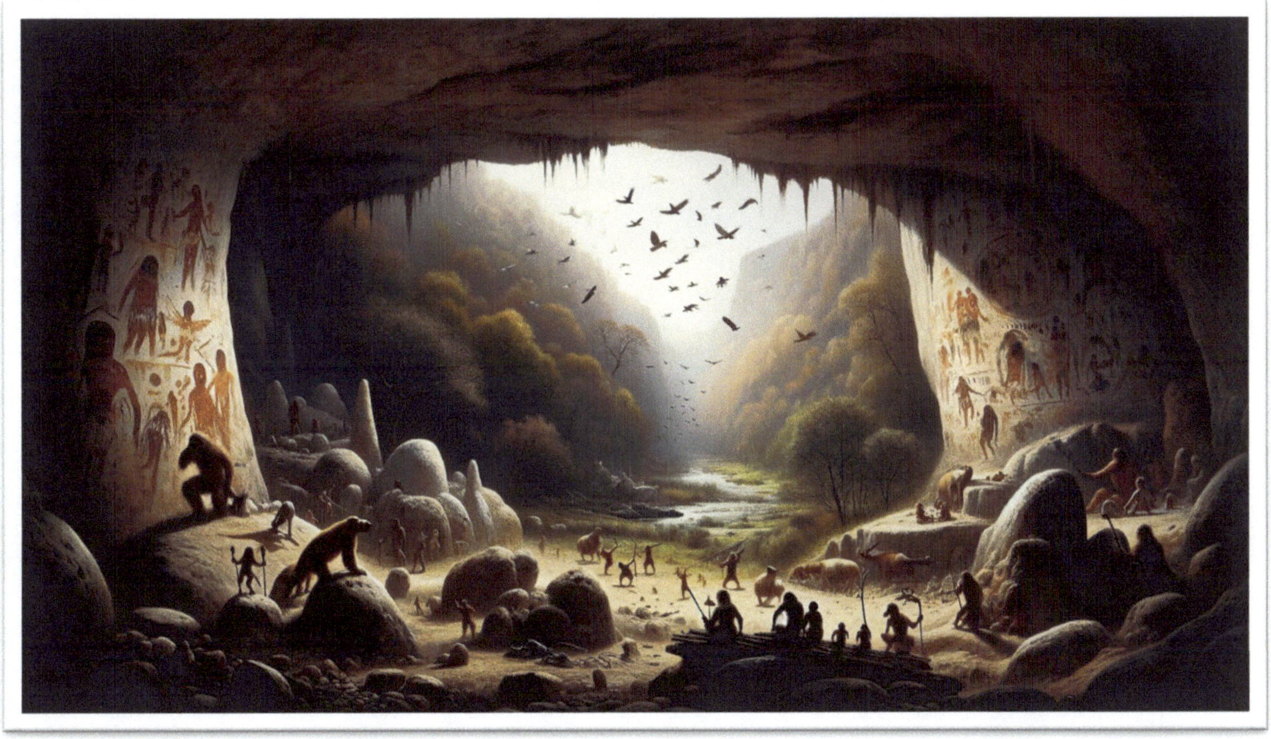

Ancient Art (c. 3,000 BCE - c. 400 CE)

Encompasses Egyptian, Greek, Roman, and Byzantine art. Known for its architecture, sculpture, and pottery.

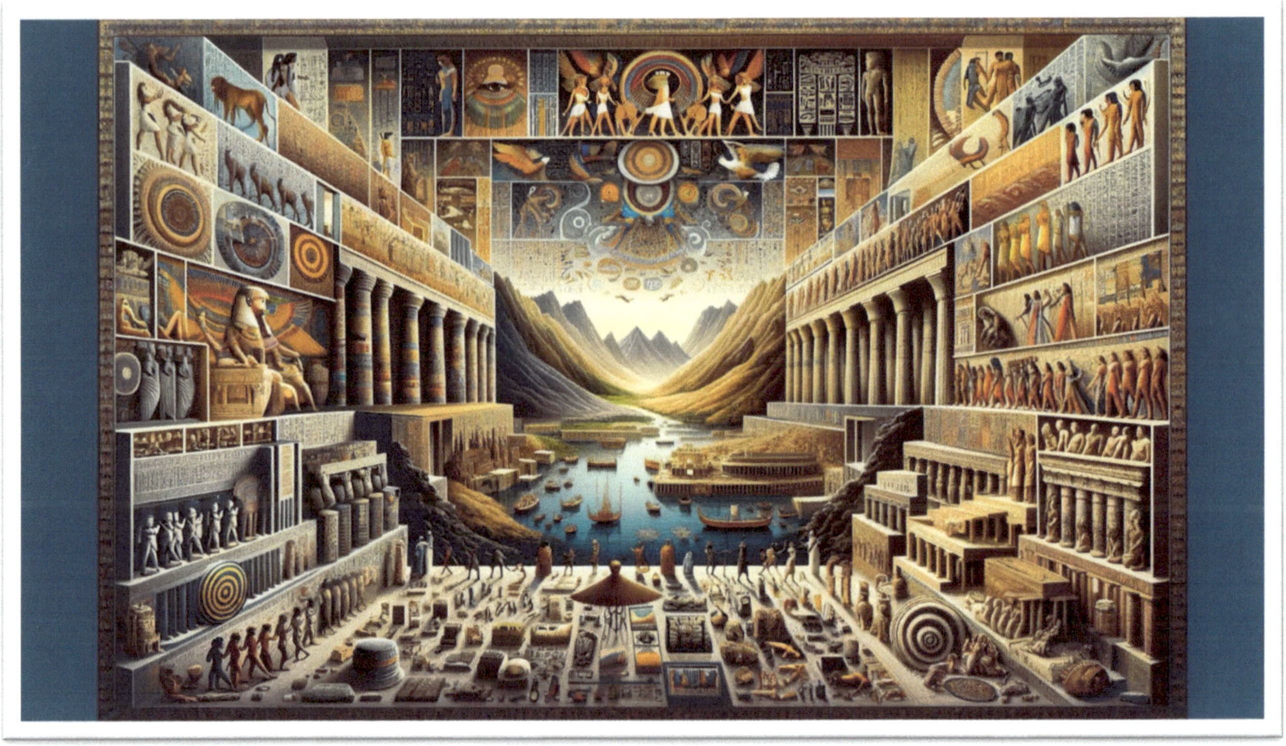

Medieval Art (c. 5th - 15th century)

Includes Byzantine, Romanesque, and Gothic styles. Focuses on religious themes; often found in cathedrals and illuminated manuscripts.

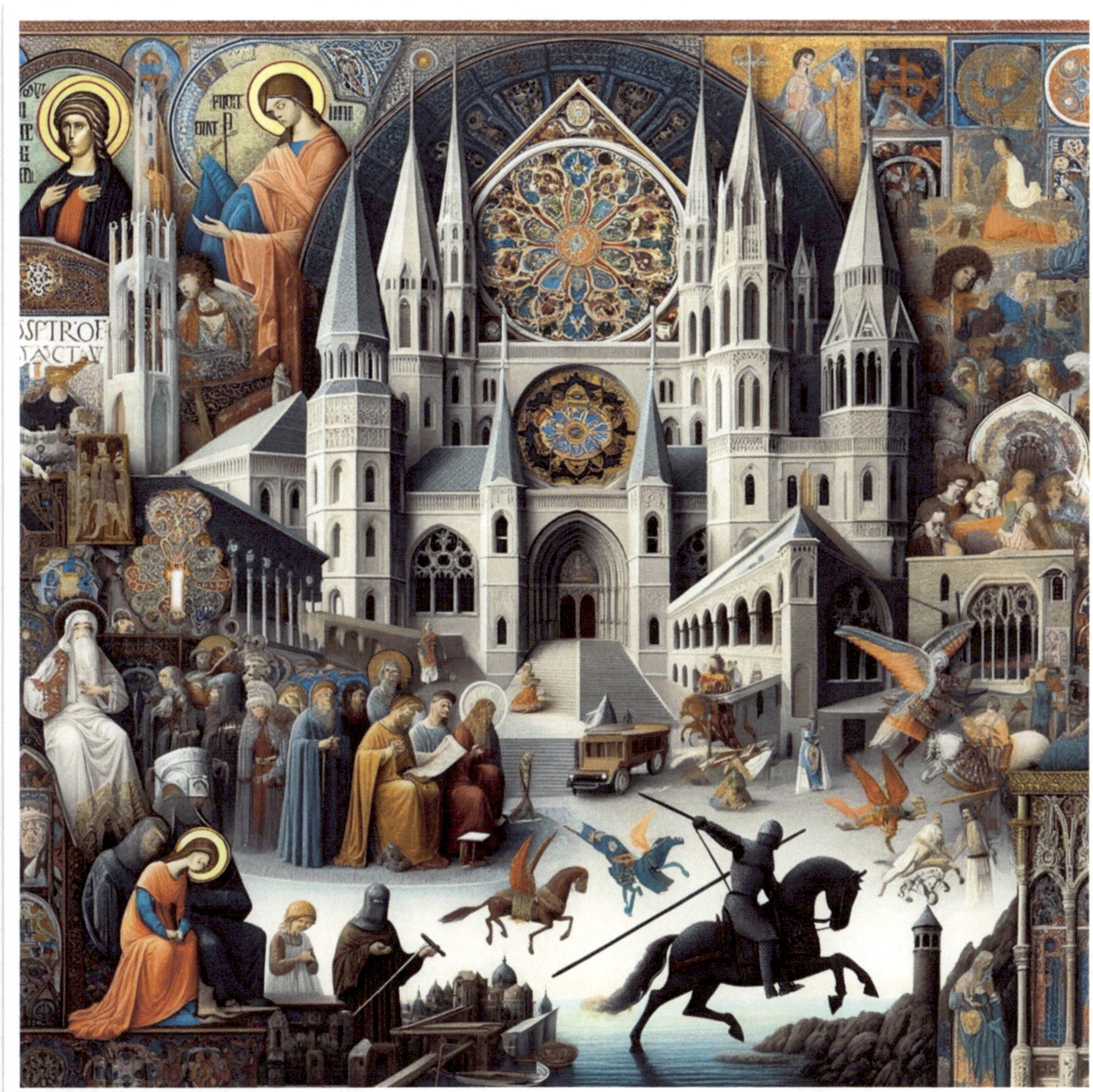

Renaissance (14th - 17th century)

The Renaissance was a profound cultural movement that emerged in Italy during the 14th century and spread across Europe. It marked a renewed interest in classical learning and values, evident in advancements in art, literature, and sciences. This period witnessed the creation of detailed, perspective-rich artworks that emphasized humanism, as depicted in the intricate figures and architectural precision in this piece. Renaissance art celebrated the beauty of the natural world and human form, blending intellectual exploration with artistic expression.

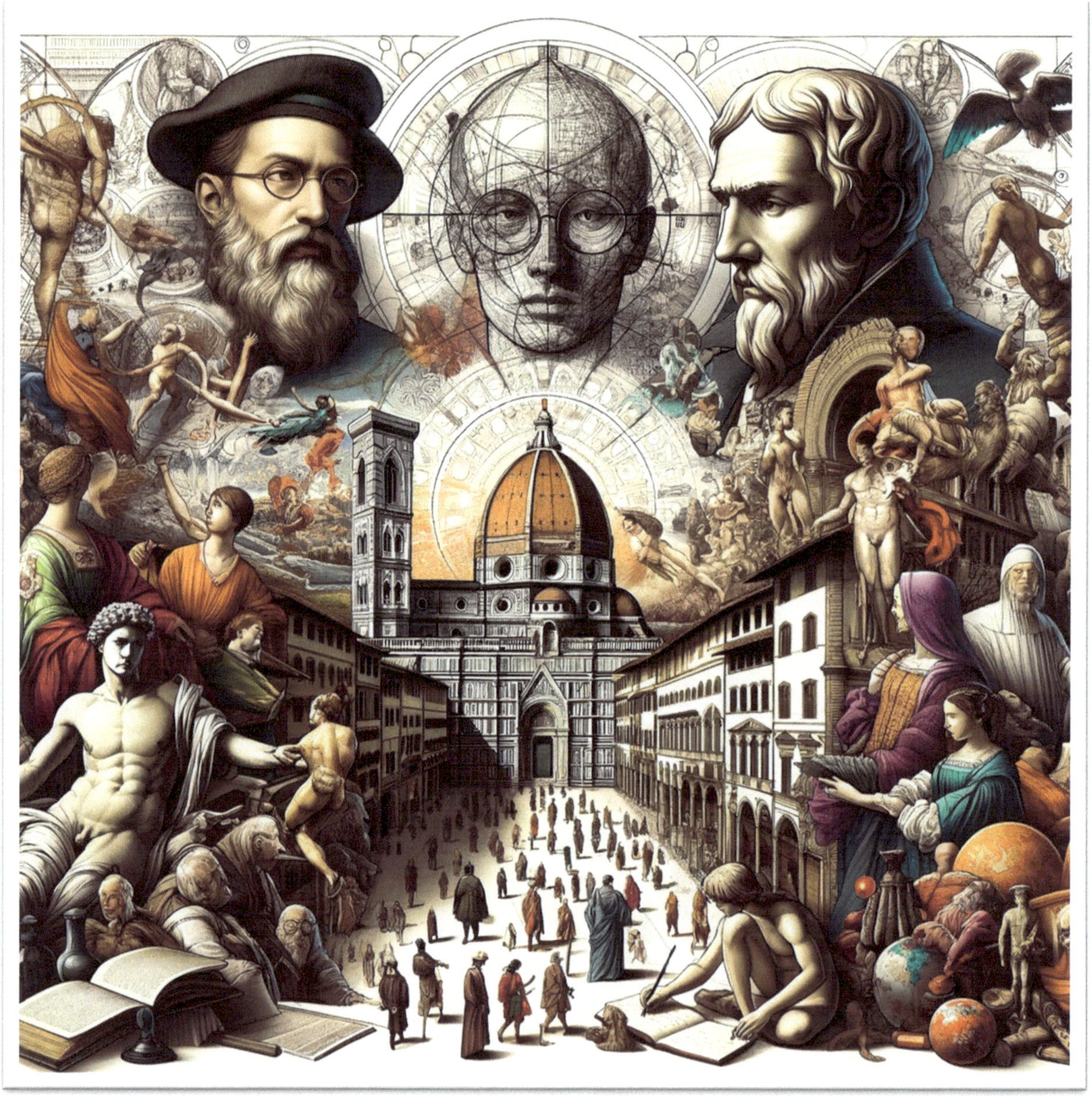

Baroque (17th century)

The Baroque era, flourishing in the 17th century, is known for its dramatic use of light and shadow, intricate details, and emotional intensity. This artwork exemplifies Baroque style through its dynamic composition, swirling clouds, and animated figures, conveying movement and theatricality. Baroque art often featured grandiose scenes and was used to evoke awe and spirituality, particularly in religious and monumental settings, showcasing the era's fascination with spectacle and the power of visual persuasion.

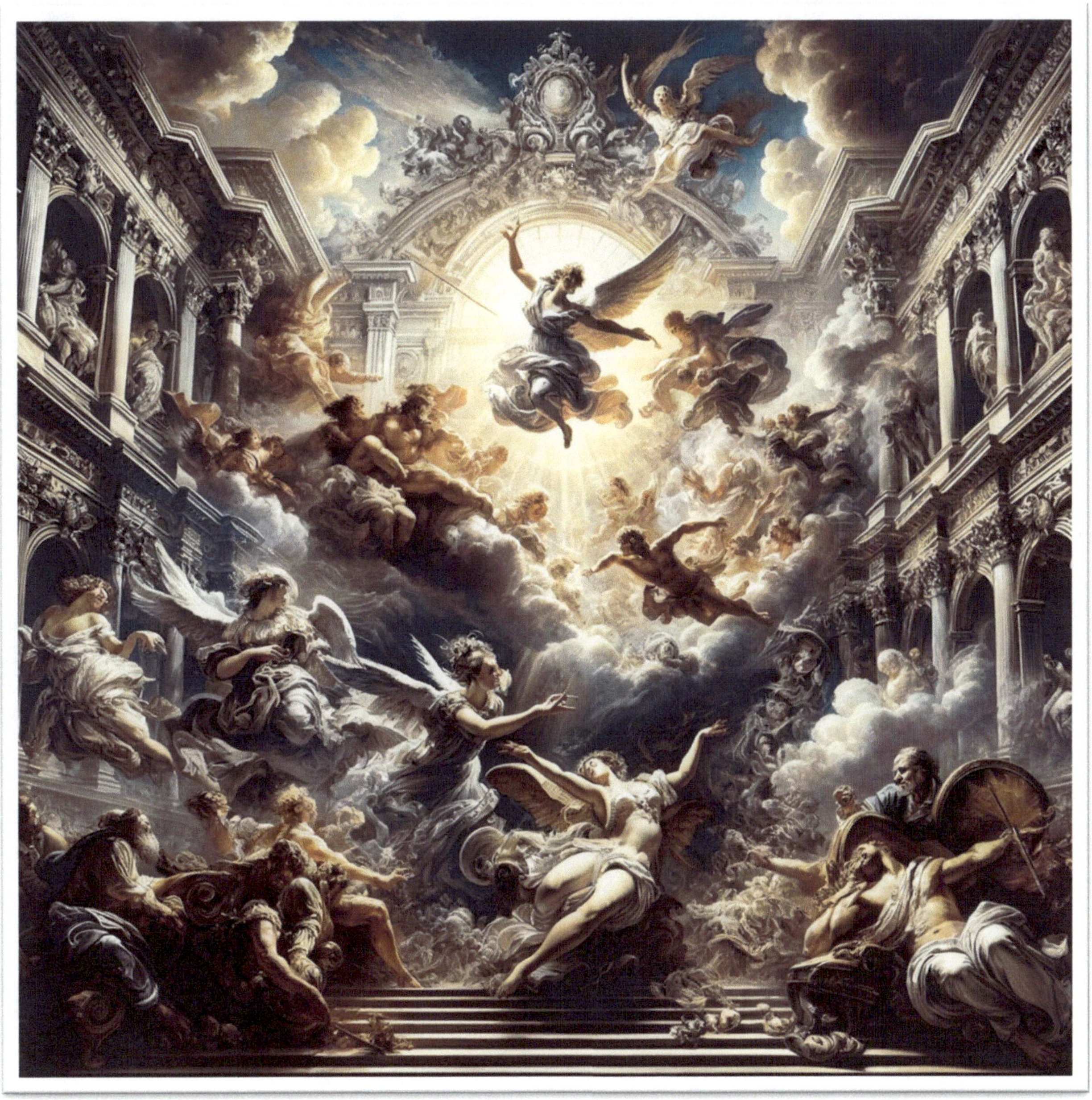

Rococo (early 18th century)

Rococo, an art style that developed in early 18th-century France, is celebrated for its ornate decorativeness, lightness, and elegance. This artwork displays Rococo's characteristic pastel color palette, playful themes, and elaborate ornamentation. The scenes are infused with a sense of frivolity and leisure, typical of the Rococo love for depicting the aristocracy's indulgent lifestyles. The intricate details and fluid curves in architecture and décor emphasize the style's focus on beauty and sophisticated grace.

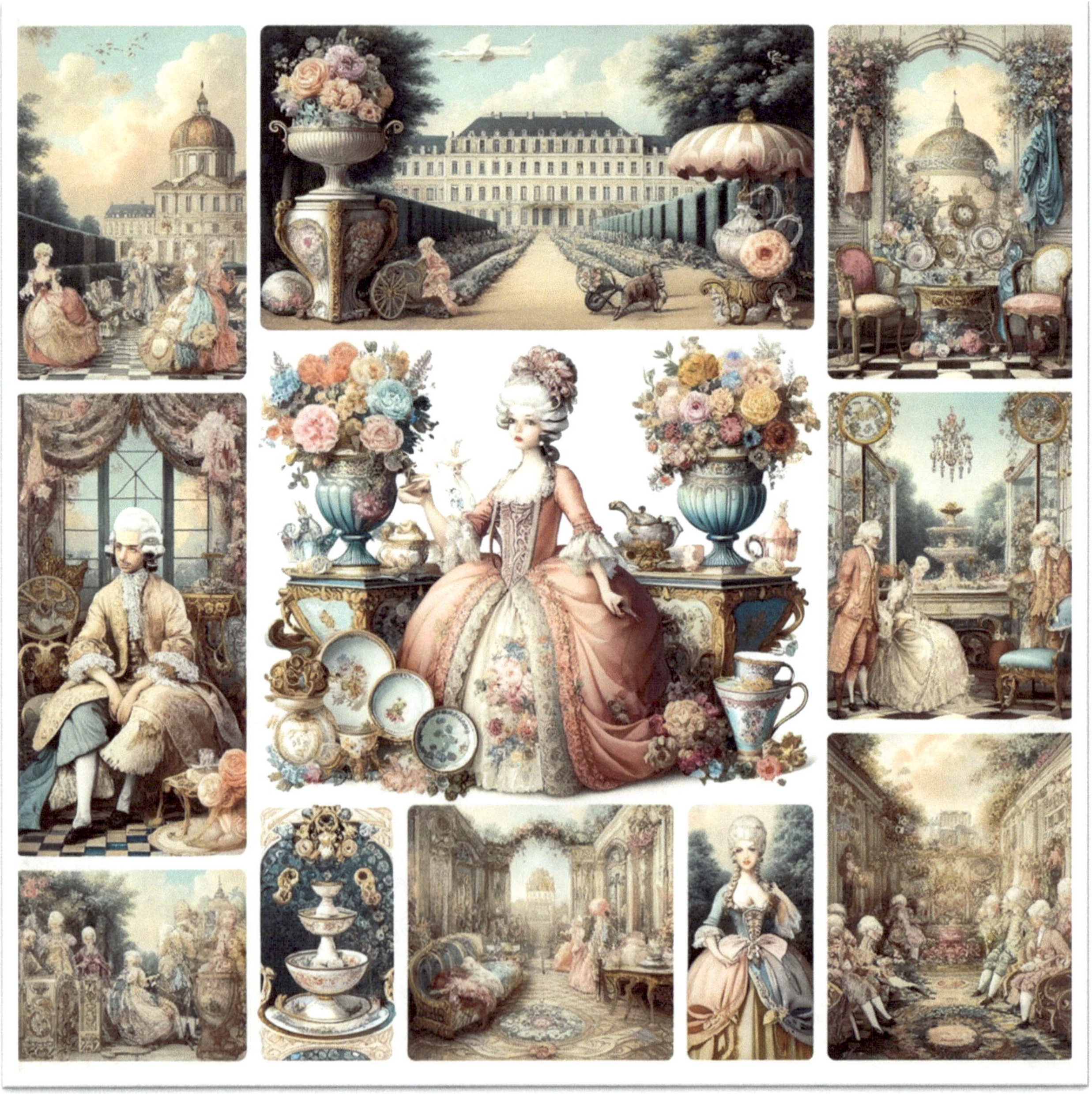

Neoclassicism (mid-18th - early 19th century)

Neoclassicism, a revival of classical art and architecture, emerged in the mid-18th century as a reaction to the ornate Rococo style. This artwork exemplifies Neoclassicism through its use of Greco-Roman motifs, structured composition, and emphasis on idealized forms. The scene, with its harmonious proportions and stoic figures, reflects the Neoclassical virtues of rationality and civic duty, aiming to inspire moral rectitude and intellectual clarity through the grandeur of ancient civilizations.

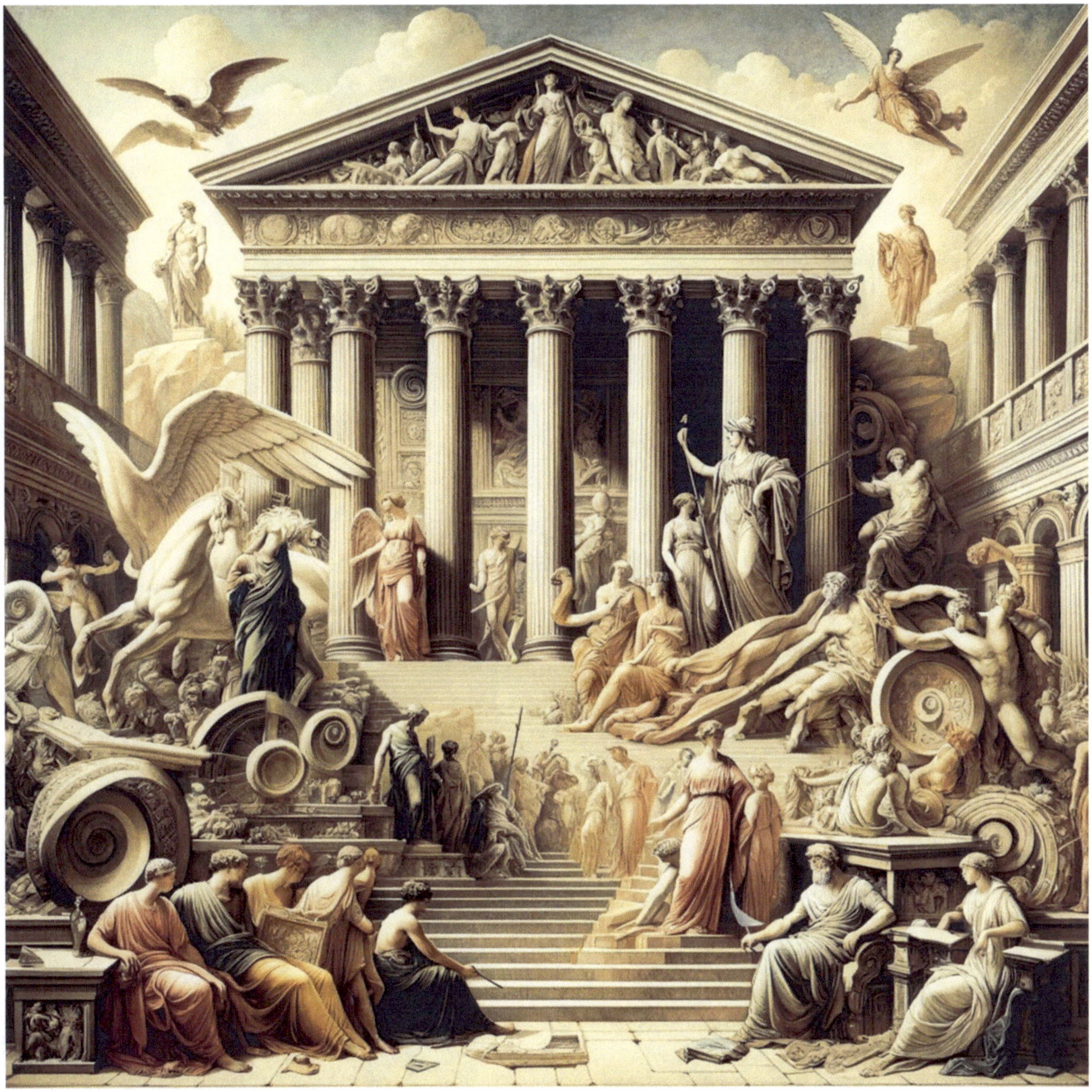

Romanticism (late 18th - mid-19th century)

Romanticism, flourishing from the late 18th to mid-19th century, emphasized emotion, individualism, and nature's sublime power. This artwork encapsulates Romanticism's focus on dramatic intensity and complex human experiences. It portrays a dynamic array of human endeavors and natural forces, merging reality with fantasy. The use of vivid, contrasting colors and dramatic lighting enhances the emotional depth and celebrates the triumph of the human spirit amidst turmoil and the overwhelming beauty of the natural world.

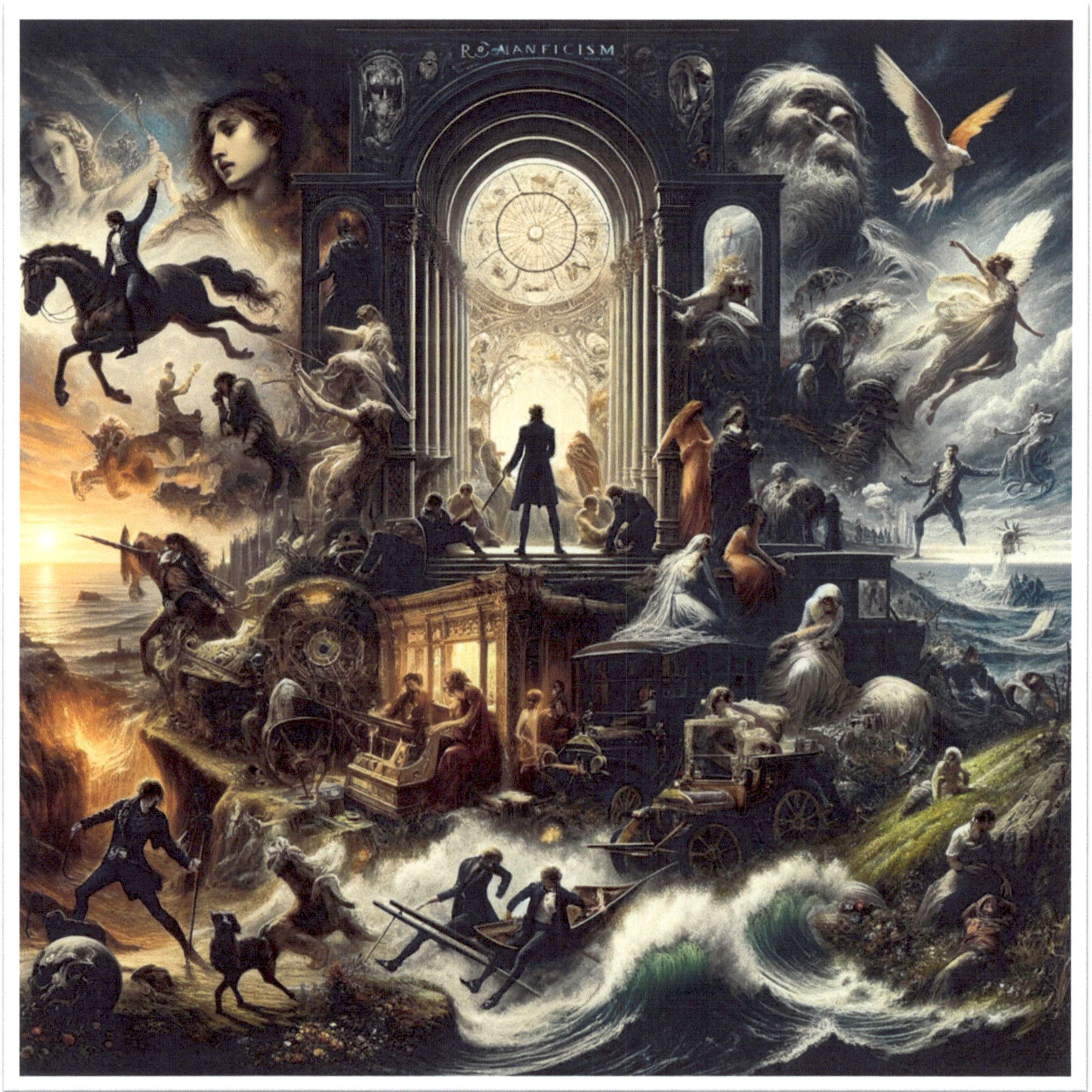

Realism (mid-19th century)

Realism, emerging in mid-19th century France, sought to depict everyday life with truth and accuracy, eschewing romanticized or idealized representations. This artwork exemplifies Realism through its focus on ordinary people and daily activities, highlighting the harsh realities of working-class life. The scenes, set in both rural and industrial environments, showcase meticulous detail and a subdued color palette, emphasizing the dignity and struggles of common folk without embellishment.

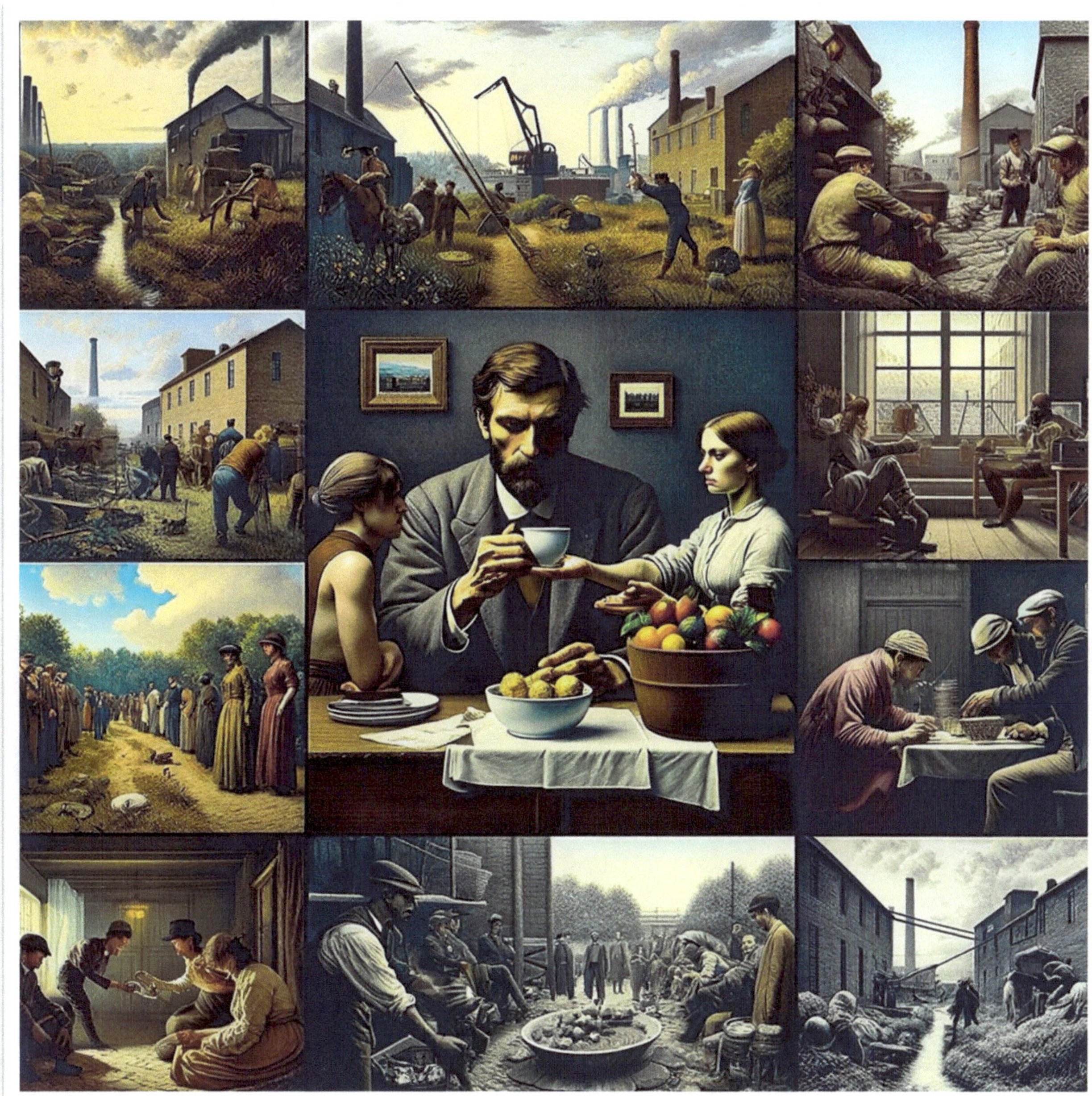

Impressionism (late 19th century)

Impressionism, emerging in late 19th century France, emphasizes light, color, and everyday scenes. This painting captures Impressionism's essence through its vibrant brushstrokes and emphasis on light effects and atmosphere rather than detail. The artist portrays a leisurely outdoor scene with fluid, visible brushwork that conveys the transient effects of light and color, inviting viewers to experience the momentary sensations of the landscape and the relaxed, joyful mood of the figures.

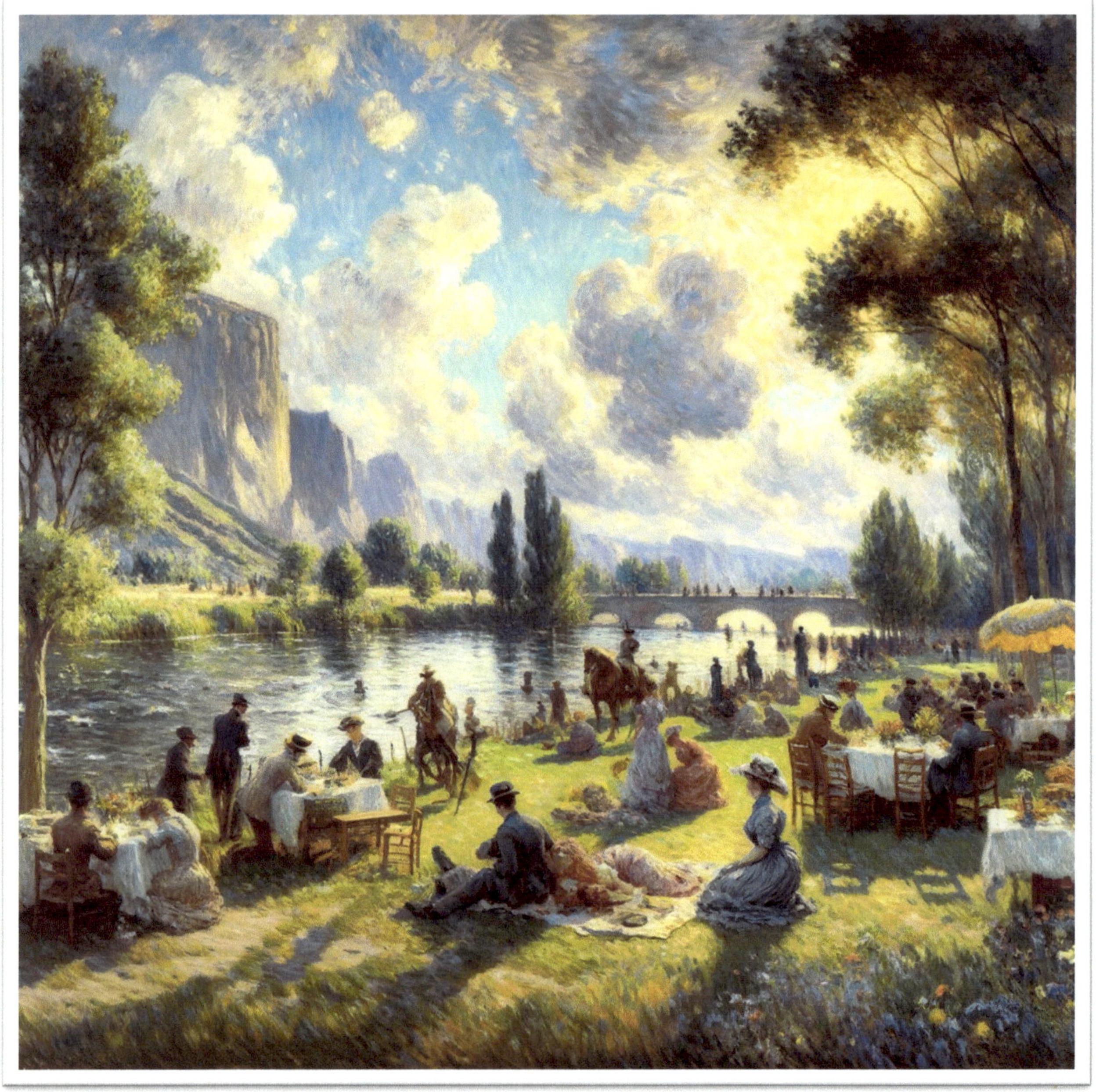

Post-Impressionism (late 19th - early 20th century)

Post-Impressionism, evolving from Impressionism in the late 19th century, emphasized a more structured form, vibrant colors, and symbolic content. This artwork reflects Post-Impressionist influences through its vivid, bold color palette and the use of geometric shapes to construct form and depth. The piece transcends mere representation, expressing deeper emotional resonance and personal perspective. It combines real and abstract elements, showcasing the artist's subjective response to the world around them.

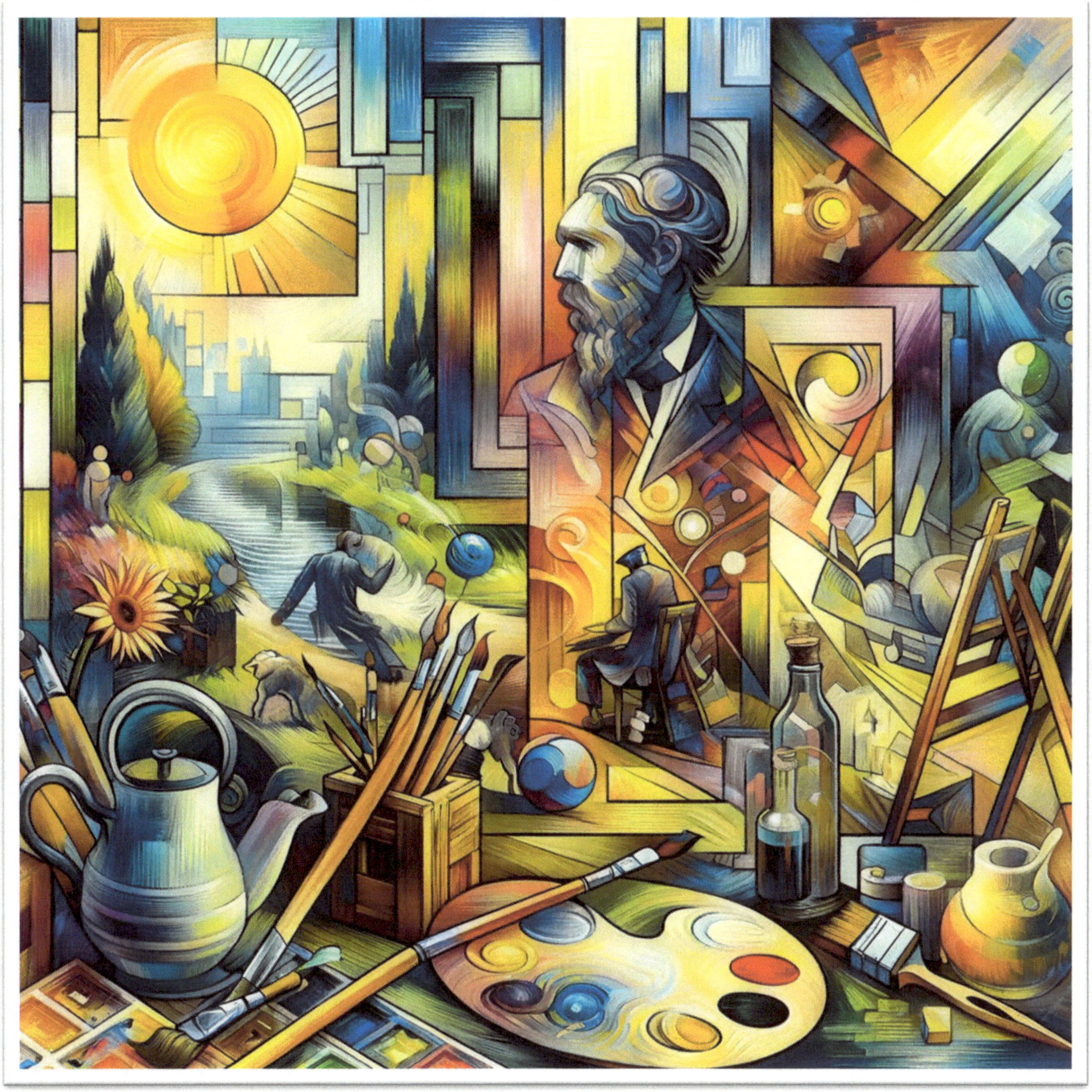

Fauvism (early 20th century)

This vibrant artwork is a brilliant example of Fauvism, characterized by its use of vivid, exaggerated colors and bold brushwork. Fauvism, an early 20th-century art movement led by figures like Henri Matisse, emphasizes painterly qualities and strong color over representational or realistic values retained by Impressionism. This piece likely aims to convey emotion through intense color contrasts and dynamic, swirling compositions, rather than through precise depictions of the natural world.

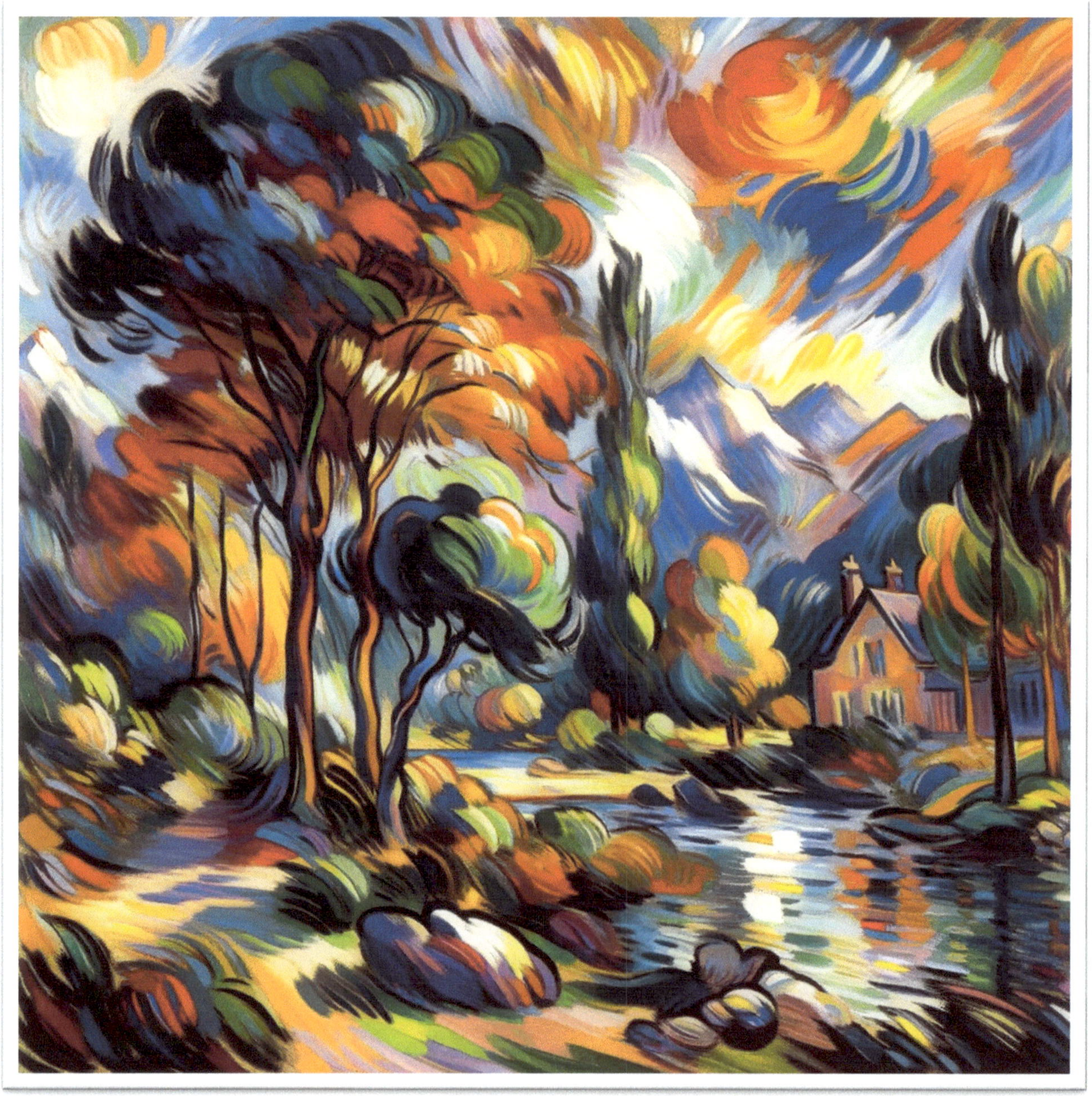

Expressionism (early 20th century)

This piece embodies Expressionism, a movement focused on conveying emotional experience rather than physical reality. Expressionist art, prevalent in the early 20th century, is marked by its use of vivid colors, exaggerated forms, and dramatic, often distorted imagery. This artwork captures the essence of human emotion and existential angst through intense colors and swirling, dynamic lines, inviting the viewer into a deeply personal and subjective visual narrative.

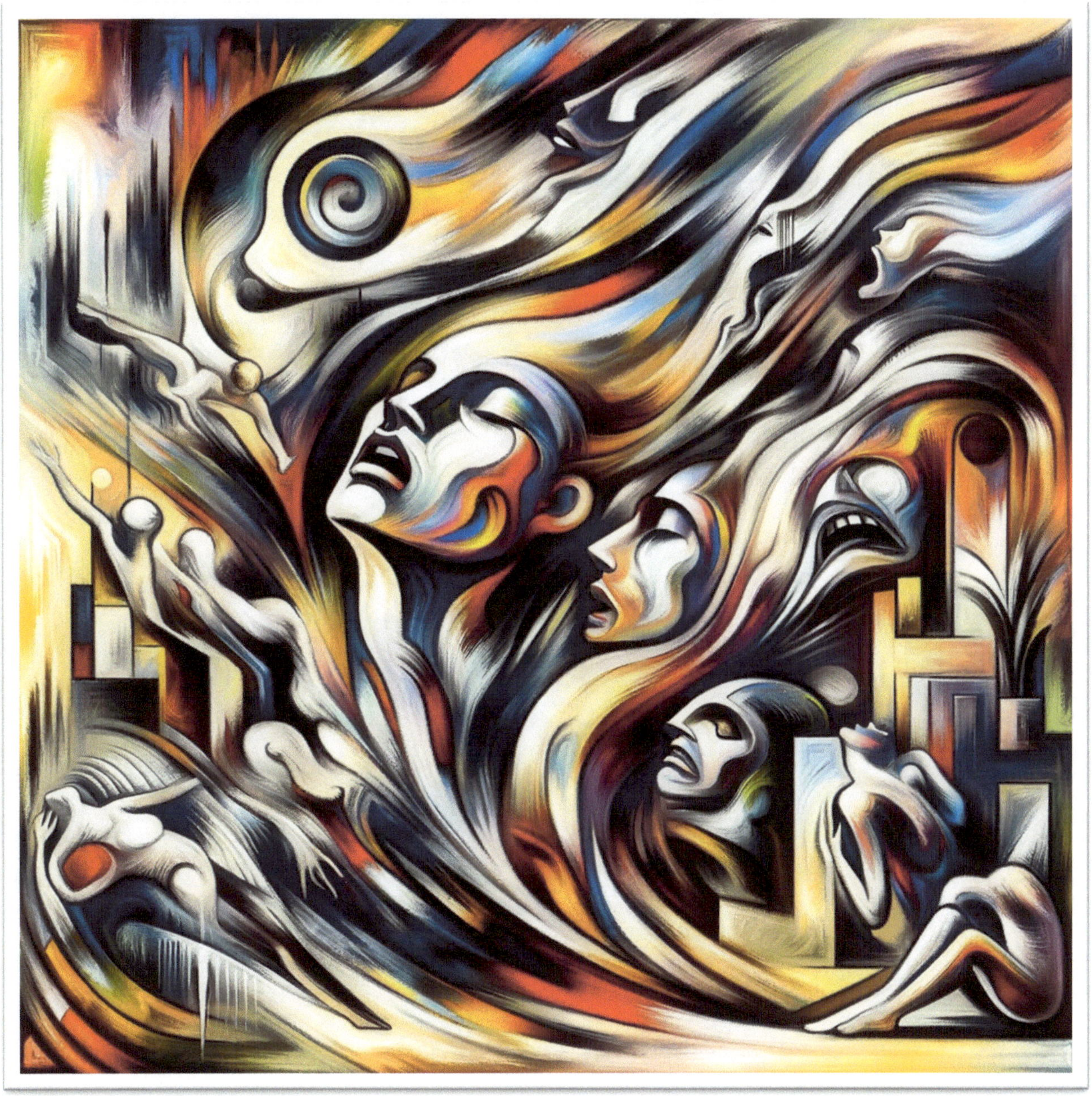

Cubism (early 20th century)

This artwork epitomizes Cubism, an early 20th-century movement that revolutionized European painting and sculpture. Cubism is characterized by fragmented objects and multiple perspectives combined into a single plane, challenging conventional forms of representation. This piece particularly illustrates these traits with its complex geometric shapes and interlocking segments, inviting the viewer to perceive the subject from different angles simultaneously, thereby deconstructing reality and emphasizing the abstract structure over realistic depiction.

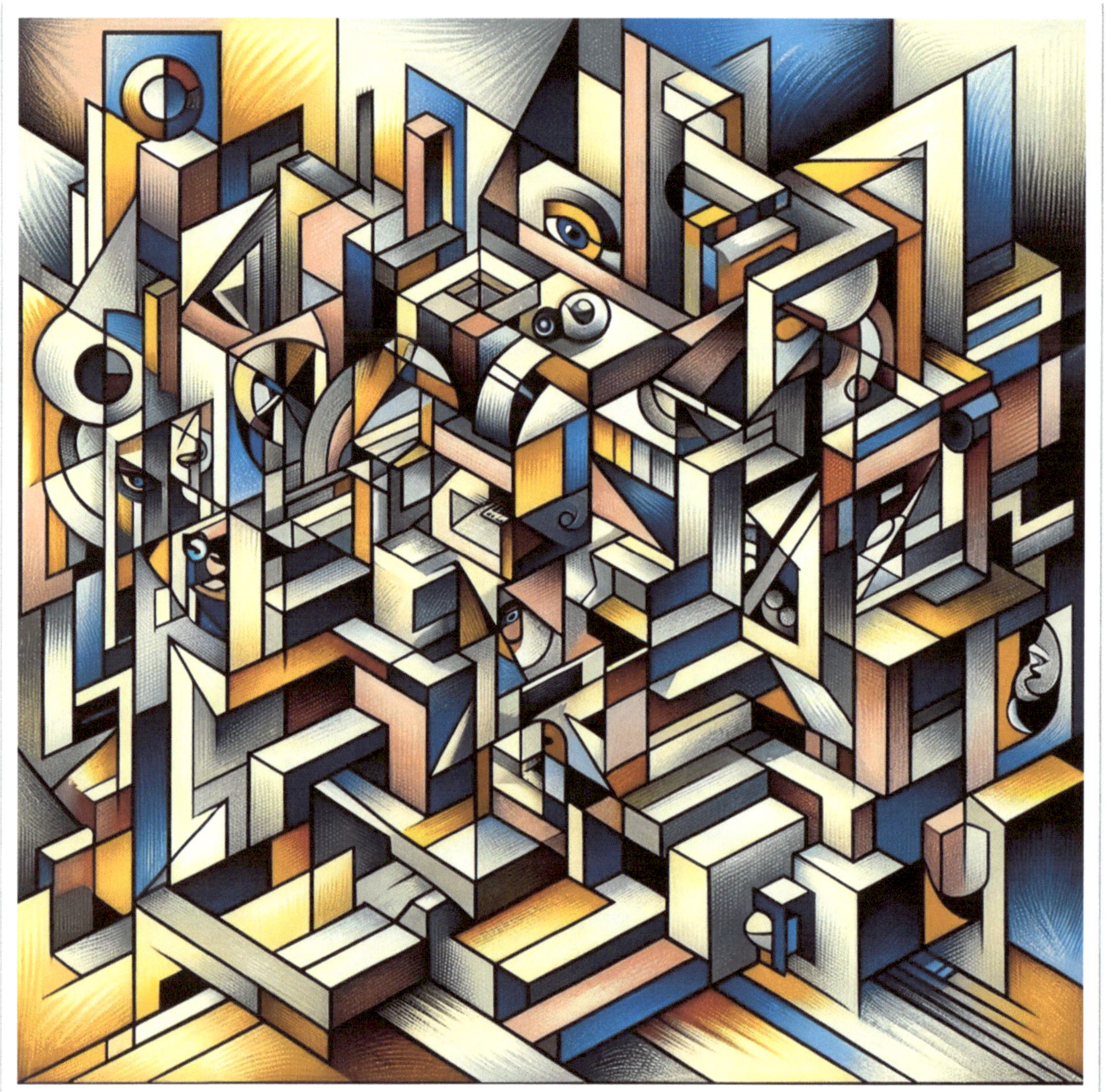

Futurism (early 20th century)

This artwork captures the essence of Futurism, an early 20th-century art movement that emphasized speed, technology, and industrial progress. Futurism celebrated the dynamism of the modern world, often portraying movement through overlapping and intersecting forms. In this piece, the sleek lines and streamlined forms convey the exhilaration of rapid movement and technological advancement, with motifs of cars, planes, and urban architecture symbolizing the futuristic aspirations and energetic ethos of the movement.

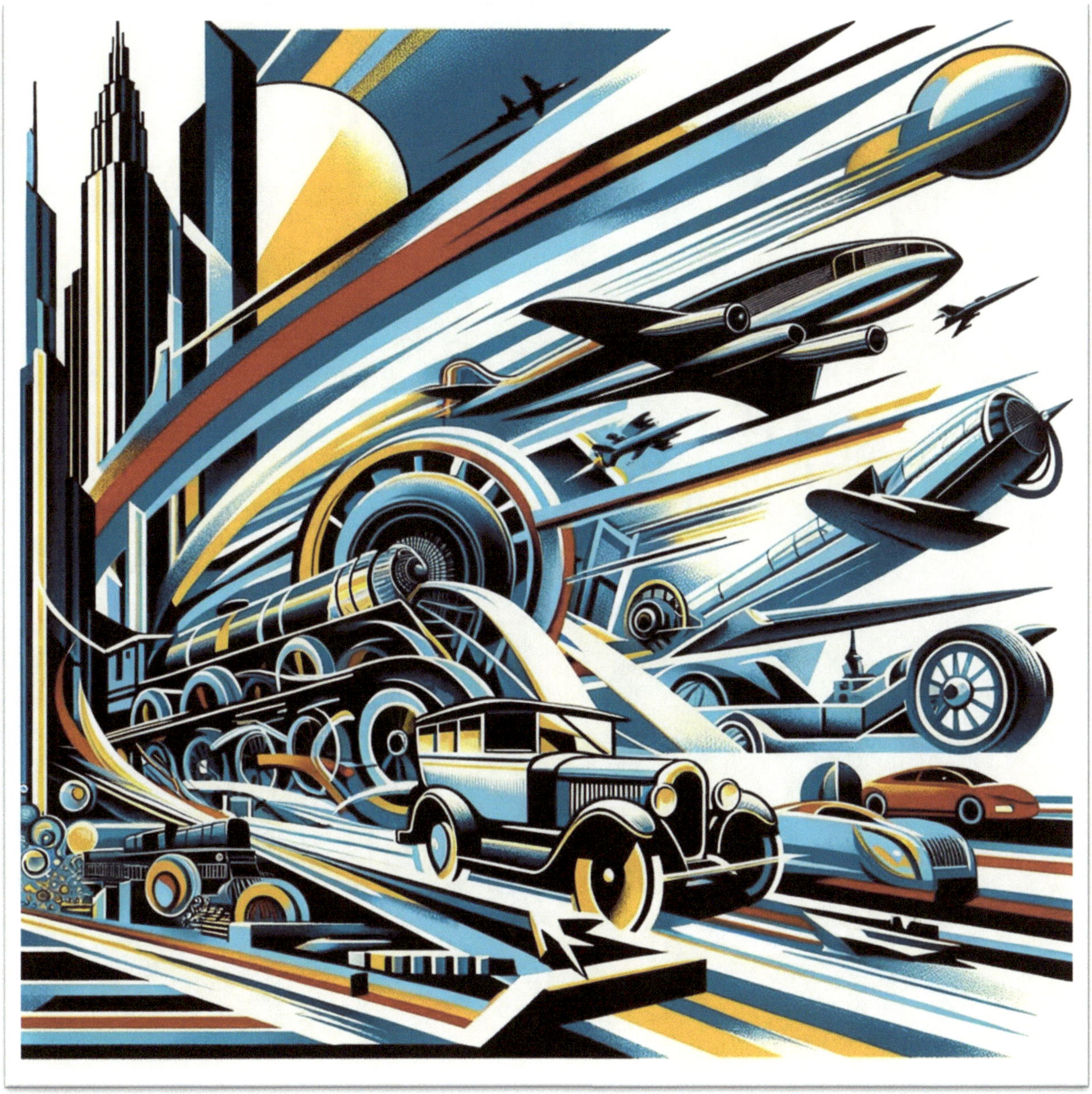

Dada (1916-1924)

This artwork embodies Dada, a movement marked by its disdain for conventional art and its embrace of absurdity. Dadaists used non-traditional materials and random methods to challenge the status quo, reflected here in the chaotic assembly of everyday objects. This piece uses a collage of disparate elements to create a complex, visually striking composition that criticizes materialism and traditional artistic values, embracing chaos and the irrational as a form of protest against the rationalism that led to war.

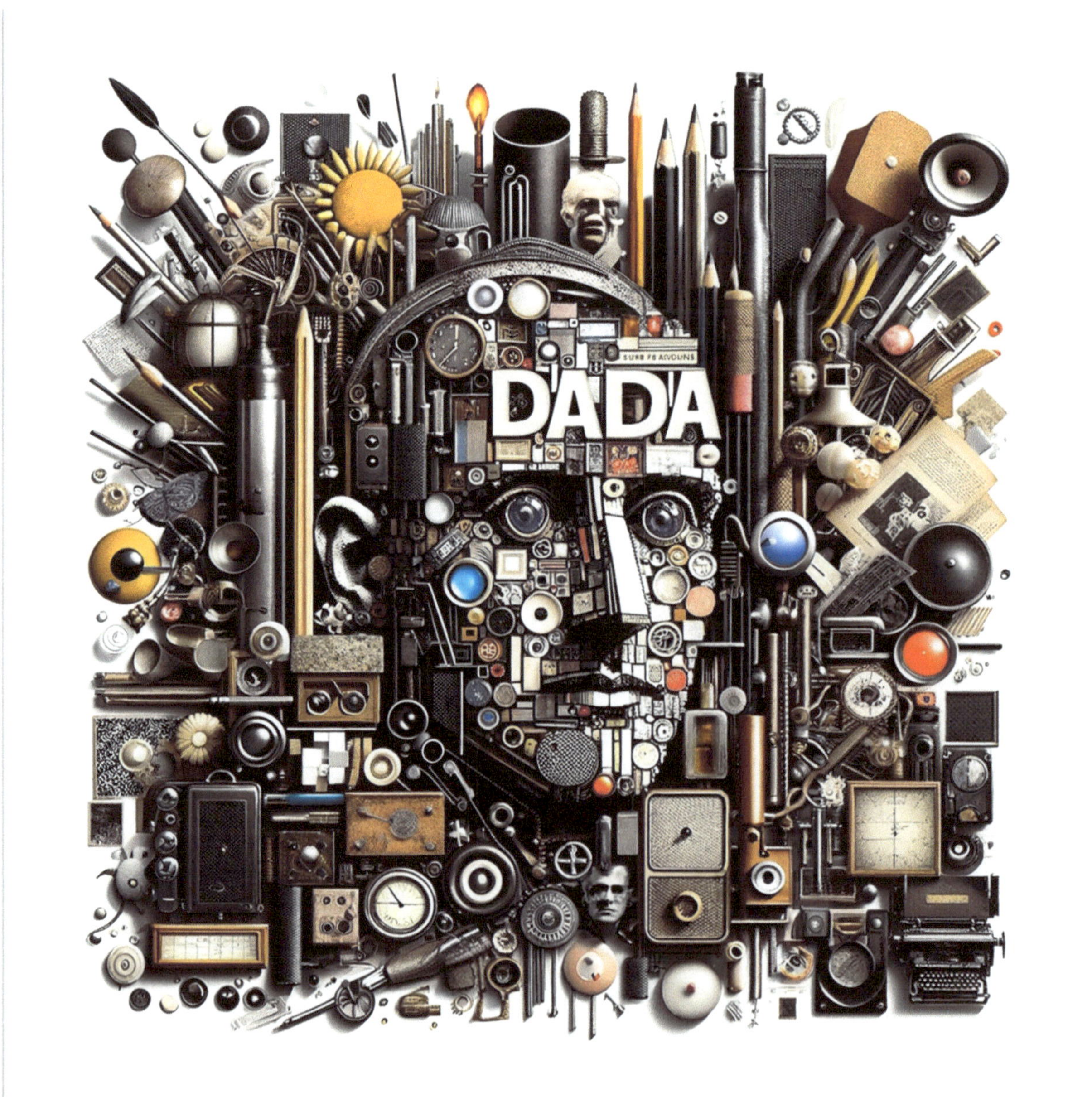

Surrealism (1920s)

This artwork is a quintessential representation of Surrealism, a movement from the 1920s known for exploring the unconscious mind through dream-like scenes and bizarre, illogical imagery. Surrealism blends reality with fantasy, as seen in the intricate, imaginative landscapes and the juxtaposition of familiar objects in unfamiliar contexts. This piece uses meticulous detail and surreal combinations to provoke thought and explore deeper truths, challenging the viewer's perception of reality.

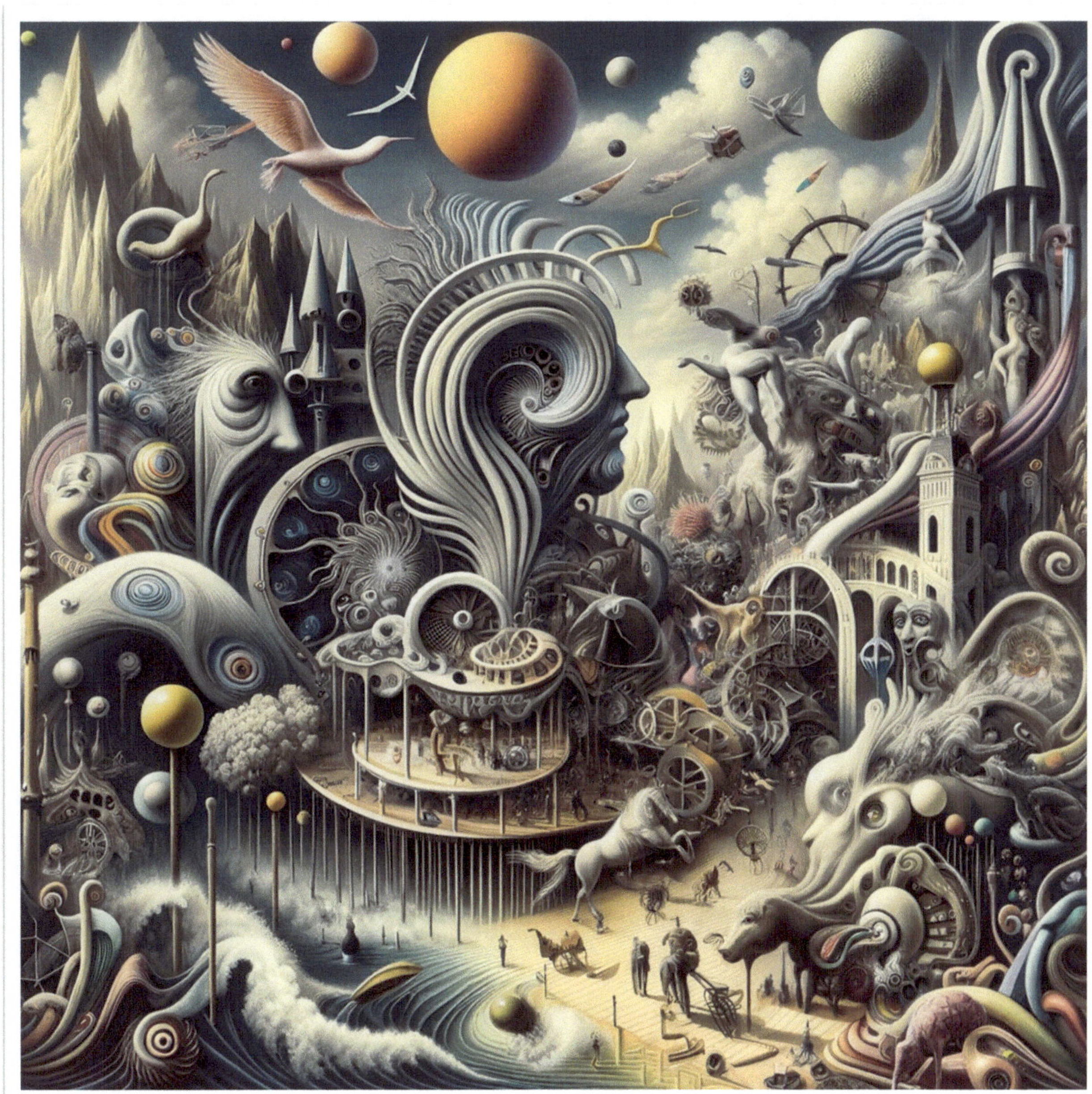

Abstract Expressionism (1940s-1950s)

This artwork exemplifies Abstract Expressionism, a movement from the 1940s and 1950s focused on conveying emotion through spontaneous, abstract forms. Abstract Expressionists prioritized individual expression and the act of painting itself. This piece features dynamic, sweeping brushstrokes and a vivid interplay of colors and forms, capturing the intensity and drama characteristic of the movement. It invites an emotional and subjective response, emphasizing the artist's freedom in both technique and expression.

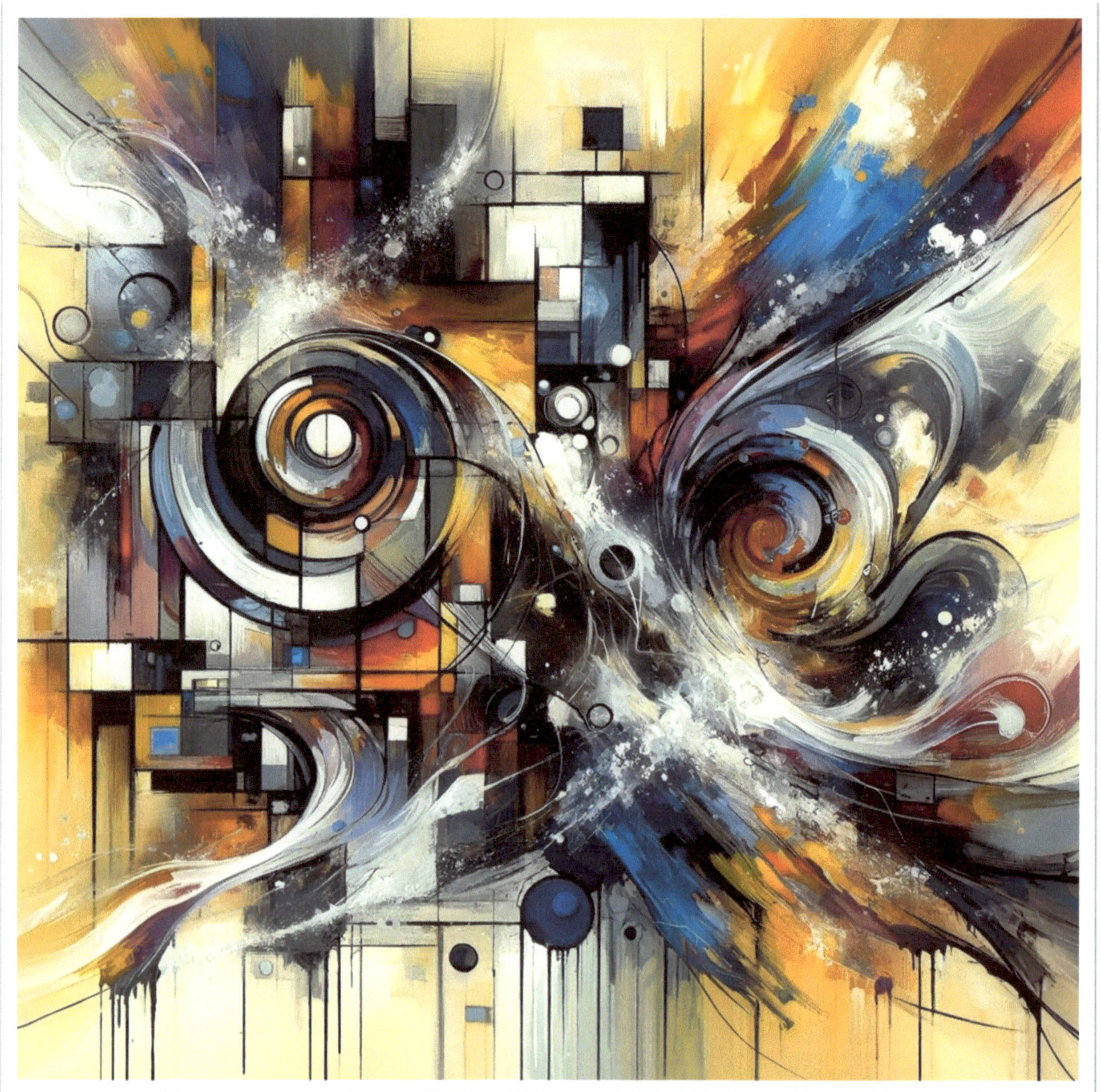

Pop Art (1950s-1960s)

This vibrant collage is quintessential Pop Art, a movement that emerged in the 1950s and 1960s, characterized by its embrace of mass culture and consumerism. Pop Art often repurposes commercial imagery and everyday objects, reflecting and critiquing the post-war boom in consumer culture. This artwork employs a bold, graphic style drawn from advertising and comic books, using bright colors and popular cultural icons to create a visually striking, ironic commentary on contemporary society.

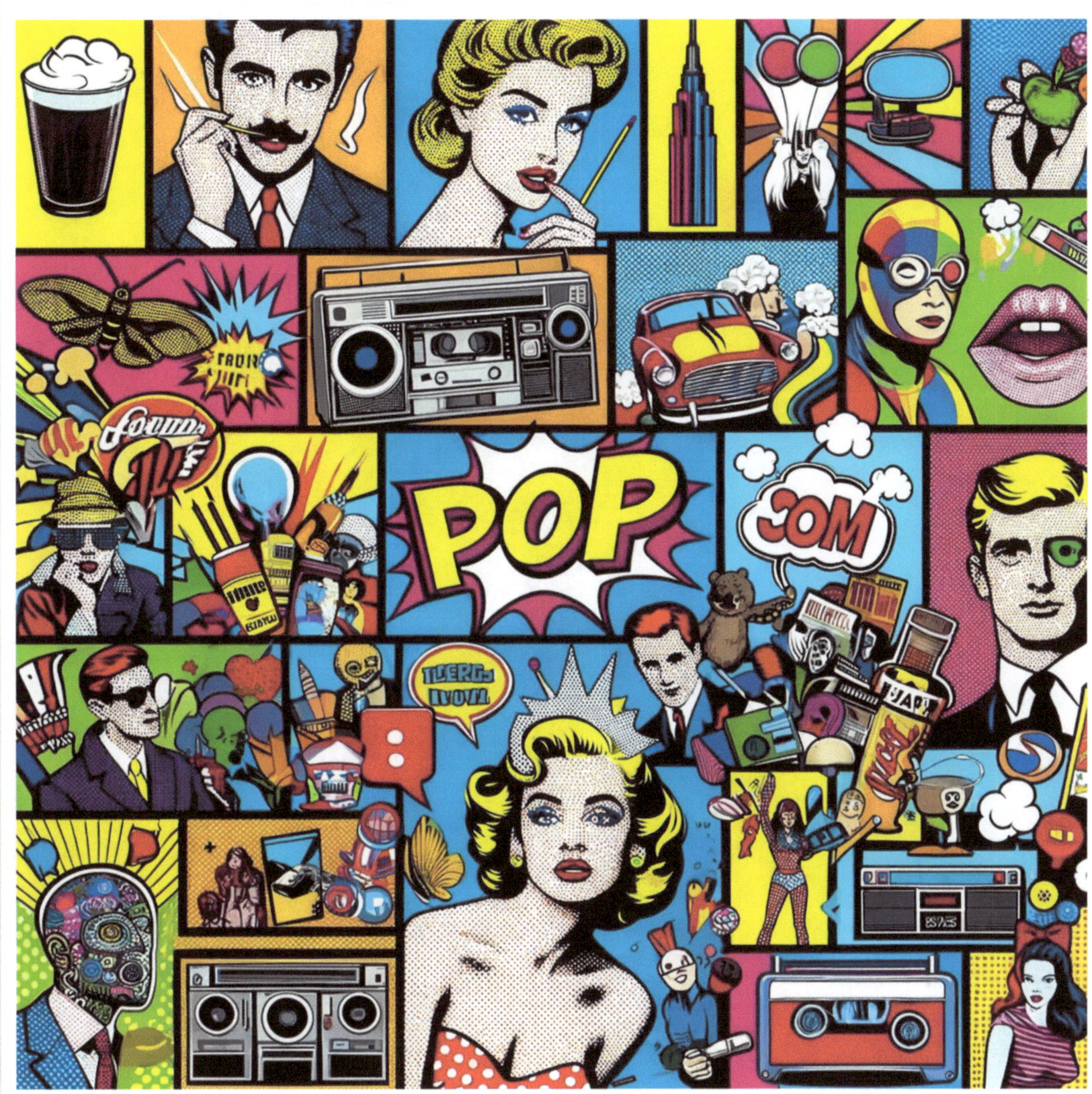

Minimalism (1960s-1970s)

This piece exemplifies Minimalism, a movement from the 1960s and 1970s focused on simplicity and abstraction. Minimalism strips away the non-essential, using geometric shapes and monochromatic palettes to highlight the purity of the form. This artwork, featuring a serene arrangement of cubes, rectangles, and a sphere in a muted color scheme, emphasizes form and space, inviting contemplation on the object itself, devoid of any representational content.

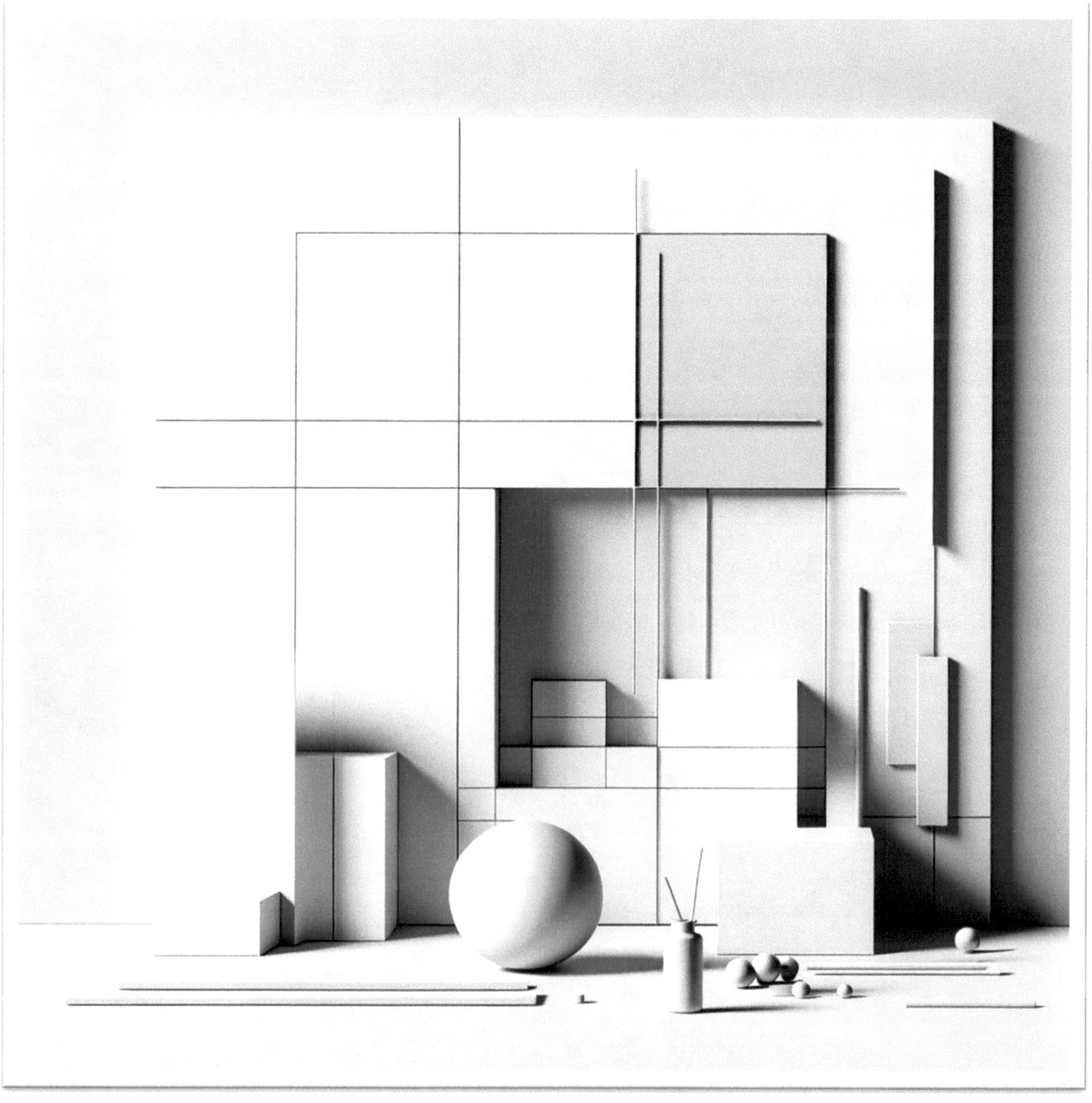

Postmodernism (late 20th century)

This artwork illustrates Postmodernism, a late 20th-century movement known for its eclectic approach and challenging traditional boundaries. Postmodern art often incorporates pastiche, irony, and a bricolage of styles and media. This piece densely layers historical and cultural references, blending classical and contemporary elements to critique or celebrate complexity and contradiction in modern society. It uses surreal juxtapositions and rich detail to question the notion of a single, unified perspective, embodying postmodernism's diverse and inclusive ethos.

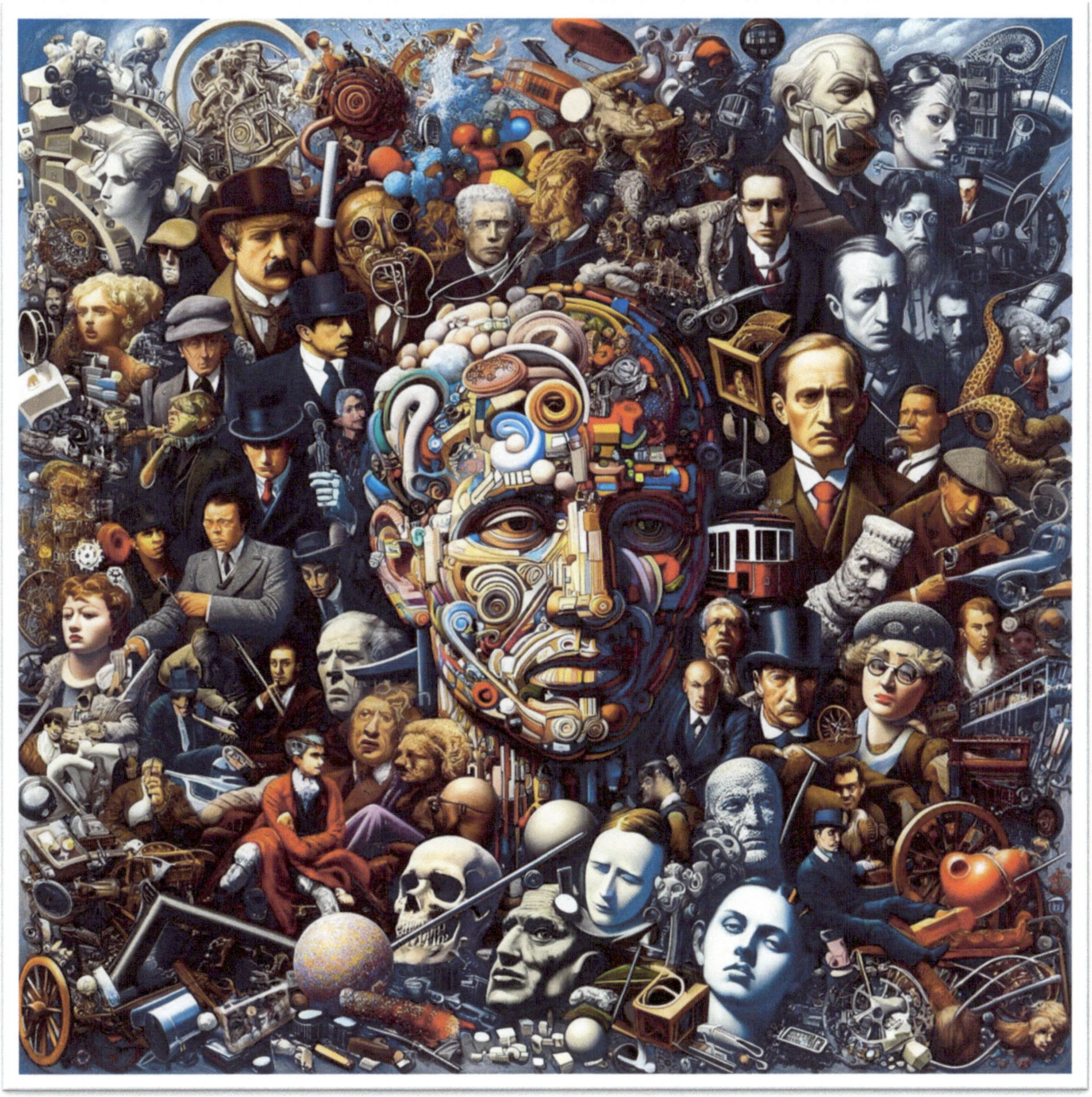

Contemporary Art (late 20th century - present)

This piece is emblematic of Contemporary Art, which often explores global and digital realities, combining diverse cultural and technological elements. The artwork features a complex assemblage of symbols from various eras and technologies, emphasizing connectivity and the impact of globalization. It uses a hyper-detailed, almost overwhelming collage style to reflect on how modern lives are intertwined with technology, media, and historical narratives, capturing the chaotic essence of contemporary existence in a visually rich tableau.

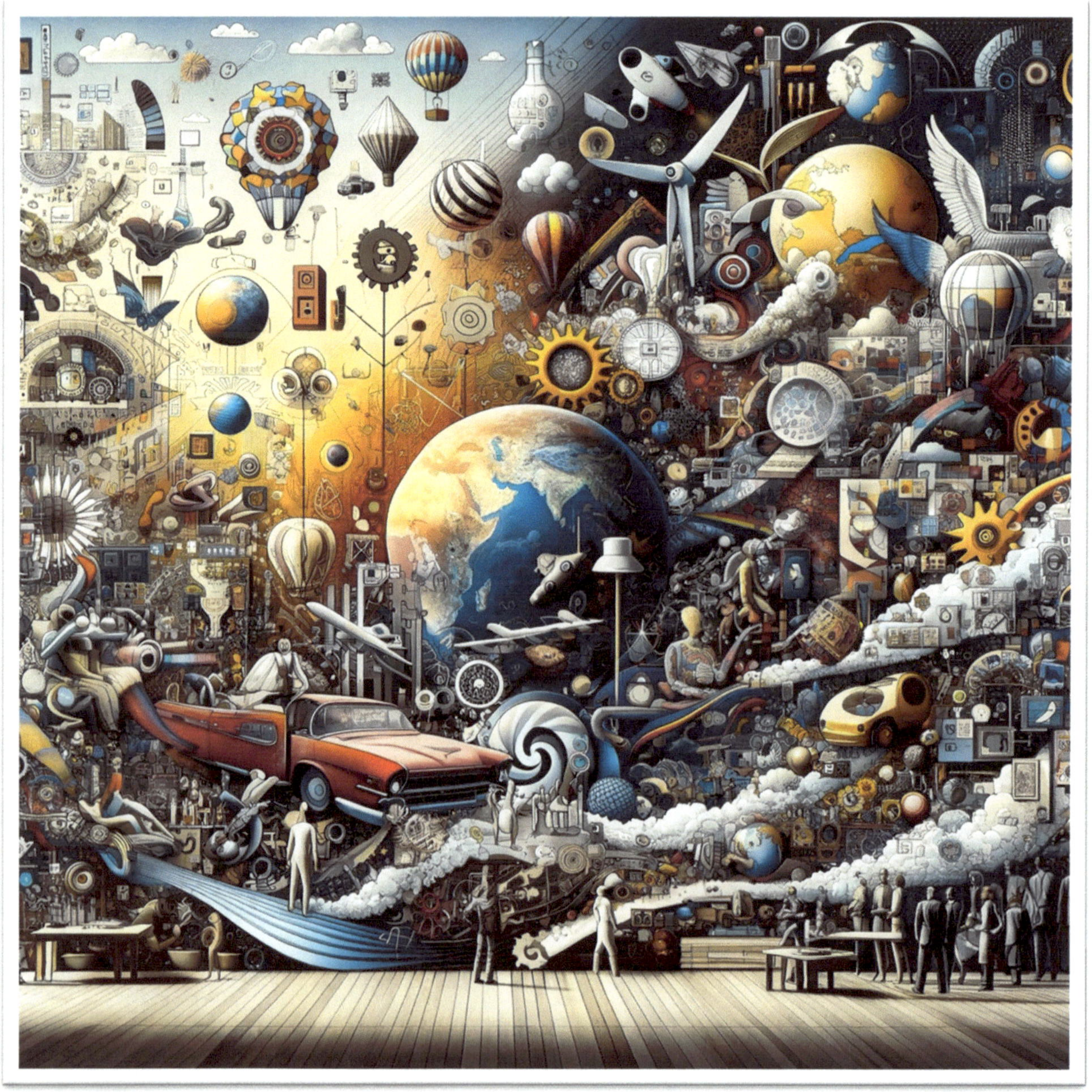

Contours of Expression: Impressionism, Cubism, and Surrealism

In the ever-evolving landscape of art history, certain movements not only reflect the aesthetic tendencies of their times but also pioneer new visions that challenge and expand our understanding of reality and perception.

This section of the book, "Contours of Expression," delves into the rich and complex worlds of Impressionism, Cubism, and Surrealism—three movements that have indelibly shaped the visual arts. Each of these styles introduces a distinct approach to the interplay of form, color, and concept, revealing the multifaceted nature of artistic expression.

- **Impressionism**, emerging in the late 19th century, marks a departure from the rigidity of academic painting, favoring instead the fleeting qualities of light and color through loose brushwork and open compositions. This movement captures moments as if they were glimpses through the artist's eyes, prioritizing spontaneity and sensory experience over detailed accuracy.

- **Cubism**, born in the early 20th century and led by pioneers such as Pablo Picasso and Georges Braque, breaks away from conventional perspectives. It deconstructs familiar objects and figures into abstracted forms, often viewed simultaneously from multiple angles. This radical approach not only altered the course of artistic expression but also influenced how viewers perceive the physical world.

- **Surrealism**, which took the stage in the 1920s, dives into the world of the unconscious mind, exploring dreams, bizarre juxtapositions, and illogical scenes. This movement seeks to unlock the power of the imagination to disrupt the everyday and explore the irrational, with artists like Salvador Dalí and René Magritte leading the charge.

By examining these three pivotal movements, we gain insight into the artists' challenges to traditional boundaries and their quests for new means of expression. This exploration not only enriches our appreciation of their historical impact but also illuminates their ongoing influence in contemporary artistic discourse.

Impressionism: Key Characteristics

Impressionism, a revolutionary art movement that emerged in the late 19th century, is celebrated for its distinctive approach to painting, which broke away from the conventions of traditional art. One of the hallmark characteristics of Impressionist artwork is the application of loose, visible brushstrokes that give a sense of immediacy and movement to the depicted scenes. Artists in this movement utilized vivid, pure colors, often placing them side by side on the canvas without much blending to achieve a vibrant, luminous effect. This technique allowed them to capture the fleeting qualities of light, showcasing how its presence could transform a scene at different times of day. Moreover, Impressionists turned their attention to the ordinary subject matter, drawing inspiration from everyday life and its myriad, often overlooked, beauties. From bustling city streets to tranquil countryside scenes, Impressionist paintings invite viewers to see the world through a lens that appreciates the momentary, sensory experience of life.

Impressionism: Summary of Key Characteristics

- ✓ **Visible Brush Strokes**: Impressionist paintings often display loose, visible brushstrokes.
- ✓ **Vivid Colors:** This style is known for its use of pure, unblended colors, often applied side by side with little mixing.
- ✓ **Emphasis on Light:** Impressionist artists were fascinated with the effects of light and often depicted scenes at different times of day.
- ✓ **Ordinary Subject Matter:** The focus is often on ordinary subject matter, like scenes of everyday life.

Impressionism: Effective Prompts

To craft a detailed and precise prompt for generating an artwork in the style of Impressionism that showcases appreciable creativity, consider the following variations. Each variation aims to capture the essence of Impressionism, a style known for its emphasis on light, movement, and everyday subjects, painted with visible brush strokes to capture the momentary, sensory effect of a scene. Each of these prompts is designed to guide GenAI in creating artworks that are not only reflective of the Impressionist style but also filled with creativity and emotional depth, true to the spirit of capturing the impression of a moment.

Diving deeper into the world of Impressionism, remember that the magic lies in the subtleties. As you explore these prompts, let the nuances of color, the play of light, and the fluidity of movement inspire your creative direction. Impressionism isn't just about what you see; it's about what you feel. By embedding your prompts with sensory details and emotional undertones, you encourage GenAI to transcend the mere replication of style, venturing into the realm of artistic innovation and expression.

This approach honors the tradition of Impressionism and paves the way for new interpretations and discoveries, making each artwork a unique conversation between artist, viewer, and the timeless language of art.

1. **Luminous Landscape at Sunrise**

   Prompt: "Create an artwork in the Impressionist style that depicts a lush, vibrant landscape at sunrise. The scene should be filled with a soft, golden light casting long shadows and reflecting off a tranquil river. Use loose, visible brushstrokes to capture the fleeting moment, emphasizing the interplay of light and color. Include elements such as blooming wildflowers and a distant, misty forest to enhance the depth and texture."

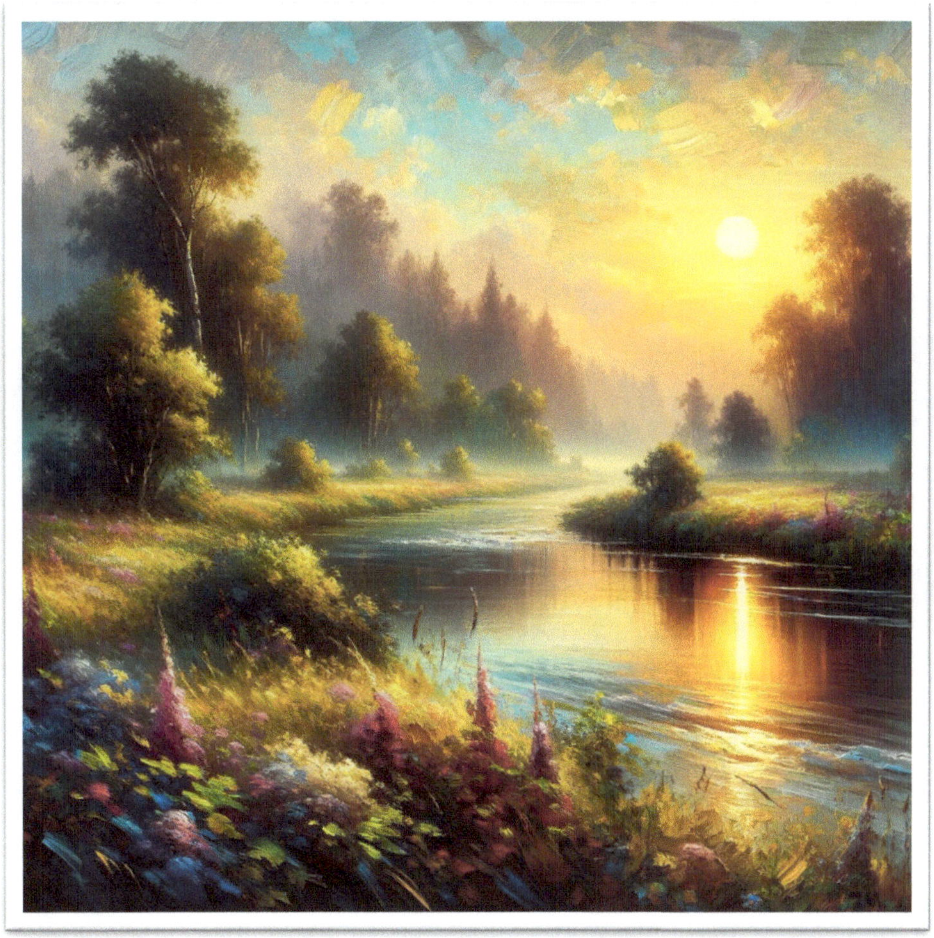

2. **Bustling City Street Scene**

Prompt: "Craft an artwork reflecting the Impressionist style, showcasing a bustling city street in the late afternoon. The painting should capture the dynamic movement of people and carriages, with the setting sun casting a warm, diffused light across the scene. Focus on using quick, thick brushstrokes to convey the vibrancy and energy of urban life, incorporating vivid colors and the effect of shifting light on buildings and the street."

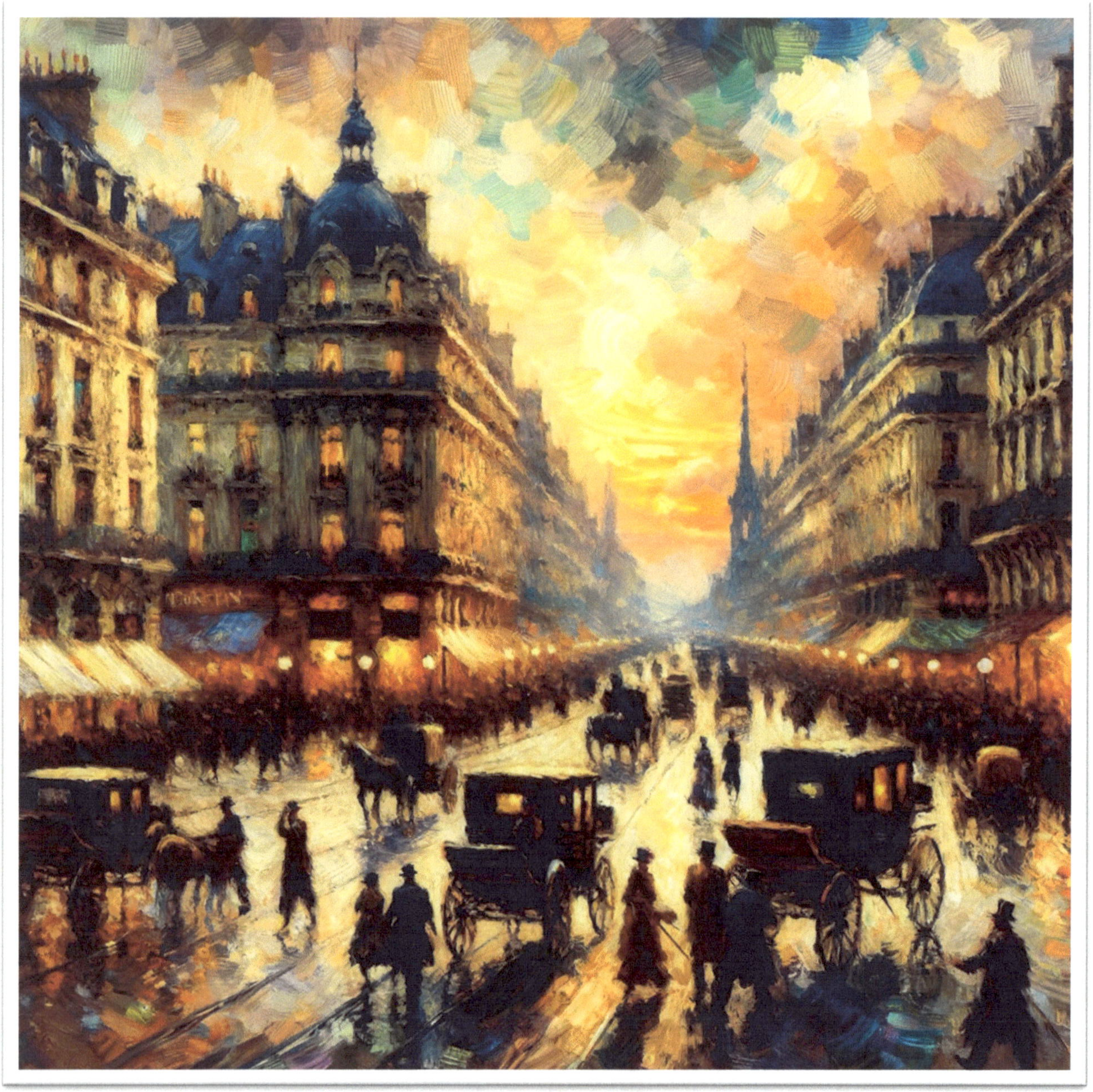

3. **Seaside Impression at Dusk**

   Prompt: "Design an artwork in the Impressionist style that captures the serene beauty of a seaside scene at dusk. Highlight the changing colors of the sky as it transitions from blue to shades of pink, orange, and purple, reflecting on the gentle waves. Employ spontaneous, textured brushstrokes to depict the movement of the water and the soft, fading light. Add figures on the shore in harmony with the landscape to convey a sense of peaceful coexistence with nature."

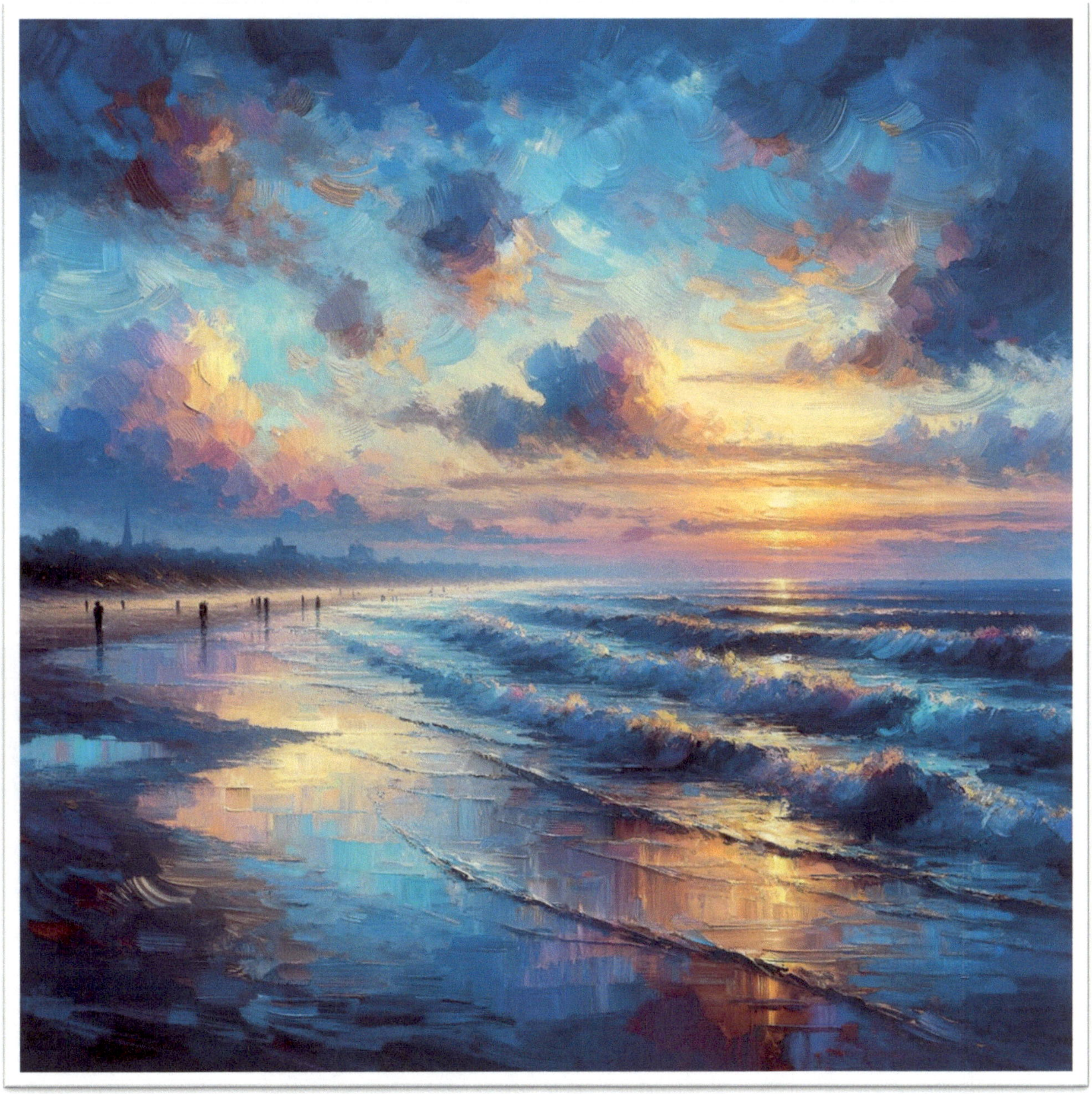

4. **Intimate Garden in Full Bloom**

   Prompt: "Generate an artwork using the Impressionist approach, focusing on an intimate garden scene in full bloom under the bright midday sun. The painting should burst with a spectrum of colors from various flowers and plants, captured with quick, dappled brushstrokes to create a lively, textured surface. Aim to evoke the warmth of the sun and the cool shadows cast by trees, creating a balanced composition that invites the viewer to experience the garden's tranquil beauty."

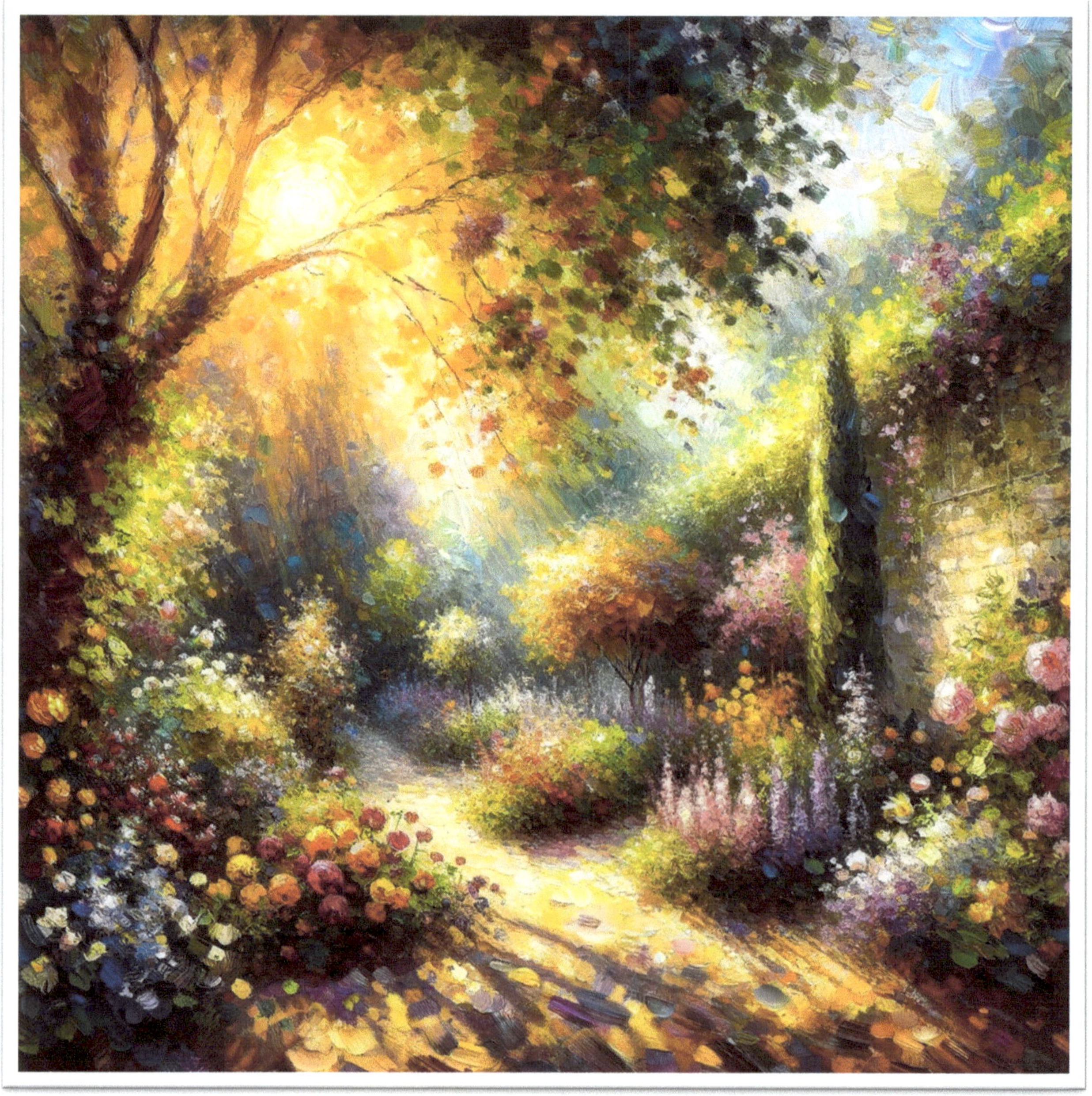

Impressionism I

This artwork depicts a modern cityscape in the style of Impressionism.

Challenge: Imagine the series of prompts that the artist supplied to the GenAI tool to achieve this output.

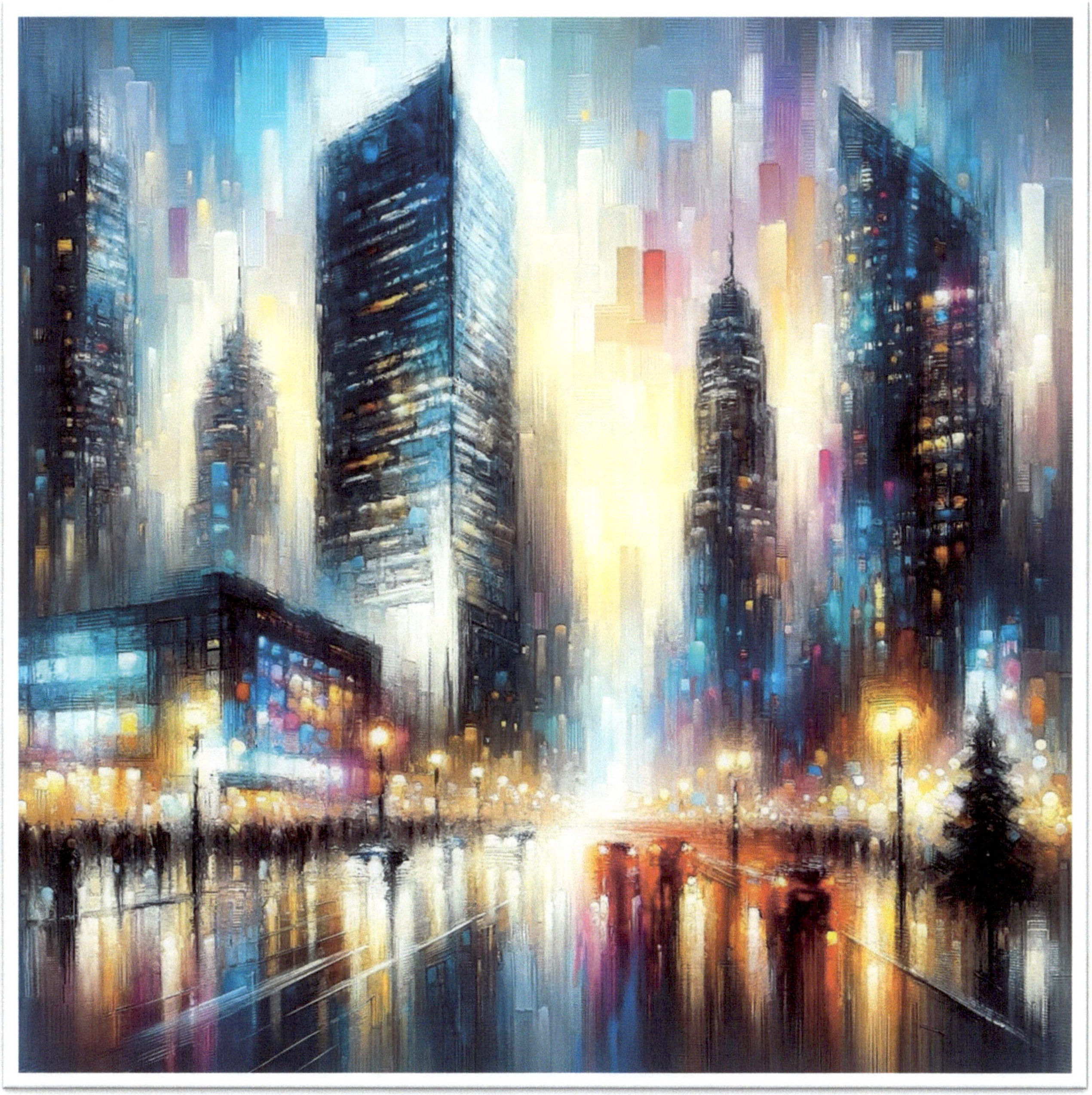

Impressionism II

This is a companion artwork depicting a modern cityscape in the style of Impressionism. To achieve this iteration the artist added subtle descriptors to the prompt.

Challenge: Use your GenAI tool to create a new image that an art critic would consider to be a companion artwork that be join the collection with Impressionism I and Impressionism II.

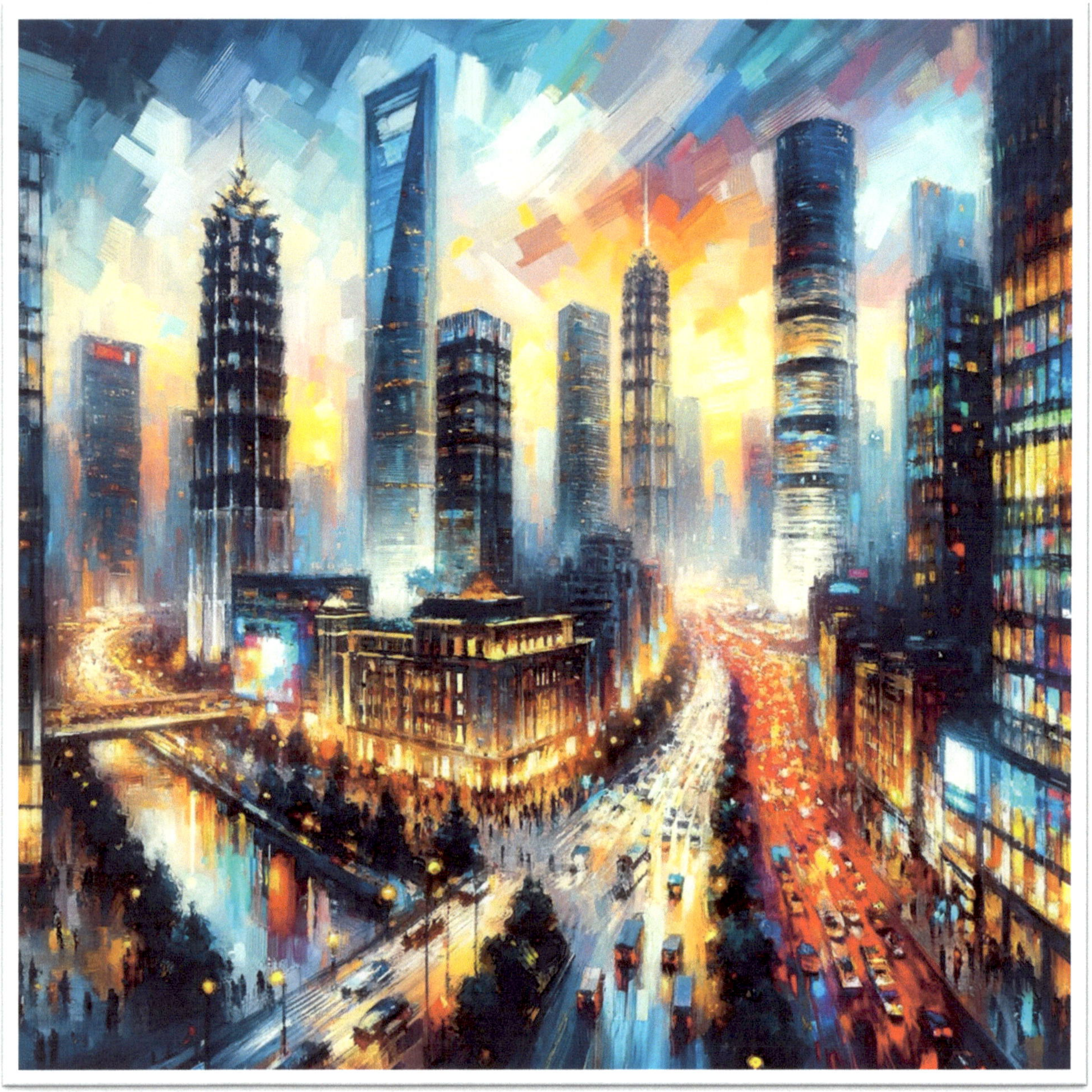

Cubism: Key Characteristics

Cubism, an avant-garde art movement that flourished in the early 20th century, introduced a radical new approach to representation that challenged conventional perspectives of art and reality. At the heart of Cubism is the innovative use of geometric shapes; artists deconstructed objects and figures into cubes, rectangles, and other geometric forms, reassembling them in abstracted compositions that defy traditional viewpoints. This style is characterized by a profound abstraction, where reality is not merely depicted but is instead distorted and reinterpreted, often merging multiple perspectives within a single piece to offer a more dynamic understanding of the subject. Cubists typically favored a limited color palette, eschewing the bright hues of Impressionism in favor of more subdued tones like browns, grays, and blacks, which further emphasized the structure and form over color. Additionally, Cubism was among the first movements to embrace collage, incorporating mixed media elements into their works to blur the lines between painting and sculpture, and between art and life. Through these innovations, Cubism challenged viewers to reconsider their perception of the world, making it one of the most influential movements in modern art.

Cubism: Summary of Key Characteristics

- ✓ **Geometric Shapes:** Cubism is marked by the use of geometric shapes. Images are broken down into cubes, rectangles, and other geometric forms.

- ✓ **Abstract Representation:** This style often abstracts and distorts reality, sometimes combining different perspectives in a single artwork.

- ✓ **Limited Color Palette:** The color palette in Cubism is often subdued, with a focus on browns, grays, and blacks.

- ✓ **Collage Elements:** Some Cubist works incorporate mixed media or collage elements.

Cubism: Effective Prompts

Crafting a prompt for GenAI to create artwork in the Cubist style involves specifying elements that characterize Cubism, such as geometric abstraction, multiple viewpoints, and fragmentation.

Below are four variations of how you might invoke Cubism to craft a detailed and precise prompt. Each of these prompts provides a clear description of what is desired from GenAI's output, ensuring that the resulting artwork reflects the unique aspects of Cubism while also demonstrating appreciable creativity.

1. **Geometric Abstraction and Fragmentation**

   Prompt: "Create an artwork in the Cubist style that features a cityscape. Use geometric shapes to abstractly represent buildings, streets, and vehicles. Incorporate fragmented elements to depict different perspectives of the city simultaneously, emphasizing sharp angles and contrasting colors to highlight the multifaceted nature of urban life."

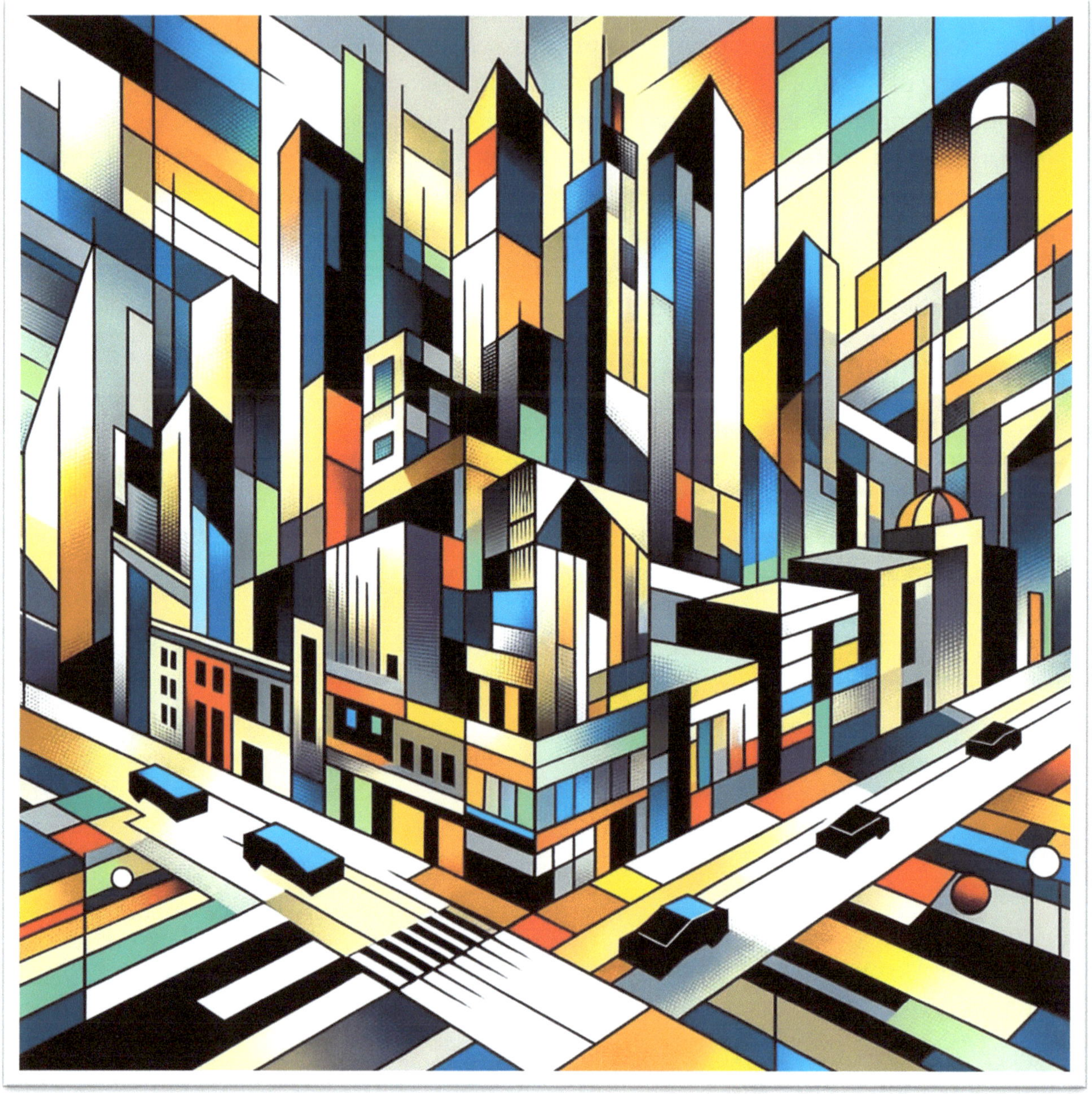

2. **Cubist Portrait with Multiple Viewpoints**

   Prompt: "Design a Cubist portrait of a figure using a palette of blue, gray, and brown. Fragment the face and body into geometric shapes, presenting multiple viewpoints within a single composition. Emphasize the interplay of light and shadow to add depth, and include abstracted elements that hint at the subject's personality or background."

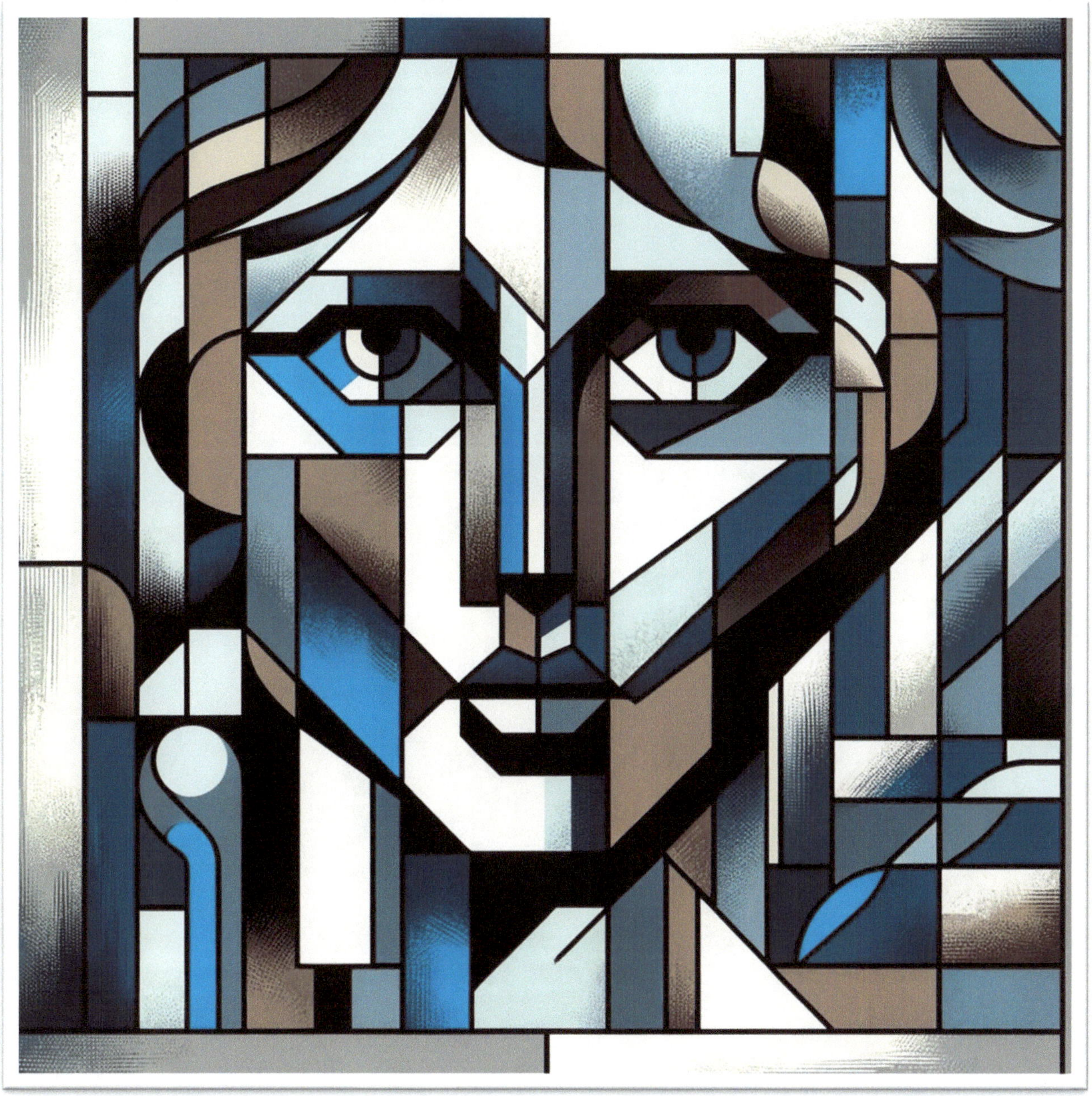

3. **Still Life with Cubist Influence**

Prompt: "Construct a still life in the Cubist style, focusing on everyday objects such as a fruit bowl, a wine bottle, and a guitar. Break these objects into their basic geometric forms, showcasing them from various angles in a single, cohesive piece. Use a muted color scheme with splashes of vibrant red or yellow to draw attention to specific elements, creating a dynamic yet harmonious composition."

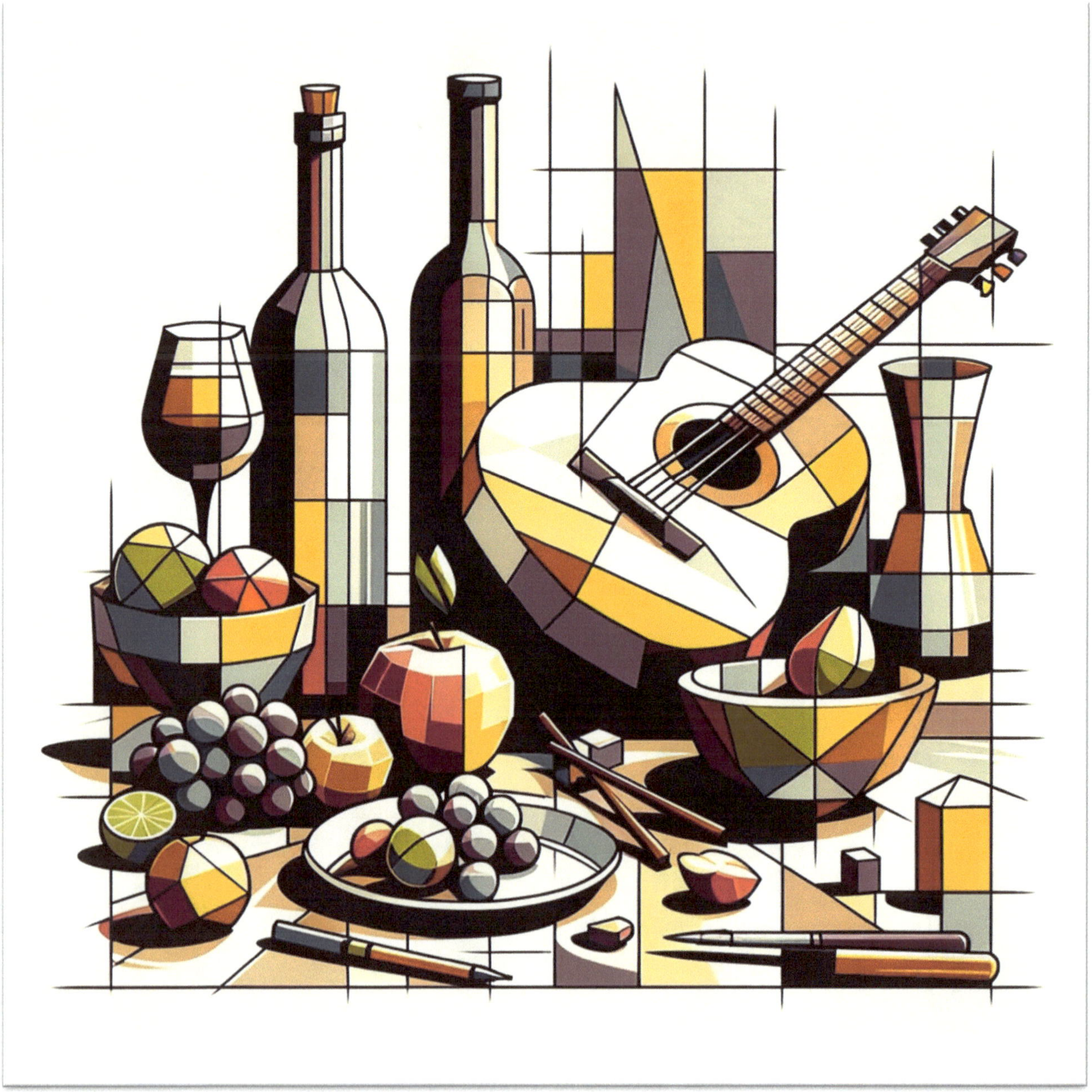

4. Cubist Landscape with Layered Perspectives

Prompt: "Generate a landscape artwork influenced by Cubism, depicting a natural scene with trees, a river, and mountains. Apply a layered approach, with geometric shapes overlapping to form the landscape's components, offering a fragmented yet recognizable view of nature. Utilize a mix of cool and warm colors to distinguish between different layers and perspectives, blending abstraction with hints of realism."

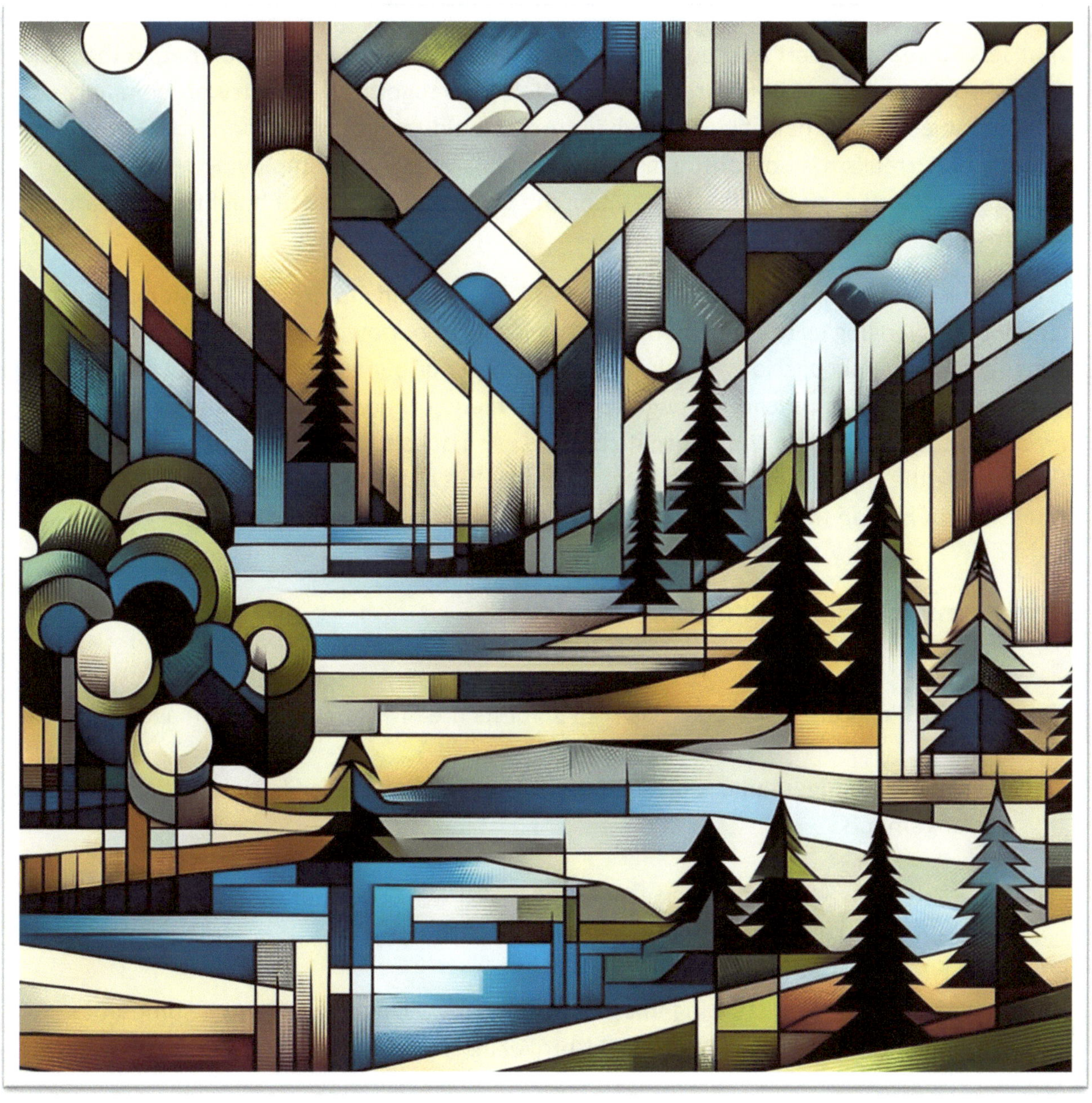

Surrealism: Key Characteristics

Surrealism stands as a beacon of creativity and imagination in the art world, having burst onto the scene in the early 20th century. This movement invites us on an extraordinary journey into the depths of dreams and the unconscious mind, crafting landscapes that stretch beyond the confines of ordinary life. With its hallmark of fantastical and dream-like imagery, Surrealism opens the door to a world unbound by the rational laws that dictate our day-to-day existence. Here, objects and figures take on bizarre and irrational arrangements, painting scenes that elude logical explanation and wrap the viewer in an enigmatic aura.

What sets Surrealism apart is its audacious approach to combining elements that, in the real world, would never meet. This daring juxtaposition knits together a tapestry of seemingly disparate objects into a narrative that, while surreal, holds an intrinsic coherence. The visual language of Surrealism is not for the faint-hearted; it is vivid, often employing elements designed to disturb or shock, thus catapulting the viewer into a state of heightened awareness and introspection.

Surrealism is more than just an art movement; it is a profound inquiry into the human condition, challenging us to confront the hidden facets of our own minds. It encourages a dialogue with our subconscious, inviting us to question our perceptions of reality and delve into the complexities of the psyche. Through its unique blend of the bizarre and the beautiful, Surrealism doesn't just depict dreams; it compels us to question the very nature of reality itself. In embracing the surreal, we find not just an escape, but a deeper understanding of the myriad dimensions of human thought and emotion.

Surrealism: Summary of Key Characteristics

- ✓ **Dream-like Scenes:** Surrealism is known for its dream-like, fantastical imagery.
- ✓ **Irrational Arrangements:** Objects and figures are often placed in irrational, unexpected arrangements.
- ✓ **Juxtaposition of Unrelated Elements:** Surrealist works frequently combine elements that don’t usually go together in reality.
- ✓ **Vivid, Sometimes Disturbing Imagery:** The imagery can be vivid and is sometimes intended to be disturbing or thought-provoking.

Surrealism: Effective Prompts

Surrealism stands as a profound exploration of the mind's untapped territories, offering a lens through which the ordinary world is transformed into a realm of extraordinary visions. At its core, Surrealism is not merely an art movement; it is a gateway to liberating the boundless creativity nestled within the unconscious mind. This movement thrives on the creation of bizarre, dream-like scenes that challenge the mundane constraints of logic and traditional aesthetics, inviting both creators and viewers alike to question the fabric of reality itself.

To navigate the vast landscapes of Surrealism, one must wield prompts like keys, unlocking the myriad doors behind which lie unexplored vistas of imagination. These prompts serve as conduits, guiding the generation of artwork that not only exhibits remarkable creativity but also embodies the quintessence of the Surrealist vision. With each variation, you are offered a passage into realms where the impossible not only becomes possible but is celebrated, blurring the once-clear demarcations between the real and the surreal.

Embracing Surrealism means to journey through the dreamscapes of the mind, where the familiar dissolves into the bizarre, and every image holds the potential to unsettle, provoke, and inspire. As you craft your prompts, think of them as brushes with which you paint upon the canvas of the AI's capabilities, encouraging it to dive into the depths of your imagination and bring forth visions steeped in the surreal.

These carefully constructed prompts are more than mere instructions; they are an invitation to the AI to traverse the uncharted territories of the subconscious, to challenge the perceived boundaries of reality, and to meld the ordinary with the extraordinary. In doing so, each piece of art generated becomes a narrative, a visual poem that speaks to the transformative power of the imagination when set free. Through this collaborative dance with GenAI, guided by the principles of Surrealism, each artwork promises to be not just a depiction, but a discovery—a vibrant testament to the endless possibilities that await when we dare to dream beyond the confines of the conventional.

As you embark on this journey through the dreamscapes of Surrealism, embrace the boundless realms of your imagination. These four variations are your gateway to worlds where the impossible becomes possible, where the line between the real and the surreal blurs into insignificance. Encourage GenAI to delve deep into the recesses of your creativity, drawing upon the rich tapestry of your subconscious.

1. **Dreamscape with Floating Elements**

   Prompt: "Create surrealistic artwork depicting a dreamscape where gravity seems to be defied. Imagine a landscape under a twilight sky, where islands float mid-air, and waterfalls run upwards. Trees with luminous leaves and wildlife with unexpected patterns roam freely. Use vivid, contrasting colors to enhance the dream-like quality, ensuring that the scene blends elements of the natural world with fantastical, impossible features."

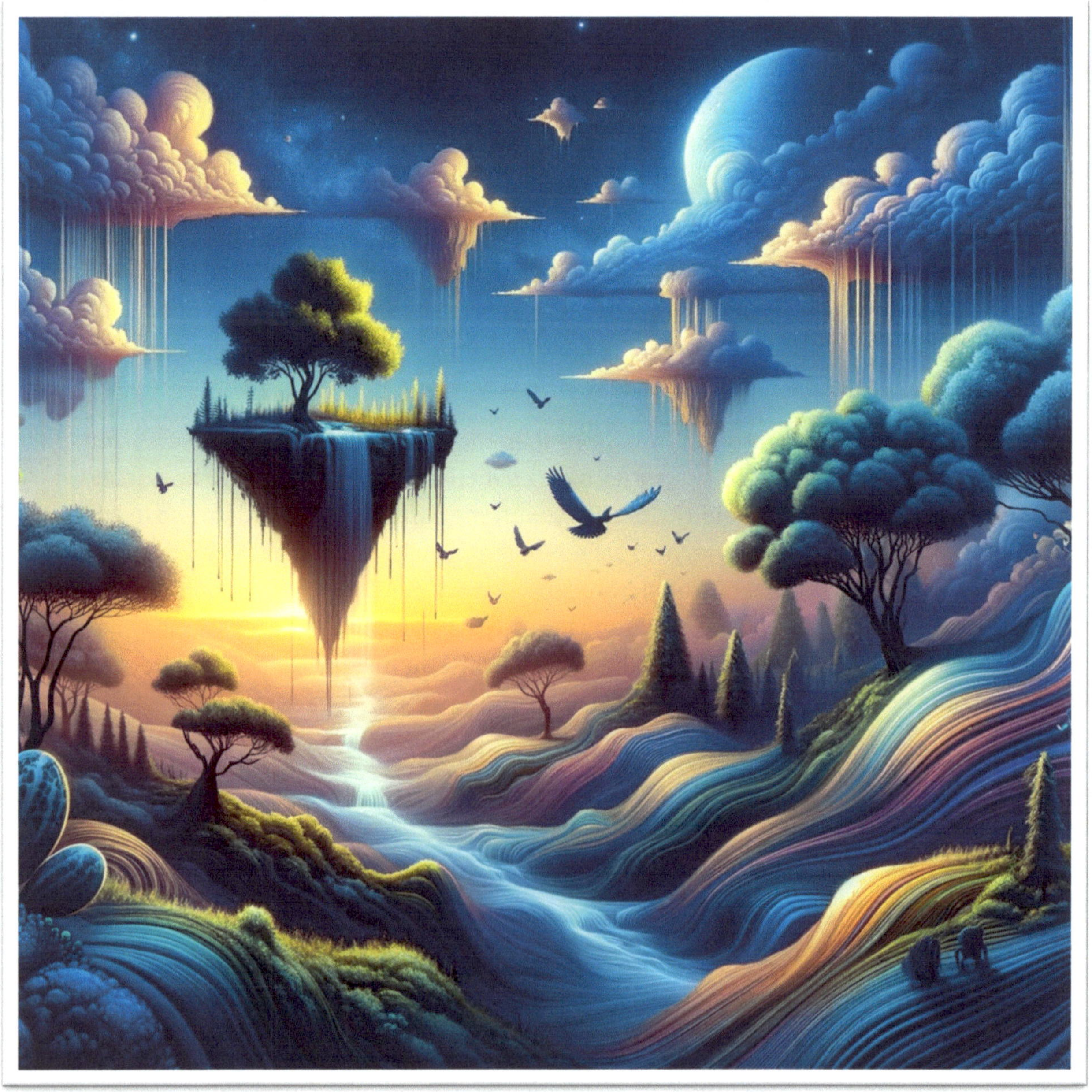

2. **Metamorphosis in a Timeless Void**

   Prompt: "Design a surreal artwork that showcases the theme of metamorphosis within a timeless void. Picture a space where human figures merge with elements of nature and machinery in unexpected ways, creating new forms of existence. This scene should challenge perceptions of reality, with a backdrop that transitions from organic textures to geometric shapes, suggesting a fluid, ever-changing universe."

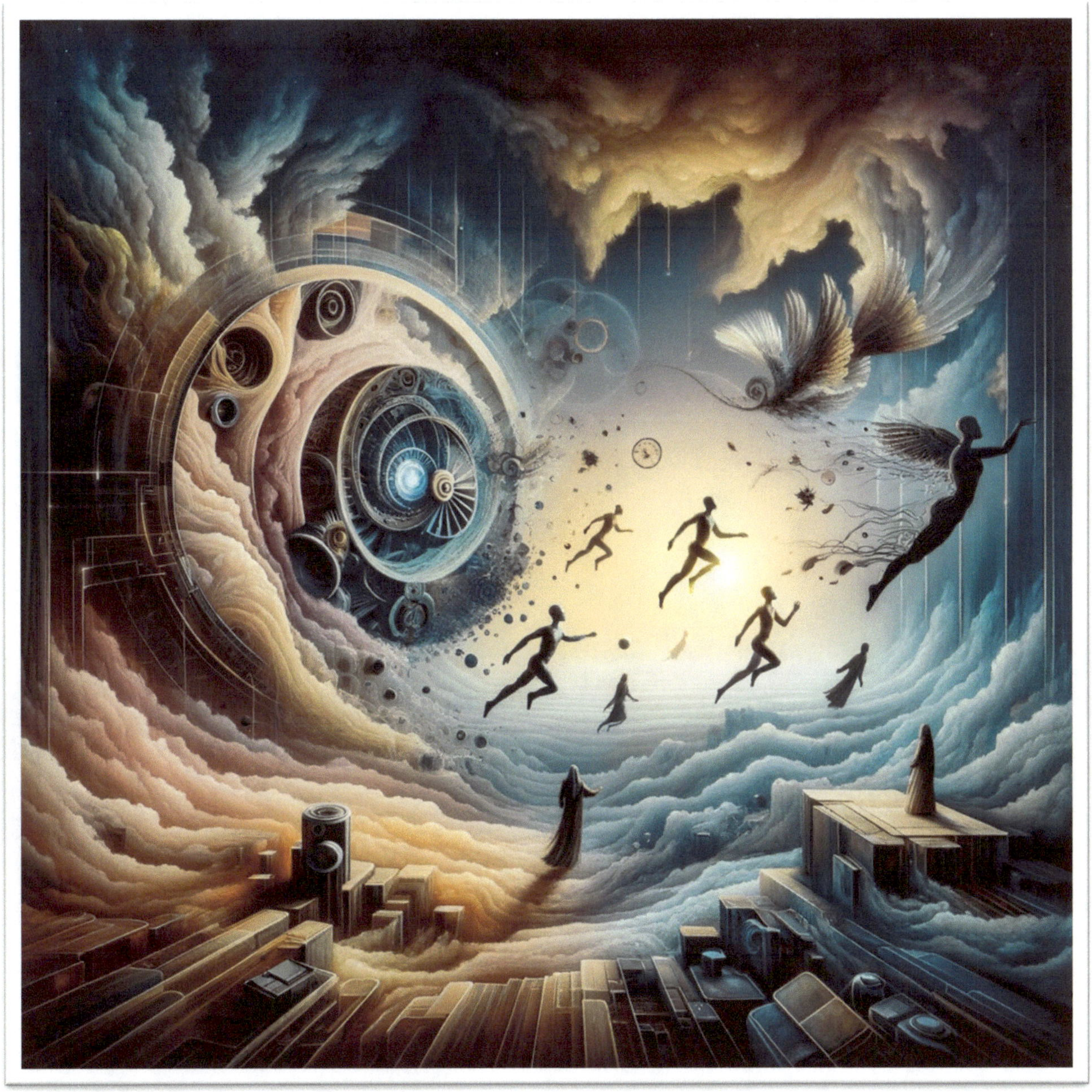

3. **Juxtaposition of the Mundane and the Extraordinary**

   Prompt: "Craft an artwork in the style of Surrealism that juxtaposes mundane everyday scenes with extraordinary, fantastical elements. A living room where the furniture defies physics, walls dissolve into open skies, and household objects transform into living creatures. This scene should provoke thought by blending the familiar with the bizarre, using a palette that adds a sense of unreality to the composition."

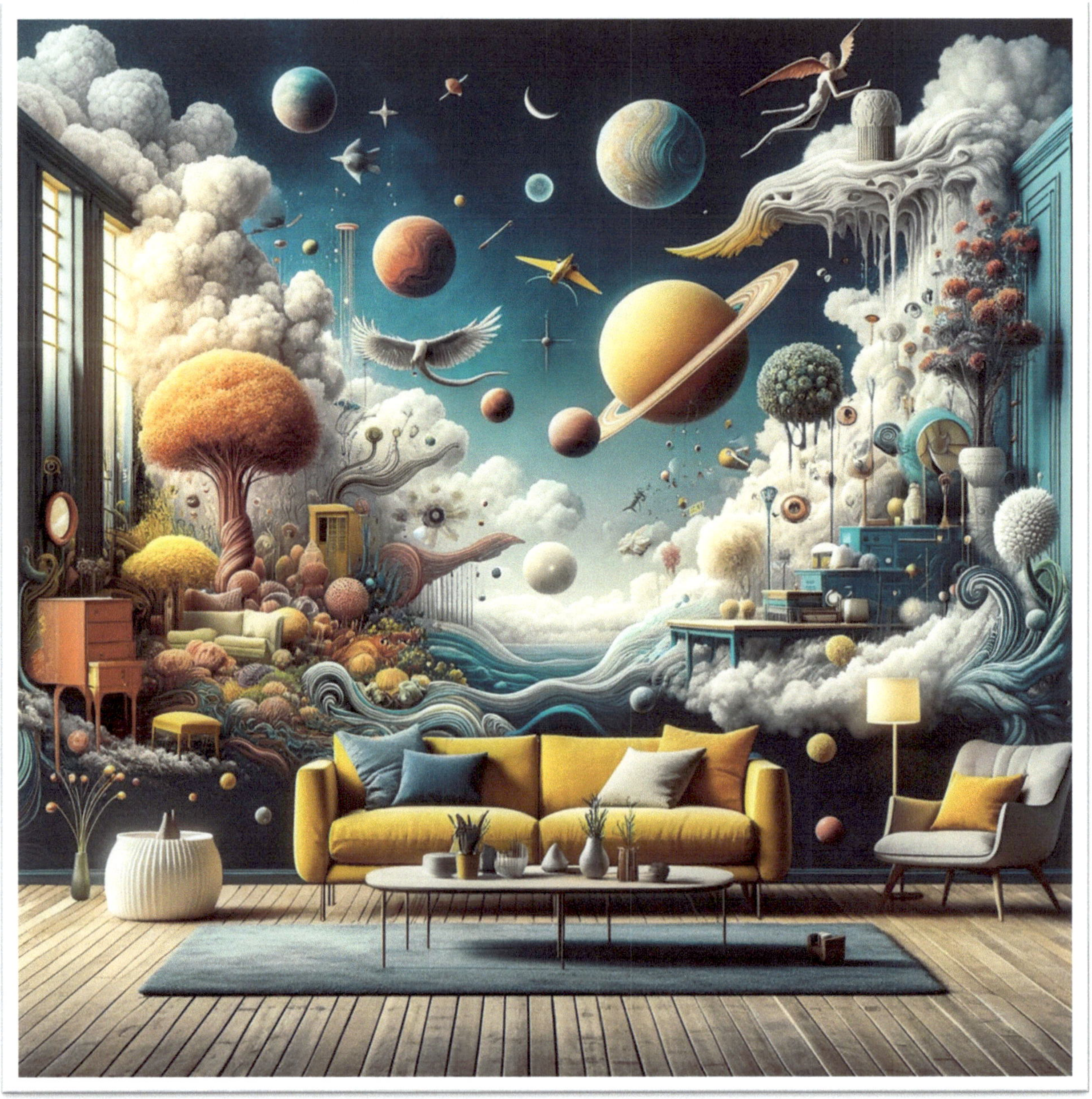

4. **Labyrinth of Mirrors Reflecting Alternate Realities**

   "Generate a surrealistic painting that explores a labyrinth of mirrors, each reflecting an alternate reality. This labyrinth is set in an ethereal landscape where the laws of physics and logic do not apply. Within it, characters navigate through paths that loop in impossible ways, encountering versions of themselves from different dimensions. Emphasize the use of light and shadow to create a sense of depth and mystery, making the viewer question what is real and what is reflection."

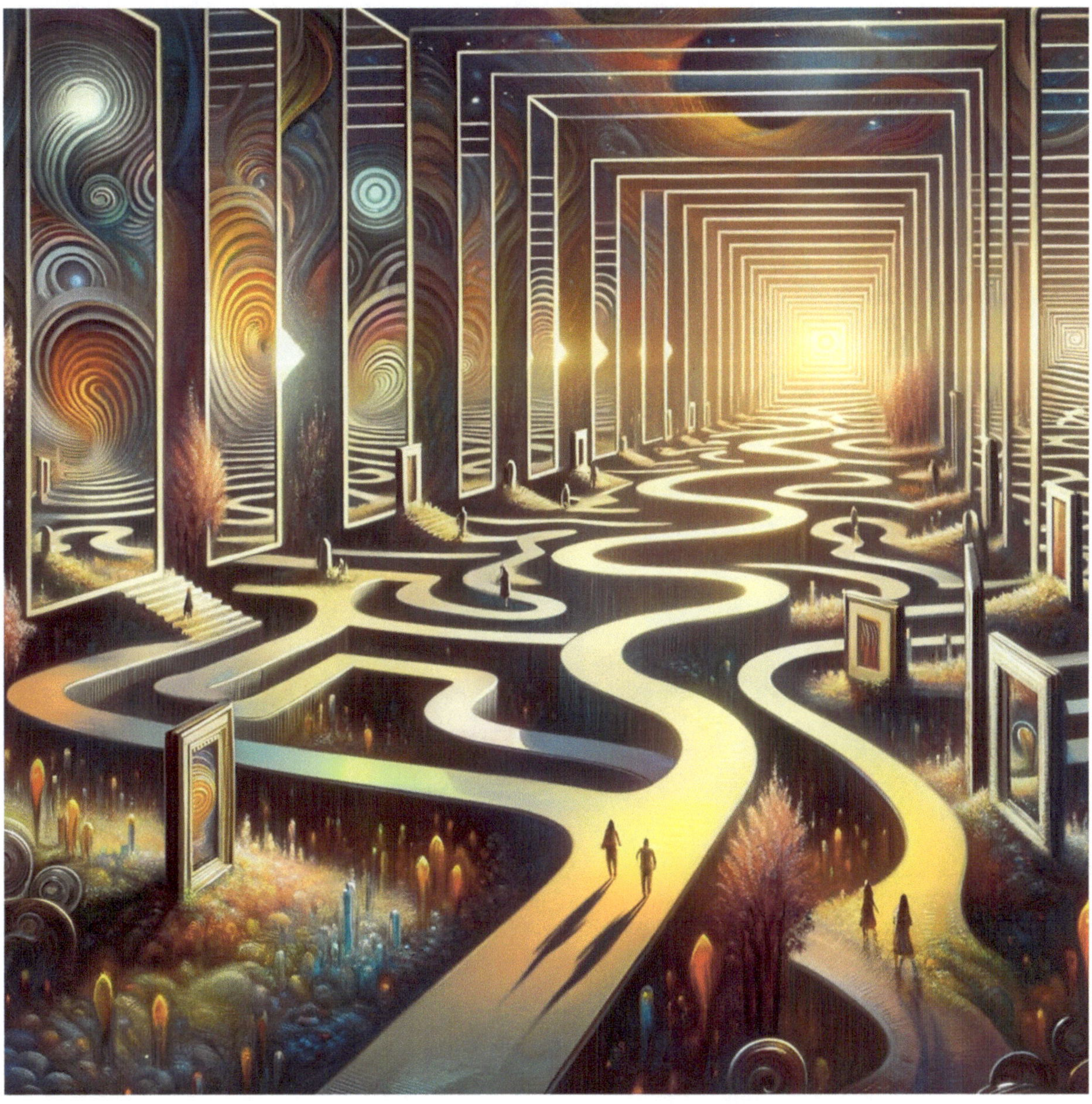

Adapting Styles and Modern Forms

You can use GenAI to adapt these styles into new forms.

Your challenge here, if you choose to accept it, is to analyze the image below and then devise a series of prompts to help GenAI achieve a comparable level of visual acuity.

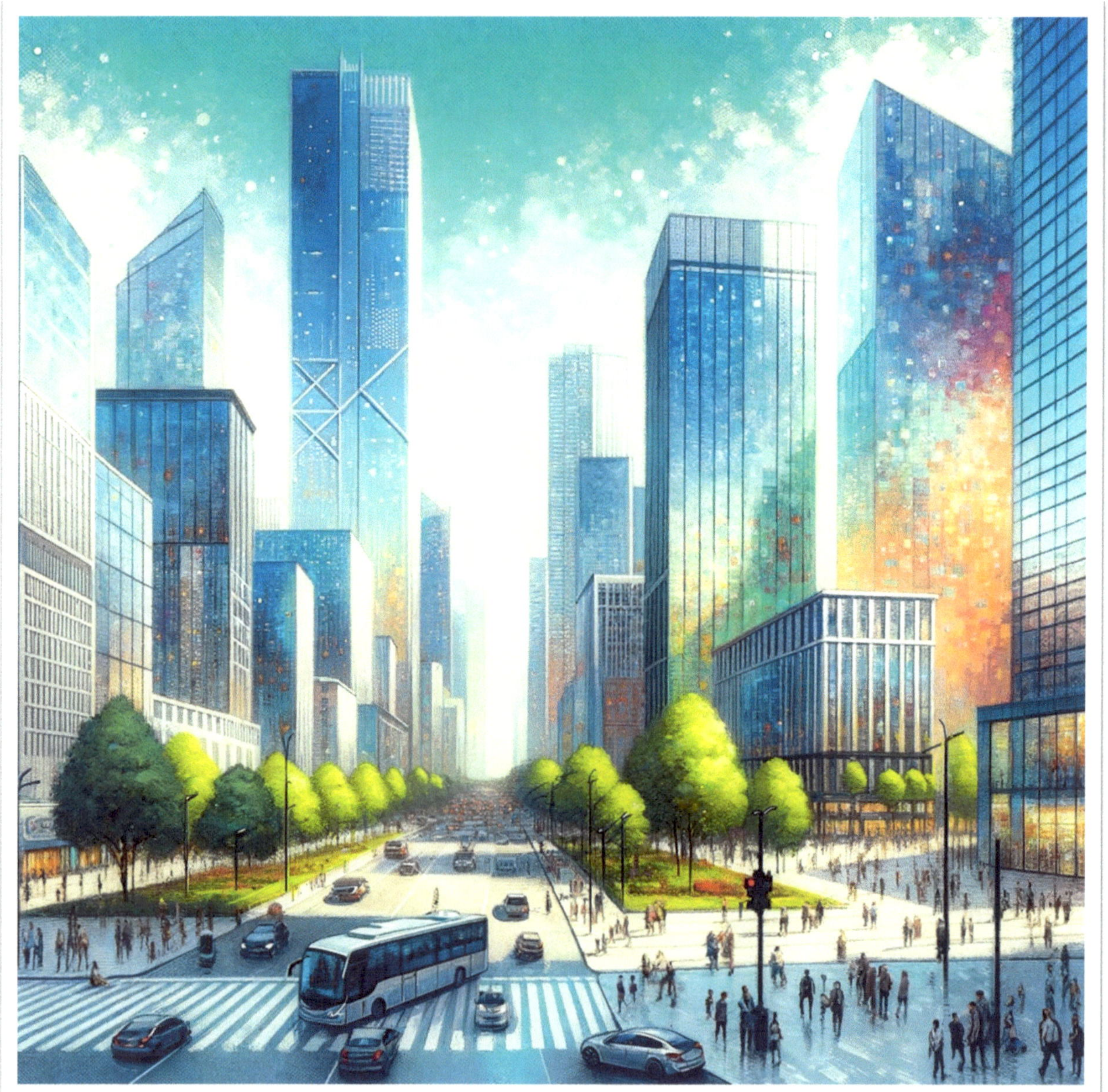

Regarding the above-described challenge, to guide an AI in creating substantially similar artwork, a series of detailed prompts that progressively build the scene could be used.

Here is how you might break it down:

1. **Basic Structure and Environment**

   Prompt: "Create an image of a wide, bustling urban street lined with modern skyscrapers. The street is filled with cars and a central bus lane. It's a clear day with a blue sky overhead. Include green trees along the sidewalks."

2. **Architectural Details**

   Prompt: "Add a variety of modern skyscrapers with glass facades that reflect the sky. Some buildings should feature unique structural designs, like cross bracing or irregular shapes. The buildings vary in height and are positioned to form a canyon-like street view."

3. **Activity and Life**

   Prompt: "Fill the sidewalks with diverse pedestrians walking or standing in groups. Some pedestrians are crossing the street. Include vehicles like cars and a city bus in the street, depicting a lively urban scene."

4. **Lighting and Atmosphere**

   Prompt: "Ensure the scene is brightly lit with sunlight that casts soft shadows on the buildings and street. Add a light haze to the atmosphere, making distant skyscrapers appear slightly obscured and dreamlike."

5. **Color and Texture**

   Prompt: "Use a palette of warm and cool colors for the building facades, creating a vibrant mosaic effect. The trees should be lush green, contrasting with the urban setting. The street should have reflections and subtle texture to show realism."

By providing these detailed prompts sequentially or as a single comprehensive prompt, an AI would have clear instructions on constructing an image that closely matches the original in terms of layout, detail, and mood.

Blending Traditional and Contemporary Art Concepts

In the realm of visual arts, the dialogue between the past and present has continually shaped the evolution of aesthetic expressions, giving rise to compelling syntheses of style, theme, and technique. This section, "Blending Traditional and Contemporary Art Concepts," explores the innovative intersections where classical art forms and modern visions converge, revealing the dynamic evolution of art through the ages. As we journey through the varied landscapes of art history and contemporary practices, we engage with the dual concepts of blending and iteration—key to understanding how artists today merge traditional techniques with modern ideas to create something wholly unique.

Blending and Iteration in Art

Blending in art refers to the seamless integration of elements from different styles, periods, or cultures to create new forms that resonate with both familiarity and innovation. This process involves taking identifiable features from historical art movements and amalgamating them with contemporary influences, thereby crafting artworks that speak to a broad spectrum of viewers across time.

Iteration, on the other hand, involves the repetitive process of refining and evolving art concepts or techniques. In the context of generative AI, iteration plays a crucial role as artists and programmers continuously refine prompts and algorithms to achieve the desired aesthetic output. Each iteration can introduce subtle changes that refine the blending of traditional cues with modern sensibilities, progressively enhancing the artwork's relevance and impact.

Exploring the Subtopics

1. **Renaissance-era Architectural Details Blended with Futurism**: This subtopic examines how the ornate and humanistic elements of Renaissance architecture can be reimagined through the lens of futuristic design principles, creating spaces that bridge time through form and function.
2. **Modern Interpretations of Classic Art**: Here, we delve into how contemporary artists reinterpret the masterworks of the past, infusing them with modern themes and techniques to comment on current societal issues or to reintroduce historical narratives in a new light.
3. **Thematic Exploration in AI Art**: This section explores how artificial intelligence can be used to develop new artistic themes by blending vast arrays of historical art data, enabling the creation of works that are both innovative and deeply rooted in traditional practices.

4. **Emotional and Conceptual Themes**: Focusing on the emotional depth and conceptual frameworks that guide the fusion of old and new artistic ideas, this subtopic highlights how artists convey timeless human emotions through a modern palette.
5. **Historical Style with Modern Elements**: Discussing specific examples where elements of historical art styles are fused with modern artistic expressions, this part showcases how this blend can both honor and transform the original works.
6. **Nature and Technology**: Reflecting on the juxtaposition and synthesis of the organic with the synthetic, artists today are creating works that highlight the complex relationship between the natural world and technological advancements.
7. **Cultural Fusion**: This subtopic addresses the merging of artistic elements from diverse cultures, which not only enriches the artistic tapestry but also fosters a greater understanding and appreciation of global cultural diversity.
8. **Abstract and Realism Mix**: Investigating how the abstract manipulation of forms and colors can be intertwined with realistic elements to create visually striking and intellectually engaging artworks.

Through this exploration of blending traditional and contemporary art concepts, we gain insight into how artists and creators utilize historical contexts and modern technologies, such as generative AI, to push the boundaries of artistic expression. This iterative blending process not only respects and revitalizes our cultural heritage but also propels it into new realms of relevance and beauty.

Renaissance-era Architectural Details Blended with Futurism

Initial Prompt: "Illustrate a futuristic scene with Renaissance-era architectural details."

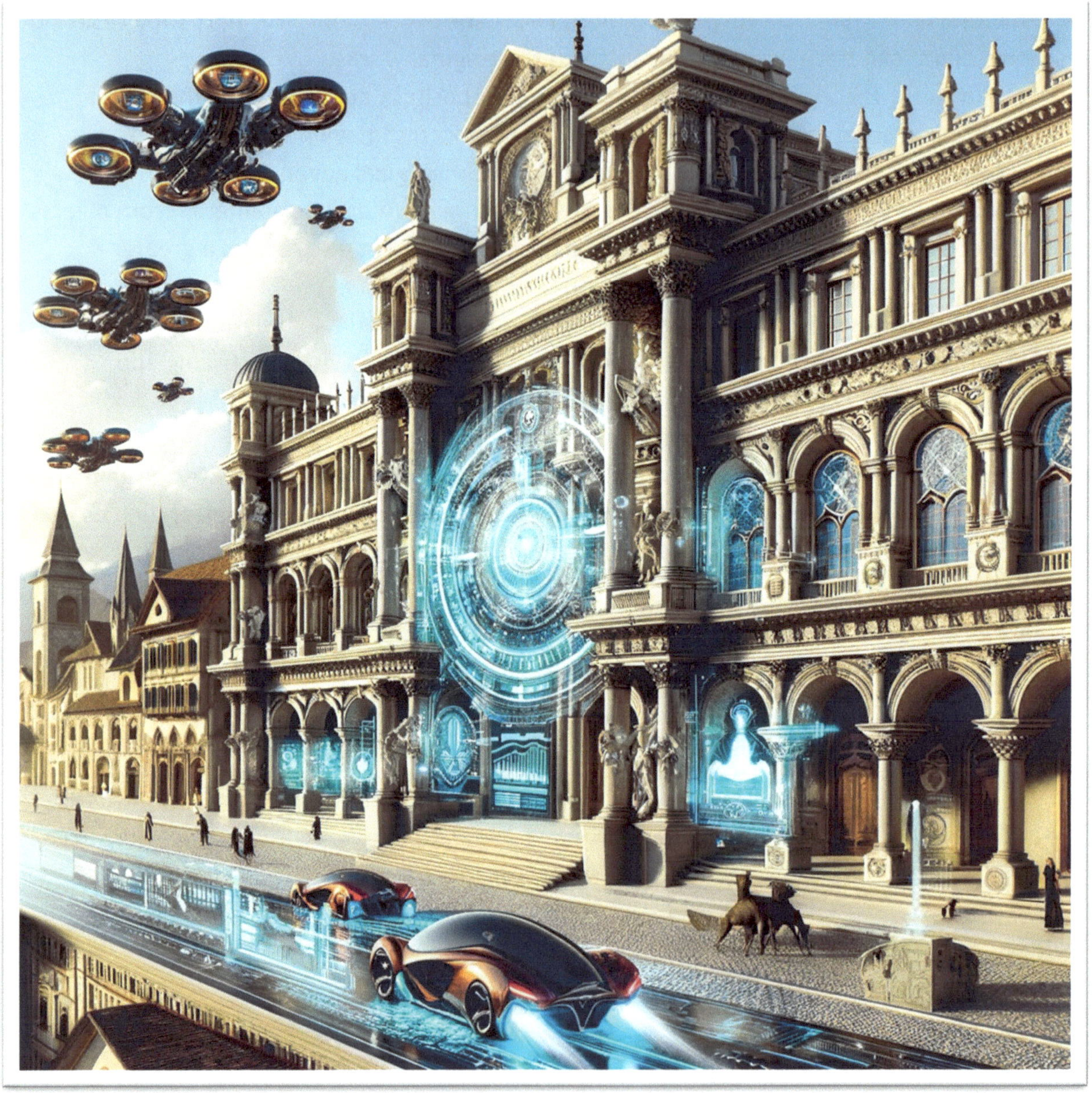

Blending and iteration explained: The process of blending and iteration appears to have involved the meticulous integration of various visual elements to create a cohesive scene that juxtaposes historical architecture with advanced technology. The artist has gone through several iterations, adjusting the placement of futuristic vehicles, the intricate holograms, and the flying objects to achieve a believable fusion that respects the perspective and lighting of the classical setting. Each iteration refines the details and the overall composition, ensuring the image is both aesthetically striking and thematically consistent.

Modern Interpretations of Classic Art

Initial Prompt: "Render an image that depicts a contemporary digital art version of Van Gogh's Starry Night with neon colors."

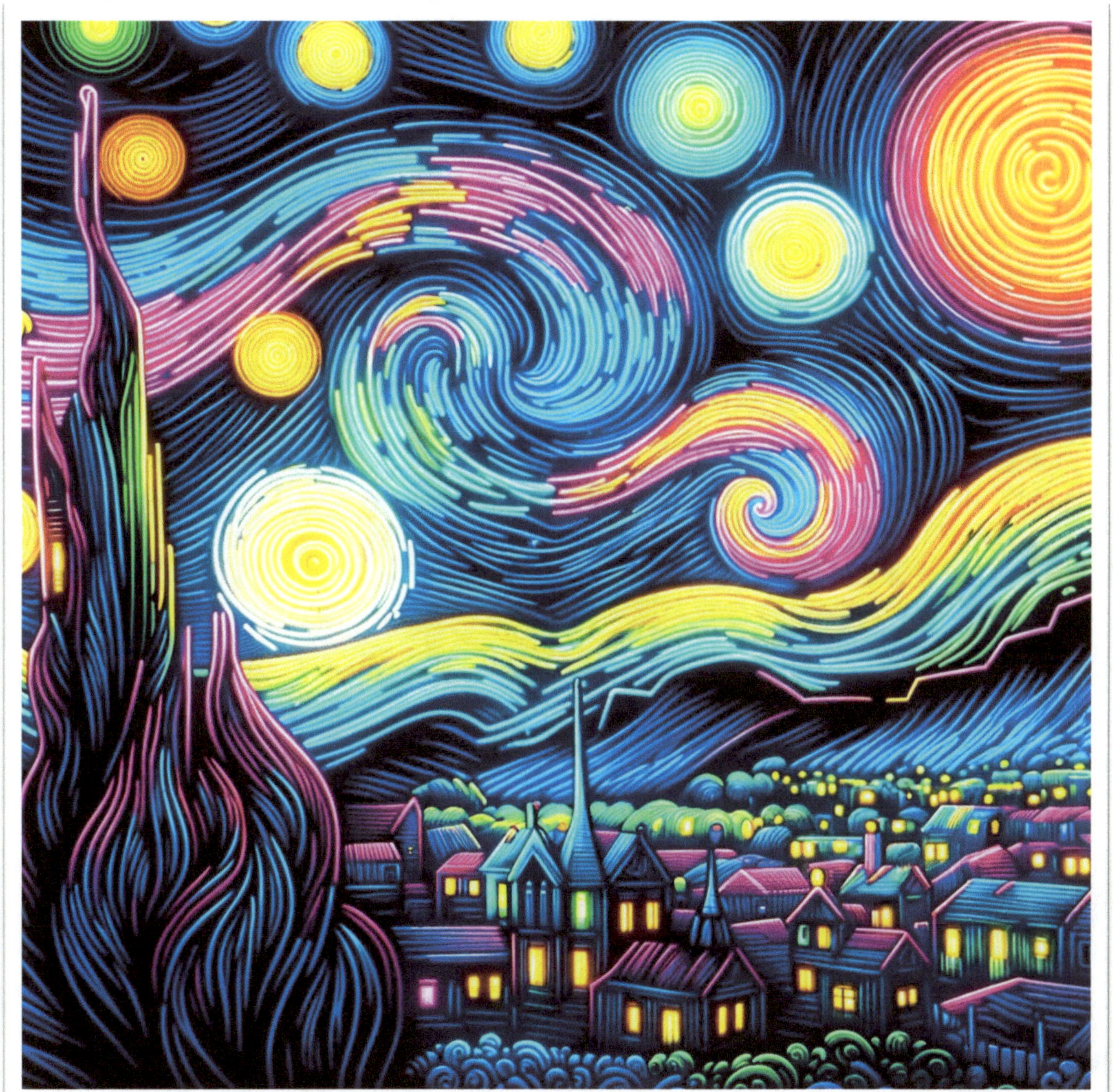

Blending and iteration explained: In this vivid reimagining of Van Gogh's *Starry Night* ,the process of blending and iteration involves the skillful fusion of iconic swirling patterns with a neon color palette to create a strikingly modern interpretation. The artist iteratively adjusts the hues and saturation to ensure that the luminosity and vibrancy enhance, rather than overwhelm, the original composition's dynamic movement. The result is a harmonious balance between the homage to Van Gogh's expressive brushwork and a fresh, electrifying aesthetic that resonates with contemporary sensibilities.

Thematic Exploration in AI Art

Initial Prompt: "Prepare thematic image that depicts a trio of heroes on an epic journey through a dystopian landscape."

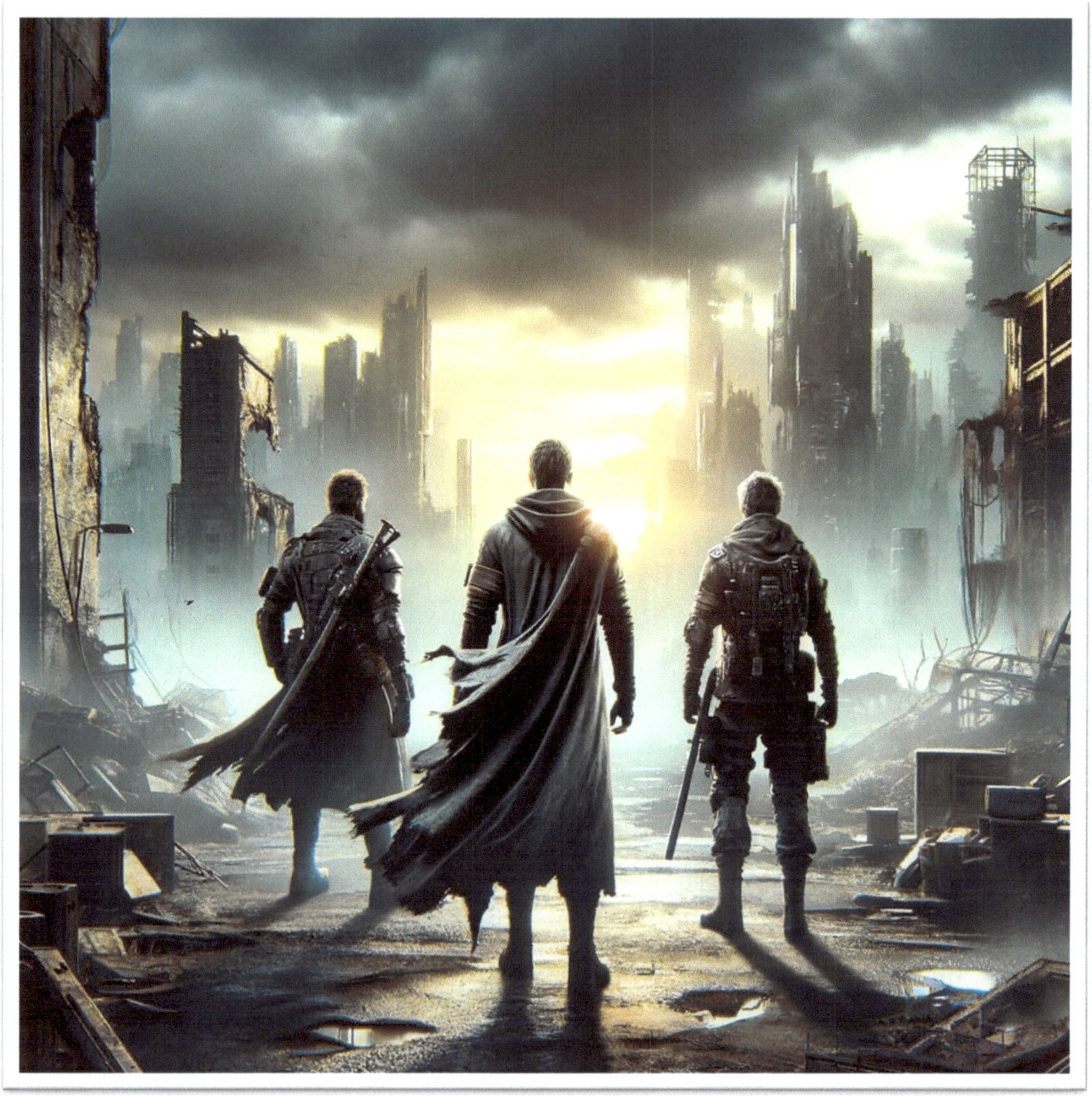

Blending and iteration explained: The artist has combined elements of dystopian decay with rays of hope shining through the skyline, creating a layered narrative. Through iteration, the artist refines each detail, from the texture of the characters' cloaks to the play of light and shadow, contributing to the image's emotional impact. The result is a powerful visual story that balances the harshness of a post-apocalyptic world with a suggestion of resilience or potential redemption as the figures look towards the light.

Emotional and Conceptual Themes

Initial Prompt: "Create a piece that visualizes the feeling of solitude in an abstract form."

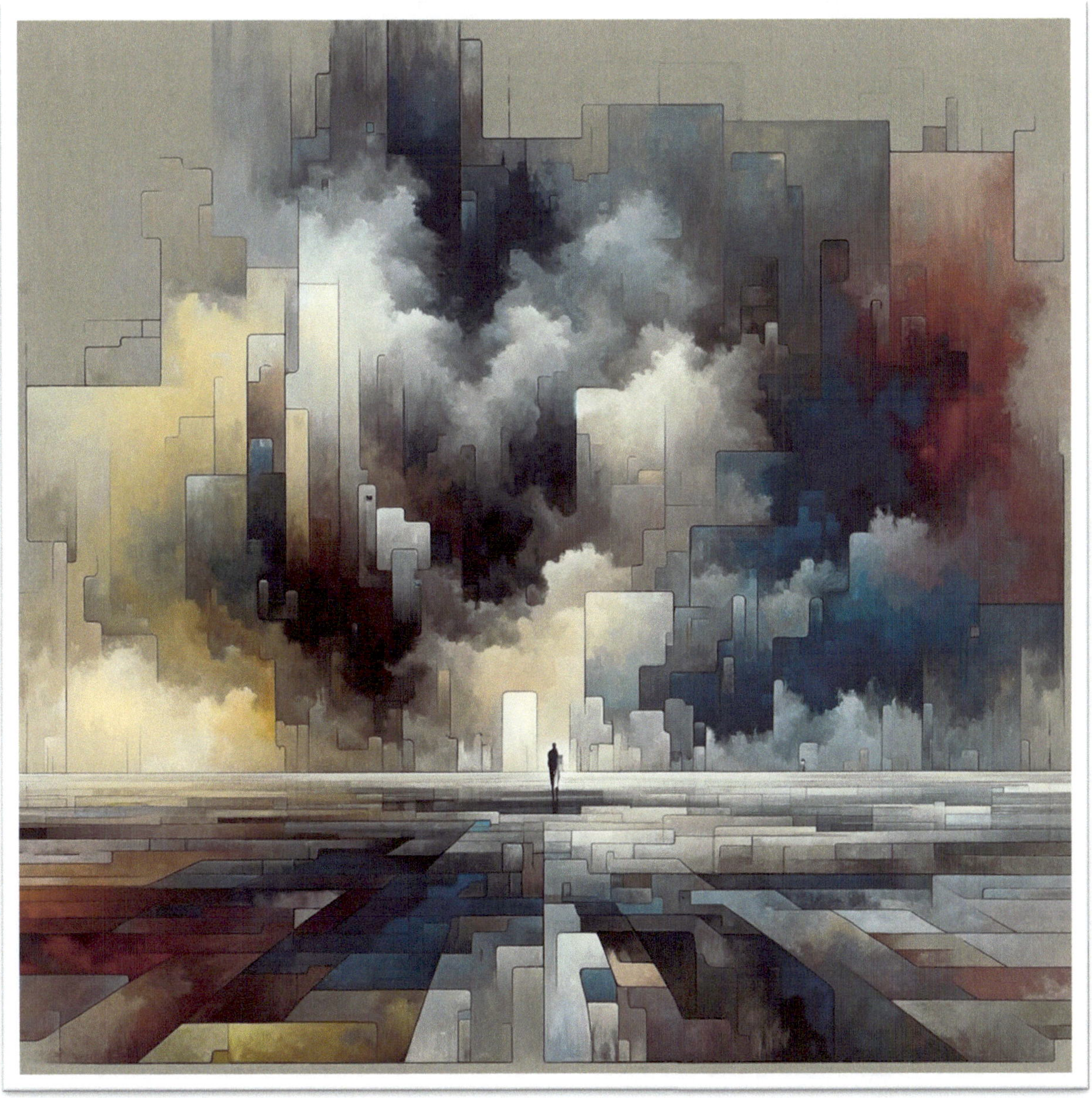

Blending and iteration explained: This artwork captures the feeling of solitude in an abstract form. Through a series of iterations, the artist specified abstract imagery, including colors, shapes, and textures, to convey a sense of being alone. The composition might depict isolated elements or vast empty spaces, evoking a feeling of emptiness and introspection. The color palette, with its muted, cool tones or stark contrasts, further enhances the mood of solitude. This artwork aims to evoke the emotional depth and introspective nature associated with solitude.

Historical Style with Modern Elements

Initial Prompt: "Generate a Baroque-style portrait with modern-day fashion elements."

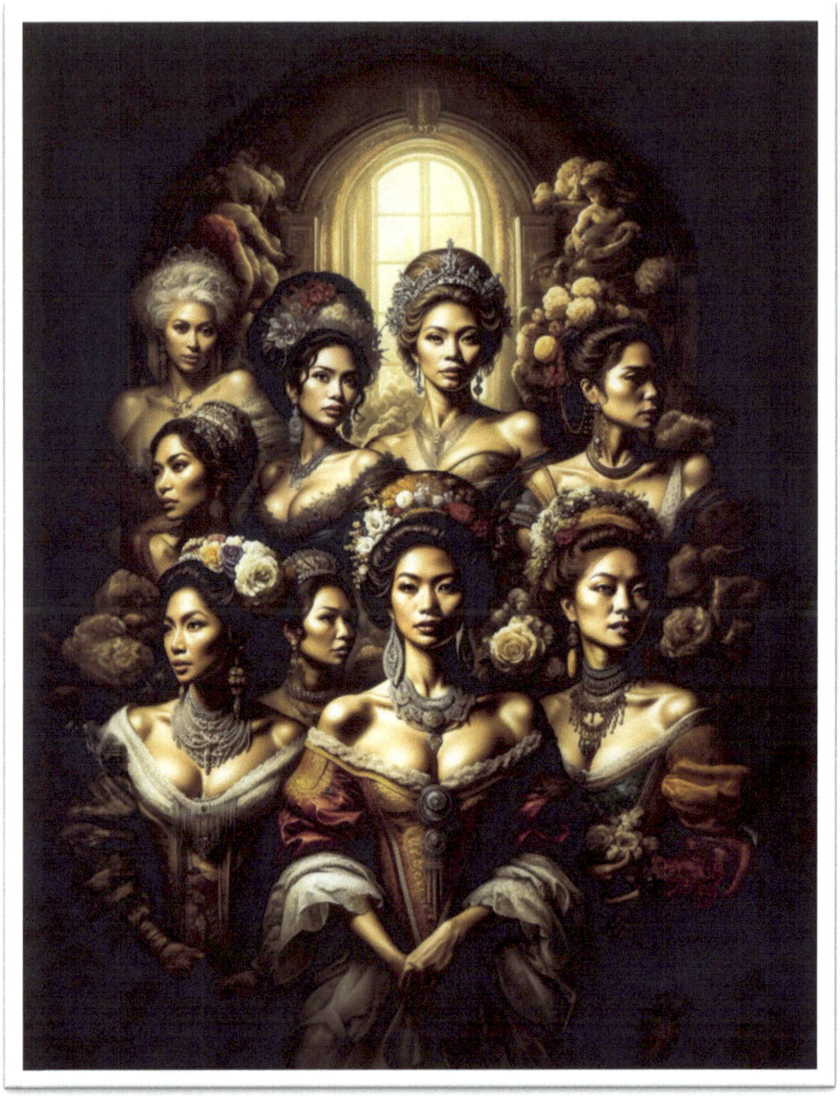

Blending and iteration explained: This compelling image presents a blend of classical portraiture with modern aesthetics, showcasing figures dressed in regal, historical attire juxtaposed against a contemporary representation of beauty and poise. The blending process here involves the fusion of traditional fashion elements with modern lighting and composition techniques to create a timeless piece that bridges different eras. Through iteration, the artist has carefully refined each subject's pose and expression, as well as the intricate details of their garments and the ambient lighting, to produce a unified and captivating tableau that celebrates diversity and grandeur. After successive attempts to capture the artist's vision, a refined version of the initial prompt achieved this new artwork that portrays a Baroque-style portrait with modern-day fashion elements.

Nature and Technology

Initial Prompt: "Illustrate a scene where nature and futuristic technology exist in harmony."

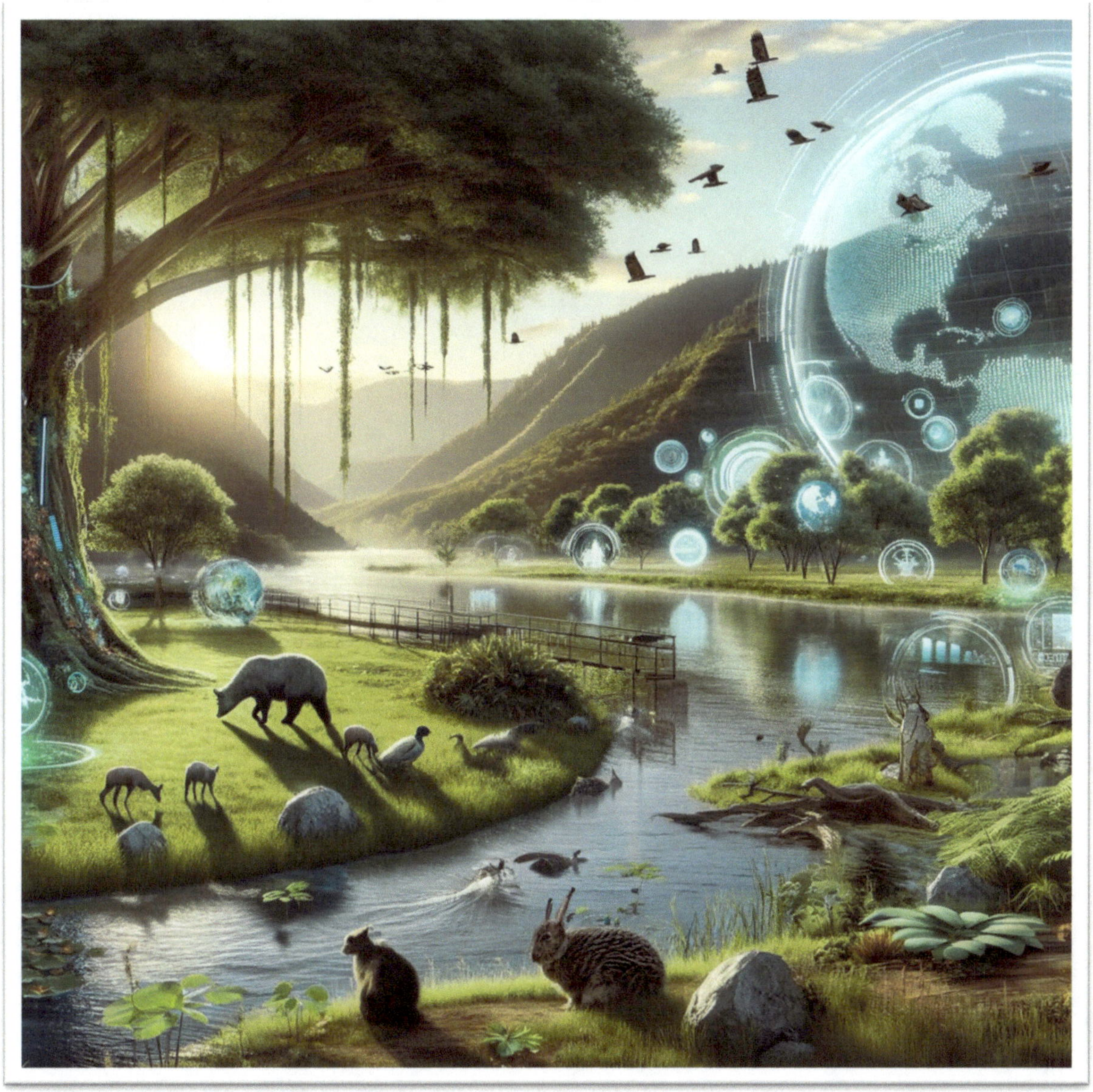

Blending and iteration explained: This artwork illustrates the final version of multiple iterations. Blending is exemplified by the harmonious combination of a serene natural landscape with elements of advanced technology, creating a scene that feels both pastoral and futuristic. The artist has iterated on this concept, thoughtfully adjusting the placement and transparency of the technological elements to ensure they complement rather than overwhelm the organic environment. This iterative process allows the piece to maintain a sense of natural beauty while also intriguing the viewer with subtle hints of a sophisticated, possibly utopian world where technology integrates seamlessly with nature.

Cultural Fusion

Initial Prompt: "Create an artwork combining Japanese traditional art styles with Western pop art influences."

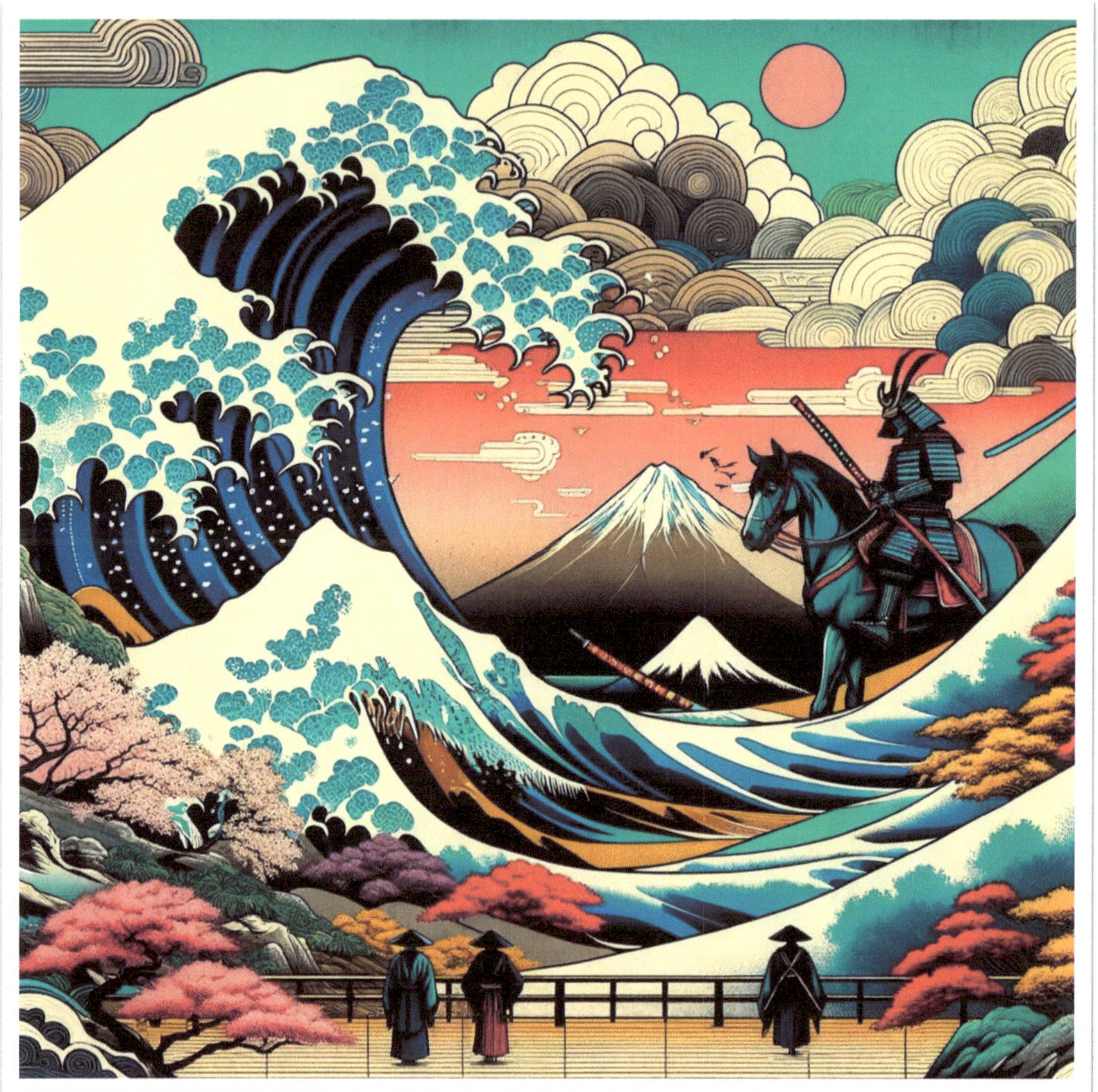

Blending and iteration explained: This artwork showcases a blend of traditional Japanese woodblock print elements with a stylized, almost graphic novel-like modernity, particularly in the vibrant color palette and dynamic wave forms. Through iteration, the artist has refined these elements, ensuring the waves, the iconic Mount Fuji, and the figures observing the scene carry both the weight of historical artistry and a contemporary aesthetic. The metaprompt for this artwork required a synthesis of classic and modern motifs, driving the iterative process to honor traditional Japanese art while infusing it with modern sensibilities, thus creating a piece that bridges time through its design.

Abstract and Realism Mix

Initial Prompt: "A surreal landscape that combines realistic animal figures with abstract geometric shapes."

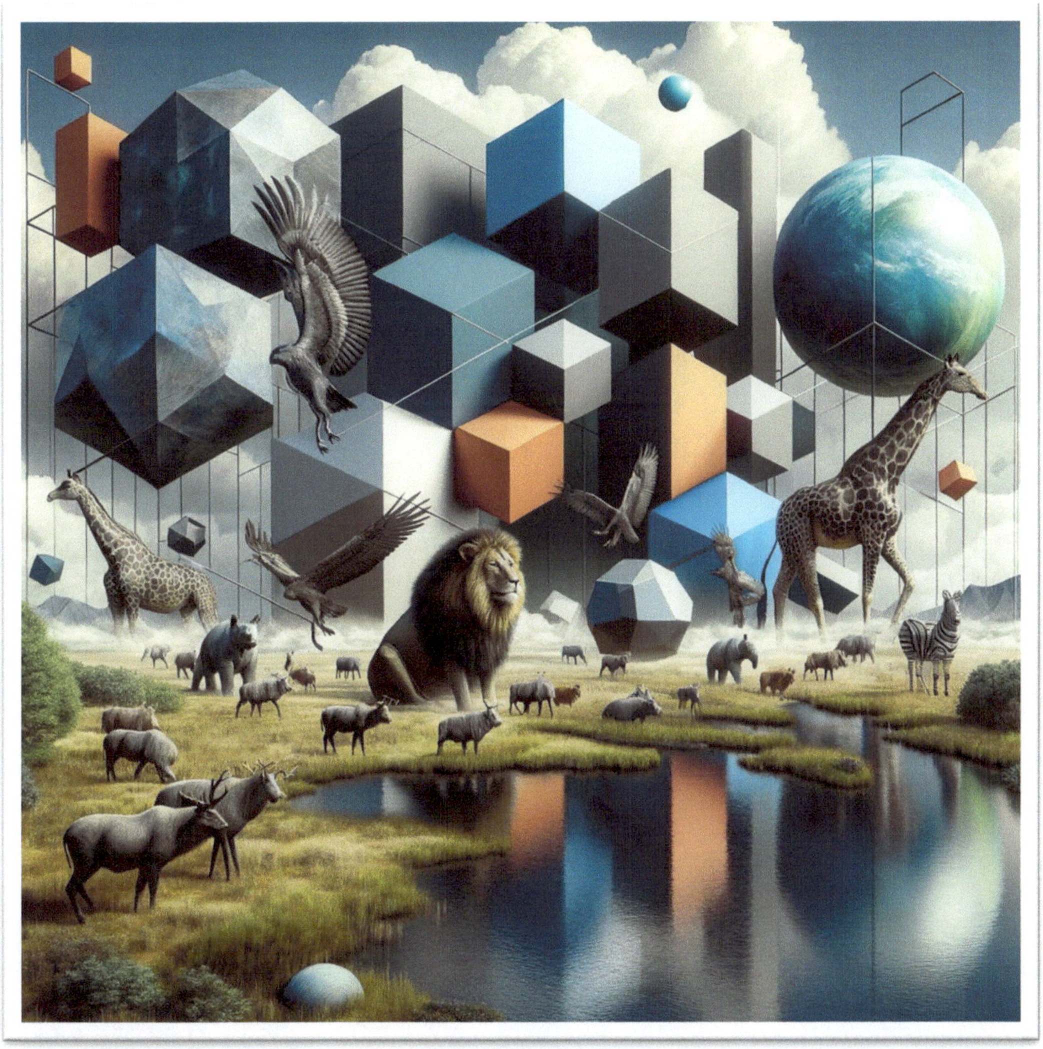

Blending and iteration explained: This artwork presents a surreal landscape that combines realistic animal figures with abstract geometric shapes. There is an intricate blending of the natural and the abstract, combining realistic wildlife with surreal, geometric shapes floating in a clear blue sky. The artistic process clearly involved iteration, with the artist carefully adjusting the scale, perspective, and shading of both the animals and the floating elements to create visual harmony. The concept appears to stem from metaprompts that explore the juxtaposition of nature with human perception or imagination, suggesting multiple creative iterations to balance realism with fantastical design.

Chapter 10: Advanced Prompt Techniques

Artists who explore advanced prompt techniques within the framework of digital evolution actively transform their craft into an academic exploration, enhancing their creative potential. Language nuances enable you to refine AI into your sophisticated tool of creativity. By skillfully utilizing these techniques, you position yourself as a digital artisan, directing AI to create works that are visually compelling and deeply enriched with narrative complexity and personal significance.

Crafting sophisticated, multi-dimensional prompts is akin to orchestrating a symphony of visual elements, themes, and artistic styles, all working in concert to direct the AI towards producing works that are detailed and layered with meaning. This chapter is your academic guide to such craftsmanship, pushing the envelope of what AI can achieve artistically.

As you navigate the intricacies of advanced prompt techniques, you will learn to articulate your creative intent with precision, allowing for an artistic collaboration with AI that transcends simple imagery. These methods stand in stark contrast to rudimentary sketches, elevating AI-generated art into realms of elaborate composition and storytelling. Through the scholarly lens of this chapter, we shall explore the architecting of prompts that go beyond the canvas, where every stroke is informed by intention, and every color choice is a deliberate step towards a masterpiece of digital artistry.

Incorporating Narrative Elements in AI Art Prompts

- **Storytelling Through Art**

  Introduce characters, plots, and settings. For instance, "Illustrate the journey of a lone astronaut discovering a garden on Mars."

- **Emotional and Conceptual Narratives**

  Use prompts that tell a story through emotions or concepts, like "An artwork depicting the struggle and triumph of overcoming adversity."

Experimenting with Abstract Concepts and Surrealism

- **Abstract Ideas**

  Translate intangible concepts into visual forms, such as "Visualize the feeling of serenity as an abstract landscape."

- **Surrealistic Imagery**

  Create surreal scenes by combining unrelated elements, like "A dreamlike sequence where gravity doesn't exist, and everyday objects float amidst clouds."

Best Practices for Complex Prompts

1. **Clarity in Complexity**

   Despite the complexity, ensure prompts are clear and cohesive.

2. **Balance Between Detail and Openness**

   Provide detailed guidance but leave room for AI's interpretation and creativity.

3. **Iterative Approach**

   Experiment with different versions of a prompt to see how slight changes can significantly impact the outcome.

Understanding Superhuman Power Prompts

Superhuman power prompts are advanced, intricate input requests designed to push AI systems beyond conventional output limits, leveraging their full potential to generate extraordinary, often unforeseen artistic results. You can use superhuman power prompts to make new art. Such prompts differ significantly from standard AI prompts in several key aspects.

Complexity and Depth
Superhuman power prompts are typically more complex than standard prompts. They contain multiple layers of instructions or queries that compel the AI to engage in deeper levels of processing and creativity. This complexity might involve intricate descriptions, nuanced emotional tones, or the blending of diverse artistic styles and elements.

High-Level Abstraction
These prompts often operate at a higher level of abstraction, asking the AI to interpret and implement conceptual or thematic elements rather than just literal instructions. For example, a prompt might ask the AI to create art that embodies the concept of "chaos theory" or "the interplay of light and shadow," which requires the AI to interpret and artistically represent abstract ideas.

Contextual and Cultural Awareness
Superhuman power prompts may incorporate an understanding of cultural, historical, or contextual nuances. This involves the AI recognizing and integrating culturally significant elements, historical references, or current socio-political themes into the artwork.

Emotional Intelligence and Sensitivity
These prompts often require a level of emotional intelligence, asking the AI to create art that evokes or represents specific emotions, moods, or psychological states. This requires a sophisticated understanding of how different artistic elements can convey emotional depth.

Adaptability and Learning
Superhuman power prompts are designed to utilize AI's ability to learn and adapt. They can include feedback loops where the AI refines its output based on previous successes or failures, leading to a more refined and targeted artistic output over time.

Incorporation of Multimodal Elements
Unlike standard prompts that may focus on a single mode (like visual art), superhuman power prompts can be multimodal, combining various forms of media and sensory inputs. For instance, a prompt might combine visual art with music or poetry, asking the AI to create a cohesive piece that integrates these different elements.

Unpredictability and Novelty
A defining feature of superhuman power prompts is their ability to yield unpredictable and novel results. You're encouraged to experiment with AI and unconventional combinations or approaches, which can lead to unique and innovative artistic creations.

Sample Images and Texts
Provide sample images and texts. Ask the AI to analyze and then mimic or otherwise generate output in response to your prompt.

Triple Quotes: Providing Specific Context

Examples:

- Analyze text within triple quotes and then rewrite in a concise manner using a professional and scholarly tone: """Add text here"""

- Refer to text in triple quotes for art design requirements and then create image that meets all art design requirements: """Add text here""" Image dimensions must be 1024x1792.

- Consider context at the URL in triple quotes and then prepare a detailed summary: """Add URL here"""

Dimensions: Specifications for Image Output

These DALL-E options allow for flexibility, depending on the aspect ratio for the image output that you request:

- Square: 1024x1024 pixels

- Wide: 1792x1024 pixels

- Tall/Portrait: 1024x1792 pixels

The Science Behind the Superhuman Element

In essence, superhuman power prompts are designed to exploit the advanced capabilities of AI in generating art, pushing the boundaries of creativity, and exploring new artistic horizons that might be beyond the scope of traditional human-led processes. They represent a fusion of technology, creativity, and deep cognitive processing, leading to the creation of art that is not only aesthetically pleasing but also intellectually and emotionally profound.

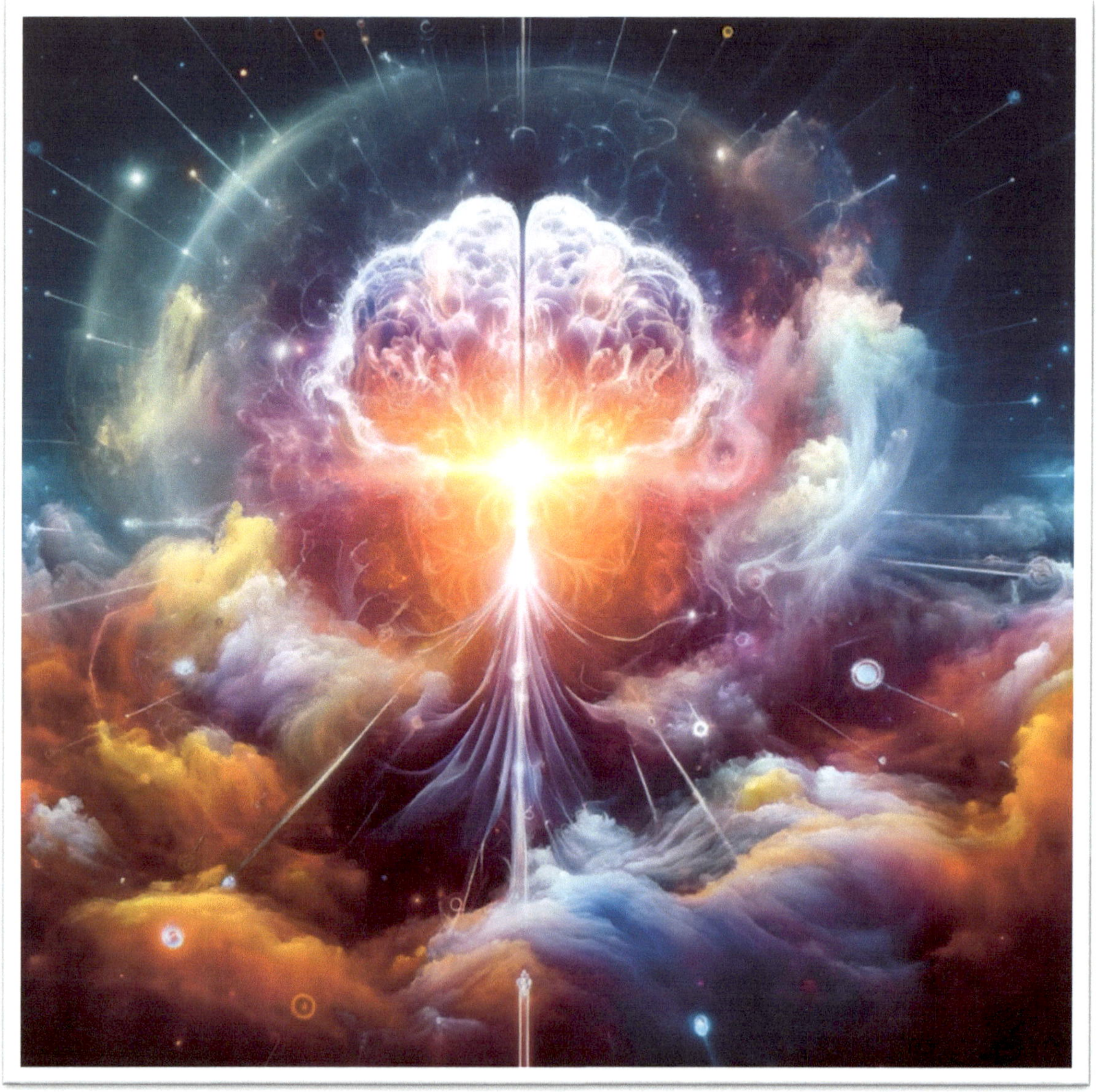

The science behind the superhuman element in Generative AI, particularly in the realm of artistic creation, hinges on several advanced technologies. These include deep learning, neural networks, and sophisticated algorithms, each playing a crucial role in enabling AI systems to interpret and respond to superhuman power prompts effectively.

Deep Learning

1. **Concept**
   Deep learning is a subset of machine learning where artificial neural networks — algorithms inspired by the human brain — learn from large amounts of data.

2. **Function in Art**
   In the context of art, deep learning enables AI to recognize and generate complex patterns, understand styles, and even emulate artistic techniques. This learning process is not just about replicating what it has seen but also about creatively combining elements to create something new and original.

3. **Layered Processing**
   Deep learning involves multiple layers of processing, allowing the AI to break down an artistic prompt into different elements (such as style, texture, color scheme) and synthesize them to produce a coherent piece of art.

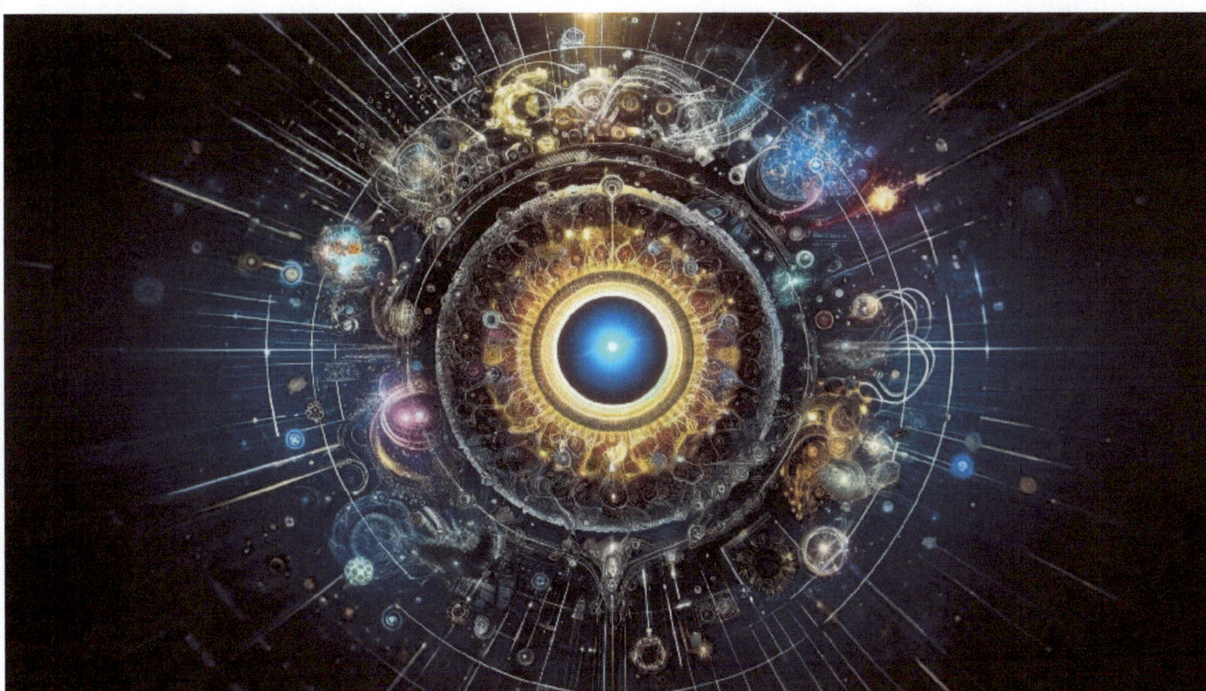

Neural Networks

1. **Structure**
   Neural networks consist of nodes (neurons) arranged in layers: an input layer, several hidden layers, and an output layer. Each neuron processes input and passes its output to the next layer.

2. **Artistic Application**
   In art, neural networks can analyze artistic elements from various artworks, learning intricate details and applying this knowledge to generate new creations. Convolutional Neural Networks (CNNs), for instance, are particularly adept at processing visual data, making them ideal for image-based art generation.

3. **Generative Models**
   Neural networks form the basis of Generative Adversarial Networks (GANs) and Variational Autoencoders (VAEs), both widely used for generating new, high-quality artistic content. GANs, for instance, use two neural networks — a generator and a discriminator — that work against each other to produce increasingly sophisticated outputs.

Advanced Algorithms

1. **Complex Problem Solving**
   Advanced algorithms in AI art encompass a range of techniques from optimization algorithms to probabilistic models. These algorithms can solve complex problems, like determining the best way to combine different artistic elements to convey a certain emotion or theme.

2. **Personalization and Adaptation**
   Algorithms can be tailored to adapt to specific artistic preferences or styles, learning from feedback and previous outputs. This adaptability is crucial for responding effectively to superhuman power prompts, which often require a high degree of personalization.

3. **Interdisciplinary Integration**
   Some advanced algorithms integrate knowledge from other fields, such as psychology (to understand emotional impact) or cultural studies (to incorporate cultural elements into art), enriching the AI's capability to create art that resonates on multiple levels.

The Superhuman Aspect

The science behind the superhuman element in Generative AI art engages a sophisticated interplay of deep learning, neural networks, and advanced algorithms. These technologies empower AI to not only emulate human artistic abilities but to also transcend them, creating art that is innovative, complex, and deeply integrated with a myriad of artistic influences and styles.

1. **Beyond Human Capacity**
   The "superhuman" aspect comes from the AI's ability to process and analyze more data and variables than a human could reasonably manage, and at a much faster rate. This includes assimilating diverse artistic styles, historical art movements, and complex patterns.

2. **Innovative Combinations**
   AI, armed with these technologies, can combine elements in novel ways that might not occur to human artists, leading to groundbreaking and innovative artistic creations.

3. **Learning and Evolving**
   Perhaps most importantly, these AI systems can continuously learn and evolve, improving their artistic outputs over time in ways that might be challenging for human artists, especially at the same scale and speed.

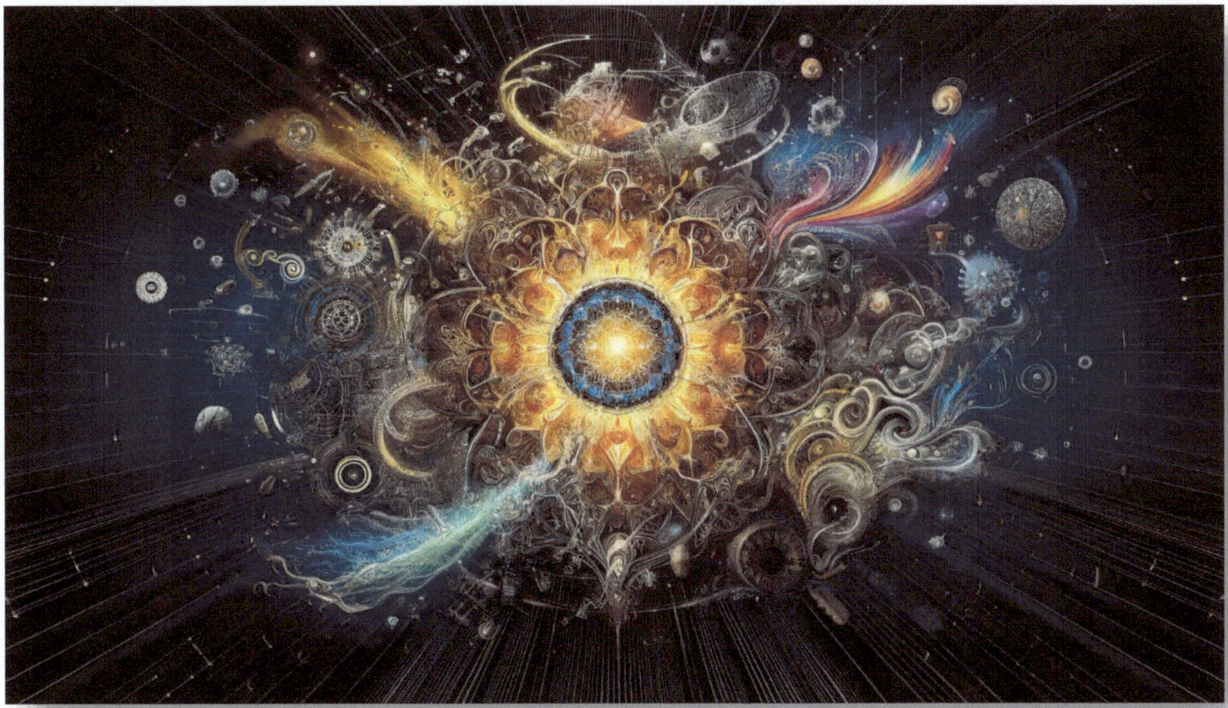

Crafting Effective Superhuman Power Prompts

Creating prompts that maximize the potential of AI, especially in the realm of generative art, requires a careful balance between providing specific guidance and allowing for creative freedom. Here's a step-by-step guide to crafting such prompts:

Step 1: Define the objective.

- **Identify the goal.**
  Clearly define what you want the AI to achieve with the prompt. This could range from creating an artwork in a specific style to generating ideas for a novel plot.

- **Understand the audience.**
  Consider who the end audience will be. Tailor the complexity and nature of the prompt to suit their preferences and expectations.

Step 2: Research and gather information.

- **Understand AI capabilities.**
  Familiarize yourself with the AI's strengths and limitations. Knowing what your AI tool is capable of is crucial in formulating effective prompts.

- **Gather inspirational material.**
  Collect examples, ideas, or elements you want the AI to consider. This could include artistic styles, themes, or specific imagery.

Step 3: Craft the prompt.

- **Start with specificity.**
  Begin your prompt with specific instructions. This could include the type of art, the mood, the main elements to include, or a particular theme.

- **Incorporate open-ended elements.**
  After the specific instructions, add open-ended elements that encourage the AI to explore and be creative. For instance, you might ask the AI to interpret a theme in an unexpected way or to surprise you with its interpretation of a concept.

- **Use descriptive language.**
  Be descriptive in your language to provide a clear picture of what you're looking for, but avoid overloading the AI with too much detail, which can restrict its creative process.

Step 4: Test and observe.

- **Initial testing.**
  Run the prompt through the AI and observe the output. Note how closely it aligns with your initial objective and where it diverges.

- **Analyze and iterate.**
  Analyze the strengths and weaknesses of the output. Refine your prompt based on this analysis, adjusting the balance of specificity and open-endedness as needed.

- **Continuous improvement.**
  Remember that crafting prompts is an iterative process. Continually refine your approach based on the results and your growing understanding of the AI's capabilities.

Step 5: Ethical and practical considerations.

- **Ensure ethical compliance.**
  Make sure your prompts do not lead to the creation of harmful, offensive, or plagiarized content. Stay within ethical and legal boundaries.

- **Incorporate feedback loops.**
  If possible, use feedback loops where the AI's output is evaluated and the prompt is modified in response, creating a dynamic and evolving creative process.

Step 6: Document and learn.

- **Keep a record.**
  Document your prompts and the corresponding outputs. Keeping a record helps in understanding what works and what doesn't.

- **Learn and adapt.**
  Use your growing repository of prompts and outputs to learn more about effective prompt crafting. Adapt your strategy based on these insights.

Step 7: Collaborate and engage with the community.

- **Engage with others.**
  Share your prompts and outcomes with other users or creators. Collaborative learning can offer new perspectives and ideas.

- **Stay informed.**
  Keep up with the latest developments in AI and generative art. Join forums, attend webinars, and read the latest research to stay informed.

Creating effective prompts for AI in art is a dynamic and evolving process that combines technical understanding with creativity. By following these steps and continuously refining your approach, you can effectively harness the AI's capabilities to produce creative, innovative, and engaging art.

Case Studies and Examples

Analyzing successful implementations of superhuman power prompts in various art projects can provide valuable insights into what makes these prompts effective. Superhuman power prompts have been utilized in various art projects to explore themes of identity, capability, and imagination.

Regarding case studies, here are several examples of successful implementations and insights into their effectiveness:

Case Studies

"The Machine to be Another" by BeAnotherLab
https://beanotherlab.org/home/work/tmtba

- **Implementation**
  This project involved using virtual reality (VR) technology to enable participants to experience life from the perspective of another person. Participants would wear VR headsets connected to cameras worn by someone else. Through synchronized movements and audiovisual cues, participants would feel as though they inhabited the body of the other person.

- **Insights**
  The project effectively challenged participants' perceptions of identity and empathy by allowing them to temporarily inhabit the body of someone else. By creating an immersive experience, it enabled participants to gain deeper insights into the lived experiences of others, fostering empathy and understanding.

"Augmented Hand Series" by Golan Levin, Chris Sugrue, and Kyle McDonald
https://csugrue.com/augmented-hand-series

- **Implementation**
  This interactive art installation used augmented reality (AR) to augment participants' hands with additional fingers or altered proportions. Participants could see their hands transformed in real-time through a screen or projection, allowing them to interact with their augmented selves.

- **Insights**

  By altering participants' perceptions of their own bodies, the project prompted reflections on the nature of human embodiment and the boundaries of physical capabilities. It highlighted the malleability of perception and the ways in which technology can reshape our understanding of ourselves.

"Superflux: Mitigation of Shock" by Superflux
https://futurehumanbydesign.com/2019/09/designers-using-futures-thinking

- **Implementation**
  This speculative design project presented a series of immersive scenarios depicting potential future environments shaped by technological advancements and environmental changes. Through multimedia installations, including videos, props, and interactive elements, participants were invited to explore these speculative worlds and engage with their implications.

- **Insights**
  By extrapolating current trends and imagining possible futures, the project encouraged critical reflection on the societal, environmental, and ethical implications of emerging technologies. It prompted viewers to consider the consequences of technological progress and the importance of proactive mitigation strategies.

Overall, these examples demonstrate that effective superhuman power prompts in art projects often leverage immersive technologies to create engaging and thought-provoking experiences. By enabling participants to temporarily transcend their physical limitations or inhabit alternate perspectives, these projects prompt reflections on identity, embodiment, and the implications of technological progress. Additionally, they highlight the importance of interactivity, storytelling, and speculative thinking while engaging audiences and fostering meaningful dialogue about the future of humanity and technology.

In the next section we'll look at four examples – hypothetical – and dissect key factors contributing to their success.

Four Examples

Example 1: Interactive AI Sculpture

Project Overview

An interactive sculpture created by AI, responding to environmental stimuli like weather, sound, and human interaction.

Effective Prompt

The prompt for the AI was to create a sculpture that changes its form based on real-time environmental data and human presence, embodying the concept of "dynamic harmony".

Success Factors

- **Multimodal Integration**
  The prompt successfully integrated multiple data sources (weather, sound, human interaction), while allowing the AI to interpret and respond in a complex, multidimensional way.

Conceptual Depth

The theme of "dynamic harmony" encouraged the AI to think abstractly, leading to an innovative interpretation of data in a physical form.

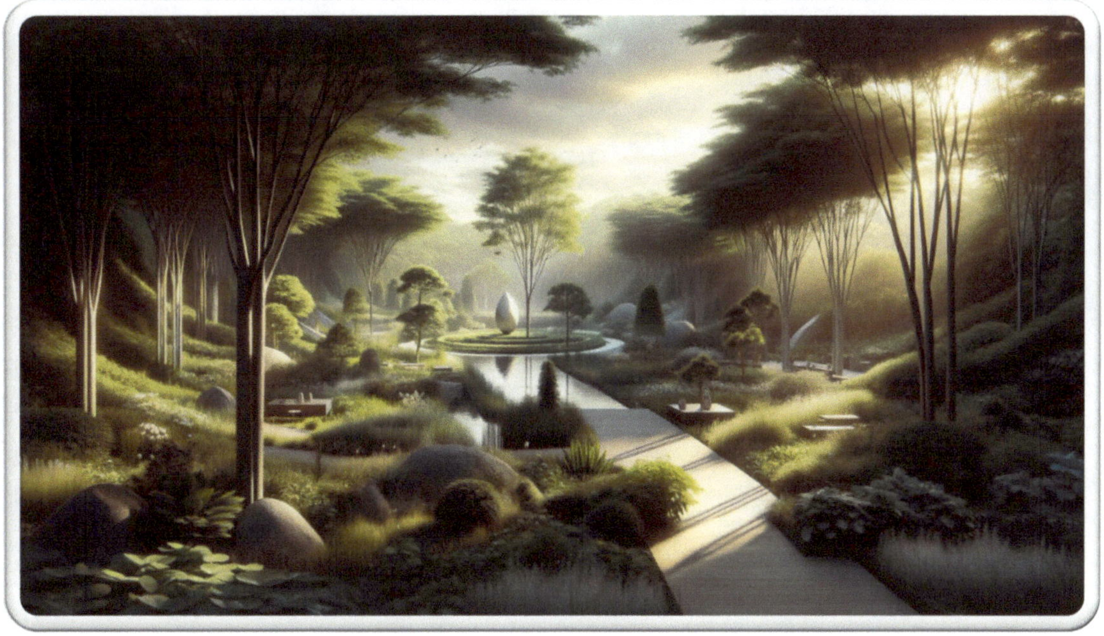

Example 2: AI-Generated Film

Project Overview

An AI-generated short film where the plot, visuals, and music were created by AI, based on a set of thematic prompts.

Effective Prompt

The AI was prompted to create a narrative exploring the theme of "identity in a digital age", incorporating specific visual styles and musical genres.

Success Factors

- **Narrative Complexity**
  The prompt encouraged the AI to weave a complex narrative, showing its ability to handle abstract and nuanced storytelling.

- **Sensory Cohesion**
  The AI's integration of visual and auditory elements based on specific styles and genres resulted in a cohesive and immersive experience.

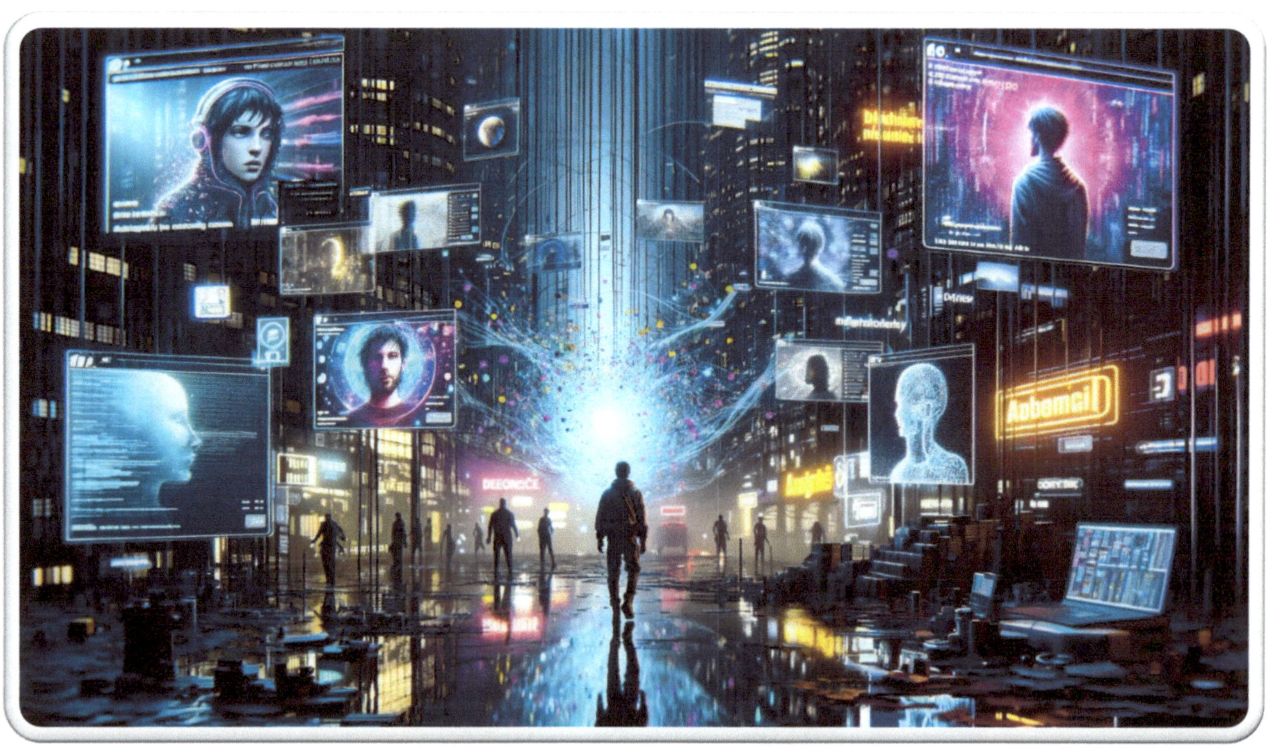

Example 3: AI-Painted Mural

Project Overview

A large-scale mural painted by an AI system, designed to reflect the cultural history and future aspirations of a community.

Effective Prompt

The prompt involved creating a visual representation that captures the essence of the community's past, present, and future, using a blend of traditional and futuristic artistic styles.

Success Factors

- **Cultural Sensitivity**
  The AI's ability to understand and depict cultural themes showed the effectiveness of the prompt in guiding AI through complex social and historical concepts.

- **Style Fusion**
  The blend of traditional and futuristic styles demonstrated the AI's capacity to merge diverse artistic influences creatively.

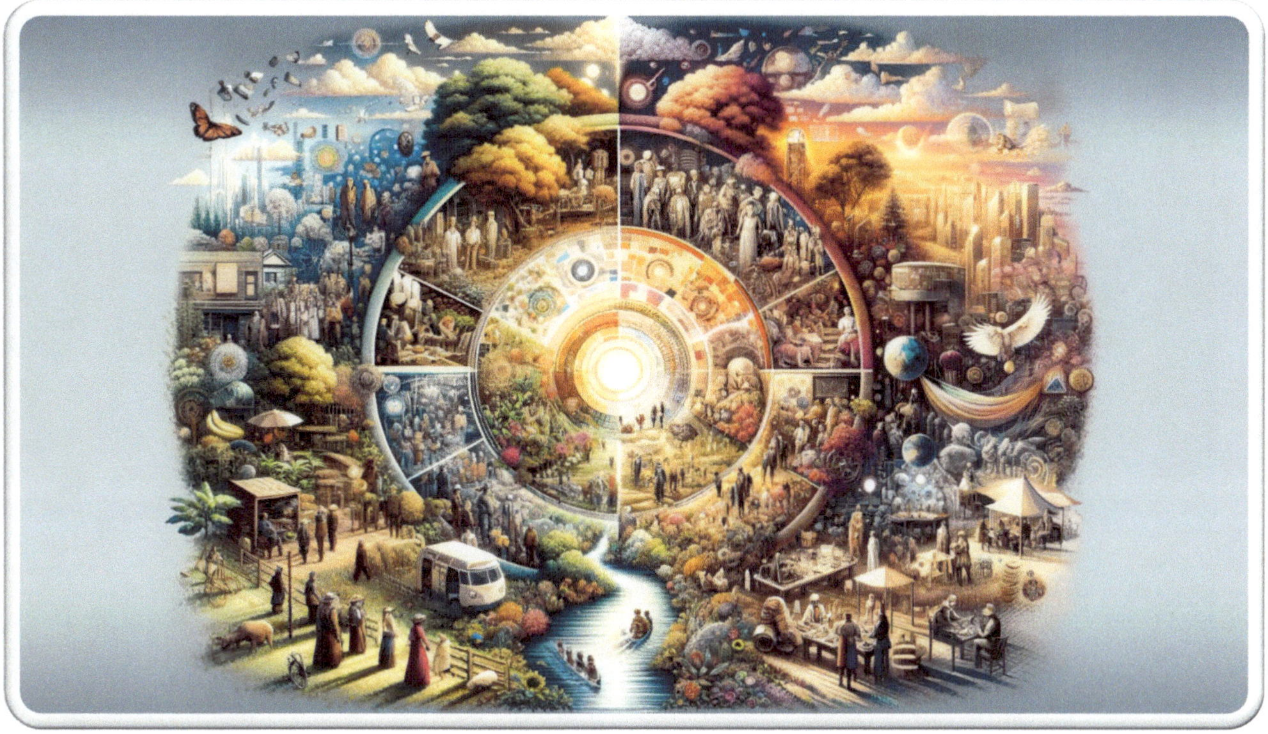

Example 4: AI-Created Virtual Reality Experience

Project Overview

A virtual reality (VR) experience generated by AI, allowing users to explore an abstract, evolving world.

Effective Prompt

The AI was prompted to create a VR environment that evolves based on user interactions, themed around the concept of "consciousness expansion".

Success Factors

- **User Interaction**
  The prompt effectively utilized AI's ability to modify the environment in real-time based on user input, demonstrating adaptability and interactivity.

- **Abstract Visualization**
  The theme of "consciousness expansion" pushed the AI to create abstract, thought-provoking visualizations, showcasing its ability to interpret complex concepts.

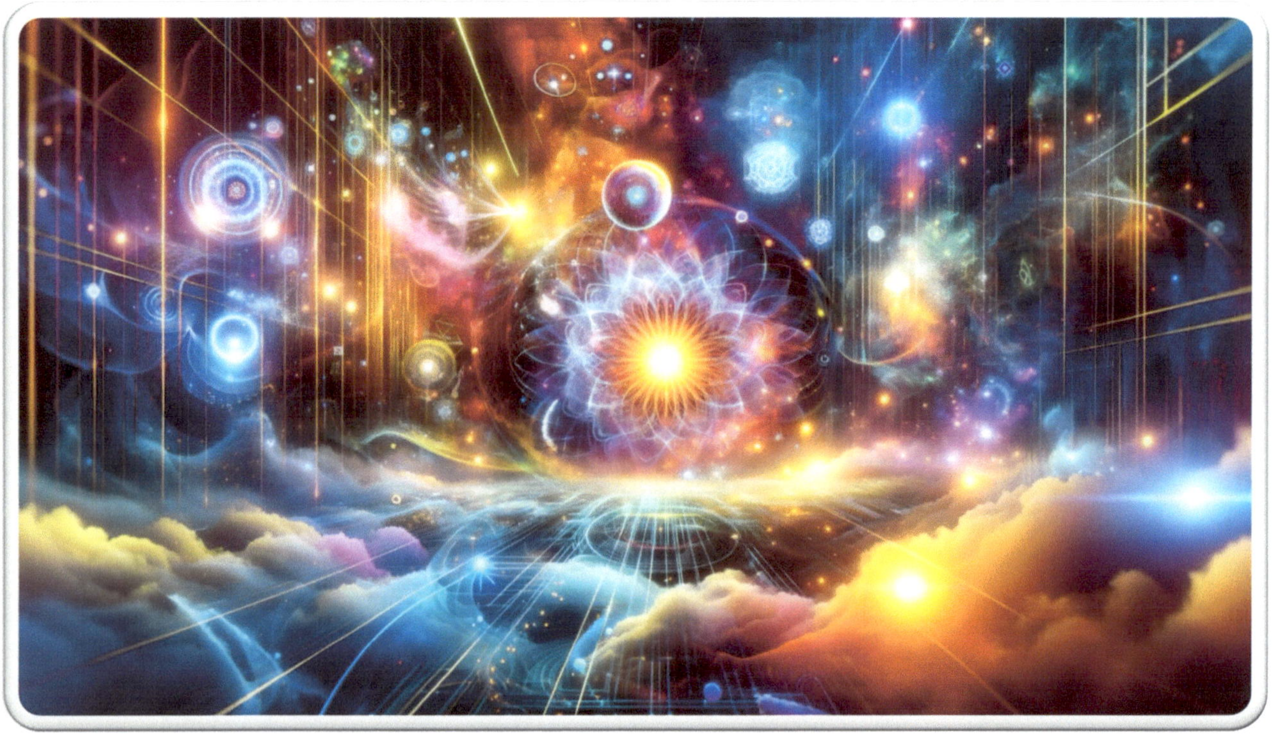

Analysis and Insights

The four examples we've discussed show that the most effective AI prompts leverage the system's advanced capabilities while encouraging creativity, abstraction, and emotional depth. This approach does more than display AI's technical abilities; it produces art that is both meaningful and powerful. The key factors common to these successful prompts underline their excellence:

Conceptual Depth and Creativity
Prompts that challenge the AI to interpret and visualize abstract or complex themes lead to innovative and thought-provoking art.

Multimodal and Multidisciplinary Approach
Effective prompts often integrate various data types and artistic disciplines, allowing AI to create more dynamic and rich outputs.

Adaptive and Interactive Elements
Prompts that leverage AI's ability to adapt and interact with data or human input result in more engaging and immersive art projects.

Cultural and Emotional Intelligence
Incorporate cultural sensitivity and emotional depth in prompts enabled AI to create art that resonates more profoundly with human experiences.

Crafting Complex, Multi-layered Prompts

Combine multiple elements.
Layer different elements, such as settings, characters, and objects. For example, "Create a bustling cyberpunk cityscape with neon-lit streets, diverse characters, and flying vehicles."

Incorporate time and movement.

Infuse prompts with a sense of time or motion, like "A timelapse view of a medieval village transforming into a modern city."

Layer themes and styles.
Merge various themes and artistic styles, for instance, "A painting that combines the tranquility of a Japanese Zen Garden with the chaotic energy of abstract expressionism."

Artistic Process: Collaboration Between You and AI

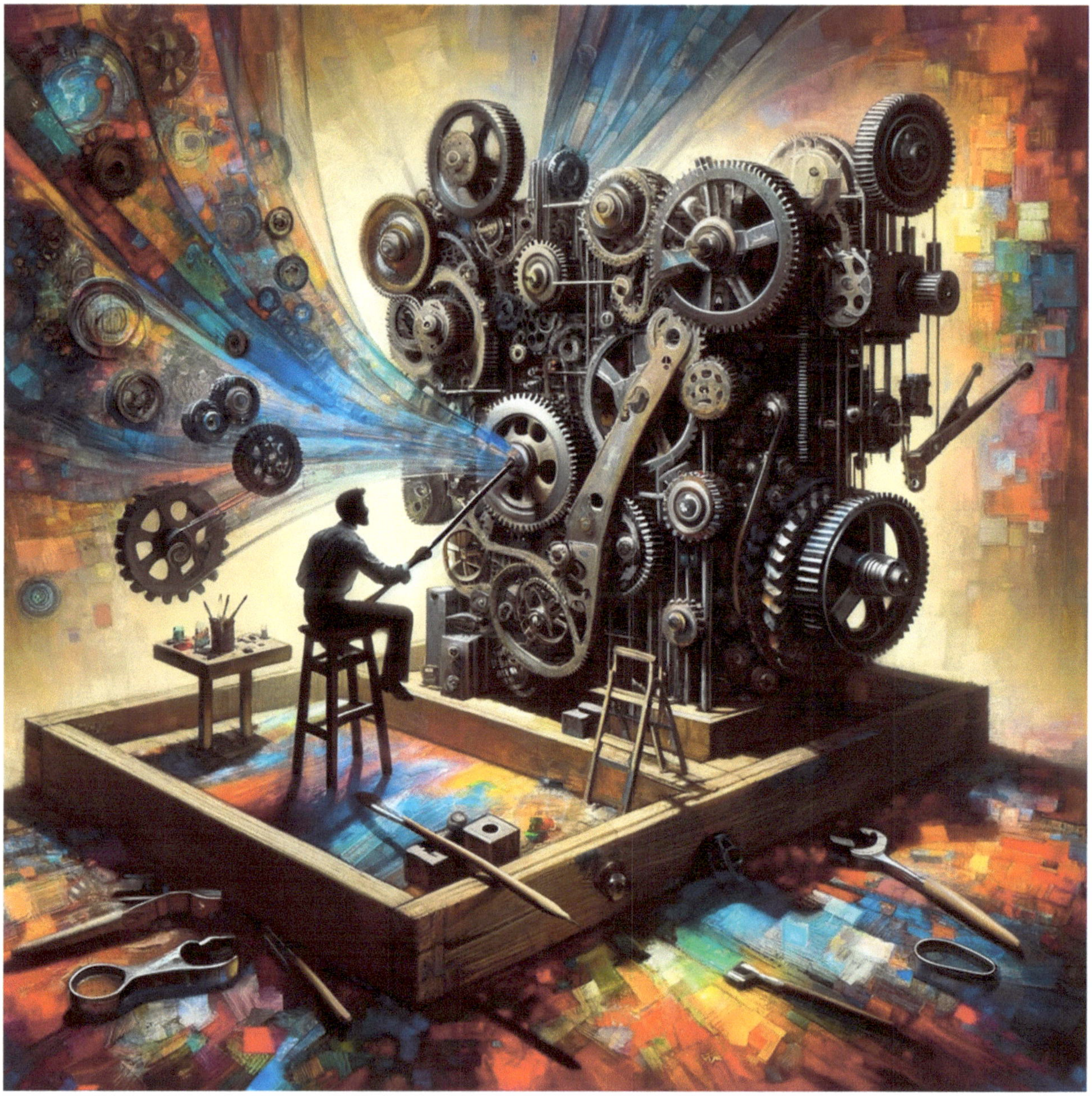

Exploring the symbiotic relationship between the artist's vision and AI's execution is crucial for understanding how these two elements can complement and enhance each other. This relationship is built on effective communication, understanding, and collaboration, ensuring that artistic output aligns with the artist's intent while leveraging AI's unique capabilities.

Elements of the Symbiotic Relationship

Artist's Vision

The artist brings creativity, conceptual thinking, emotional intelligence, and cultural understanding. This vision forms the foundation of what the art should communicate or represent.

AI's Execution

AI contributes with its ability to process large amounts of data, identify patterns, and execute complex tasks rapidly and efficiently. It can bring a new perspective to the artistic process, often uncovering patterns and possibilities that might not be immediately apparent to the human mind.

Complementary Strengths

The artist's vision provides direction and purpose, while the AI's execution offers new tools and methods for realizing that vision. Together, they can create art that is innovative, intricate, and resonant in ways that neither could achieve alone.

Prompt Engineering for Art Creation

By utilizing one or more of these strategies, you can turn your creative vision into a profitable venture. Prompt engineering optimized for monetizing art involves these critical aspects:

Originality and Creativity

While it's possible to prompt AI to emulate existing styles, the most monetizable art often incorporates unique elements or novel combinations. Prompt engineering should, therefore, focus on creating original pieces that stand out in the market. This involves using imaginative descriptions and avoiding overused themes.

Clarity and Specificity

A well-engineered prompt should be clear and specific to produce art that closely aligns with the intended vision. This means using detailed descriptions of the desired style, composition, color scheme, mood, and subject matter. Clear prompts lead to higher quality outputs, which are more likely to attract customers and generate revenue.

Audience Understanding

Successful monetization requires an understanding of the target audience. Prompts should be engineered with the preferences and tastes of the intended market in mind. This might involve researching current trends, understanding color theory, or incorporating elements known to resonate with the target demographic.

Marketing Language

Incorporating persuasive and appealing language into the prompts can sometimes influence the AI's output in subtle ways that make the art more attractive to potential buyers. This might include the use of vivid, evocative descriptions or the inclusion of elements known to evoke emotional responses.

Scalability

For those looking to monetize at scale, prompts should be designed in a way that they can be slightly modified to produce a wide range of outputs. This allows for the creation of collections or series, which can be more appealing to customers than one-off pieces.

Testing and Iteration

Before finalizing a piece for sale, it's important to test various prompts and iterate based on the results. This process helps in refining the details and ensuring the final product meets quality standards and audience expectations. Iteration can also help in discovering unexpected and innovative art forms that might appeal to a broader audience.

Legal and Ethical Considerations

When monetizing AI-generated art, it's crucial to ensure that the prompts don't infringe on copyrights or other intellectual property rights. This means avoiding specific references to protected characters, artworks, or styles. Additionally, ethical considerations should be addressed, like ensuring the art is culturally sensitive and doesn't perpetuate harmful stereotypes.

Communicating Effectively with AI

Clear and Detailed Instructions
When communicating with AI, clarity is key. Provide detailed instructions and specify the desired outcomes. This might include details about style, mood, themes, and specific elements that should or should not be included.

Understanding AI Capabilities and Limitations
Familiarize yourself with what the AI can and cannot do. This knowledge allows for more realistic and focused instructions, aligning the artist's expectations with the AI's capabilities.

Use of Examples and References
Providing examples, such as images, texts, or other artworks, can help guide the AI. These references can serve as a basis for the AI to understand the desired aesthetic or thematic elements.

Iterative Process
Art creation with AI is often an iterative process. Initial results should be reviewed and refined. Feedback should be given to the AI to adjust its output in subsequent iterations.

Balancing Specificity and Flexibility
While specific instructions are important, leaving room for AI to interpret and add its own creative input can lead to more innovative outcomes. Find a balance between guiding the AI and allowing it some creative freedom.

Emotional and Conceptual Input
Besides technical specifications, communicate the emotional or conceptual goals of the project. If the artwork is meant to evoke a certain feeling or represent a complex idea, make this clear in your instructions.

Collaborative Dynamics

Artist as Guide and Collaborator
The artist should act as a guide, steering the AI towards the envisioned outcome, but also as a collaborator, open to the AI's unique contributions to the creative process.

Adaptation and Evolution
Both the artist and the AI need to adapt and evolve together. As the artist learns more about the AI's strengths and weaknesses, these co-creators can refine their approach. And, as the AI receives more input and feedback, it can better align with the artist's vision.

Chapter 11: Ethical Considerations for Art Created Using GenAI

As AI continues to evolve and become more integrated into the art world, it brings with it a host of ethical considerations and questions about the future. This chapter explores the ethics of AI in art creation, intellectual property concerns, and predictions for how AI will continue to shape the art world.

Originality and Authorship

Central to ethical considerations are the originality of AI-generated art and the implications for artistic authorship. Without the benefit of developing case law, it might remain nebulous how much of a creation can be attributed to AI and attribution shared with the human creator.

See Appendix A for Profiles of Artists Using AI; and see Appendix B for Influential Artists.

The Philosophical Debate: What Constitutes Originality in AI Art?

The advent of AI in art raises fundamental questions about the nature of originality and creativity. Philosophically, there is a debate on whether AI can truly be creative or if it is merely mimicking human creativity. Some argue that AI, lacking consciousness and subjective experiences, cannot be genuinely original. Others contend that AI's ability to combine and transform existing art into something seemingly new constitutes a form of originality.

Transparency is a key consideration, especially when it comes to public display or sale of AI art and derivative works. There is no question that AI art impacts cultural representation. AI art has the potential for perpetuating or challenging social norms and biases, and its impact ultimately depends on how the human interacts and shapes AI output.

Intellectual Property Considerations

From a legal standpoint, the originality of art created by a human using AI can be presumed if a human contributed to its creation in an appreciable way. Traditionally, copyright law protects works that are original and created by humans. AI complicates this, as it can create art without direct human intervention.

Appreciable

In copyright law, 'appreciable' refers to the necessary level of creativity for a work to qualify for copyright protection. While not an exceedingly high bar, the work must demonstrate some originality and be the result of the author's creative efforts. To meet the 'appreciable' standard, a work cannot simply be a copy; it needs a basic level of creativity, perhaps shown through how its content is selected, coordinated, or arranged. Works produced mechanically or routinely without creative input typically fail to meet this criterion. Conversely, works that embody even modest artistic choices, creativity, or intellectual effort are likely to satisfy the requirement.

De Minimis

When an artist's input in a creation is labeled as 'de minimis,' it means the contribution is too minor to qualify for copyright protection. Derived from Latin, 'de minimis' refers to matters too trivial for legal consideration. The assessment of what counts as de minimis is subjective and hinges on the work's specific context and characteristics. Courts evaluate both the qualitative and quantitative value of the contribution against the entire work to make this judgment. Despite the inherent subjectivity, the distinction between a significant and a de minimis contribution is clear-cut, with no middle ground. For legal scholars examining copyright issues in AI-generated art, like those involving ChatGPT, these distinctions are crucial.

The Role of the Human Prompter

In the creation of AI-generated art, the human prompter plays a pivotal role. Far from being mere spectators, humans are active contributors to the artistic process. Their prompts are a key form of creative expression, steering the AI towards producing specific artistic outcomes.

Nature of AI as a Tool

Much like a painter uses a brush or a writer uses a pen, humans use AI to realize a creative vision. The AI, in this context, does not act independently but follows the guidance embedded in the human-provided prompts.

Legal Precedent and Interpretation

Current copyright law generally requires a work to be authored by a human for it to be eligible for copyright protection. The human prompter, in providing detailed, creative instructions to the

AI, can be seen as playing a sufficiently creative role to meet this requirement. The AI's output, in this case, is a direct result of the human's creative input.

Threshold of Creativity

For a work to be copyrighted, it must possess a certain level of creativity. When a human crafts a prompt that is original and creative, and the AI produces a work based on that prompt, the resulting artwork meets the threshold of creativity needed for copyright protection.

Ownership and Attribution

The human who designed the prompt could reasonably assert ownership of the copyright for the AI-generated art, especially where that creative input significantly influenced the final product. This aligns with the principle that copyright protects the expression of ideas (i.e. the prompts, guidance, and resulting output). It does not protect the ideas themselves or the tools used to express them (the AI).

As an example of ownership relating to attribution, OpenAI Terms of Service provides as follows:

> "**Ownership of Content**. As between you and OpenAI, and to the extent permitted by applicable law, you (a) retain your ownership rights in Input and (b) own the Output. We hereby assign to you all our right, title, and interest, if any, in and to Output."
> https://openai.com/policies/terms-of-use (Effective January 31, 2024)

Based on these considerations, it's reasonable for a human—who provides specific, creative prompts to ChatGPT—to assert ownership of the copyright in the resulting artwork. However, as AI continues to evolve and play a more significant role in creative processes, these legal interpretations may be challenged and could evolve. Ongoing legal discourse and potentially new legislative measures might be necessary to address these emerging complexities fully.

Copyright Infringement Risks

If AI is used to replicate or modify copyrighted artworks without authorization, it can constitute copyright infringement, especially if the new work is substantially like the original and does not qualify as fair use.

Fair Use

It's crucial to understand the four factors that are considered when determining whether a use qualifies as fair. These four factors are weighed on a case-by-case basis, and no single factor will determine fair use definitively.

1. **Purpose and Character of the Use**
   This factor considers whether the use is of a commercial nature or for nonprofit educational purposes. Transformative use (modifying, adding to, or recontextualizing the original work) often favors fair use.

2. **Nature of the Copyrighted Work**
   The use of factual or non-fictional works is more likely to be deemed fair use compared to highly creative works like fiction, music, and art.

3. **Amount and Substantiality of the Portion Used**
   This looks at the quantity and value of the portion used in relation to the copyrighted work as a whole. Smaller, less significant portions favor fair use.

4. **Effect on the Potential Market**
   If the use adversely affects the market for or value of the original work, it's less likely to be considered fair use.

Moral Rights and Artist Integrity

Many jurisdictions recognize moral rights of human artists, which include the right to attribution and the right to object to derogatory treatment of the creators' work. AI modifications that distort or misuse the original work could potentially violate these moral rights.

Moral rights are designed to protect the personal and reputational relationship between an author and their creation. The core components of moral rights typically include the right of attribution (the right to be recognized as the creator of a work) and the right of integrity (the right to object to any distortion, mutilation, or other modification of a work that would be prejudicial to the author's honor or reputation).

Legally, moral rights can be asserted by authors to prevent unauthorized use or alteration of their works that might be deemed harmful to their artistic integrity or personal reputation. In countries that strongly recognize these rights, such as those adhering to the Berne Convention for the Protection of Literary and Artistic Works, an author can take legal action to enforce these rights. However, the extent of these rights and the mechanisms for their enforcement vary significantly from one jurisdiction to another. In some jurisdictions, moral rights are inalienable and cannot be transferred, whereas in others, like the United States under the Visual Artists Rights Act (VARA), these rights are more limited in scope and duration and typically apply only to certain works of visual art. Therefore, the ability to assert moral rights depends largely on the specific legal context of the country in question.

Issues with Posthumous Modifications

Using AI to modify the works of deceased artists raises questions about respecting the artistic integrity and intended message of the original creator.

Cultural Sensitivity

When AI modifies artworks that are culturally significant, it raises concerns about cultural sensitivity and appropriation, especially if the AI-generated modifications are seen as disrespectful or misrepresentative.

Preservation of Artistic Heritage

AI modifications of classic artworks might affect the public's understanding and appreciation of historical art, potentially leading to confusion about the original context and meaning. Respect for artistic heritage is an ethical consideration for humans to grapple with. AI will undoubtedly also be attuned to such nuanced concerns. While AI offers innovative ways to engage with art, there's a need to balance this with the preservation of artistic heritage and historical accuracy.

Licensing and Usage Rights

If you are not certain how licensing and usage rights of AI-generated art apply to you in a commercial context, consult with an attorney who specializes in Intellectual Property (IP) law.

Determining Copyright

A primary legal complexity is determining who holds the copyright for AI-generated art. Is it the creator of the AI software, the user who provided the prompts, or, in some interpretations, the AI itself? The answer varies based on jurisdiction and the specific involvement of the AI and the human user.

Work for Hire and Commissioned Works

In commercial contexts, questions arise around works created as “work for hire” or commissioned pieces. The usual rules that apply to human-created works may not straightforwardly apply to AI-generated works.

Licensing Agreements

When licensing AI-generated art, it's crucial to have clear terms defining who is licensing the art and the scope of the license.

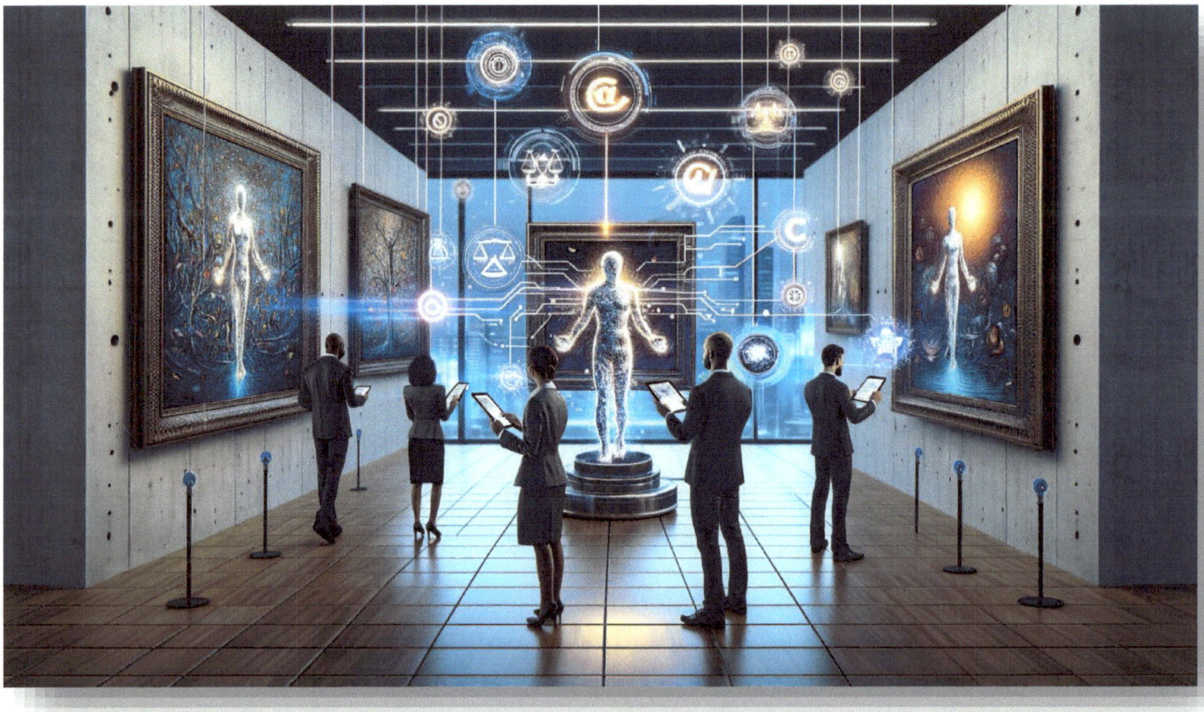

Usage Rights and License Terms

It's important to note that the specifics of a copyright license can vary greatly depending on the agreement between the copyright holder and the licensee. Additionally, different jurisdictions may have variations in how these rights are defined and enforced. Therefore, when drafting or signing a copyright license, it's crucial to be clear about which rights are being licensed and any limitations or conditions attached to each right.

License agreements must specify what the licensee is permitted to do with the artwork – whether it's for digital use only, if print reproductions are allowed, and so forth. Here are the various permissions that can be granted to a licensee regarding the use of a copyrighted work:

1. **Reproduction**
   The right to make copies of the copyrighted work.

2. **Distribution**
   The right to sell, rent, lease, or otherwise distribute copies of the work to the public.

3. **Public Performance**
   The right to perform the work publicly, such as for plays, music, or films.

4. **Public Display**
   The right to display the work publicly, applicable to paintings, photographs, sculptures, and other works that can be viewed.

5. **Derivative Work**
   The right to make derivative works based on the original copyrighted work. This includes adaptations, translations, or other transformations.

6. **Digital Transmission**
   The right to digitally transmit the work, particularly important in the context of digital media and online platforms.

7. **Synchronization**
   The right to synchronize music with visual media, such as in movies, TV shows, or advertisements.

8. **Adaptation**
   Like derivative work rights, this specifically covers adaptations of the work into new formats or styles.

9. **Translation**
   The right to translate the work into other languages.

10. **Archival**
    The right to archive the work for preservation, especially in institutional contexts like libraries or museums.

11. **Performance in Public**
    The right to play sound recordings publicly, such as on the radio or in a public venue.

12. **Moral Rights**
    While not universally recognized and varying greatly by jurisdiction, moral rights typically include the right of attribution and the right to object to derogatory treatment of the work.

13. **Broadcasting**
    The right to broadcast the work via media like television or radio.

14. **Rental and Lending**
    The right to rent or lend copies of the work, typically relevant for video and audio recordings.

15. **Merchandising**
    The right to use the work for merchandising purposes, such as on T-shirts, mugs, etc.

16. **Commercialization**
    The right to use the work for commercial purposes, beyond mere distribution or sale.

Royalties: Exclusivity and Territory

Royalty amounts are negotiated. Factors include the territorial scope of the license and whether the license is exclusive or non-exclusive.

Royalty Arrangements

Determining how royalties are managed and distributed for AI-generated art can be challenging. Commercial exploitation of AI-generated art depends on the use rights discussed above.

Adaptation of Existing Legal Frameworks

The legal system is still catching up with technological advancements in AI. Existing copyright and licensing laws may need adaptation or reinterpretation to accommodate the unique nature of AI-generated art. There is also the added complexity of international legal variations, especially relevant in the global digital art market.

Predictions for the Future of AI in the Art World

In envisioning the future of AI in the art world, one of the most exciting prospects lies in the increased collaboration between human artists and AI technologies. This symbiotic relationship is poised to lead to the emergence of new forms of art that intricately blend human creativity with the capabilities of AI.

The Evolution of Collaborative Art

Future AI systems are anticipated to become more intuitive and responsive to human input, allowing for a more dynamic creative process. Artists will be able to interact with AI in real-time, using it as a creative partner rather than just a tool. AI's ability to process and analyze vast amounts of data will provide artists with new perspectives and ideas.

Art Forms and Media

Emerging hybrid artworks combine traditional artistic media with digital and AI-generated elements, creating multisensory experiences. AI's capability to adapt and learn can be used to create art that evolves over time, reacts to its environment, or interacts with audiences in innovative ways. AI art is a versatile field that spans various media, reflecting the diverse ways AI can be incorporated into the creative process. Here's a list of media in which AI art is commonly exhibited:

- **Digital Images.** Perhaps the most common medium, digital images include everything from paintings and drawings to complex visualizations, all created or manipulated using AI algorithms.

- **Interactive Installations.** These are immersive spaces or setups where viewers can interact with AI elements, often leading to real-time changes in the art based on viewer input or environmental factors.

- **Video and Animation.** AI is used to create or alter moving images, producing everything from short films and animations to video art.

- **Sculpture.** While more traditional in form, sculptures can be designed or conceptualized using AI, with some even being 3D printed based on AI models.

- **Performance Art:** In some cases, AI is part of live performances, where it might control aspects of the performance or interact with the performers in real-time.
- **Virtual Reality (VR) and Augmented Reality (AR):** AI-generated art can be experienced in a fully immersive environment or overlaid onto the real world, providing interactive and immersive experiences.
- **Sound and Music:** AI is used to compose music or create soundscapes, which can either stand alone or accompany other forms of art.
- **Text and Poetry:** AI-generated text or poetry can be considered a form of art, especially when it's part of a larger installation or performance.
- **Generative Art:** This includes artworks that continuously change or evolve based on algorithms, often creating never-repeating patterns or sequences.
- **Photography:** AI can alter or enhance photographs to create new, artistic images or can even generate photorealistic images from scratch.
- **Fashion:** AI is used to design clothing or accessories, which are then made into physical items or presented in digital formats.
- **Light Displays:** Using AI to control or design light patterns, artists can create dynamic visual experiences on buildings, in rooms, or across other surfaces.

These media demonstrate the flexibility and breadth of AI art, showing how technology can augment and expand traditional artistic practices into new and innovative territories. As AI technology continues to evolve, it's likely that even more media will emerge, further broadening the horizons of AI art.

Important Considerations

Derivative Works

Generally, users are permitted to create derivative works based on the output from ChatGPT. This means you can modify, build upon, or incorporate the output into other works.

Copyright Ownership
In terms of copyright, the situation can be complex. While you may claim copyright on your original contributions to the derivative work, the output generated directly by ChatGPT itself may not be eligible for copyright protection, as it is produced by an AI system. The degree to which the output is transformed or augmented by your input could play a role in determining copyright ownership.

Commercial Use
If you plan to use the output for commercial purposes, it's important to review the terms for any specific conditions or limitations regarding commercialization.

Attribution and Acknowledgment
Although not typically a legal requirement, it's often considered good practice to acknowledge or attribute the role of AI tools like ChatGPT in the creative process, especially if their contribution to the final work is substantial.

Terms and Conditions
Always review the most current version of OpenAI's Terms of Service. Terms and conditions can change, and they may include specific clauses related to the use of outputs, intellectual property rights, and other legal considerations.

Legal and Ethical Considerations
Beyond the terms of use, consider any legal and ethical implications, especially if the outputs include sensitive or regulated content.

Given the rapidly evolving nature of AI and its applications, it's recommended to consult the latest terms of service and, if necessary, seek legal advice, particularly for uses with significant legal, ethical, or commercial implications.

Prompts as Art

The aim of a copyright statement is to clarify ownership and rights, which is especially important in works where AI plays a role in the creative process. The copyright status of your prompts for ChatGPT can be complex and depends on several factors. Generally, copyright protects original works of authorship that are fixed in a tangible medium of expression. For a prompt to be protected by copyright, it must be appreciable to fully meet the criteria of originality and creativity.

- **Originality and Creativity**
  If a prompt is sufficiently creative or original, it may be eligible for copyright protection. For instance, a creatively constructed scenario or a detailed and imaginative description could potentially be copyrighted.

- **Fixation**
  The prompt must be "fixed" in a tangible medium of expression. In the case of generative AI, when a user inputs a prompt, it is fixed in a digital medium.

- **User's Rights**
  If you are the original creator of a prompt and it qualifies for copyright protection, you would typically hold the copyright. This is contingent, however, on the prompt not being based on or derived from any previously copyrighted material owned by others.

- **Practical Considerations**
  In practice, certain prompts submitted to ChatGPT might be too simple to qualify for copyright protection. Simple questions or requests for information, for instance, are unlikely to meet the threshold of originality required for copyright.

- **Terms of Service and Agreements**
  The terms of service or user agreements associated with ChatGPT or its platform could also play a role in determining the rights associated with prompts submitted by users. Users typically agree to certain terms that might affect how their inputs (including prompts) are treated.

In summary, while it is possible for your AI prompts to be protected by copyright if they are original and creative, unappreciable prompts may not meet the requisite criteria. Additionally, the terms of service of the generative AI platform and the nature of the input's originality are important considerations.

Copyright Statements for Art Created by Humans Using AI

An appropriate copyright statement for work created with the assistance of AI can vary depending on several factors, such as the nature of the AI's contribution, the originality of the input provided by the human creator, and the terms of use of the AI tool itself.

Key Points Relating to Copyright Protection:

1. **Authorship Acknowledgment**
   Clearly state your authorship as you would in any creative work. If the AI's role is significant, it's good practice to acknowledge it.

2. **Year of Creation**
   Include the year when the work was created.

3. **Rights Reserved**
   Specify that all rights are reserved, which indicates that you hold the copyright and others cannot reproduce, distribute, or create derivative works without your permission.

4. **AI Tool Mention**
   If the AI tool's Terms of Service require, or if you wish to acknowledge the tool used, include its name.

5. **Terms of Use of AI Tool**
   Be aware of the terms of use of the AI software or tool. Some AI tools might have specific requirements or limitations regarding copyright claims on the output.

Consult Legal Advice

For commercial works or if you have any doubts about the correct form of the copyright statement, it's advisable to consult with a legal professional, particularly as laws regarding AI and copyright can be complex and vary by jurisdiction.

The Role of AI in the Creative Process

AI can assist in the conceptual phase of art creation, suggesting themes, styles, or compositions based on the artist's initial ideas. AI tools can help you with ideation. AI provides welcome suggestions when effectively prompted. Co-creating alongside the artist, AI brings a new dimension to the creative process.

Art Education in the Era of AI

The integration of AI in the field of art presents both exciting opportunities and significant challenges for art education. As AI continues to reshape the landscape of creative expression, art education must adapt to these changes, balancing traditional artistic skills with new technological competencies.

Challenges

- **Technological Integration**
  One of the primary challenges is integrating AI technology into the traditional art curriculum. This includes not only the acquisition of equipment and software but also updating the curriculum to include AI-based art techniques.

- **Skill Set Adaptation**
  Educators and students alike are required to develop a new set of skills that blend artistic sensibilities with technological proficiency. This learning curve can be steep for those accustomed to traditional art forms.

- **Conceptual Understanding**
  Understanding AI's capabilities and limitations in the context of art requires a deep conceptual grasp of both technology and art, which can be challenging to impart in an educational setting.

- **Ethical and Philosophical Questions**
  AI in art raises ethical questions about originality, authorship, and the value of human vs. machine-generated art. Addressing these in an educational context is complex.

Opportunities

- **Expanding Creative Boundaries**
  AI promotes new avenues for creative expression by humans. It allows students to experiment with styles and techniques that would be difficult or impossible to achieve by traditional means.

- **Interdisciplinary Learning**
  The use of AI in art education fosters an interdisciplinary approach, merging science, technology, engineering, art, and mathematics.

- **Innovation and Collaboration**
  AI encourages innovation and can facilitate collaborative projects that bring together students with diverse skills and interests, promoting teamwork and diverse thinking.

- **Accessibility and Inclusivity**
  AI tools can make art creation more accessible. For example, they can assist students who may have physical disabilities or those who find traditional art mediums challenging.

- **Preparing for the Future**
  Incorporating AI into art education prepares students for a future where technology and art increasingly intersect, equipping them with relevant skills for the evolving job market.

In balancing these challenges and opportunities, art education can provide a rich, dynamic learning environment that prepares students for the future of art. By embracing AI, educators can not only enhance the artistic capabilities of their students but also encourage critical thinking about the role of technology in creative expression. The key lies in integrating AI not as a replacement for traditional art, but as an additional tool that expands the scope and potential of what art can be.

Chapter 12: Valuable Art Created Using AI Tools

Art is inherently subjective. The concepts of creativity and originality can vary widely among different cultures, time periods, and legal jurisdictions.

Indisputable Proof Artwork Possesses Requisite Degree of Creativity

Establishing indisputable proof that your artwork has the requisite degree of creativity can be complex, especially since the assessment of appreciable creativity and originality in art is often subjective. In legal contexts, defined criteria used to assess this.

- **Distinctiveness from Prior Art**
  Your artwork should show clear differences from existing works. This doesn't mean it can't be inspired by or referenced by other art, but there should be evident creative choices that set it apart. This can be assessed through comparative analysis.

- **Artistic Choices and Techniques**
  Evidence of your deliberate artistic choices in elements like composition, technique, medium, and style can demonstrate creativity. These choices should reflect your personal creative expression rather than just technical skill or replication of existing styles.

- **Conceptual Innovation**
  Sometimes, originality lies not in the aesthetic but in the concept behind the artwork. If your artwork introduces a new idea or a unique interpretation of a subject, this can be seen as evidence of creativity.

- **Artist's Testimony and Process Documentation**
  Your explanation of your artwork and your creative process can be crucial. Documentation showing the evolution of your work, sketches, drafts, or notes that illustrate the creative journey can serve as proof of originality.

- **Expert Opinions**
  Art historians, curators, critics, and other experts can provide insights into the originality of a piece based on their knowledge of art history and trends. Their analysis can help in identifying unique aspects of your artwork.

- **Legal Precedents and Standards**
  In copyright law, the bar for originality is relatively low. The work must simply possess some original elements that are not entirely derived from other works.

- **Cultural and Historical Context**
  Understanding the context in which artwork was created is important. What might be considered original in one cultural or historical context might not be in another.

- **Public Perception and Acceptance**
  While not always a definitive measure, the way an artwork is received by the public and the art community can sometimes reflect its originality. A work that inspires discussion, interpretation, or spawns a new artistic movement can be seen as having a significant degree of creativity.

Notable Artworks Created Using AI

The recognition these artworks have received highlights the growing interest and value in AI-generated art within the traditional art market. The five artworks that follow exemplify how AI is a tool for artistic creation.

AI Generated Nude Portrait #7 Frame #64 by Robbie Barrat

https://www.sothebys.com/en/buy/auction/2022/the-now-evening-auction/ai-generated-nude-portrait-7-frame-64

- **Auction Price**: Listed by Sotheby's with estimated value between $890,330 - $1,526,280

- **Details:** This artwork, created by AI researcher Robbie Barrat, is an early example of AI-generated art. Part of series of 300 AI-generated nude art known as *The Lost Robbies*, it showcases a unique interpretation of the nude portrait genre using neural networks.

Portrait of Edmond de Belamy by Obvious

https://obvious-art.com/portfolio/edmond-de-belamy

- **Auction Price:** Sold for $432,500 at Christie's in October 2018.

- **Details:** Crafted by the Paris-based art collective Obvious, this artwork was brought to life using a Generative Adversarial Network (GAN). The piece features a portrait of a fictional character and forms part of a series that delves into the intriguing intersection of art and artificial intelligence. Notably, the artist's signature, elegantly printed in a cursive Gallic script at the bottom of the artwork, plays a pivotal role in the creation process. This signature is an integral part of the algorithm's code that generated the artwork, embedding the artist's touch directly within the digital fabric of the piece.

The Butcher's Son by Mario Klingemann

https://www.artsy.net/artwork/mario-klingemann-imposture-series-the-butchers-son

- **Auction Price**: Not publicly disclosed, but it is possible that this original artwork was sold at an auction at Sotheby's for an estimated $50,000.

- **Details:** At the time of publication, Mario Klingemann's *The Butcher's Son* was available for sale at Artsy as a giclée print on cotton paper.

Memories of Passersby I by Mario Klingemann

https://www.sothebys.com/en/auctions/ecatalogue/2019/contemporary-art-day-auction-l19021/lot.109.html

- **Auction Price:** Reportedly sold for $42,000 at Sotheby's in March 2019.

- **Details**: Created by artist Mario Klingemann, this AI-generated artwork uses a neural network to create an ever-evolving series of portrait-like images displayed on two screens.

Le Comte de Belamy by Obvious

https://obvious-art.com/portfolio/le-comte-de-belamy

- **Auction Price**: $12,000

- **Details**: Created by Artificial Intelligence Creative Adversarial Network (AICAN), an AI program developed by Dr. Ahmed Elgammal, this artwork is part of a series, like the Belamy portraits. AICAN's work is known for pushing the boundaries of AI's role in creative expression.

Non-Fungible Tokens (NFTs) Certify Ownership and Authenticity

NFTs are digital assets that use blockchain technology to certify ownership and establish the authenticity of various digital items, including digital art, music, videos, virtual real estate, collectibles, and more. Blockchain technology is a decentralized, distributed ledger that stores the record of ownership of digital assets. It's a type of shared database that differs from a typical database in the way it stores information; blockchains store data in blocks that are linked together via cryptography.

NFTs work by creating a unique, verifiable record on a blockchain, typically on the Ethereum blockchain. This record contains information about the specific digital asset, its ownership history, and a cryptographic signature that ensures its authenticity and scarcity. When someone purchases an NFT associated with a digital item, they are essentially buying a digital certificate of ownership for that item, and the blockchain provides a transparent and immutable ledger of ownership.

It's important to note that while NFTs can certify ownership and authenticity of digital assets, NFTs do not necessarily guarantee the copyright or intellectual property rights associated with the underlying content. Ownership of the NFT and ownership of the intellectual property rights to the digital content are separate concepts. It's essential for buyers and creators to understand the terms and rights associated with both the NFT and the digital asset they are acquiring or selling.

NFT Platforms

Prominent NFT platforms that have played a pivotal role in this new technology include:

1. MakersPlace
2. OpenSea
3. Rarible
4. SuperRare

MakersPlace @ https://makersplace.com

MakersPlace is a marketplace for discovering and collecting unique digital creations as NFTs. Founded in 2016 in San Francisco, it supports artists, photographers, writers, and others to showcase and sell their digital art utilizing blockchain technology. The platform verifies every NFT to ensure authenticity and represent artists well.

Security and Wallets

MakersPlace undergoes multiple layers of security for quality and safety. It's an invite-only platform requiring extensive application. Users must have a verified email address to buy and sell, and the platform uses blockchain technology to ensure authenticity and ownership of digital content.

Fees and Royalties

MakersPlace charges transparent fees: 2.5% on each secondary sale and 10% creator royalty, which aligns with other marketplaces. For primary sales, the commission is 5%. MakersPlace also covers minting fees on the Ethereum blockchain but sets a minimum list price to offset this cost.

Lazy Minting

MakersPlace allows creators to mint NFTs without incurring upfront Ethereum blockchain transaction costs (aka gas fees). MakersPlace covers gas fees for creators. Creators can dictate terms of their sales, such as rarity, pricing, and auction parameters.

Usage and Accessibility

MakersPlace offers a user-friendly interface, simplifying the process of minting, buying, and selling. While it supports credit card payments for select NFTs, some features might require a wallet connection, which can be less intuitive for users unfamiliar with blockchain technology.

Blockchain and Currency Support

MakersPlace primarily uses the Ethereum blockchain and supports Ether (ETH) for transactions. It also allows the use of credit cards for some purchases. The platform provides a digital wallet, but users can also link their existing crypto wallets.

Recent Developments

MakersPlace has seen growth in its trading volume and creator base. It emphasizes quality, authenticity, and fairness, and has collaborated with renowned artists and celebrities for exclusive drops. The platform focuses on education, offering resources and webinars for budding NFT artists.

OpenSea @ https://opensea.io

OpenSea, founded in 2017 by Devin Finzer and Alex Atallah, is the world's first and largest web3 marketplace for NFTs and crypto collectibles. It acts as a user-friendly interface for blockchain technology, supporting a wide range of digital assets like art, games, music, and more.

Security and Wallets

OpenSea offers compatibility with multiple wallets and blockchains, enhancing security for transactions. Users can connect to hardware wallets, like MetaMask. This connection requires some technical expertise but ensures a higher level of transaction security.

Fees and Royalties

OpenSea charges a service fee of 2.5% on every successful transaction. Additionally, gas fees, paid to blockchain miners, vary depending on the blockchain used. Creators have the option to set secondary market royalties of up to 10% on their NFTs, receiving a percentage of sales whenever their NFT is resold.

Lazy Minting

OpenSea employs lazy minting, which allows users to upload digital assets and have them visible on the marketplace before tokenizing them; no gas fees are incurred until the item is sold. The party completing the transaction (buyer or seller) pays the gas fees.

Usage and Accessibility

OpenSea offers an intuitive user interface, making buying, selling, and creating NFTs a simple process. OpenSea also provides free educational videos on blockchain technology and tools for NFT creation to attract and educate new users.

Blockchain and Currency Support

OpenSea supports multiple wallets and blockchains for transactions, primarily using Ethereum. The platform facilitates various sale structures, including price floors, auctions, and fractionalized tokens, to improve the liquidity and value of NFTs.

Recent Developments

OpenSea faced a significant drop in users and daily transaction volume in 2022, indicating market volatility. Despite this, it remains a leading platform in the NFT space, with a series of successful funding rounds and a valuation of $13.3 billion as of January 2022.

Rarible @ https://rarible.com

Rarible, established in 2020, is a significant and widely used NFT marketplace that enables users to create, buy, and sell NFTs across various blockchains. It's known for its community-centric approach and offers a vast array of NFT projects, catering to both beginners and experts in the NFT space.

Security and Wallets

Rarible supports multiple wallets across its platform, allowing users to connect and transact with ease. In terms of security, while there have been no reported sitewide incidents, a vulnerability was discovered in April 2022 that could potentially allow malicious actors to create harmful NFTs. Rarible promptly acknowledged and addressed this issue.

Fees and Royalties

Rarible imposes a 2.5% listing fee on transactions. Additionally, the platform offers creators the option to defer minting gas fees until an NFT is sold, a feature known as "lazy minting." This approach is beneficial for creators as it reduces upfront costs associated with minting NFTs.

Lazy Minting

Rarible offers "lazy minting," allowing creators to list NFTs without incurring immediate gas fees. This feature is particularly advantageous for creators starting out or for those who wish to mint NFTs on the more expensive Ethereum blockchain, as it defers the gas fee until the NFT is sold.

Usage and Accessibility

Rarible is user-friendly, with a simple and navigable website and app interface. The platform allows users to buy, sell, and list NFTs easily, with features like fixed-price, timed auction, and open auction sales. However, the mobile app currently only allows users to view NFTs and their details, but not to buy, sell, or mint them.

Blockchain and Currency Support

Rarible is a multichain platform, supporting various blockchains like Ethereum, Tezos, Polygon, Solana, and Immutable X. This multi-blockchain approach offers flexibility to users in terms of choosing a blockchain that best suits their needs.

Recent Developments

Rarible has introduced the ability for users to create their own NFT community marketplaces. This feature enables creators to set up custom marketplaces for specific NFT collections, adding a new dimension to the platform's functionality.

SuperRare @ https://superrare.com

SuperRare, launched in 2018, is a curated NFT art market built on the Ethereum blockchain. It distinguishes itself by focusing on exclusive, one-of-a-kind digital artworks. SuperRare's model resembles that of a traditional art dealer, emphasizing the quality and uniqueness of each piece. The platform is known for hosting high-end digital art, attracting experienced collectors and investors in fine art.

Security and Wallets

The platform uses the Ethereum blockchain for minting, transacting, and verifying NFTs. NFTs listed on SuperRare are locked in smart contracts and remain in the seller's wallet until sold. Funds from buyers are also secured in a smart contract until a successful bid. For wallet support, SuperRare is compatible with popular digital wallets like MetaMask, Fortmatic, and Wallet Connect.

Fees and Royalties

SuperRare charges a 15% gallery fee on primary sales and a 3% marketplace fee on purchases. These fees are relatively high compared to other NFT marketplaces. Additionally, artists are responsible for gas fees when minting artwork. For secondary sales, artists receive a 10% commission as royalties.

Lazy Minting

There is no explicit mention of lazy minting on SuperRare.

Usage and Accessibility

SuperRare is considered less beginner-friendly due to its high-end nature and price points; average sale price for digital artwork on this platform is over $4,000. Artists must be approved or invited to mint on SuperRare, making it an exclusive platform for creators. It is best suited for experienced collectors and fine art investors.

Blockchain and Currency Support

Built on the Ethereum blockchain, SuperRare requires an Ethereum-compatible wallet and ether (ETH) for transactions. The marketplace also has its own governance token, RARE, which allows token holders to vote on community decisions.

Recent Developments

SuperRare's recent advancements are not explicitly detailed in the sources, but its continued focus on high-quality, exclusive digital art keeps it at the forefront of luxury NFT marketplaces.

Chapter 13: Hands-On Tutorials: Guided Projects

Step-by-Step Guides to Create Specific Types of Art

Creating art with GenAI is an iterative process. It often takes several attempts to get the desired result, so don't be afraid to experiment with different prompts and settings. Each iteration can bring you closer to the vision in your mind.

To gain hands-on experience, challenge yourself and complete the "Exercises for GenAI Prompt Crafting" in Appendix F. In the meantime, the following guided projects can support you in your process.

Guided Project #1: Creating a Surreal Landscape

Step 1: Choose your GenAI tool.

- Select a Generative AI art tool such as DALL·E, Artbreeder, or DeepArt. Each has unique features, so choose one that aligns with your artistic goals.

Step 2: Conceptualize your landscape.

- Decide on the elements you want in your landscape. Think about the terrain (mountains, valleys, rivers), sky (daytime, nighttime, auroras), and any surreal elements (floating islands, unusual color schemes).

Step 3: Crafting the prompt.

- Write a detailed prompt that describes your landscape. Include specific details like "a river glowing with bioluminescence under a starry sky" or "giant floating islands over a misty forest."

Step 4: Experiment with settings.

- Adjust settings like style, complexity, or color palette if your chosen tool allows it. These settings can drastically change the outcome.

Step 5: Generate and Iterate

- Create your artwork. If the first result isn't quite right, tweak your prompt or settings and try again.

Step 6: Refinement

- Once you have a result you like, you can refine it using image editing software if necessary.

Step 7: Save and Share

- Save your final artwork. Consider sharing it on social media or art communities to get feedback and inspiration.

Guided Project #2: Creating a Futuristic Cityscape

Step 1: Select your GenAI platform.

- Choose a platform like DALL·E, Midjourney, Deep Dream Generator, or another AI art generator that suits your needs.

Step 2: Visualize your cityscape.

- Think about the elements of your futuristic city. Consider architecture, technology, and atmosphere (e.g., neon lights, flying vehicles, towering skyscrapers).

Step 3: Compose your prompt.

- Write a descriptive prompt. Include details like "futuristic city with neon-lit skyscrapers and hovering cars under a twilight sky."

Step 4: Tweak AI settings.

- Play with any available settings to influence the style or mood of the artwork. This might include adjusting realism, abstractness, or brightness.

Step 5: Generate the artwork.

- Use the platform to generate your artwork. If the result isn't perfect, modify your prompt or settings and regenerate.

Step 6: Post-processing.

- You may want to use photo editing software to make final adjustments to your cityscape.

Step 7: Finalize and display.

- Save your artwork. Consider printing it or sharing it online in art forums or social media.

Chapter 14: Showcasing and Monetizing AI Art

Tips for Presenting AI Art in Portfolios and Exhibitions

Presenting AI art in portfolios and exhibitions requires a thoughtful approach that highlights both the artistic value and the unique aspects of AI as a medium. Here are three practical tips to effectively showcase AI-generated art.

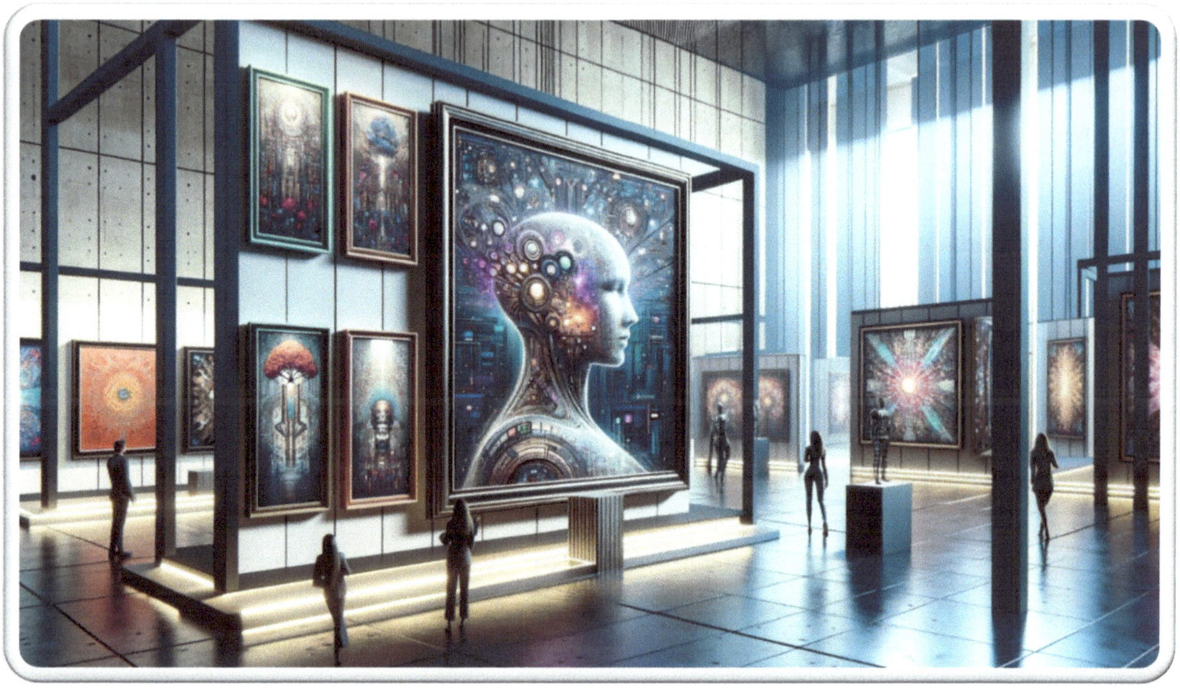

1. Curate with a narrative or theme.

- **Narrative Focus**
  AI art often excels in creating unique and intriguing visuals. Building a narrative or thematic focus for your portfolio or exhibition can help contextualize AI art and give viewers a framework to understand and appreciate it. For instance, a theme like "Dreamscapes and Visions: An AI Journey" can set the tone for the surreal and imaginative nature of the artwork.

- **Storytelling**
  Leverage the descriptions of each artwork to narrate its creation journey. This can encompass the initial inspiration, the AI's contribution to the creative process, and the subtleties of human-AI collaboration. This approach fosters a deeper connection between the viewers and the artwork.

2. Highlight the AI's unique contribution.

- **AI as Collaborator**
  Clearly communicate the role of AI in the creation of each piece. Treat the AI as a collaborator in your artistic process. This might involve explaining how the AI's capabilities influenced the direction of the artwork or showcasing how AI-generated elements were combined with traditional techniques.

- **Technical Insights**
  For an audience that may be intrigued by the technological aspect, include information about the AI model used (like GPT-4 or DALL·E), the training process, and how prompts were developed. This can be particularly engaging in exhibitions where the blend of art and technology is a focal point.

3. Create an interactive and engaging presentation.

- **Digital Displays**
  Given that AI art is often digital, utilize high-resolution displays to showcase the work in its best light. Interactive screens where viewers can zoom in to details or see variations of a piece (if available) can enhance engagement.

- **Interactive Elements**
  Consider incorporating interactive elements, such as a station where visitors can enter prompts and see live AI art generation (if feasible). This not only makes the exhibition more engaging but also educates the audience about the process.

- **Online Portfolio Considerations**
  For online portfolios, ensure high-quality image hosting. Consider interactive elements like hover-over text for artwork details or a blog section discussing the AI art creation process. Accessibility and ease of navigation are key.

Bonus Tip: Art Process Documentation

Showing the process of how the AI artwork was created, including initial sketches, prompt evolution, and different iterations, can be fascinating for viewers. This peek behind the curtain can demystify AI art and enrich the viewer's understanding and appreciation.

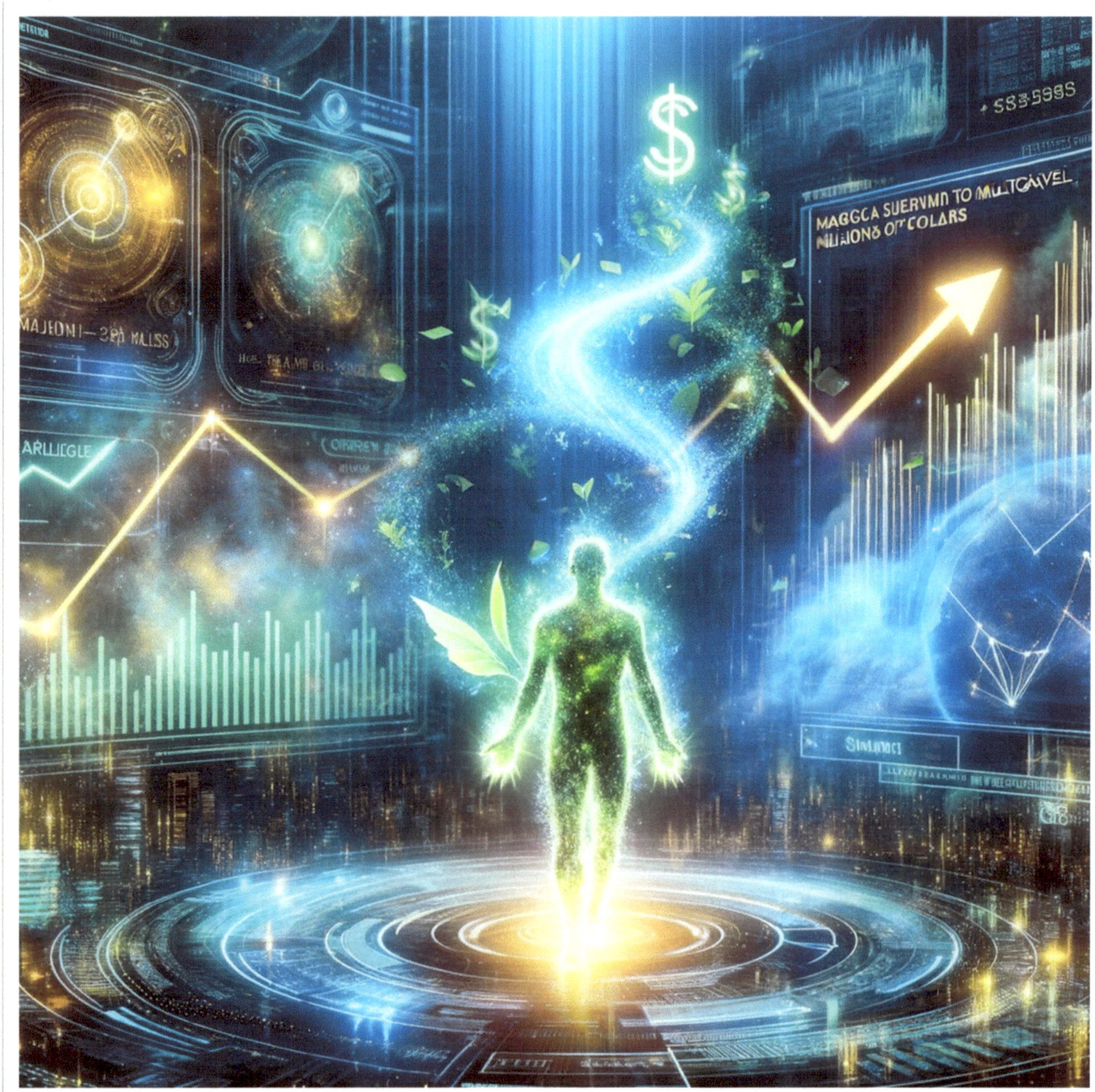

Monetize Your Artworks

Monetizing AI-generated artworks involves innovative strategies that match the unique nature of AI creations. The generation of AI art and its subsequent monetization depend on numerous factors, including market demand, the uniqueness of the artwork, the reputation of the artist, and current trends in the art world. No specific prompt can inherently ensure a certain amount of earnings.

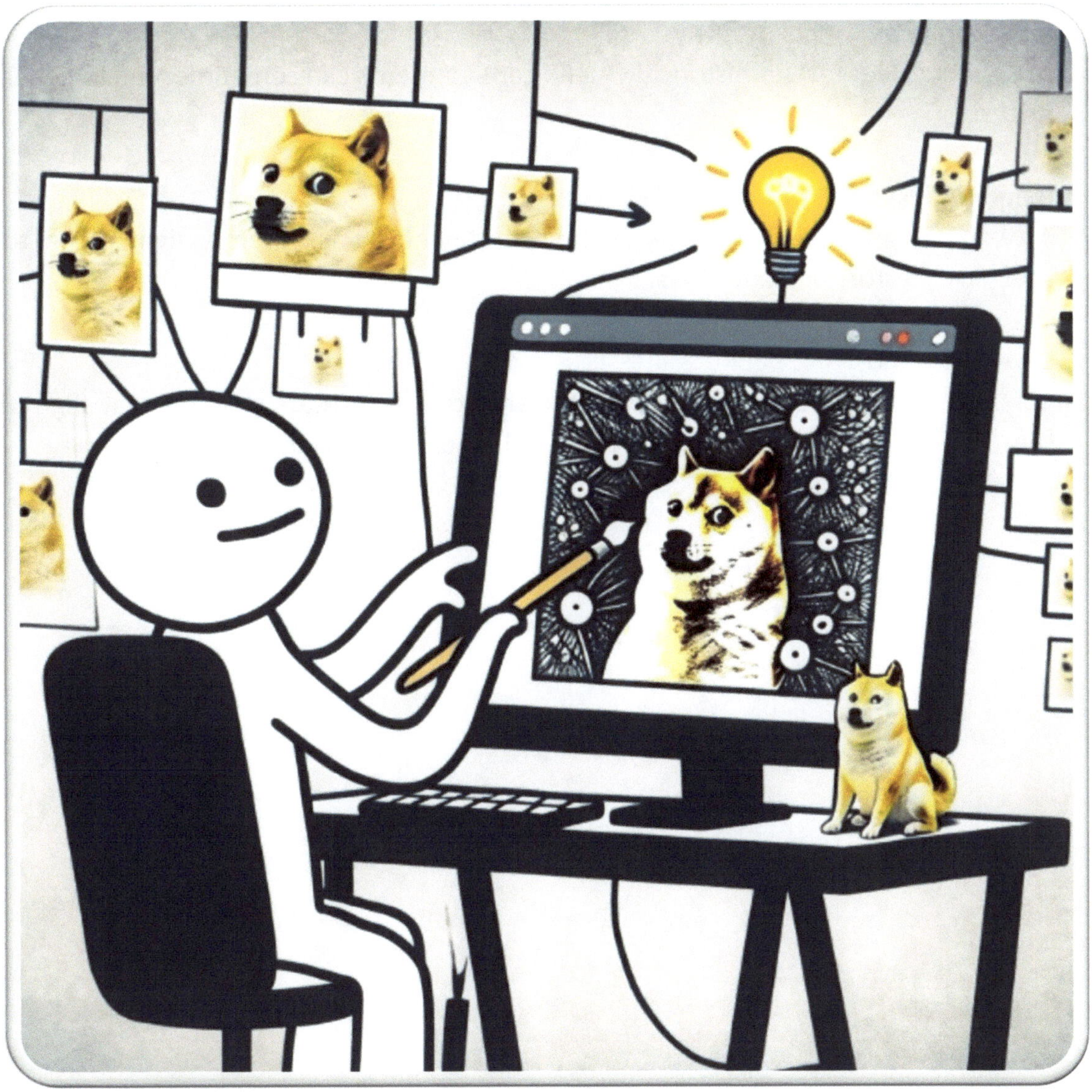

Focus on creating something truly unique, potentially high in demand, and appealing to a specific, wealthy audience or collector. Here are some considerations for crafting a prompt that might create high-value art.

- **Target high-value art markets.**
  Understand the tastes and trends in high-value art markets. Creating something that resonates with collectors of high-end art could potentially increase the value of the artwork.

- **Create unique and complex compositions.**
  Craft a prompt that leads to complex, intricate, and unique compositions, which are often more valued in the art world.

- **Incorporate elements of rarity.**
  Art that includes rare or historically significant elements can sometimes fetch higher prices.

- **Blend with cultural or historical significance.**
  Artwork that resonates with a particular cultural or historical theme might appeal to specific collectors or institutions.

- **Leverage trends.**
  Stay informed about current trends in the art world and create prompts that align with these trends, as this can sometimes lead to higher demand and value.

Twelve Strategies for Successful Monetization of Your Artwork

The art market is subjective and unpredictable. While these strategies have great potential to increase the value of AI-generated art, they do not guarantee a specific financial outcome.

The success of selling art, AI-generated or otherwise, often also relies on marketing, networking, and sometimes a bit of luck. They can also be combined for diversified income streams. Building a reputation and following can significantly enhance monetization potential.

Diversification across multiple channels and exploring different revenue streams can maximize the potential for monetization. Each of these strategies can be tailored to fit the artist's style, target audience, and the nature of the AI artwork.

1. Limited Edition Prints

- **Strategy**
  Produce high-quality, limited edition prints of your AI-generated artworks. Number and sign each print to ensure authenticity and collectability.

- **Monetization Potential**
  Limited editions create a sense of exclusivity and value, often appealing to collectors. By controlling the number of prints, you can maintain scarcity and demand, potentially increasing the artwork's value over time.

2. Digital Art Platforms and NFTs

- **Strategy**
  Utilize digital art platforms and Non-Fungible Tokens (NFTs) to sell unique digital ownership of your AI artworks. Platforms like OpenSea, Rarible, and Foundation provide a marketplace for digital art sales.

- **Monetization Potential**
  NFTs have gained significant attention as they provide a way to authenticate and own digital art uniquely. They have opened up new revenue streams for digital artists, with some AI-generated pieces selling for substantial amounts. The digital scarcity and ownership proof can significantly increase the perceived value.

3. Commissioned Work and Customization

- **Strategy**
  Offer to create customized AI art based on client specifications. This could range from personal portraits to unique business logos or thematic artwork for an event.

- **Monetization Potential**
  Customization adds a personal touch that clients are willing to pay a premium for. As an artist, you can set prices based on the complexity and usage of the artwork. Ongoing relationships with clients can provide a steady income stream.

4. Licensing for Commercial Use

- **Strategy**
  License your AI-generated artworks for commercial use. This can include book covers, album art, advertising, merchandise, or even as part of design elements in video games and movies.

- **Monetization Potential**
  Licensing can be lucrative, especially if you secure deals with high-profile clients or popular products. You can negotiate one-time fees or ongoing royalties based on sales, providing a potential recurring revenue.

5. Teaching and Workshops

- **Strategy**
  Offer courses, workshops, or online content teaching others how to create AI art. As an expert in the field, you can share your knowledge on the technology, techniques, and business aspects.

- **Monetization Potential**
  Education is a powerful revenue stream. You can monetize through direct course sales, subscriptions, or sponsored content. As the field of AI art grows, so does the audience eager to learn about it, ensuring a market for such educational offerings.

6. Art Galleries and Exhibitions

- **Strategy**
  Partner with art galleries or participate in art exhibitions that are open to digital and AI-generated artworks. This can include both physical galleries and online exhibitions.

- **Monetization Potential**
  Exhibiting in galleries can attract collectors and art enthusiasts who are willing to pay for unique pieces. It also offers the opportunity to sell prints or digital versions on-site. Additionally, showing your work enhances your visibility and credibility as an artist.

7. Collaborations with Other Artists and Designers

- **Strategy**
  Collaborate with traditional artists or designers to create mixed-media works, combining AI art with other art forms.

- **Monetization Potential**
  Collaborative pieces can appeal to a broader market and can be sold as unique art pieces. These collaborations can also open doors to new networks and markets, potentially leading to higher sales and exposure.

8. Merchandising

- **Strategy**
  Use your AI-generated artwork to create merchandise such as clothing, stationery, home decor, or accessories.

- **Monetization Potential**
  Merchandising can significantly extend your revenue streams. With the popularity of custom and unique designs, especially those with artistic value, this approach can appeal to a wider audience beyond art collectors.

9. Social Media and Online Portfolios

- **Strategy**
  Leverage online portfolios and social media platforms to showcase your work and attract buyers. Platforms like Instagram, Pinterest, and Behance are excellent for visual art.

- **Monetization Potential**
  A strong online presence can attract direct purchases, commission work, and even sponsorships. Social media platforms can also drive traffic to your own website or online store where you can sell your art.

10. Crowdfunding and Patronage Platforms

- **Strategy**
  Use crowdfunding or patronage platforms like Kickstarter or Patreon. You can fund specific projects or offer subscription-based access to your artwork and creative process.

- **Monetization Potential**
  This can provide upfront funding for projects and a steady income from supporters. It's also a great way to build a community around your work.

11. Stock Image and Video Marketplaces

- **Strategy**
  Sell your AI-generated images or videos on stock content platforms like Shutterstock, Adobe Stock, or Getty Images.

- **Monetization Potential**
  These platforms can provide a passive income stream as businesses and content creators license your art for commercial use.

12. Corporate Commissions and Partnerships

- **Strategy**
  Seek out commissions or partnerships with businesses for unique AI art that can be used in corporate settings, like offices, hotels, or advertising campaigns.

- **Monetization Potential**
  Corporate clients can offer larger-scale projects with potentially higher budgets, providing significant earnings and opportunities for high-profile exposure.

Conclusion

The relationship between an artist's vision and AI's execution in art is a symbiotic one, built on effective communication, mutual understanding, and collaboration. By leveraging each other's strengths, artists and AI can together create artworks that are not only technically impressive but also emotionally and conceptually profound.

Ponder the impact AI wields in the art world's evolution. In the preceding chapters we've explored the intricate relationship between human creativity and artificial intelligence, unveiling the vast potential and possibilities that AI brings to the art world. Now much clearer are the nuances of how to craft effective prompts that generate valuable art.

Your innate artistic talents can be even more valuable, leveraging output you realize with your powerful AI prompts. With your awareness of ethical considerations and legal intricacies surrounding AI-generated art, you're well-prepared to venture further into this domain.

The profiles of artists and the exploration of galleries and exhibitions have also illustrated the vibrant and evolving landscape of AI art. These insights have shown us that the fusion of AI and art is not just a fleeting trend but a significant shift in how we perceive and create art.

As AI technology continues to advance, the collaboration between human artists and AI will deepen, leading to the birth of new art forms and expressions. This book has equipped you with the knowledge and tools to be a part of this exciting evolution, encouraging you to experiment, explore, and push the boundaries of creativity.

In closing, *Visual Art Design Using Generative AI* is not just a guide but an invitation to embark on a unique artistic journey, one that intertwines the time-honored tradition of art with the boundless possibilities of AI. Whether you are an artist, a technologist, or simply an enthusiast of the arts, the future of AI-generated art is a canvas awaiting your contribution. Embrace it with curiosity, creativity, and an open mind, and be part of shaping the next chapter in the story of art and technology.

Appendix A: Profiles of Artists Using AI

Refik Anadol

Refik Anadol is a distinguished Turkish-American media artist, born in 1985, known for integrating advanced technology and data into his artwork, particularly through the use of artificial intelligence and machine learning. Anadol's innovative work often explores themes of data aesthetics, digital consciousness, and the interaction between the physical and virtual worlds.

Anadol has showcased his art internationally, with significant exhibitions including "Machine Hallucinations" at the Museum of Modern Art (MoMA) in New York, where he employed AI to reinterpret and transform over two centuries of art history into digital visualizations. His work, "Unsupervised," part of the Machine Hallucinations series, is notable for its use of AI to create immersive, abstract environments from large data sets, exploring the boundary between digital and physical realms. Check out the Refik Anadol Studio: https://refikanadolstudio.com

Sofia Crespo

Sofia Crespo is an Argentine visual artist born on April 7, 1991, currently based in Lisbon. She is renowned for her work that intersects the realms of biology and artificial intelligence. Crespo's art primarily investigates how organic life utilizes artificial mechanisms to mimic and evolve itself, challenging the conventional separation between technology and its biological origins.

Her notable works include "Neural Zoo," "Artificial Remnants," and "This Jellyfish Does Not Exist," which showcase her fascination with AI's potential to reimagine natural forms and processes. Crespo's installations and digital artworks often feature a mix of neural networks and generative techniques to create intricate and surreal representations of natural entities. She collaborates with Feileacan Kirkbride McCormick in the artistic duo Entangled Others, focusing on themes of ecology, nature, and the more-than-human world.

Crespo's art has been featured in various prestigious venues worldwide, such as Kunstverein Hannover and Fotomuseum Winterthur, and has been part of innovative projects that explore digital ecosystems and biodiversity through artificial intelligence. Her work not only provides a speculative glance at unseen natural worlds but also prompts discussions on the creative and cognitive intersections between humans and AI. https://aiartists.org/sofia-crespo

Dr. Ahmed Elgammal

Dr. Ahmed Elgammal is a professor at Rutgers University's Department of Computer Science and a leading figure in the intersection of art and artificial intelligence. He directs the Art and Artificial Intelligence Laboratory at Rutgers, where his innovative research focuses on the capabilities of AI in understanding and generating new artistic creations. Dr. Elgammal's work with AI explores how machines perceive and create art, challenging traditional notions of creativity and artistic expression.

One of Dr. Elgammal's notable contributions to AI in art is the development of AICAN, an autonomous AI system designed to produce original artworks. AICAN's creations, which have been exhibited internationally, are based on the system's understanding of art history and its ability to generate new visual forms that challenge human perceptions of art made by machines. https://aiartists.org/ahmed-elgammal

Mario Klingemann

Mario Klingemann is a prominent German artist celebrated for his innovative work at the intersection of artificial intelligence, neural networks, and artistic expression. Born in 1970 in Laatzen, Lower Saxony, Klingemann has been a pivotal figure in the AI art movement. He was a resident artist at Google Arts and Culture from 2016 to 2018 and has been actively involved with ONKAOS, a new media artist support program.

Klingemann's art primarily explores the capabilities of AI and machine learning to reimagine and reinterpret human perception and creativity. His notable works, like "Memories of Passersby I" and "Uncanny Mirror," utilize generative adversarial networks (GANs) to challenge and expand our understanding of art. "Memories of Passersby I" gained particular attention for being one of the first AI-generated artworks auctioned at a traditional auction house, Sotheby's.

He is known for his critical approach to the art world, viewing it as a complex system influenced significantly by social dynamics and narratives rather than merely the artworks themselves. His art often questions and explores these dynamics, aiming to expose and understand the underlying structures of cultural perception and classification. Klingemann’s contributions to digital and AI art have been recognized with awards such as the 2018 Lumen Prize Gold Award and an honorary mention at the Prix Ars Electronica in 2020.

Klingemann's work is exhibited internationally, including prestigious venues like the Ars Electronica Festival, the ZKM Karlsruhe, and the Museum of Modern Art in New York. https://aiartists.org/mario-klingemann

Anna Ridler

Anna Ridler is a London-based artist and researcher renowned for her innovative work at the intersection of data, AI, and art. She primarily engages with themes surrounding the natural world, using machine learning as a tool to explore and reinterpret these themes through her art. Ridler is particularly known for creating detailed datasets which she uses to train machine learning models, thus generating unique artistic narratives and visual representations.

One of Ridler's notable projects is "Myriad (Tulips)," which involves an installation of ten thousand hand-labeled photographs of tulips. This work not only reflects on historical economic bubbles, like the 17th-century tulip mania, but also on contemporary issues such as cryptocurrency speculation. Another significant work, "Mosaic Virus," uses AI to manipulate images of tulips based on the fluctuations in Bitcoin prices, visually critiquing the speculative nature of value in modern economies. https://aiartists.org/anna-ridler

Helena Sarin

Helena Sarin is a multifaceted artist and software engineer known for her innovative work at the intersection of AI and visual arts. Sarin has a strong background in technology, having started her career at Bell Labs before moving on to become an independent consultant specializing in computer vision and deep learning. This technical expertise greatly informs her artistic practice, particularly her use of Generative Adversarial Networks (GANs) to create complex, aesthetically pleasing artworks.

Her artistic works often involve a critical engagement with AI technologies, crafting her own datasets and integrating them into her pieces to ensure each work is unique. This approach allows her to maintain a personal touch and avoid the homogeneity that can arise from using common datasets. Sarin's art is characterized by its exploration of still life compositions, where she combines elements like food and flowers, reminiscent of traditional masterpieces but reinterpreted through modern computational techniques. https://aiartists.org/helena-sarin

Appendix B: Influential Artists

Artist	Full Name	Synopsis
Abanindranath Tagore	Abanindranath Tagore (अबनीन्द्रनाथ ठाकुर)	Prominent figure of the Bengal School of Art, Abanindranath Tagore played a pivotal role in the revival of traditional Indian art forms and techniques, emphasizing Indian subjects and themes.
Ai Weiwei	Ai Weiwei (艾未未)	Contemporary artist and activist, Ai Weiwei is known for his political commentary and works that challenge the Chinese government's stance on democracy and human rights.
Amaral	Tarsila de Aguiar do Amaral	Pioneering figure in the modernist movement in Brazil, Amaral played a crucial role in developing the Brazilian aesthetic identity, particularly through her involvement in the Anthropophagy Movement.
Baselitz	Georg Baselitz	Influential contemporary artist, Baselitz is known for his figurative, expressive compositions. He gained recognition for his upside-down paintings, challenging viewers' perceptions and conventions of art.
Basquiat	Jean-Michel Basquiat	American artist of Haitian and Puerto Rican descent who became one of the most famous artists of the 20th century for his raw, provocative imagery blended with graffiti-inspired work.
Bearden	Romare Bearden	African American artist who worked with many types of media including cartoons, oils, and collages, drawing on his experiences in the American South and Harlem.
Beuys	Joseph Beuys	Multifaceted artist involved in sculpture, performance, and conceptual art. His works, emphasizing social and political activism, have left a profound impact on the contemporary art scene.

Artist	Full Name	Synopsis
Bose	Nandalal Bose (नंदलाल बोस)	Student of Abanindranath Tagore, Bose was instrumental in establishing modern Indian painting, incorporating indigenous motifs and techniques in his works.
Braque	Georges Braque	20th-century French painter and sculptor who, along with Pablo Picasso, developed the art style known as Cubism.
Bravo	Manuel Álvarez Bravo	Considered one of the greatest photographers of the 20th century, Álvarez Bravo's work captures the essence of Mexican life, blending elements of surrealism with social and political commentary.
Britto	Romero Britto	Contemporary pop artist known for his vibrant, iconic style that combines elements of pop art, graffiti, and expressionism, reflecting optimism and hope.
Cai Guo-Qiang	Cai Guo-Qiang (蔡国强)	Contemporary artist widely known for his use of gunpowder in art and his installation and explosion projects, reflecting on contemporary social issues and traditional Chinese culture.
Carrington	Leonora Carrington	Though born in Britain, Carrington became a significant figure in the Mexican art scene. Her work in the surrealist tradition explores themes of feminism, mysticism, and the subconscious.
Cassatt	Mary Cassatt	American painter and printmaker who was part of the impressionist movement, known for her paintings of women and children.
Cezanne	Paul Cézanne	French artist and Post-Impressionist painter whose work laid the foundations of the transition from the 19th-century conception of artistic endeavor to a new and radically different world of art in the 20th century.

Artist	Full Name	Synopsis
Chagall	Marc Zakharovich Chagall	A Russian-French artist, Chagall was known for his colorful and whimsical paintings that blended fantasy, nostalgia, and folklore with a unique style. Chagall was associated with the École de Paris as well as several major artistic styles and created works in a wide range of artistic formats, including painting, drawings, book illustrations, stained glass, stage sets, ceramics, tapestries and fine art prints.
Chen Cheng-po	Chen Cheng-po (陳澄波)	An important figure in Taiwanese art history, Chen was known for his landscape and urban paintings. He played a significant role in Taiwan's art education and was a prominent figure in the Taiwanese cultural scene before his execution in 1947 during the 228 Incident.
Chen Chieh-jen	Chen Chieh-jen (陳界仁)	A contemporary artist known for his video and photography work, Chen's art often reflects on Taiwan's history, social issues, and the impact of globalization.
Chung Sang-hwa	Chung Sang-hwa (정상화)	Key figure in the Dansaekhwa movement, Sang-hwa is celebrated for his rigorous, process-oriented approach to painting, creating textured, monochromatic surfaces.
Clark	Lygia Pimentel Lins	Clark was a leading artist in the Neo-Concrete Movement, known for her innovative work that transcended traditional forms of art to include viewer participation and therapeutic elements.
Courbet	Jean Désiré Gustave Courbet	French painter who led the Realism movement in 19th-century French painting. Courbet was committed to painting only what he could see, rejecting academic convention and the Romanticism of the previous generation of visual artists.

Artist	Full Name	Synopsis
Dali	Salvador Domingo Felipe Jacinto Dalí i Domènech, Marquis of Dalí de Púbol	Prominent Spanish surrealist born in Figueres, Catalonia, Spain.
Danwon	Kim Hong-do (김홍도), also known as Danwon (단원)	Leading painter of the Joseon Dynasty, known for his depictions of daily life, landscapes, and genre paintings.
Degas	Edgar Degas	French artist famous for his paintings, sculptures, prints, and drawings. He is especially identified with the subject of dance; more than half of his works depict dancers. He is regarded as one of the founders of Impressionism, although he rejected the term and preferred to be called a realist.
Dürer	Albrecht Dürer	Painter, printmaker, and theorist of the German Renaissance. Born in Nuremberg, Dürer established his reputation and influence across Europe when he was still in his twenties due to his high-quality woodcut prints. He was also known for his engravings and detailed paintings.
Ernst	Max Ernst	A pioneer of the Dada movement and Surrealism, Ernst's inventive techniques, including frottage and grattage, and his experimental use of materials have had a lasting impact on the art world.
Fan Kuan	Fan Kuan (范宽)	Active during the Song Dynasty, Fan Kuan is celebrated for his landscape paintings that emphasize harmony between man and nature, demonstrating profound Taoist influences.

Artist	Full Name	Synopsis
Friedrich	Caspar David Friedrich	A 19th-century Romantic landscape painter, Friedrich is known for his evocative and melancholic paintings that often explore humans' relationship with nature, featuring contemplative figures amidst vast landscapes.
Goncharova	Natalia Sergeevna Goncharova (Наталья Сергеевна Гончарова)	A leading avant-garde artist, painter, costume designer, and writer, Goncharova was influential in several modern art movements, including Futurism and Rayonism.
Goya	Francisco José de Goya y Lucientes	Spanish Romantic painter and printmaker regarded both as the last of the Old Masters and the first of the moderns. Goya was a court painter to the Spanish Crown and a chronicler of history.
Gu Kaizhi	Gu Kaizhi (顾恺之)	A painter and poet of the Eastern Jin Dynasty, Gu Kaizhi is known for his contributions to the development of Chinese figure painting, particularly for his detailed brushwork and expressive figures.
Gyeomjae	Jeong Seon (정선), also known as Gyeomjae (겸재)	Prominent landscape painter of the Joseon Dynasty, known for his true-view landscape paintings that realistically depicted Korean scenery.
Hockney	David	Prominent British painter, draftsman, printmaker, stage designer, and photographer. Key elements of Hockney's style include a vibrant palette, playful manipulation of perspective, and a blend of realism with abstraction. His work often features a flatness in depth, yet remains spatially complex, engaging with the viewer's perception.
Holbein	Hans Holbein the Younger	A German-Swiss painter and printmaker, Holbein became one of the greatest portraitists of the 16th century, known for his detailed and realistic depictions of Henry VIII and other Tudor court figures.

Artist	Full Name	Synopsis
Hsia Yan	Hsia Yan (夏陽)	A member of the Fifth Moon Group, Hsia Yan is known for his unique fusion of Eastern and Western artistic principles, creating distinctive figural paintings with a modern twist.
Huang Gongwang	Huang Gongwang (黄公望)	Active during the Yuan Dynasty, Huang Gongwang is revered as one of the Four Masters of the Yuan Dynasty and is highly regarded for his influential landscape paintings, which emphasize spontaneity and the rhythm of nature.
Huang Hua-cheng	Huang Hua-cheng (黃華成)	A pioneering figure in Taiwan's Avant-garde art movement, Huang's contributions span across painting, film, and experimental art, influencing generations of Taiwanese artists.
Ingres	Jean-Auguste-Dominique Ingres	French neoclassical painter who was considered one of the greatest of his time and was known for his portrait work and historical paintings.
Kahlo	Frida Kahlo (Magdalena Carmen Frida Kahlo y Calderón)	Mexican painter best known for her self-portraits and works inspired by the nature and artifacts of Mexico. Kahlo is celebrated for her deeply personal and symbolic paintings, often self-portraits, that explore themes of identity, post-colonialism, gender, class, and race in Mexican society.
Kandinsky	Wassily Wassilyevich Kandinsky (Василий Васильевич Кандинский)	Often credited as one of the pioneers of abstract art, Kandinsky's work had a profound influence on the development of abstract expressionism.
Khakhar	Bhupen Khakhar (भूपेन खख्खर)	Khakhar was a leading artist in the Indian contemporary art scene, known for his vibrant and candid depictions of the lives of middle-class Indians and open expressions of homosexuality.

Artist	Full Name	Synopsis
Kim Whanki	Kim Whanki (김환기)	Pioneer of abstract art in Korea, is known for his abstract compositions that combine traditional Korean motifs with modern abstract expressionism.
Klee	Paul Klee	Klee was a painter deeply influenced by expressions of color and form. His work is associated with Expressionism, Cubism, and Surrealism, contributing significantly to the development of modern art.
Klimt	Gustav Klimt	Austrian symbolist painter and one of the most prominent members of the Vienna Secession movement. Klimt is noted for his paintings, murals, sketches, and other objets d'art. His primary subject was the female body, and his works are marked by a frank eroticism.
Kollwitz	Käthe Kollwitz	Kollwitz was a printmaker and sculptor whose work reflects the hardships of the working class, the horrors of war, and the human condition, showcasing deep empathy and social critique.
Lee Bul	Lee Bul (이불)	Prominent contemporary artist known for her diverse artistic practice which spans sculpture, installation, performance, and video art. Her art has been exhibited widely across the globe in numerous solo and group exhibitions. Notable solo exhibitions include shows at the Museum of Modern Art in New York, the Hayward Gallery in London, and the Mori Art Museum in Tokyo.
Lee Jung-seob	Lee Jung-seob (이중섭)	Known for his paintings of bulls, a symbol of resilience and strength, reflecting the hardships of life during the Korean War.
Lee Ming-tse	Lee Ming-tse (李明則)	An influential sculptor, Lee Ming-tse is celebrated for his abstract works in metal, which explore the relationship between space, form, and the spiritual world.

Artist	Full Name	Synopsis
Lempicka	Tamara de Lempicka	Polish painter known for her polished Art Deco portraits of aristocrats and the wealthy, and for her highly stylized paintings of nudes.
Leonardo	Leonardo di ser Piero da Vinci, commonly known as Leonardo da Vinci	Italian polymath of the Renaissance whose areas of interest included invention, painting, sculpting, architecture, science, music, mathematics, engineering, literature, anatomy, geology, astronomy, botany, writing, history, and cartography.
Lichtenstein	Roy Lichtenstein	American painter, sculptor, and lithographer. Lichtenstein was a founder and foremost practitioner of Pop art, a movement that countered the techniques and concepts of Abstract Expressionism with images and techniques taken from popular culture. His work was influenced by popular advertising and the comic book style.
Liu Kuo-sung	Liu Kuo-sung (劉國松)	Often regarded as the father of modern ink painting in Taiwan, Liu Kuo-sung's work blends traditional Chinese techniques with modern abstract expressions, pioneering a new direction in Chinese ink painting.
Magritte	René Magritte	Belgian surrealist artist born on November 21, 1898, in Lessines, Belgium. Magritte is best known for his witty and thought-provoking images that challenge observers' preconditioned perceptions of reality.
Malevich	Kazimir Severinovich Malevich (Казимир Северинович Малевич)	Russian avant-garde artist and art theorist, whose pioneering work and writing had a profound influence on the development of abstract art in the 20th century. His concept of Suprematism sought to develop a form of expression that moved as far as possible from the world of natural forms (objectivity) and subject matter to access "the supremacy of pure feeling" and spirituality.

Artist	Full Name	Synopsis
Mantegna	Andrea Mantegna	Italian painter, a student of Roman archeology, and son-in-law of Jacopo Bellini. Mantegna was an important Renaissance artist known for his use of perspective and foreshortening and for the stark clarity of his figures.
Maqbool Fida Husain	M. F. Husain (मकबूल फिदा हुसैन)	Maqbool Fida Husain, often referred to as the "Picasso of India," was a prolific and controversial modernist painter known for his bold, vibrantly colored narrative paintings in a Cubist style.
Marinetti	Filippo Tommaso Emilio Marinetti	Italian poet, editor, art theorist, and founder of the Futurist movement. His manifestos played a crucial role in shaping the ideology and aesthetics of Italian Futurism.
Marshall	Kerry James Marshall	African American artist known for his paintings, sculptures, and other works that explore the experiences of African Americans and narratives of American history.
Matisse	Henri-Émile-Benoît Matisse	Often regarded as the most important French painter of the 20th century, Matisse is widely known as a painter. He was the leader of the Fauvist movement around 1900, and he pursued the expressiveness of color throughout his career.
Mehretu	Julie Mehretu	Ethiopian-born American contemporary visual artist, known for her large-scale, abstract, and multi-layered paintings and prints.
Mehta	Tyeb Mehta (तैयब मेहता)	Mehta was a noted modern Indian painter, known for his bold, emotive, and powerful expressionist works that often-depicted themes of existential despair.
Meireles	Cildo Meireles	Meireles is a conceptual artist known for his politically charged installations and artworks that critique social and economic issues in Brazil and beyond.

Artist	Full Name	Synopsis
Mérida	Carlos Mérida	A Guatemalan-born painter who became a key figure in the Mexican muralism movement, Mérida is known for integrating modern European painting techniques with Latin American themes.
Michelangelo	Michelangelo di Lodovico Buonarroti Simoni	Italian sculptor, painter, architect, and poet of the High Renaissance born in the Republic of Florence, who exerted an unparalleled influence on the development of Western art. His most famous works include the frescoes on the ceiling of the Sistine Chapel and the sculpture of David.
Milhazes	Beatriz Ferreira Milhazes	Milhazes is known for her colorful, abstract paintings and installations that draw on Brazilian cultural imagery, incorporating elements from baroque, folk art, and tropicalia.
Mondrian	Pieter Cornelis Mondrian, often known as Piet Mondrian	Dutch painter and theoretician who is regarded as one of the greatest artists of the 20th century. He made a significant contribution to the development of abstract art and was a pioneer of the De Stijl movement.
Monet	Oscar-Claude Monet	French painter, a founder of French Impressionist painting, and the most consistent and prolific practitioner of the movement's philosophy of expressing one's perceptions before nature, especially as applied to plein air landscape painting.
Morisot	Berthe Morisot	French painter who was a member of the circle of painters in Paris who became known as the Impressionists.
Munch	Edvard Munch	Norwegian painter and printmaker whose intensely evocative treatment of psychological themes built upon some of the main tenets of late 19th-century Symbolism and greatly influenced German Expressionism in the early 20th century. One of his most well-known works is *The Scream* (1893).

Artist	Full Name	Synopsis
Muniz	Viktor Muniz	Muniz is a contemporary artist best known for his innovative use of materials and mediums to recreate famous artworks and photographs, often with a social commentary.
Nam June Paik	Nam June Paik (백남준)	Considered the founder of video art, utilizing television and video technology to create groundbreaking multimedia installations.
Nesterov	Mikhail Vasilyevich Nesterov (Михаил Васильевич Нестеров)	A significant figure in Russian Symbolism, Nesterov's works are noted for their spiritual and mystical themes.
Niemeyer	Oscar Ribeiro de Almeida Niemeyer Soares Filho	A revolutionary architect known for his design of Brasília's civic buildings, Niemeyer's work is characterized by its free-flowing forms and use of concrete, making him a key figure in modern architecture.
Oiticica	Hélio Oiticica Filho	Oiticica was a visual artist and a key member of the Neo-Concrete Movement, famous for his interactive art that encouraged viewer participation, exploring color, form, and social engagement.
O'Keeffe	Georgia O'Keeffe	American artist who was known for her paintings of enlarged flowers, New York skyscrapers, and New Mexico landscapes. O'Keeffe has been recognized as the "Mother of American modernism."
Orozco	José Clemente Orozco (José Clemente Ángel Orozco Flores)	A pioneer of the Mexican Mural Movement, Orozco's powerful murals depict the struggles of the Mexican people, emphasizing social and political messages.

Artist	Full Name	Synopsis
Park Soo-keun	Park Soo-keun (박수근)	Modern Korean painter, is celebrated for his simplistic yet poignant portrayals of the everyday lives of ordinary people, using unique brush techniques and earthy colors.
Parks	Gordon Parks	African American photographer, musician, writer, and film director who became prominent for his photo essays in Life magazine and his work focusing on civil rights, poverty, and African Americans.
Picasso	Pablo Diego José Francisco de Paula Juan Nepomuceno María de los Remedios Cipriano de la Santísima Trinidad Ruiz y Picasso	Spanish painter, sculptor, printmaker, ceramicist, and stage designer considered one of the greatest and most influential artists of the 20th century and the co-founder of the Cubist movement.
Pissaro	Jacob Abraham Camille Pissarro	Danish-French Impressionist and Neo-Impressionist painter born on the island of St Thomas (now in the US Virgin Islands, but then in the Danish West Indies). His importance resides in his contributions to both Impressionism and Post-Impressionism. Pissarro studied from great forerunners, including Gustave Courbet and Jean-Baptiste-Camille Corot. He later adopted a loose brushwork and began painting landscapes that highlighted the beauty of nature.
Portinari	Candido Torquato Portinari	One of Brazil's most famous painters, Portinari's work covers a wide range of themes, from social issues and historical events to everyday life, with a focus on the Brazilian people.

Artist	Full Name	Synopsis
Qi Baishi	Qi Baishi (齐白石)	A prominent 20th-century Chinese painter, Qi Baishi is celebrated for his whimsical, often simplistic depictions of everyday life and nature, utilizing traditional Chinese ink brush techniques.
Ravi Varma	Raja Ravi Varma (राजा रवि वर्मा)	A celebrated painter of the 19th century, Ravi Varma is known for his depictions of scenes from Indian epics and mythology, blending European techniques with Indian sensibilities.
Repin	Ilya Yefimovich Repin (Илья Ефимович Репин)	A leading Russian realist painter, Repin is best known for his portrayal of historical scenes, Russian folklore, and the Russian peasantry.
Richter	Gerhard Richter	Richter is known for his diverse painting styles, seamlessly moving between photorealistic depictions, abstract color planes, and glass works. His exploration of the medium's possibilities has made him one of the most important contemporary artists.
Rivera	Diego Rivera (Diego María de la Concepción Juan Nepomuceno Estanislao de la Rivera y Barrientos Acosta y Rodríguez)	A prominent muralist, Rivera's works are known for their depiction of Mexican society and reflect his political beliefs in communism. His murals adorn public buildings, blending indigenous Mexican culture with European artistic traditions.
Rodchenko	Alexander Mikhailovich Rodchenko (Александр Михайлович Родченко)	Rodchenko was one of the founders of Constructivism and Russian design; his work in photography, graphic design, and sculpture was innovative and influential in the development of modern art.

Artist	Full Name	Synopsis
Rodin	François-Auguste-René Rodin	French sculptor widely regarded as the progenitor of modern sculpture. Rodin was prolific in his work, and his most famous sculptures include "The Thinker" and "The Kiss."
Rousseau	Henri Julien Félix Rousseau	French post-impressionist painter in the Naïve or Primitive manner. He is also known as Le Douanier (the customs officer), a humorous description of his occupation as a toll and tax collector. He was self-taught and is known for his richly colored and meticulously detailed pictures of lush jungles, wild beasts, and exotic figures.
Roy	Jamini Roy (जामिनी रॉय)	Roy was a significant figure in Indian art, known for his work that drew inspiration from folk and tribal art, moving away from Western traditions to create a distinct style rooted in Indian cultural heritage.
Serov	Valentin Alexandrovich Serov (Валентин Александрович Серов)	Known for his portraits and historical paintings, Serov played a key role in the development of Russian Impressionism.
Sher-Gil	Amrita Sher-Gil (अमृता शेर-गिल)	Sher-Gil is considered one of the most important Indian painters of the 20th century, known for her paintings that blend Western and Indian art forms, depicting the daily lives of Indian people in a style reminiscent of the European masters.
Shin Saimdang	Shin Saimdang (신사임당)	Poet, calligrapher, and artist from the Joseon Dynasty, is renowned for her detailed nature paintings, particularly of insects and plants.
Shishkin	Ivan Ivanovich Shishkin (Иван Иванович Шишкин)	Renowned for his landscape paintings, Shishkin was a master of depicting the Russian forest landscape with detail and realism.

Artist	Full Name	Synopsis
Shiy De-jinn	Shiy De-jinn (席德進)	A renowned painter who played a significant role in the development of Taiwanese modern art, Shiy's work is known for integrating traditional Chinese painting techniques with Western artistic concepts.
Siqueiros	David Alfaro Siqueiros	Siqueiros was one of the most influential muralists of his time. His work is known for its dynamic and dramatic use of colors and forms to convey social and political messages.
Stavrides	Nick Stavrides	Stavrides is a autodidact painter based in New York City, well-known for his *Fish Series* paintings. His other vibrant works are also inspired by various cultures, urban life, and a deep commitment to ocean conservation. Stavrides' work often includes large-scale projects that engage the community and reflect his passion for the arts and environmental advocacy.
Subramanyan	K. G. Subramanyan (के. जी. सुब्रमण्यन)	A prolific artist, Subramanyan was known for his expertise in painting, sculpture, and mural-making, blending traditional Indian aesthetics with contemporary themes.
Syed Haider Raza	S. H. Raza (सैयद हैदर रज़ा)	Syed Haider Raza is known for his abstract works focusing on Indian iconography and deeply rooted in his fascination with Indian metaphysical concepts, particularly the Bindu.
Tamayo	Rufino Tamayo (Rufino del Carmen Arellanes Tamayo)	Tamayo was known for his unique style that blended Mexican folk themes with modernist aesthetics. Unlike his contemporaries, he focused more on Mexican identity through color and form rather than overt political messaging.
Toledo	Francisco Benjamín López Toledo	Toledo was known for his efforts to preserve and promote indigenous Mexican culture and arts, his work spans painting, sculpture, and graphic arts, deeply influenced by Oaxacan traditions.

Artist	Full Name	Synopsis
Van Gogh	Vincent Willem van Gogh	Dutch post-impressionist painter who is among the most famous and influential figures in the history of Western art.
Varejão	Adriana de Oliveira Varejão	Varejão's work explores themes of colonialism, cultural identity, and social integration through a diverse range of mediums, including painting, sculpture, and installation art.
Varo	Remedios Varo (María de los Remedios Alicia Rodriga Varo y Uranga)	A Spanish-born artist who became an integral part of the Mexican surrealist movement, Varo's paintings feature highly detailed dreamscapes and mystical themes.
Velazquez	Diego Rodríguez de Silva y Velázquez	Spanish painter and one of the leading artists in the court of King Philip IV. Velázquez is among the most important painters of the Spanish Golden Age and a master of Western art history, well known for his portraits of the Spanish royal family and other European notables.
Vermeer	Johannes Vermeer	Dutch painter who specialized in domestic interior scenes of middle-class life. Vermeer was a moderately successful provincial genre painter in his lifetime but was forgotten after his death; he was subsequently rediscovered in the 19th century, and he is now regarded as one of the greatest painters of the Dutch Golden Age.
Vrubel	Mikhail Alexandrovich Vrubel (Михаил Александрович Врубель)	Vrubel is known for his unique style, which combined elements of the Russian Byzantine style with Art Nouveau, and his work had a significant influence on Russian Symbolism.
Walker	Kara Walker	African American contemporary artist known for her exploration of race, stereotypes, gender, and identity themes mainly through her silhouetted figures.

Artist	Full Name	Synopsis
Warhol	Andy Warhol	American artist and filmmaker, an initiator and leading exponent of the Pop art movement of the 1960s whose mass-produced art apotheosized the supposed banality of the commercial culture of the United States.
Wu Guanzhong	Wu Guanzhong (吴冠中)	Wu Guanzhong is considered a major figure in 20th-century Chinese art, bridging traditional Chinese and Western art forms by integrating modern abstract principles with traditional Chinese painting techniques.
Wu Tien-chang	Wu Tien-chang (吳天章)	Renowned for his digitally manipulated photographs and installations, Wu's work deals with Taiwan's complex identity and historical memory, employing a vivid, surreal aesthetic.
Xu Beihong	Xu Beihong (徐悲鸿)	Xu Beihong is known for his contributions to modern Chinese painting, particularly his realistic paintings of horses and birds. He was instrumental in bringing Chinese art into the modern era by incorporating Western techniques.
Yang Mao-lin	Yang Mao-lin (楊茂林)	A prominent figure in Taiwanese contemporary art, Yang is known for his satirical and often humorous commentary on Taiwan's society and political landscape through multimedia works.
Yuan Jai	Yuan Jai (袁旃)	A painter whose work beautifully merges traditional Chinese painting techniques with vibrant, contemporary aesthetics, creating lush, imaginative landscapes and scenes.
Yun Hyong-keun	Yun Hyong-keun (윤형근)	Prominent figure in the Dansaekhwa (monochrome painting) movement, known for his minimalist abstract paintings that emphasize materiality and nature.
Zeng Fanzhi	Zeng Fanzhi (曾梵志)	One of the leading contemporary Chinese artists, Zeng Fanzhi is known for his *Mask* series, reflecting on the complexities of human emotion and the duality of modern society.

Artist	Full Name	Synopsis
Zhang Daqian	Zhang Daqian (张大千)	Known as one of the best-known and most prodigious Chinese artists of the twentieth century, Zhang Daqian was famous for his splashed-ink landscapes, a modern interpretation of traditional Chinese painting.

Appendix C: AI Art Generation Software

AI art generation software has become increasingly popular, offering both open-source and commercial options. These tools use advanced AI algorithms, typically based on neural networks, to create artworks in various styles.

Here is a list of AI art generation software, categorized into open-source and commercial offerings.

Open-Source AI Art Software

DeepArt

- Description: Uses deep neural networks to transform photos into artworks based on famous styles.
- Features: Allows users to upload a photo and choose an art style, and the AI recreates the photo in that style.

Deep Dream Generator

- Description: Inspired by Google's Deep Dream, this software creates surreal, dream-like images by over-interpreting and enhancing the patterns it finds in an image.
- Features: Known for its distinctive, hallucinogenic effects, it's popular for creating highly stylized and abstract images.

RunwayML

- Description: A more comprehensive AI software platform that integrates various machine learning models, including those for art generation.
- Features: Offers a user-friendly interface and is geared towards creators who want to experiment with AI without requiring deep technical knowledge.

Commercial AI Art Software

Adobe Sensei

- Description: Adobe's AI and machine learning platform, integrated into many of Adobe's creative cloud applications.
- Features: Provides a range of AI-driven tools for image enhancement, pattern generation, and style transfer, among others.

DeepArt.io

- Description: A commercial version of the DeepArt technology offering higher resolutions and more customization options.
- Features: Ideal for creating high-quality art prints and digital artworks with unique artistic styles.

Artbreeder

- Description: Allows users to merge various images to create new artworks using a technique called Generative Adversarial Networks (GANs).
- Features: Especially known for its ability to blend and morph faces, landscapes, and other types of images to create fantastical, hybrid artworks.

DALL-E (by OpenAI)

- Description: A powerful AI image generator capable of creating highly detailed and specific images from textual descriptions.
- Features: Known for its ability to generate creative, high-quality images and art from complex prompts.

DeepAI

- Description: Offers a suite of different AI tools, including ones for art generation.
- Features: Its API can be integrated into other software or websites, making it versatile for different creative projects.

Appendix D: Conferences and Symposiums

These conferences and symposiums offer a platform for presenting cutting-edge research, artistic works, and discussions on the implications and future of AI in the art world. They are excellent opportunities for networking, learning, and staying updated with the latest trends and developments in this dynamic field. Academics, artists, technologists, and theorists converge to discuss, present, and explore the intersection of human creativity and machine learning. Here are some key annual events focused on AI in art, including workshops and conferences:

1. **NeurIPS Creativity Workshop**
   https://neurips.cc
   Held as part of the larger Conference on Neural Information Processing Systems (NeurIPS), this workshop focuses on the creative applications of AI. It brings together researchers and practitioners to explore how AI technologies can be used in artistic creation, including visual art, music, literature, and design.

2. **SIGGRAPH Art Gallery**
   https://www.siggraph.org/siggraph-events/conferences
   SIGGRAPH, the premier conference on computer graphics and interactive techniques, hosts an annual Art Gallery that often includes AI-generated art. The event showcases innovative digital and technologically assisted art created by artists worldwide.

3. **Ars Electronica Festival**
   https://ars.electronica.art/festival
   Held in Linz, Austria, the Ars Electronica Festival is a prominent annual gathering that celebrates the confluence of art, technology, and society. The festival includes exhibitions, conferences, and workshops, often featuring AI in art.

4. **ISEA - International Symposium on Electronic Art**
   https://www.isea-international.org/symposia/upcoming
   This annual event focuses on electronic and digital art and includes discussions and exhibitions on AI's role in contemporary art.

5. **AI in Music and Art Conference**
   https://aimusiccreativity.org
   This specialized conference explores the role of AI in music and visual arts. It includes presentations on AI algorithms used in creating and interpreting art and music.

6. **AI Art and Aesthetics Research Meeting**
   https://www.aibigeiken.com/index_e.html
   Typically held in Japan, this event focuses on the aesthetic aspects of AI-generated art. It brings together researchers working on AI models that analyze, interpret, or create art.

7. **ACM Creativity & Cognition**
   https://cc.acm.org/2024
   Organized by the Association for Computing Machinery, this conference explores the intersection of creativity and technology, including the role of AI in the creative process.

8. **Lumen Prize and Symposium**
   https://www.lumenprize.com
   Accompanying the Lumen Prize, an international award for art created with technology, this symposium addresses topics related to digital art, including the use of AI.

9. **The Artificial Intelligence Conference**
   https://aiconference.com
   Organized by O'Reilly Media, this conference covers a wide range of AI topics, including sessions and panels on AI's impact on art and creativity.

10. **AI & Art Pavilion at the Venice Biennale**
    https://decentralartpavilion.io
    As part of the Venice Biennale, the AI & Art Pavilion explores the integration of AI in contemporary art, featuring discussions, exhibitions, and workshops.

Appendix E: Academic Journals

The field of AI art is a rapidly evolving area of study that intersects technology, art, and often philosophy. Here are some reputable academic journals where you might find interesting research on AI art:

Leonardo

Leonardo is a leading international journal that covers the application of contemporary science and technology to the arts. It often features articles on AI art and its intersections with technology and creativity. Website: https://www.leonardo.info

Computers in Entertainment (CIE)

CIE is an ACM (Association for Computing Machinery) journal that covers a wide range of topics related to the intersection of computer science and entertainment, including AI-generated art and media. Website: http://cie.acm.org

Journal of Artificial Intelligence Research (JAIR)

JAIR is a respected journal in the field of artificial intelligence. While it covers a wide range of AI topics, it may occasionally feature research related to AI-generated art. Website: https://www.jair.org

Entertainment Computing

This Elsevier journal focuses on the use of computing technologies for entertainment purposes, which can encompass AI art and creative applications. Website: https://www.journals.elsevier.com/entertainment-computing

Appendix F: Exercises for GenAI Prompt Crafting

Try these exercises for GenAI prompt crafting.

These exercises are designed to refine your skills in various aspects of prompt crafting, from detailed description to abstract conceptualization. As you practice, you'll develop a deeper understanding of how to communicate effectively with GenAI to bring your creative visions to life. These exercises are an excellent way to enhance your skills in directing AI to produce specific and complex outputs.

Exercise #1: Specificity and Detail

Objective: Develop a highly detailed prompt to generate a specific scene.

1. **Theme**: Choose a historical era and a specific location (e.g., Renaissance Italy, a marketplace).

2. **Task**: Write a prompt that includes specific details like the time of day, weather, types of people present, their activities, architectural details, and any notable objects.

3. **Challenge**: Ensure that each sentence adds a new layer of detail to the scene.

Exercise #2: Abstract Concepts

Objective: Translate abstract concepts into visual elements.

1. **Theme**: Pick an abstract concept or emotion (e.g., solitude, joy, chaos).

2. **Task**: Write a prompt that personifies this concept in a scene or an object. Describe colors, shapes, and elements that you associate with this concept.

3. **Challenge**: Avoid using the name of the concept or emotion directly in your prompt.

Exercise #3: Cross-Genre Fusion

Objective: Combine elements from different genres or styles.

1. **Theme**: Select two distinct art styles or genres (e.g., cyberpunk and impressionism).
2. **Task**: Craft a prompt that merges these styles into a coherent image. Describe how elements from each style will be integrated.
3. **Challenge**: Maintain a balance where both styles are equally represented.

Exercise #4: Progressive Complexity

Objective: Gradually increase complexity within a single prompt.

1. **Theme**: Start with a simple object or scene (e.g., a tree).
2. **Task**: Begin your prompt with a basic description, then add layers of complexity with each sentence, such as the time of year, the surrounding environment, activity around the object, and emotional ambiance.
3. **Challenge**: Each new sentence should transform the scene, adding depth and richness.

Exercise #5: Narrative Scene Creation

Objective: Create a prompt that tells a story.

1. **Theme**: Choose a narrative theme (e.g., a discovery, an encounter).
2. **Task**: Write a prompt that sets a scene for this narrative. Include characters, settings, and objects that hint at an unfolding story.
3. **Challenge**: The image generated from your prompt should allow a viewer to infer the past and future progression of the story.

Exercise #6: Contrasting Elements

Objective: Juxtapose contrasting elements in a harmonious way.

1. **Theme**: Select two contrasting ideas (e.g., fire and water, ancient and modern).
2. **Task**: Craft a prompt that blends these elements into a single, cohesive image.
3. **Challenge**: Achieve a balance where the contrasting elements enhance each other rather than clash.

Exercise #7: Mood and Atmosphere

Objective: Evoke a specific mood or atmosphere.

1. **Theme**: Decide on a mood or atmosphere (e.g., eerie, tranquil).
2. **Task**: Write a prompt focused on evoking this mood. Consider time of day, weather, lighting, environment, and any characters or objects that might contribute to the atmosphere.
3. **Challenge**: The mood should be perceptible without directly stating it in the prompt.

About the Author

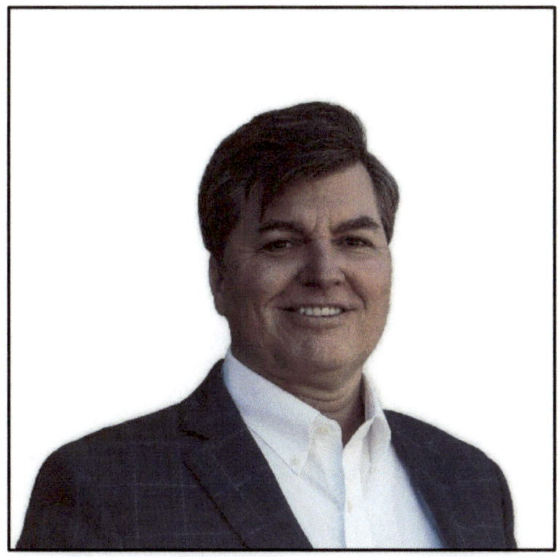

Marcus Ledergerber plays a pivotal role in the ongoing evolution of digital technology. As an eDiscovery expert deeply engaged with technology, he passionately merges his interests in innovation and digital art, making notable contributions to AI design. His understanding of how to apply artificial intelligence in various fields marks him as a pioneer in teaching about AI's transformative effects on art.

In his book, *Visual Art Design Using Generative AI,* Marcus introduces readers to the fascinating world of art created using generative AI. This book provides guidance, ideas, and practical examples for artists who are actively exploring AI as a powerful technology to augment creative expression.

www.ingramcontent.com/pod-product-compliance
Lightning Source LLC
LaVergne TN
LVHW070933210926
848482LV00003B/236
* 9 7 9 8 9 9 0 5 8 9 7 0 4 *